Dictionary of Forestry and Wildlife Sciences

By the Same Author

- Forest Planning at Landscape Level: A Case Study of Working Plan Revision in Chhattisgarh.
- Forest Resources and Sustainable Development Principles: Perspectives and Practices.
- Planning for Forest Resources and Biodiversity Management

About the Author

Kailash Chandra Bebarta, an officer from Indian Forest Service presently works in a senior position in Forest Department, Government of Chhattisgarh. Getting Master's Degree in Zoology, he earned postgraduate diploma in forestry from Indira Gandhi National Academy of Forestry, Dehradun. He also holds a Diploma in Business Administration. Mr. Bebarta has to his credit four books entitled, *Teak: Ecology, Silviculture, Management and Profitability, 'Planning for Forest Resources and Biodiversity Management, Forest Resources and Sustainable Development* and *Forest Planning at Landscape Level.* He has contributed a couple of technical papers published in Scientific and Technical Journals of India. He developed a fully functional **Forest Information System** (FIS) for the State of Chhattisgarh, using the state-of-the art technologies, like Geographic Information System (GIS), Remote Sensing (RS), Geoscience, and Information and Communication Technology (ICT), etc. His current interest lies in developing and adopting appropriate technologies for mainstreaming sustainable forest management practices.

Dictionary of Forestry and Wildlife Sciences

Kailash Chandra Bebarta
Indian Forest Service

CONCEPT PUBLISHING COMPANY PVT. LTD.
NEW DELHI-110059

ISBN-13: 978-81-8069-719-7 (HB)

First Published 2011

Published and Printed by

Concept
Since 1974

Concept Publishing Company Pvt. Ltd.
Regd. Office:
A/15-16, Commercial Block, Mohan Garden,
New Delhi-110059 (India)
Phones : 25351460, 25351794, *Fax* : 091-11-25357109
Email : publishing@conceptpub.com
Website: www.conceptpub.com

Editorial Office:
H-13, Bali Nagar, New Delhi-110 015. India.

Cataloging in Publication Data--*Courtesy:* D.K. Agencies (P) Ltd. <docinfo@dkagencies.com>

Bebarta, K. C. (Kailash Chandra)
Dictionary of forestry and wildlife sciences / Kailash Chandra Bebarta.
p. cm.
ISBN 9788180697197

1. Forests and forestry--Dictionaries. 2. Wildlife management--Dictionaries. I. Title.

DDC 634.903 22

Preface

Dictionaries are the cornerstone of any information and knowledge system. They draw contextual and conceptual boundaries around any word or phrase in any science including forestry. They remain dynamic if words or phrases are constantly updated. Development of dictionary showing changes is always necessary for producing compatible information in consonance with the changes. This apart, use of right word or understanding a word in its correct perspective can result in greater efficiency in any subject.

The last few decades had seen dramatic changes in the diversity of societal perceptions of the uses, needs and values of forests. There has been a paradigmatic shift in forest management all over the globe. A transition from the conventional forestry of Sustained Yield (timber) management to the present practice of Sustainable Forest Management (SFM) is distinctly evident. Existing terminologies and glossaries on forestry are traditionally focused on words and phrases primarily relating to timber management. They do not reflect the changes taking place in management practices. In order to develop a modern dictionary on forestry and wildlife science, the author took this initiative.

Definitions and meanings found in this dictionary are based on traditional forestry books, conventional glossaries found in print or in the web as well as modern books on forestry and allied subjects. My own experiences in the field of forestry helped to redefine certain words and phrases. Since a large list of definitions and meanings was assembled and developed gradually over time, it is no longer possible to mention source of information. More than any other reference, I consulted the British Commonwealth Forest Terminology, N.K. Gulati's 'A Glossary of Forestry Terms,' FAO's various publications on forestry and forest glossaries, MOEF's

Website, 'Dictionary of Environmental Economics' and 'Terminology of Forest Science Technology' developed by Society of American Foresters. Some terms do have multiple definitions. All such multiple definitions have been presented against word or phrases wherever necessary.

I hope that this dictionary will be a useful resource for the reader in understanding words and phrases relating to forestry and wildlife sciences. Definitions are written so as to be comprehensible to all types of academic and other general readers, whilst including the technical details necessary to elucidate the key concepts.

Raipur,
30-6-2010

Kailash Chandra Bebarta
bebarta@indiatimes.com

List of Abbreviations

BIS	Bureau of Indian Standard
BCFT	British Commonwealth Forest Terminology
CAI	Current Annual Increment
CBD	Conservation on Biodiversity
CCD	Convention to Combat Desertification
CIDA	Canadian International Development Agency
CIFOR	Centre for International Forestry Research
CITES	Convention on International Trade in Endangered Species of Wild
CSD	Commission on Sustainable Development
DBMS	Database Management System
EIA	Environmental Impact Assessment
EEC	European Economic Community
ESIA	Environmental and Social Impact Assessment
ESRI	Environmental Systems Research Institute
FAO	Food and Agriculture Organisation of the United Nations
FCA	Forest Conservation Act, 1380
FMU	Forest Management Unit
FRM	Forest Resource Management
FSI	Forest Survey of India
GDP	Gross Domestic Product
GEF	Global Environment Facility
GMO	Genetically Modified Crop
GIS	Geographic Information System

GNP	Gross National Product
GOI	Government of India
ha	Hectare(s)
HDI	Human Development Index
ICFRE	Indian Council of Forestry Research and Education
INSAT	Indian National Satellite
IPF	Intergovernmental Panel on Forests
ICRAF	International Centre for Research in Agro-forestry
ISDN	Integrated Service Digital Network
ITTO	International Tropical Timber Organisation
IUCN	International Union for the *Conservation* of Nature and Natural Resource
IUFRO	International Union of Forestry Research Organisations
JFM	Joint Forest Management
km	Kilometre(s)
LO	Local Organisation
m	Metre(s)
MAI	Mean Annual Increment
MBI	Market Based Instruments
MIS	Management Information System
MoEF	Ministry of Environment and Forests
NAEB	National Afforestation and Eco-Development Board
NBSAP	National Biodiversity Strategy and Action Plan
NCA	National Commission on Agriculture
NFAP	National Forestry Action Programme
NFP	National Forestry Policy
NNP	Net National Product
NPV	Net Present Value
NWDB	National Wasteland Development Board
NWFP	Non-Wood Forest Product
OECD	Organisation of Economic Cooperation and Development
PA	Protected Area
PP	Precautionary Principle
PPP	Poluter's Pay Principle

PRA	Participatory Rural Appraisal
SFM	Sustainable Forest Management
SNA	System of National Accounts
SOE	State Owned Enterprise
sq.km	Square Kilometre(s)
t	tonnes
TOF	Tree Outside Forests
UN	United Nations
UNCED	United Nations Conference on Environment and Development
UNDP	United Nations Development Programme
UNEP	United Nations Environmental Programme
UNESCO	United Nations Educational, Scientific and Cultural Organisation
UNFCCC	United Nation's Framework Convention on Climate Change
USAID	United States Agency for International Development
VFC	Village Forest Committee
WB	World Bank
WGS 84	World Geodetic Service 1984
WII	Wildlife Institute of India
WLDB	Wasteland Development Board
WP	Working Plan
WTP	Willingness to Pay
WTTRC	World Tourism Travel Environment Research Centre
WWF	World Wide Fund for Nature
yr	Year

About the Book

This Dictionary of Forestry and Wildlife Science is intended to provide an updated resource for the present day readers in understanding words in its current perspective from forestry, wildlife science and many other allied subjects such as ecology, environmental economics, geomatics , etc. Illustrations and examples are provided in a simple manner to make every word or phrase easily comprehensible. The dictionary has been designed to make it useful and appropriate for academic readers as well as a practicing foresters.

Aa

Abhyaranya A forest where animals can roam without fear of man. *See* National Park, Sanctuary, sanctum sanctorum.

Abiotic Non-living parts of the environment, e.g., air, water, coal, geological structures, temperature, topography.

Absolute Geo-reference The referencing in space of the location of a point using a predefined coordinate system such as latitude and longitude or a national grid.

Absorptive Capacity Also known as assimilative capacity. The ability of the environment to assimilate waste products from the economy. Limits to this capacity may be determined locally, regionally or globally. To the extent that waste emissions exceed the absorptive capacity of the environment, pollutants accumulate and damage results. *See* Precautionary Principle (PP); Polluter's Pay Principle (PPP).

Abstraction The division of real world phenomena into individual, distinct items.

Abundance, Index of Relative Any expression of relative abundance, e.g., a useful approximation of the total number of individuals of a species relative to time or space.

Abundance, Relative The frequency of encountering an organism in a given time and place relative to the frequency of encounter in another time or place. Typically the smaller divided by the larger number, thus a proportion.

Abundance, Species An estimate of the total number of individuals of a species in a defined area, population, or community. (Confusion between abundance and density can be avoided if density is viewed as abundance per unit of area or volume).

Abundance 1. The number of organisms in a population, combining density within inhabited areas and number and size of inhabited areas. 2. It refers to the total number of a particular species in an area. *See* frequency.

Accelerated Erosion Abnormally rapid erosion in an environment disturbed mainly by man. Not in vogue.

Access Time A measure of the time interval between the instant that data are called from storage and the instant that delivery is complete.

Acclimatization 1. Adjustment to environmental change by an individual. The physiological adjustment or increased tolerance shown by an individual organism to environmental change. 2. Adaptation to a different climate. 3. A genetically determined characteristic that enhances the ability of an individual to cope with its environment. 4. The process (es) whereby populations, species, or individuals (or parts of individuals), change in structure, form, and/or function in such a way as to better survive under given environmental conditions. 5. Evolutionary process by which an organism becomes fitted to its environment. 6. A reversible change in the morphology or physiology of an organism in response to environmental change.

Accuracy Assessment Comparison of a classification with ground-truth data to evaluate how well the classification represents the real world.

Accuracy Conformance to a recognizable standard; can often mean the number of bits is computer word available in a given system. The statistical meaning of accuracy is the degree with which an estimated mean differs from the true mean.

Acid Deposition 1. It involves the atmospheric deposition of sulphur dioxide (SO_2), nitrogen oxide (NO_2), ammonia (NH_3). Acid wet and dry deposition has effects on water, soil and forests. (Stanners and Bourdeau, 1995). 2. Precipitation and dry particulate fallout with low *p*H linked to other components of air pollution. *See* acid rain.

Acid or Sour Humus Humus resulting from decomposition under an aerobic condition.

Acid Rain Atmospheric stocks of sulphur dioxide (SO_2) and nitrous oxide (N_2O) accumulate primarily from coal and heavy oil fired for power generation. As a result, acid rain occurs through two principal processes. In dry deposition, particulate matter is physically deposited, subsequently taking acidic form in conjunction with surface water. Wet deposition is characterised by acidic substances, particularly sulphuric and nitric acid, being formed in the atmosphere, and subsequently being deposited through rain precipitation or simply movements of moist air. (Perman *et al.*, 1999). *See* acid deposition.

Acid Soil Soil with a low *p*H, less than 7.0 but practically less than 6.6.

Acidity The extent to which the *p*H value of a solution falls below 7.

Activity A measure, course of action, or treatment that is undertaken to directly or indirectly, produce, enhance, or maintain forest and rangeland and related rural land outputs or achieve administrative or environmental quality objectives.

Adaptability The ability to alter structure or function in response to changes in the environment in such a way that fundamental life processes can continue to cope with (or continue to function in) an uncertain environment.

Adaptable. Capable of undergoing inheritable (and/or non-heritable) structural or functional changes in response to environmental changes that could otherwise impair life processes.

Adaptation 1. The result of the process of (a) long-term evolutionary adjustment of a population to environmental changes, or (b) short-term physiological/behavioural responses compensating for environmental changes. Frequently a short-term behavioural or physiological response, if it is generally adaptive, will be reinforced by genetic adaptation that ensures the longevity of the short-term response. 2. Adaptation refers to changes in ecological, social or economic systems in response to changes in conditions. This term is often applied when discussing climate change issues and includes changes in processes, practices and structures in order to moderate damages or to yield benefits from potential opportunities arising from climate change. There are two reasons why adaptation is important to climate change strategies. The first is that estimating the impact of climate change requires estimates of the extent to which adaptation will reduce the net damage. The second is that adaptation policy strategies should be developed to minimize the risks arising from climate change. Adaptation is needed as a policy strategy since, even with reductions in greenhouse gas emissions, climate change is expected. For example, climate change is expected to lead to a sea-level rise resulting in erosion, flooding and saltwater intrusion in coastal areas. Adaptation here could include the building of sea defences, and will significantly reduce the costs of climate change. It is important that adaptation to climate change be built into coastal zone management. Another type of adaptation is the development of crop species that are more tolerant to climatic variations. Adaptation policy includes three approaches to managing global change: (1) blocking, or preventing, unfavourable impacts of such change on any valuable resources; (2) adjusting or correcting environmental policy to prevent, or make up for, welfare losses resulting from global environmental change; and (3) anticipatory adjustment to strengthen the social systems to lessen losses from uncontrolled environmental change. (Markandya *et al.*, 2002)

Adaptive Management 1. An approach to natural resource management wherein actions are designed and executed to achieve objectives, but also effects are monitored for the purpose of learning and adjusting future management actions, thereby improving the efficiency and responsiveness of management. 2. Sustainable management practices for ecosystems and species that are responsive to uncertainties and ecological fluctuations, as well-being reversible and flexible.

Adult Sexually mature; an animal that has contributed to new individuals to a population.

Advance Growth Seedling, sapling and pole of species of the overwood that have been established naturally in a forest before regeneration felling are started. *See* advance reproduction; advance regeneration.

Advance Reproduction/ Advance Regeneration True seedlings or sprouts of the tree species that occupy the overstory existing as part of the understory vegetation. The root systems of sprout advance reproduction are usually older than the stems, are relatively large, and are capable of supporting much greater stem growth than the root stems of true seedlings.

Adventitious Bud 1. A bud from any part of the stem, leaves or roots that is not connected with the strands of bud-bearing tissue arising from the axis of the leaves. 2. A bud from a tree bole or stem usually resulting from a branch being broken or the bole being exposed to sunlight.

Adverse Impact. An effect that causes harmful interference (beyond limits of acceptable change) with the structure or functioning of a person, place, ecosystem, or object.

Aeration, Soil The process by which air and other gases in the soil are renewed. The rate of soil aeration depends largely on the size and number of soil pores and on the amount of water clogging the pores. A soil with many large pores open to permit rapid aeration is said to be well aerated, while a poorly aerated soil either has few large pores or has most of those present blocked by water.

Aerial Photograph 1. A photograph of the Earth's surface taken (either directly downward or obliquely) from an aeroplane. 2. Aerial photograph. Photograph taken from an aerial platform (usually an aeroplane), either vertically or obliquely.

Aerial Strip Census A census of wildlife taken from both sides of an aircraft flying along specified lines. Sampling techniques are used to compute the results.

Aerobic 1. Life processes occurring in the presence of free oxygen. 2. Applied to soil organisms that can live only in the presence of oxygen and to conditions in which free oxygen is available.

Aeroplankton The small living organisms, ranging from minute arthropods and seeds to microscopic fungal spores and bacteria, that are suspended in the atmosphere.

Aesthetic(s) Relating to or dealing with perceptions of beauty; the philosophy dealing with beauty and with judgements or perception of beauty; also esthetic.

Aestivation 1. The process of passing a period of hot season or prolonged drought in an inactive state. It can also be stated as the state or condition of torpidity or dormancy induced by heat and dryness of summer as opposed to hibernation. Also see hibernation. 2. The arrangement of the parts of a flower within a bud.

Afforestation The establishment of forest cover on land not previously forested. Afforestation may be necessary, for example, to increase the net capacity of the Earth's forests to absorb carbon dioxide (CO_2) and other greenhouse gases. (Mintzer, 1992). 2. The establishment of a tree crop on an area from which it has always been or for very long been absent. 3. Artificially establishing forest crops by planting or sowing on land that has not previously, or not recently, grown tree crops. *See also* reforestation.

After-Ripening Biochemical or physical changes occurring in seeds, bulbs, tubers and fruits after harvesting when ripe in the ordinary way; often necessary for subsequent germination or growth.

Age Class 1. One of the intervals into which the range of age of trees growing in a forest is divided for classification or use; also the trees falling into such an interval age gradation. 2. A distinct group of trees or portion of growing stock recognized on the basis of age. 3. A general term applied to organisms which are born, hatched, etc. within a specified time period; also a life stage. Age class time frame varies with generation time of organisms. For example, the young, juvenile, and adult age classes of many small mammals occur within a single year, whereas for trees, the young age class encompasses several years, typically 10. Age intervals into which wildlife or timber stands are divided into commonly 10 years. Age classes are "balanced" when the whole forest has an approximate equal number of plots or patches having same extent in each 10-year class from age zero through rotation age.

Age Class Distribution, Normal A complete series of age class in such proportions as will permit equal volumes from annual or periodic fellings under the given rotation and silvicultural system. *See* normal forest, normal growing stock, normal age gradations.

Age Class Distribution The local occurrence, or proportionate representation, of different age class in a forest.

Age Classification The division of a crop according to differences in age; or the allotment of woods to age class.

Age Composition 1. An array of age classes. 2. The arrangement of age classes in a population which describes the relative strengths of the age classes. It is synonymous with age structure.

Age Distribution (Age Class Distribution) Individuals of a population classified according to age classes or periods such as pre-reproductive or sub-adult, reproductive, and post-reproductive. An age pyramid is a diagram of the proportions within each age class of a population.

Age Gradation An age class with one year as the interval. Loosely used sometimes as synonymous with age class.

Age Gradations, Normal Series of A complete series of age gradation from the seedlings to the mature stage in proper proportions.

Age Ratio Age ratio is a proportion of young to adults, suggesting a measure of productivity. This provides an indication of population density where numbers cannot be readily counted as among rabbits and ducks. *See* density.

Age, Average The arithmetic mean age of a population or group.

Age, Crop The age of a regular crop corresponding to its crop diameter.

Age, Exploitable The age at which an individual tree of crop attains the size or stage of growth required to fulfil the management objects. *See* rotation.

Age, Mean The average age of the dominant trees in a crop. *See* crop age.

Age, Predominant Applied to a crop of mixed ages and is the age of that diameter or girth class of the species, principal which is most numerously represented age.

Age, Top Age corresponding to the top diameter.

Agenda 21 The global sustainable development agenda set out in the Rio Declaration on Environment and Development, which was established at the Earth Summit in 1992. Agenda 21 consists of 40 chapters, and 21 principles. There are four broad sections which cover a range of issues: social and economic dimensions; conservation and management of resources for development; strengthening the role of major groups; and implementation. Agenda 21 is an Earth Charter setting out basic principles and programmatic action required to move towards sustainability. It established a negotiated framework for co-operative action between Government, agencies, and programmes of the United Nation's system, Non-Governmental Organisations and the private sectors. It laid an emphasis on people, communities and organisation in all matters of natural resources management. This approach is called as 'bottom-up approach'. It stresses that most effective planning evolves gradually through participatory process that allows different social groups to debate the gains and losses in reconciling development and environment (David Reid, p. 188). The programme of action on environment and development is divided into four main sections. They are: (1) Social and economic development encompassing issues of inequities between rich and poor; wasteful consumption; the population explosion; integration of development and environment. (2) The conservation and management of resources for development. (3) Strengthening the role of major groups involved in achieving sustainable development. (4) Means of implementation. Chapter 38 of Agenda 21 calls for the establishment of a Commission on Sustainable Development (CSD) that will provide the active involvement of organs, programme and organisation of the United Nation's system, international financial institutions and other relevant inter-Governmental organisations, and encourage the participation of Non-Governmental Organisations, including industry and the business and scientific communities. The most relevant functions of the Commission are: (1) To monitor progress in the implementation of Agenda 21; (2) To consider the information submitted by Governments, including their national reports; (3) To review progress in the implementation of commitments contained in the Agenda 21, such as those related to provision of financial resources and transfer of technology and to receive and analyse relevant inputs from competent Non-Governmental Organisation, including the private and scientific sector. The agenda focuses on the role of National Governments in promoting sustainable development. It urges on every Government to prepare a national strategy for sustainable development, which should integrate development and environment policies at all levels and at all sectors of economy. It also advised all Governments to build a national consensus on every issue pertaining to sustainable development of resources. Besides, it called upon South to devise ways and means of 'capacity building', so that the environmental problems are appropriately dealt with. Capacity building is a major theme in the section — Means of Implementation. It involves in developing the abilities and resourcing of institutions to manage the various changes and activities required of them. The ways suggested for capacity building are: developing human resources, strengthening the capacity of existing institutions in research and development, developing management techniques for programme implementation, undertaking and co-ordinating reviews of sectoral needs, addressing the larger issues of technology transfer and delineation of terms for such transfer and negotiation over intellectual property rights.

Aggradation 1. The geologic process in which inorganic materials carried downstream are deposited in stream beds, flood plains and other water bodies resulting in a rise in elevation. 2. One of four phases of forest biomass accumulation beginning soon (approximately 5-15 years) after a harvest and dependent on species.

Aggregation 1. In GIS, it is the process of combining smaller spatial units, and the data they contain, into larger spatial units by dissolving common boundaries and lumping the data together. 2. Grouping following establishment of scattered colonizing invaders as a result of propagation.

Agro-Climatic Indices This is one of two general techniques for examining the response of agricultural crops to climate change; these involve the measurement of crop suitability, whereas the others (crop-climate models) provide an estimate of potential productivity. Agro-climatic indices show the growth of a crop in response to climatic variables.

Agroforestry 1. A form of intercropping in which annual herbaceous crops are interspersed with perennial trees or shrubs. The deeper-rooted trees can often exploit water and nutrients not available to the herbs. The trees may also provide shade and mulch, while the ground cover of herbs reduces weeds and erosion, (FAO, 1995) 2. Agroforestry is a collective name for all land use systems and practices where woody perennials are deliberately grown on the same land management unit as agricultural crops or animals in some form of spatial arrangement or temporary sequence (ICRAF, Nairobi). 3. A form of intercropping in which annual herbaceous crops are interspersed with perennial trees or shrubs. The deeper-rooted trees can often exploit water and nutrients not available to the herbs. The trees may also provide shade and mulch, while the ground cover of herbs reduces weeds and erosion (FAO, 1995). 4. A collective name for land-use systems and practices in which trees and shrubs are deliberately integrated with non-woody crops and/or animals on the same land area for ecological and economic purposes. 5. It is a type of land-use system in which tree crops are planted on the same land for raising agricultural crop. 6. It connotes a land use system that integrates trees, crops and animals in a way that is scientifically sound, ecologically desirable, practically feasible and socially acceptable to farmers.

Albedo Ratio of the amount of electromagnetic energy reflected by a surface to the amount of energy incident upon it.

Albinism Animals or plant, otherwise healthy, but showing marked deficiency in pigmentation. Example, persons with a pale, milky skin, light hair and pink eyes; also the white tiger of Rewa in Madhya Pradesh.

Algae Simple rootless plants growing in water and in soil. Algal blooms may adversely affect water quality.

Algorithm 1. A set of logical and mathematical operations performed in a specified sequence. A repeatable set of rules for action or decision making. 2. A set of rules for solving a problem. An algorithm must be specified before the rules can be written in a computer language.

Alkalinity The extent to which the *p*H value of a solution exceeds 7 acidity. *See* soil, acid.

Alkalization A process whereby the exchangeable sodium content of the soil is increased.

All-aged Forest (Uneven-aged forest) A forest which contains trees of all ages, intermixed.

All-Aged Crop in which, theoretically, trees of all ages or gradations up to and including those of exploitable age are found.

Allelopathy The influence of plants, other than micro-organisms, upon each other, and arising from the products of their metabolism. This influence includes both inhibitory and stimulatory effects.

Alley-cropping An agroforestry system in which crops are grown on strips of land between widely spaced rows of trees. *See* agroforestry.

Alliance A physiognomically uniform group of community associations sharing one.

Allogenic Factors Factors which operate, independently of the plants themselves, to alter the habitat gradually and thus cause changes in the vegetation.

Allogenic Originating external to a system.

Allotment to Periods or to Periodic Blocks The sub-division of a forest into management blocks equal to the number of periods in the rotation so that an orderly sequence of operations is possible.

Allowable Annual Cut or Annual Allowable Cut (AAC) The amount of timber that is permitted to be cut annually from a particular area. AAC is used as the basis for regulating harvest levels to ensure a sustainable supply of timber.

Allowable Annual Harvest The volume of timber that may be harvested from an area on a perpetual basis.

Allowable Cut The amount of wood (or forest products) that may be harvested annually or periodically from a specified area over a stated period in accordance with the objectives of management.

Alluvium 1. Material such as earth, sand, gravel, or other rock or mineral materials transported and laid down by flowing water. 2. A general term for all sediment deposits resulting directly or indirectly from sediment transport within streams deposited in riverbeds, flood plains, lakes, fans and estuaries. *See* Colluvium.

Alpha Diversity 1. The variety of organisms occurring in a particular place or habitat; often called local diversity. 2. Any of a variety of definitions of diversity relating to lists of species, abundance of each, and proportional abundance within a community. It is an expression of populations co-occurring at a specific time and space.

Alphanumeric Character Any numeric digit (a number from 0 to 9), any letter of the alphabet from A to Z, or any special symbol, such as a plus sign (+) or a per cent sign (%).

Alpine A term applied to the zone of vegetation where winter is severe, snowfall heavy, the mean annual temperature below 45°F. and the mean January temperature below 30°F. In India, alpine zone occurs in the Himalayas at altitudes above 3030 metre. An alpine zone is usually characterised by grassy meadows and stunted vegetation with snow during winter.

Alternative Propositions or situations, a set of actions, usually from among thousands, only one of which may be chosen as describing actions to arrive at a desired future condition. One of several policies, plans, or projects proposed for selection by decision-makers.

Alternative Cost Approach An alternative to the Revealed Preference (RP) and the Stated Preference (SP) approaches to the valuation of environmental impacts. This approach seeks to establish the expenditure which would be required to remove the negative externality involved, or to reduce it by a specified amount. This approach has often been used in studies of pollution, and is clearly appropriate where the expenditure is actually incurred and does completely remove the externality.

Altimeter An instrument which indicates the vertical distance above a specified datum plane.

Altitude Matrix A grid of elevation values used in GIS.

Am/fm Automated mapping and facilities management.

Amensalism An interaction in which one organism or population adversely affects a second organism or population, but the second has no effect on the first.

American Standard Code for Information Interchange (ASCII) It is a widely used industry standard code for exchanging alphanumeric codes in terms of bit-signatures.

Amla The Indian Gooseberry (*Emblica officinalis* or *Phyllanthus emblica*) is a deciduous tree of the Euphorbiaceae family. It is known for its edible fruit of the same name. Common names of this tree include *amalaka* in Sanskrit, *amla* in Hindi, *amba* in Nepali Bhasa, *usirikai* in Telugu, and *nellikai* in Kannada as well as *aonla, aola, amalaki, amla* berry, *dharty, aamvala, aawallaa, emblic, emblic myrobalan,* Malacca tree, *nillika,* and *nellikya* in various other languages. The tree is small to medium sized, reaching 8 to 18 m in height, with crooked trunk and spreading branches. The leaves are very short, petioled, ovate or oblong, 7-10 cm long. The flowers are greenish-yellow. The fruit is nearly spherical, light greenish yellow, quite smooth and hard on appearance, with 6 vertical stripes or furrows. The fruits ripen in autumn. Its taste is bitter-sour. Being more fibrous than most fruits, it cannot be consumed raw in vast quantity; indeed, it is taken with salt. A glass of water taken immediately after eating a large fruit makes the water seem sweeter. For medicinal purposes dried and fresh fruits of the plant are used. Amla fruit is sour and astringent in primary taste, with sweet, bitter and pungent secondary taste, and is cooling in action. It is light and dry. It is a *rasayana* tonic that promotes longevity, and is especially good for the heart. It strengthens the lungs, helping to fight chronic lung problems as well as upper respiratory infections. Apart from this it also contains tannins; a reason why even dried form retains most of the vitamin content. The fruit is an adaptogen which means it is a food grade, nontoxic herb that normalizes body function, balances the neuroendocrine system and improves immunity. In Ayurveda the fruit alone is considered a *rasayana* for *pitta*. Particularly in Southern India, the fruit is pickled with salt, oil, and spices, and also used as a primary ingredient in the Ayurvedic *rasayana* in tonic *Chyawanprash* and in the nourishing laxative *triphala* where it is mixed with chebulic and belleric myrobalans. The *Charaka Samhita*, the main text of Ayurvedic herbal medicine, describes emblic and chebulic myrobalans as possessing the same virtues, though they have slightly different nature: They have healing virtues and are auspicious (used in sacred and ceremonial occasions). They restore the faults (*doshas*) to their normal course. They are light (as food). They enkindle digestive fire, and are good *pachanas* (digestive aids). They promote longevity and induce nourishment. They prevent the effects of age more than any other drug. They alleviate all varieties of ailments, and impart strength to the intellect and the senses. They quickly conquer vitiligo, abdominal tumors, flatulence, dropsical swellings (edema), chlorosis, alcoholism, piles, ailments of the *grahani* (duodenum), chronic intermittent fever, diseases of the chest, diseases of the head, diarrhoea, disgust for food, cough, gonorrhea, epistasis, enlargement of the spleen, abdominal dropsy when new, discharge of phlegm matter, hoarseness of the voice, discoloration or loss of complexion, anemia, intestinal worms, waste of *dhatus* (main body components), some forms of asthma, vomiting, loss of virility, weakness of the limbs, blockage of ducts of various kinds, sensation like a wet blanket covering the chest, a similar sensation in the heart, and dullness of the memory and understanding.

Amplitude, Ecological. The range of one or more environmental conditions in which an organism or a process can function. *See* Tolerance.

Anaerobic 1. Life processes that occur in the absence of free oxygen. 2. Applied to organisms that can live without free oxygen and to conditions in which free oxygen is not available aerobic.

Analogue 1. Representation of information by a continuously varying signal (contrast with discretized signals such as digital data). 2. A representation of a physical variable or phenomenon by another variable which displays proportional relationship over a specified range; for an example using a map to describe an area on the earth's surface.

Analysis, Stump Stump Analysis is an exercise, which gives ideas about diametric increment and age of the tree. In other words, it is an analysis of a stump-section by measuring annual rings in order to estimate the age of the tree and its past rate of diametric growth. There are two main objectives of the exercise. They are: (a) to determine the progress of diametric increment on stump over the past years; (b) to find out age / diameter relationship to decide the rotation age corresponding to exploitable diameter.

Analysis Area A delineated area of land subject to analyses of (1) responses to proposed management practices in producing, enhancing, or maintaining forest and rangeland outputs and environmental quality objectives, and (2) economic and social impacts.

Analysis Scheme The logical linking of spatial operations and procedures to solve a particular application problem in GIS.

Analysis, Stem Stem analysis is defined as the analysis of a complete stem by measuring annual rings on a number of cross-sections at different heights in order to determine its past rate of growth. (Chaturbedi, A.N. *et al.*, 1994). The principal objective of this exercise is to determine the relationship of the tree with respect to the whole span of its life. These relationships are: (a) Age-diameter; (b) Age-height; (c) Age-volume. In addition, it aims to assess the average rate of diameter, height and volume increment in the said tree.

Analytical Hill Shading The process of calculating relief shadows and using these as a visualization technique to enhance the portrayal of relief on a map.

Ancillary Data Data from other sources than remote sensing that can be used to aid in the classification. For an example, the secondary data pertaining to the area or classes of interest, such as topographic, demographic, or climatological data constitute ancillary data.

Anemograph A recording anemometer. *See* anemometer.

Anemometer An instrument for measuring the direction, force and velocity of wind.

Anemophilous Plants Plants pollinated by wind.

Angiospermae, Angiosperms (division Magnoliophyta). The

botanical name for the group of vascular flowering plants that produce seeds enclosed in an ovary; includes hardwoods, bamboos, and palms but not softwoods.

Note: Divided into the dicotyledones and the monocotyledones. *See* Gymnospermae.

Angle of Repose The maximum angle (or per cent slope) to the horizontal at which any soil or loose or fragmented solid material will stand without sliding, e.g., soil on a roadside cut.

Angle of Slide The slope, measured in degrees of deviation from the horizontal, on which loose or fragmented materials will start to slide, slightly greater than the angle of repose.

Angler A person who catches fish for sport or for food with rod and line. The term is also applied to a species of sea fish because the first ray of the dorsal fin is modified to form a "rod" which suspends bait for little fish; the mouth of the fish is close by, ready to seize the prey.

Animal An organized being having life, sensation, and voluntary motion-typically distinguished from a plant, which apparently has no sensation or voluntary motion. The term includes mammals, birds, reptiles, etc.

Animal Community The characteristic assemblage of animals associated with a forest type or ecological community.

Animal Unit A measure for converting types of animals to forage resources. It is based on the equivalent of the forage required by a mature cow.

Animal Unit Conversion Factor A numerical grazing measurement figure, which allows conversion from one kind or class of animal to another (e.g., equivalent animal months). Such a conversion factor expresses the amount of forage required to maintain an animal. It may have no application in determining stocking rates for range use for particular animals.

Anisotropic An adjective to describe a spatial phenomenon having different physical properties or actions in different directions.

Annotation Alphanumeric or symbolic information added to a map to improve communication.

Annual Allowable Cut (AAC) The amount of timber that is permitted to be cut annually from a particular area. It is used to ensure a sustainable supply of timber. It averages roughly the amount of new growth each year minus deductions for losses due to fire, insect or diseases.

Annual A plant species with a life cycle of 12 months or less.

Anoxic Lack of oxygen. *See* anaerobic.

Antelope Any of a group of swift, cud-chewing, horned, deer like, cloven-hoofed animals, related to oxen, goats, deer, etc. It includes the chamois and the gazelle. Deer which have deciduous horns or antlers. Antelopes found in India are: (1) FOUR-HORNED ANTELOPE OR CHOUSINGHA (*Tetracerus quadricornis*). This is found in peninsular India south of the Himalayas where the country is wooded and hilly, but not too densely forested. It is not found on the Malabar Coast. It is the only antelope with two pairs of horns of which the front pair is always the shorter. A pair of well developed glands i. found between the false hoofs of the hind legs. The colour of its coarse coat is dull red brown above and white below. (2) INDIAN ANTELOPE OR BLACK BUCK (*Antilope cervicapra*). A long-horned antelope that is brownish black above and white below. This is the sole representative in India of the genus Antilope, and is perhaps the most beautiful of all its kinds. It is found all over the Indian plains except on the Malabar coast. It avoids forest or hill tracts. It has beautiful spiralled horns. Black bucks are usually seen in herds of 20 or 30; in Rajasthan and Punjab gatherings may number several hundreds. *See* NILGAI: BLUE BULL.

Anthropocentric Environmental Ethic A view of the environment that is human-centred. More formally it refers to a comprehensive set of principles, obligations and values that are the basis of much of environmental economics. Values for the environment derive exclusively from the value that the environment has for individuals, both those alive now and those who have yet to be born. Thus it can address issues of intergenerational equity. The proposal to extend this definition to encompass the existence of moral interests of non-human but potentially conscious is known as the extended rights view. *See also* ethics; environmental ethics; intergenerational equity principle. (Markandya *et al.*, 2002)

Anthropogenic Of human origin or influence.

Anthropomorphism An interpretation of what is not human or personal in terms of human or personal characteristics, e.g., attributing to animals the same thoughts, reactions, emotions, etc., as are experienced by human beings.

Anticipatory Policy Response A type of Government policy which anticipates environmental problems and environmental changes before they occur, so that measures to limit the damage associated with the environmental problems are in place before the problem surfaces.

Apikko Movement This was a social and ecological movement that took place in state of Karnataka in India. The word '*Apikko*' in Kannada means the same thing 'to hug'. The movement represented the popular sentiment and initiative aimed at preventing felling of the trees by adopting non-violent means such as hugging them. *Apikko* movement, started in 1983 in Salkani forests in Siris district in Karnataka, has proceeded along the same lines as *Chipko*. About 160 men, women and children of the village hugged their trees and prevented the woodcutters from cutting them down. They formed an organisation by the name of Yuvak Mandali which focused the grievances on two major issues: (1) commercial felling by the contractors damaging a number of other trees, and (2) replacing of the natural forests by teak and eucalyptus monoculture plantations.

Apogee The farthest point in an elliptical orbit of a satellite from the body, e.g., the Earth, which it is orbiting.

Application Programme or Package A set of computer programmes designed for a specific task. Application is a task addressed by a computer system.

Appraisal and Evaluation *See* evaluation and appraisal; evaluation.

Appropriate Technology Technology, which provides solutions to the problems of local communities, are sustainable, in the sense that the technology can be maintained by the communities themselves and does not introduce dependence on outside support. Appropriate technologies should also be sensitive to the need to reduce pollution by using renewable energy sources and recycling materials where possible. An alternative definition of the term is a production method that most efficiently utilizes an economy's endowment of factor inputs, such as land, labour or human-made capital.

Aquatic Pertaining to standing and running water in streams, rivers, lakes, ponds, and reservoirs.

Aquifer A geologic formation, group of formations, or part of a formation that contains sufficient saturated permeable material to hold and yield significant quantities of water to wells and springs. If a well taps more than one aquifer, the principal aquifer will be the one that yields the greatest amount of water. In aquifers, water moves more readily than in adjacent formations with lower permeability. The term "water-bearing" is sometimes used synonymously with "aquifer" when a stratum furnishes water for a specific use. Aquifers are usually natural sands, gravel, and fractured or porous rock.

Arboretum (Plural Arboretums; also Arboreta) 1. A place where trees, shrubs and herbaceous plants are cultivated for scientific and educational purposes. 2. A place for cultivating and displaying trees. A botanical tree garden where trees are maintained for display purposes. *See* botanical garden.

Arboriculture The area of cultivating trees primarily for shade or landscape effects.

Arc 1. A connection between nodes in the vector GIS model. 2. A complex line connecting a sequence of co-ordinate points. Also known as a chain or string. 3. An alternative term for a line feature formed from a connected series of points.

Arc/Info A leading GIS software package developed by the Environmental Systems Research Institute (ESRI).

Archaeological Area Sites and areas which have been designated as containing important evidence and remains of the life of people on Earth between the time of their first appearance and the development of written history. Archaeological remains are the sole kind of evidence that applies to pre-history and they may provide information about all aspects of human life.

Archaeological Resource All remaining physical evidences of former occupation by now-extinct cultural groups. Evidence includes skeletons, settlement remains, implements, artifacts, monuments, and inscriptions. This resource class does not include any of the more recent physical products of contemporary native cultural groups such as may exist on Indian reservations.

Archival Storage Magnetic and optical media (types, removable disks) used to store programmes and outside the normal addressable memory units of the computer.

Area Cartogram A type of cartogram that is used to depict the size of areas relative to their importance according to the some non-spatial variable such as population or per capita income.

Area of Analysis The geographic area within which ecosystems, their components, or their processes are evaluated during analysis for one or more plans, plan revisions, or plan amendments. This area may vary in size depending on the relevant planning issue. An area of analysis may be larger than a plan area. An area of analysis may include multiple ownerships.

Area Reconnaissance Early visits to observe an area and its ecological, economic, and social conditions and to determine the scale and scope of plans and subsequent work (or visits and information collection).

Area, Geologic Areas containing scientifically or educationally significant fossilized specimens of flora and fauna from previous geologic periods, e.g., coal swamp forests, dinosaurs, etc.

Area 1. A fundamental unit of geographic information (a geographic primitive) which is a measure of a particular extent of the earth's surface (*see* point, line and polygon). 2. The entity type used to represent enclosed parcels of land with a common description.

Arenaceous A term used to indicate sandy soils.

Artesian Water that arises to the earth's surface under hydrostatic pressure from an aquifer that is confined between two impermeable stratums.

Arthropod Invertebrate animals with jointed legs and a segmented body such as insects, mites, and spiders.

Artificial Feeding Artificial feeding of wild animal life means placing food into the environment that supplements the food sources contained naturally within the home range of a wild species. Usually directed at populations of animals, it may apply to feeding individual animals.

Artificial Intelligence (AI) Field of study concerned with producing computer programmes capable of learning and processing their own 'thoughts'.

Artificial Neural Network (ANN) *See* 'neural networks'.

Artificial Regeneration or Reproduction 1. Planting or seeding to establish a new crop of trees on an area, usually when timber has been removed. 2. The process of renewal of a forest by sowing, plantings or other artificial means.

Artiodactyla Even toed ungulate mammals, with the axis of ea foot falling between the third and fourth toe. It includes de sheep, antelope, cattle, pigs, camel, giraffe and hippopotam

Aspatial Query The action of questioning a GIS database on the basis of non-spatial attributes.

Aspect 1. The direction towards which a slope faces. 2. The direction in which a unit of terrain faces. 3. The compass direction that a surface faces. Aspect is usually expressed in degrees from North. 4. The compass direction in degrees azimuth towards which a land slope faces (the direction downhill). Since plants suffer their greatest moisture losses through evapotranspiration on southwest facing slopes (which receive the greatest energy input from the sun compared to that received by other slopes), aspect can be an important factor influencing vegetation distribution. It is used as exposure such as the seasonal appearance of a community, e.g., spring aspect, summer aspect, etc.

Ass (*Equus onager, E. hemippus, E. hemionus*, etc.) A quadruped related to the horse, but smaller, with tuft at the end of tail, and long ears. It has descended from the wild ass (*E. asinus* or *E. taeniopus*) of Abyssinia. In India, the Indian Wild Ass (*E. hemionus khur*) is found in the Rann of Cutch and parts of the desert zone of North-West India. One other species, the wild Ass of Tibet, occurs in Ladakh and Tibet. The Indian wild ass is probably the only true Wild Ass left in the world. It is a handsome creature. It is bigger than domestic donkeys. It has short ears like those of zebra.

Assembly Language A low-level (primitive) programming language that uses mnemonics rather than English-like statements.

Assessment Results of analyzing and interpreting the existing social, economic, or ecological characteristics or conditions of an area using scientific principles.

Asset Conversion Human societies must evaluate the allocation between many different forms of potential assets in building up an optimal portfolio. If the current distribution of assets is different from the optimal portfolio, there will be an incentive to convert some of the assets held to other forms, implying disinvestments in some assets (often natural assets or natural capital), and investment in others that are human-preferred. The incentive to reduce the level of investment in natural assets in order to invest in the latter is called the 'conversion process'. The natural form of any resource is in competition with the other forms of same assets. Asset conversion often takes place between natural assets and human-made assets in the course of economic development, for example, the construction of a factory on a Greenfield site. (Swanson, 1994) *See also* opportunity cost.

Assimilation Anabolism or constructive metabolism; the process of taking in and converting nutrient substances into components of living tissues; the conversion of non-living matter into protoplasm.

Assimilative Capacity The capability of the environment to take wastes and convert them into harmless or ecologically useful products. This is related to the assimilative potential for the environment. (Pearce and Turner, 1900)

Associate 1. Applied to any of the dominant species associated with a given species in a plant association. 2. Also applied loosely to all species, dominant or otherwise, associated with a given species in a crop.

Association 1. A commonly-occurring relationship between two or more species which can be readily recognized in the field and treated as an ecological unit. 2. An actual or concrete community, stand, or group of organisms characterized by a definite floristic composition, presenting uniformity in physiognomy and structure, and growing under uniform habitat conditions. 3. A group of things classified together because they meet certain standards of similarity. 4. A climatic climax unit that includes all of the successional stages preceding or associated with it. Plant associations and animal associations emphasize populations of plants or animals respectively within an area. 5. A level in a classification based on ecological groupings of vegetation units with broadly defined environmental and physiognomic factors that are in common. This level is subject to revision as vegetation alliances and community associations are organized under the upper levels of the hierarchy. 6. A plant community of some particular kind or grade, usage varying greatly from one ecological school to another, but two prevalent concepts regarding it as (a) the "fundamental unit" of plant ecology (the equivalent of species in taxonomy), admitting many local sub-associations and facies (roughly equivalent to subspecies and varieties respectively in taxonomy) and defined mainly by floristic composition.

Association, Index of A measure of the probable occurrence together of one species with another.

Association, Plant A major unit of a climax formation characterized by one or more dominants peculiar to it. *See* climax units.

Associes 1. The development or successional equivalent of the plant association. 2. A seral community with two or more dominants.

Assortment Table A volume table giving the volumes of wood in the round down to various thin-end diameters. Standard volume table and commercial volume table are special classes of assortment tables.

Assumption A judgemental decision by planners which supplies missing values, relationships, or societal preferences for some informational component necessary for making a decision. The true nature of such missing information is either unknown or cannot be readily ascertained within the time and/or budgetary constraints on a decision.

Atmospheric Correction Image processing procedure that compensates for effects of selectively scattered light in multi-spectral images.

Attenuation 1. Reduction in light intensity through a forest canopy. 2. Reduction in light intensity in water because of absorption by water molecules, suspended particles and dissolved substances.

Attitude A learned predisposition, feeling, or conviction manifesting itself in a general state of readiness either to evaluate or to react towards an object or class of objects in either a favourable or unfavourable manner in a more or less consistent and characteristic way. Attitudes are relatively stable and have three components: a cognitive or belief component, an effective or feeling component, and a connotative or action-disposition component. Although behaviour may be a function of attitude at times, attitudes are not necessarily predictors of behaviour. Consequently, changes in attitudes do not always result in changes in behaviour. Attitude has a different meaning in remote sensing practices. It is angular orientation of remote sensing system with respect to a geographic reference system.

Attribute 1. A characteristic of a component. The sum of knowledge of all attributes defines a component, e.g., attributes of grass include colour, phenology, live biomass, dead biomass, litter biomass, etc. 2. Non-graphic information associated with a point, line, or area element in a GIS. Non-graphical descriptors relating to geographical features or entities in a GIS. 3. Characteristic of the feature that is being mapped.

Attributes of Goods and Services A resource can be defined in terms of the services it provides, or its attributes. For example, a park could be defined in terms of its services: boating, fishing, swimming, accessibility (the proximity to an urban centre), and so on. The value of these attributes can be measured using hedonic pricing or other valuation techniques. (Perman *et al.*, 1996)

Autecology 1. The study of plants and/or animals in relation to their environment. 2. The ecology of an individual organism or taxonomic group. 3. The study of environmental organisms and their effects on plants. *See* autecology; ecology.

Autogenic Factors Dominating factors of change which are due only to the individuals in a plant community, e.g., shade, root competition, etc. *See* factors.

Autogenic Succession Development of vegetation on account of factors originating from within a system.

Autogenic Originating from within a system.

Automated Cartography The process of drawing maps with the aid of computer driven display devices such as plotters and graphics screens. The term does not imply any information processing.

Autotrophic Organism An organism capable of synthesizing organic matter from inorganic substances. In contrast, a heterotrophic organism must have organic matter as its source of food.

Autotrophic Plants Plants, which obtain their food exclusively from the inorganic materials of soil, air and water. *See* heterotrophic plants.

Auxin Collective term for naturally occurring organic substances, which, in minute concentrations, influence the growth of plants favourably or otherwise.

Average Cost Pricing A system in which the price is determined by the average cost of production. This system often implies that new higher-cost sources of, for example, natural resources are averaged-in with existing lower-cost sources, yielding a price that is substantially lower than the true marginal cost (MC). Thus the incentive to conserve is diminished, since a reduction in consumption saves less money than it would under marginal cost pricing. The expected outcome would be a level of conservation that is less than efficient. (Tietenberg, 1992)

Average Daily Traffic (ADT) The average 24-hours volume of traffic, being the total volume of traffic during a stated period divided by the number of days in that period. Unless otherwise stated, the period is 1 year.

Average Synonymous with arithmetic mean. Sometimes used in a general way as a representative value. *See* mean, weighted.

Aves or Birds Class of vertebrates, having feathers, warm blood and wings formed from the forelimbs. Birds are known to have evolved from primitive extinct reptiles.

AVHRR (Advanced Very High-Resolution Radiometer) A meteorological satellite with multispectral imaging system used for large area of earth observation normally at 1 km spatial resolution.

AVIRIS (Airborne Visible/Infrared Imaging Spectrometer) An airborne hyper-spectral sensor with 22410 nm bands.

Azimuth 1. Compass direction from a point, measured in degrees clockwise from true North. 2. The horizontal angle or bearing measured clockwise from the astronomic north.

Azimuthal Projection It is a type of map projection in which the surface of the globe is projected on to a flat plane.

Ba

Backstop Technology A technology that is a substitute for one that uses natural resources. For example, wind turbines can be thought of as a backstop substitute for the use of coal for electricity generation. Wind power is currently a backstop technology in that it is more expensive than conventionally generated power, but as fossil fuel stocks deplete and prices increase, power generators will switch to the construction of wind turbines. The backstop technology cost is the upper boundary of the price of the natural resource in question since, if the price rose above this level, generators would switch to using the backstop. (Perman *et al.*, 1999) *See also* renewable energy.

Backup Making a copy of a file or a whole disk for safe keeping in case the original is lost or damaged.

Badger, Honey or Ratel (*Melivora Capensis*) This is an animal of Africa and South-Western Asia. In India this is found in areas starting from the base of the Himalayas to Kanyakumari. It lives in the desert and in the dry and moist deciduous zones, avoiding regions of heavy rainfall. It prefers hilly broken country where shelter is easier to find, and when living in the plains chooses the banks of streams or river where burrows are easily dug. The body of Ratel is squat and bear-like, the legs are short and stumpy, tail small, feet broad and long and the claws blunt. Under-parts are deep black contrasting vividly with the pale dorsal surface. It defends itself fiercely against attack.

Badlands More or less barren, rough, broken land that is strongly dissected or gullied by streams. Most common in semi-arid regions where streams have entrenched themselves in soft erodible materials, e.g. clays, soft shales and limestones.

Bait (Fishing) Food (bread, cheese, etc.), worms, etc. put on hook or used in spring to lure fish.

Bait (Hunting) Usually a live (domestic) animal tied up to attract and locate tiger or leopard. Also any food or substitute, used as a lure in trapping etc.

Balance of Nature (Ecological Stability) The apparent stability of the population density relationships between the many species of organisms that make up a biotic community. The concept of such a balance has been severely criticized. Population density of each of the species in a biotic community may fluctuate more or less widely from time to time (e.g., existence of population explosions, die-offs, epidemics, irregular migrations, succession etc.) and that the density of no species remains at a fixed value. The fluctuations in the numbers of each species, however, usually have fairly definite limits. Using 'balance' includes the recognition that the population densities of every species making up a community fluctuate from season to season and from year to year.

Balanced Objectivism An idealistic point of view which advocates that resource use decisions should be reached in a completely objective manner — not disproportionately influenced by any special interest group pressure tactics, no special consideration given for any particular segment of society (whether privileged or disadvantaged), and not based on any of the other determinants of planning value — biophysical, social, or economic. Balanced objectivism is conceptually unrealistic because it seeks to ignore the political reality of pressure groups, fails to recognize that issues (i.e., value conflicts between resource use audience members) are typically the impetus for any planning effort and that most value system clashes cannot be satisfactorily resolved by rational arguments.

Balanced Population Natural population in a particular land area or body of water that maintains itself year after year with little fluctuation in number of individuals in spite of regulated hunting or fishing.

Bamboo Bamboo is called poor man's timber and conspicuously in great demand. It is a grass widely distributed in India. Over 150 species of bamboo are found to grow in various parts of India. They are markedly gregarious. Distribution of bamboo follows the distribution of rainfall, temperature and altitudes. The commonest Indian bamboo is *Dendrocalamus strictus*. It thrives in somewhat open types of mixed deciduous tree forests or where trees are almost absent, on well drained, light soil on hill sides and extends into drier regions more than any other species. The other bamboo of Indian peninsula *Bambusae arundinacea* is found in richer and moist soil, often on alluvial ground along the sides of streams. The most interesting phenomenon relating to flowering of bamboos is that of gregarious flowering. A felling cycle of 3-4 years is adopted for harvesting bamboo forests on the basis of culm selection principle. About 10 clumps are required to be kept per clump comprising all new culms of the year and some of the previous year. Bamboos are used in basket making, *agarbati* making, and paper pulp.

Band 1. Data values for a portion of the electromagnetic spectrum, sometimes called a channel. 2. A wavelength interval in the electromagnetic spectrum. For example, in INSAT images the bands designate specific wavelength intervals at which images are acquired.

Bandicoots (*Genus Bandicota*) The mole bandicoot is largely a creature of fields and forest, but the other bandicoots found in India are essentially parasites on man, living in or about human dwellings. Because of their burrowing habits they do much damage to grounds and floorings. Their large size is sufficient to distinguish bandicoots from other house rats. Four species are known from peninsular India.

Bandwidth The number of cycles per second between the limits of a frequency band; also the range of frequencies recorded by an antenna.

Bar A submerged or exposed ridge-like accumulation of sand, gravel, or other alluvial material formed in a lake or in the channel, along the banks, or at the mouth of a stream where a decrease in velocity induces deposition.

Barbel Any of various species of fish belonging to the genius Barbus (so-called as they are equipped with barbels on the upper jaw). Barbus mosal is the mahseer of India. It is by far the finest fish from the anglers point of view. It is found in most hill streams.

Bark Tissues of stem and root of a tree outside the cambium layer; in older trees usually divisible into inner (living) and outer (dead) bark.

Bark Gauge An instrument for measuring the thickness of bark.

Barking Deer *See* Deer.

Bark Scotch Localized injury to bark and cambium caused by exposure of a stem to intense sunlight or high temperature, often resulting in wounds.

Bark, Over and Bark, Under Refers to girth or diameter measurements which include or exclude the bark.

Barograph A recording barometer.

Barren An area with sparse vegetation usually owing to some physical or chemical property of the soil.

Basal Area The area of the cross-section of a stem at breast height. When applied to a crop, it is called the "crop basal area"; it denotes the sum of basal areas of all the stems or the total basal area per unit of area.

Base Exchange Capacity The total capacity of a soil for holding cations.

Base Exchange The process whereby a soil absorbs certain positively charged ions from the soil solution and gives up other cations in equivalent quantities and in which the colloidal fraction of the soil is primarily concerned. The term "cation exchange" is tending to be substituted.

Base Map A map showing certain fundamental information, on which is compiled additional data of specialized nature. Also a map to which all other maps and GIS map layers are registered and re-scaled.

Base Status (High or Low) The quantity of nutrient bases available in the soil.

Basel Convention Also known as the Convention on the Transboundary Movement of Hazardous Wastes. The Basel Convention came into force in 1992 and stipulated that hazardous wastes could not be moved except between those nations party to the convention. The conditions of this convention stipulate the pre-notification and consent of the recipient country. These restrictions were established to encourage the proper management and reduction of hazardous waste at source, and to prevent the transfer of damaging pollution to countries which were not able to control the wastes effectively. (Jha, Markandya and Vossenaar, 1999)

Baseline 1. The baseline is the measure against which all other further data or information are compared to evaluate their effectiveness. 2. A line which is used as a base for further work, particularly in surveying.

Baseline Study, Ecological For a geographic area where human activities potentially affecting the environment are proposed, a study is undertaken to describe the existing conditions and trends. This description of key ecological system components and their functional relations through time provide a reference "baseline" from which the effects of the proposed action may be predicted. It also provides a benchmark against which future conditions and trends, occurring after the proposed activity begins, may be compared. Thus the purpose of such a study is to provide sound ecological information as input to the decision-making process for locating, designing, and operating new human activities which are potentially degrading to the ecological environment.

Basic (Beginner's All-Purpose Symbolic Instruction Code) A simple, high-level computer programming language, for inexperienced computer users.

Basic Spatial Unit (BSU) The smallest spatial entity to which data are encoded.

Basicole A plant that lives on soils of high base status.

Basifuge A plant that tends to avoid soils of high base status.

Basin An area in which the margins dip towards a common centre or depression, and towards which surface and subsurface channels drain. *See* drainage area.

Basin Listing The ploughing or furrowing of land, usually on the contour, with a special lister that places earth plugs at intervals in the open furrows to form small basins between them.

Basiphile A plant that tends to be restricted to basic soils.

Bast The fibrous portion of the phloem or inner bark of a tree.

Baud Rate A measure of the speed of data transmission between a computer and other devices — equivalent to bits per second.

Bay A body of water forming an indentation of the shoreline, larger than a cove.

Beach The zone of demarcation between land and lake water, or other large bodies of water, covered by sand, gravel, or larger rock fragments.

Bear A large heavy, clumsy plantigrade mammal, of the genus Ursus, and related genera, with shaggy and thick fur and a very short tail, native to temperate and arctic zones. Commonest Indian varieties are: BROWN BEAR (*Ursus arctos*). A bear with brown fur found in Europe, Africa, Asia, etc. The

Indian race is said to be distinctive from its paler coat and smaller build. It is found on higher levels of North-western and Central Himalayas. Its heavier built and brown coat will suffice to distinguish it from the Himalayan Black Bear. Himalayan Black Bear (*Selenarctos Thibetanus*). It is confined to the Asian countries, and in India it occurs in Kashmir, Himalayas and Assam. Its shorter smoother coat and black claws distinguish it from the sloth bear. Its general colour is typically black. SLOTH BEAR (*Melursus Ursinus*). A bear with a shaggy black fur, flexible snout and long white claws, found in the forested tracts of India and Sri Lanka from the base of the Himalayas southwards.

Beat 1. A territorial charge primarily protective in scope; sub-division of a range; usually in the charge of a forest guard or forester. 2. Actual beating of the forest for driving out game.

Beat (Hunting) A patch of forest which is beaten up for game. *See* beating.

Beat Up, to To restock blanks in an artificially regenerated area with fresh sowings or plantings.

Beater (Hunting) A person employed in beating or driving game from cover in a hunt.

Beating *See* Hunting (Beating).

Bed. The bottom of a lake, pond, river, stream, or other body of water.

Bedding Area A specific site selected by big game animals to lie down and rest.

Bedrock The more or less solid rock in place either on or beneath the surface of the Earth. It may be soft or hard and have a smooth or irregular surface.

Beetle An insect of the order coleoptera, having its wings covered and protected by hard outer wing-cases.

Belief An unproven assertion based on one or more fundamental assumptions. The assertion may be unprovable.

Bench 1. Shelf-like areas with steeper slopes above and below. 2. In the flood plain, a series of level areas remaining as a result of periodic deposition and erosion.

Benchmark 1. Sites for measuring natural phenomena in areas where human activity has essentially no effect. These sites would be expected to continue at least as long as natural conditions exist. 2. Certain existing examples or conditions in the field which are usable as established standards or definitions for practical comparison of "use capability" classes. Units of equal "use capability", but possessing markedly different physical features or appearances, can be recognized as being equal. 3. A set of estimates used to establish standards by which to compare alternatives considered in detail. Benchmark alternatives include minimum level, maximum resource levels, and maximum present net value levels.

Bench Terraces Level or slightly sloping platforms constructed for soil conservation along the contours of a slope, separated from one another by a much steeper slope, and with a bank, usually covered with a vegetation on their outer edges.

Beneficiary Pays Principle A principle, which states that the beneficiaries of a high quality or improved environment should compensate resource users for attributes that do not bring market benefits and are not required of all people. This principle requires that any additional costs associated with the provision of positive non-market benefits be reimbursed. It differs from the polluter pays principle (PPP) in that it assumes that citizens do not hold the costs of environmental improvement. The PPP, on the other hand, assumes that the property rights to a clean environment lie with citizens, so that a firm must compensate the public for environmental damage. Thus, the beneficiary pays principle and the PPP have different distributional implications. (Young, 1992)

Benefit (Value or Outcome) Inclusive terms used to quantify the positive expected results or outputs of a proposed activity, project, or programme expressed in monetary or non-monetary terms. Ideally, estimates of all benefits, outputs, or effectiveness expected to be received or achieved as a result of undertaking a proposed activity, programme, or project. Realistically, a particular programme and its outputs, some intended and very specific beneficial outputs, although some attendant outputs may be negative or non-beneficial.

Benefit Function Approach An example of the practice of benefit transfer, valuation studies, to measure the economic value of a non-market asset, typically model a relationship between willingness to pay (WTP), the characteristics of the affected population and the non-marketed good or service. With the benefit function approach, the entire valuation function model is then transferred to the policy site, and adjusted to conform as closely as possible to the population and physical characteristics at that site. A zonal travel cost method model for recreational trips derived at one lake, for example, may be used in conjunction with data on average travel costs, water quality conditions, socio-economic characteristics, substitute sites and so on at another lake, in order to estimate the recreational benefits of that lake.

Benefit-Cost Analysis (BCA) 1. An analytical approach to solving problems of choice which identifies for each objective, that alternative which yields the greatest total discounted benefit for a given discounted cost or that alternative which produces the required level of benefits at the lowest cost. This same analytical process has also been referred to as cost effectiveness analysis when the benefits of the alternatives cannot be quantified in terms of monetary values or when benefits are limited to those stated in objectives. 2. A tool of analysis which was originally designed to evaluate the net financial benefits of investment projects, but has lately been extended into the social, environmental and natural resource fields, BCA compares the monetary value of the streams of benefits and costs of a proposed policy, programme or project over defined space and time boundaries. It then ranks alternatives in terms of various measures such as net present value (NPV). Despite the growing use of BCA in the environmental field, critics contend that its methods are flawed, or that the approach (using monetary values for environmental goods and services) is unethical. Although current methods are in principle capable of including almost all benefits and costs, the controversy over the appropriateness of BCA as an evaluation tool continues. Five particular issues arise: (1) how to calculate direct and indirect costs; (2) how to incorporate a societal perspective (BCA has no accepted mechanism to deal with equity); (3) how to measure intangible non-market values such as air quality; (4) how to relate the benefits and costs calculated for each future year to a common scale (the use of discounting, the standard method for doing this, is much debated); and (5) how to deal with uncertainty, both in financial and biological forecasts. The main criticism is that qualitative factors related to social, environmental or other external costs and benefits are very often inadequately dealt with in such analysis and that distributional considerations are marginalized. Nevertheless, BCA is widely used and is an important tool in decision-making. When external costs are included in the analysis, it is sometimes referred to as extended benefit-cost analysis. (Tolba and El-Khaly, 1992)

Benefit-Cost Ratio An economic indicator of efficiency, computed by dividing benefits by costs. Usually, both the benefits and the costs are discounted so that the ratio reflects efficiency in terms of the present value of future benefits and costs. Benefits for projects should exceed costs or the ratio should be greater than 1.0.

Benthos The whole group of organisms in a water body (pond, lake, or river) which crawl about on the bottom, or burrow into the bottom, or grow attached to the bottom. Those aquatic organisms that are carried passively by water currents or the wind are termed plankton and those that swim actively and may move long distances for feeding or breeding purposes, nekton.

Bequest Value The value that an individual places on having an environmental resource or general environmental quality available for his or her children to experience. It is based on the desire to exchange current value for the increased well-being of one's descendants. Bequest values are considered as a non-use value of a resource, even though the value derived results from the future use of a resource. Bequest value makes up part of the total economic value of an environmental resource. (Kahn, 1998)

Berm A levee, shelf, ledge, bench along a stream bank that may extend laterally into the channel to partially obstruct the flow, or parallel to the flow to contain the flow within its stream banks. May be natural or man-made.

Best Environmental Practice (BEP) This is the best environment-friendly company practice that takes into account the following considerations: (1) dissemination of information and knowledge among the public and consumers about environmental impacts of products and services, their use and disposal; (2) elaboration and application of codes of good environmental practice covering the entire product life cycle; and (3) product labelling to inform consumers about possible hazardous effects of the product, its use and disposal. To determine the combination of measures leading to BEP, consideration is given to: (1) danger to the environment to the product, its use and disposal; (2) the feasibility of using cleaner technologies and substances; (3) the scale of product use; (4) potential environmental advantages or shortcomings of alternative materials or activities; (5) recent advances in science and research and development; (6) the time framework needed to change over to the BEP; and (7) its socio-economic effects.

Best Management Practices (BMPs) Practices or their combination that has been determined by a natural resource agency to be the most effective means of preventing or reducing an amount of degradation of forest or pollution, typically sources to a level compatible with resource (e.g., forest quality, water quality) goals.

Beta-Diversity 1. The diversity between or among more than one community present along an environmental gradient or in the same place over time (e.g., soil acidity). 2. The variety of organisms within a region arising from turnover of species among habitats.

Bharal Blue Sheep (*Pseudios nayaur*). This is a ruminant mammal, intermediate in structure and habits between a sheep and a goat; it has rounded smooth horns, curving backwards. Typically a Tibetan animal, it is found also in Ladakh, Sikkim and Nepal.

Bias The difference between the mean, population or true as sampled and the average of the sample values that would be obtained in an infinitely large number of repetitions of a sampling process. A sampling process involving such a difference is said to be "biased".

Biennial 1. A plant species that lives for two growing seasons. 2. A species with a life cycle of approximately two years with fruiting occurring in the second year.

Big Bore (of a Rifle Barrel) Having an inside diameter greater than 0.22 inch. *See* Small bore.

Big Game 1. The larger species of animals that are hunted, e.g., tiger, deer, bison, and in some areas, the wild turkey. 2. The large animals, sought or taken by hunting for pleasure, or sport. *See* game.

Bija (*Pterocarpus marsupium*) It is known as Indian Kino Tree, or the Malabar Kino. It is also known as Bija in Central India. The Indian

Kino is found in Central India, Eastern and Western Ghats regions of India. In the far Western region of Nepal, it is known as "Bijiayasal". Parts of the Indian Kino (heart wood, leaves, flowers) have long been used for their medicinal properties in Ayurveda. The heart wood is used as an astringent and in the treatment of inflammation and diabetes. The Indian Kino is a medium to large, deciduous tree and can grow up to 30 metres tall. The bark of this plant is used as an astringent and for toothaches.

Binomial Nomenclature (or Binominal Nomenclature) The system, introduced by Finnaeous, of denoting an organism by two Latin words, the first the name of the genus, the second the specific name or epithet, the two constitute the name of the species; e.g., *Homo sapiens, Acacia arabica. See* species. *See also* classification.

Bioaccumulation The uptake and retention of environmental substances by an organism by means other than the ingestion of food. *See* Biomagnification.

Bioassay 1. Determining the physiological effect of a substance (such as a drug) by comparing its effects on a test tissue, organ, or living organism with that of some standard substance; in contrast to chemical assay or analysis. 2. A technique for determining the effectiveness of a substance by measuring its effects on animals, tissues or organisms and comparing them to the effects of a standard preparation.

Biocenology (Biocoenology) Biology concerned with the study of natural communities and the interaction of the members of such a community.

Biochemical (Biological) Oxygen Demand (BOD) 1. The dissolved oxygen required to decompose organic matter in water and thus a measure of oxygen consumption in a fixed period of time. 2. The amount of molecular oxygen required to stabilize decomposable matter by aerobic biochemical action, measured in mg/l. 3. A measure of the quantity of dissolved oxygen, in milligrams per litre, required to stabilize the demand for oxygen in a water sample, usually resulting from the process of microorganisms consuming organic matter and utilizing the available dissolved oxygen in the oxidation process. Adding waste to water may cause a high BOD, deplete oxygen, and kill aquatic life. 4. The measure of the oxygen demand placed on a stream by any particular volume of effluent. It represents the amount of oxygen, measured in milligrams per litre, required in the oxidation of organic matter by biological action under specific standard test conditions. BOD is widely used to measure the level of organic pollution in waste water and streams. Sometimes referred to as biological oxygen demand. (Water Quality Association, 1997)

Bioclimatics The science of relating the climatic characteristics of a locality in which certain plants grow to those of another of similar properties where the same plants may be introduced and grown successfully.

Biocoenosis The association of animals and plants together, especially in relation to any given feeding area. Such a community comprises both animals and plants.

Biodegradable 1. A biodegradable substance is one that is easily decomposed by bacteria. Often cited on product labels, this quality is important for waste are biodegradable, but hard detergents and some pesticides are not, and these may damage ecosystems. 2. Substances which can be broken into their component parts by bacteria and fungi.

Biodiversity, India's India has a rich and varied heritage of biodiversity, encompassing a wide spectrum of habitats from tropical rainforests to alpine vegetation and from temperate forests to coastal wetlands. India figured with two hotspots — the Western Ghats and the Eastern Himalayas—in an identification of 18 biodiversity hotspots carried out in the eighties (Myers, 1988). Recently, Norman Myers and a team of scientists have brought out an updated list of 25 hotspots (Myers *et al.*, 2000). In the revised classification, the 2 hotspots that extend into India are the Western Ghats/Sri Lanka and the Indo-Burma region (covering the Eastern Himalayas). India has two major realms called the Palaearctic and the Indo-Malayan, and three biomass, namely the tropical humid forests, the tropical dry/deciduous forests, and the warm desert/semi-deserts. India has ten biogeographic regions including the Trans-Himalayan, the Himalayan, the Indian desert, the semi-arid zone(s), the Western Ghats, the Deccan Peninsula, the Gangetic Plain, North-East India, and the islands and coasts (Rodgers and Panwar, 1988). India is one of the 12 centres of origin of cultivated plants. In addition, India has 26 recognised endemic centres that are home to nearly one-third of all the flowering plants identified and described to date. Of the estimated 5—50 million species of the world's biota, only 1.7 million have been described to date (Groombridge and Jenkins, 2000), and the distribution is highly uneven. About seven per cent of the world's total land area is home to half of the world's species, with the tropics alone accounting for 5 million. India contributes significantly to this latitudinal biodiversity trend. With a mere 2.4 per cent of the world's area, India accounts for 7.31 per cent of the global faunal total with a faunal species count of 89,451 species (MoEF, 1999).

Biodiversity Biodiversity or biological diversity, can be defined as 'the variety and variability among living organisms from all sources including, *inter alia*, terrestrial, marine and other aquatic ecosystems and the ecological complexes of which they are part, this includes diversity within species, between species and of ecosystems' (Convention on Biological Diversity, Rio de Janeiro, Brazil, June 3-14, 1992, http://www.biodiv.org/). The Convention distinguishes between biological diversity and biological resources, where biological resources consist of the resources necessary for biodiversity assessments, namely conservation areas, scientific collections, genetic resource collection, information and human resources.

Biodiversity Losses Many leading natural scientists are predicting and imminent mass extinction of species. Some project losses of 25 to 50 per cent of all life forms over the next 100 years — biodiversity losses. There are various reasons for the loss of biodiversity, including overexploitation of species and the loss of habitats, also known as the global conversion process (Swanson, 1994). *See also* asset conversion; enclosure.

Biodiversity or Biological Diversity 1. The variety of life. 2. Biological diversity includes the diversity of species, genes and ecosystem and the evolutionary and functional process which link them. 3. An index of richness in a community, ecosystem, landscape and the relative abundance of these species. 4. According to The Biological Diversity Act, 2002, biological diversity means 'the variability among living organisms from all sources and the ecological complexes of which they are part, and includes diversity within species or between species and of ecosystems'. There are commonly five levels of biodiversity: (a) genetic diversity referring to the genetic variation within a species; (b) species diversity referring to the variety of species in an area; (c) community or ecosystem diversity referring to the variety of communities or ecosystems in an area; (d) landscape diversity referring to the variety of ecosystems across a landscape; and (e) regional diversity referring to the variety of species, communities, ecosystems, or landscapes with a specific geographic region. Each level of biodiversity has three different components: (i) compositional diversity or the number of parts or elements within a system and is indicated by measures such as the number of species, genes, communities, or ecosystems; (ii) structural diversity or the variety of patterns or organizations within a system, such as habitat structure, population structure, or species morphology; and (iii) functional diversity or the number of ecological processes within a system, such as disturbance regimes, roles played by species within a community, and nutrient cycling within a forest. *See* diversity.

Biodiversity, Economic Values of The total economic value of biodiversity consists of several components. Direct-use value derives from direct use of or contact with biological resources or an ecosystem, for instance the use of the reserve of a species for scientific research or to attract tourism. Indirect use value derives from the role of ecosystems in supporting human activity, for example the support given to agriculture by forests that regulate the hydrological cycle. Option value is the value placed on preserving and asset that, while not used at present, may be used in the future. An example of option value is the value that people place on preserving ecosystems and landscapes that they may wish to visit in the future. Bequest value is the value that people place on preserving natural assets to pass on to future generations, and existence value is the value that people place on the knowledge that a particular species or ecosystem exists. The tools of non-market valuation can be used to attach monetary values to biodiversity. These tools include the Contingent Valuation Method (CVM), the Travel Cost Method (TCM), and the production function approach. Valuing biodiversity is a way to estimate the extent to which natural ecosystems should be preserved in order to maximize human welfare. Destroying natural ecosystems, such as forests, often brings financial gains. The non-financial value of a forest should be offset against this gain in order to establish whether or not depleting the forest is economically efficient.

Biodynamics The branch of physiology that deals with life processes of plants and animals.

Bioecology The study of both plants and animals acting together; a combination of plant and animal ecology.

Biogenesis The theory that living organisms come only from other living organisms and not from non-living matter.

Biogenic Resulting from activity of living organisms; necessary for continuation of life processes.

Biogeochemical Relating to the chemical relationships between the geology of an area and its plant and animal life. In land use planning, the term is more often used for all of the naturally occurring objects, processes, and relationships in an area. Often used in the sense of the biogeochemical parameters of a planning area. Biogeochemical is approximately equivalent to the natural ecosystem and ecosystem functions of a planning area. This composite term is based on the assumption that all naturally occurring things can be classified as being biological, geological, or chemical.

Biogeochemical Cycle (Mineral Cycle, Nutrient Cycle, Material Cycle) The circulation (cycling) of chemical elements such as nitrogen, carbon, etc. in specific pathways from the abiotic portions of the environment into organic substances (flora and fauna) and then back again into abiotic forms.

Biogeography. 1. The study of biology on a geographical basis. An example from Swanson (1994) is the study of islands, which is instructive for looking at the global impact of conversions of habitat. This study has revealed a geometric relationship between habitat conversions and the extinction of species, in the sense that the rate of species loss increases geometrically with increased levels of habitat loss. As the technology for conversion becomes more and more efficient, the loss of species will become ever greater. This is what has been occurring on the global level, paralleling the island extinctions from which this relationship was deduced (Swanson, 1994). 2. Branch of biology dealing with the geographical distribution of a stable natural community. It is the resultant of all the effects of the constituent organisms on one another. Such effects include food chains, parasitism, predatism. It represents the evolutionary adjustment between breeding pressure and environmental resistance.

Biogeophysical A composite term often used to encompass all of the naturally occurring materials, processes, and relationships operating in an area. Often used in the sense of the "biogeophysical parameters" of a planning area. In such usage, the term is approximately equivalent to the natural ecosystem and ecosystem functions of a planning area. The word was constructed so that all the natural objects and processes operating in an area can be classified as being either biological (i.e., plant and animal species, ecological interactions, biotic productivity, etc.) or geological (i.e., rock types, soil types, geomorphic history, sedimentation, erosion, etc.), or physical (i.e., heat, light, electrical, gravitational, etc.).

Biological Amplification Small levels of pollutants can disrupt the environment through this mechanism. An example is the food chain, which amplifies the pollution problem because animals higher up the food chain receive doses of pollutants many times higher than the initial exposure. A well-known example of this is the use of dichlorodiphenyltrichloroethane (DDT) as a pesticide. DDT is persistent pollutant that is absorbed in small does by insects, but is amplified in birds and other animals including humans higher up the food chain. (Lowe and Lewis, 1980)

Biological Control 1. Using organisms or viruses to control parasites, weeds, or pests. 2. Attack on noxious organisms (e.g., insects) by interference with their ecological adjustment, such as by the introduction of parasites not previously present. Artificial application of biotic control.

Biological Diversity, Convention on The Convention on Biological Diversity (CBD) recognises the rights of countries on their genetic resources. To date 175 countries have ratified it. It has been in force since 1993. The Convention emphasises on: (1) Conservation of biodiversity. (2) Its sustainable use. (3) Fair and equitable sharing of benefits out of its use. (4) The preservation of knowledge and practices of indigenous communities. The challenges to the convention are sustainable conservation and utilisation. Southern nations need legislation to tackle bio-piracy, to document the knowledge of indigenous communities and to establish systems of benefit sharing.

International Intellectual Property Rights systems should recognise the rights of communities to traditional knowledge. Apart from this, an effective dispute settlement and compliance mechanism to settle CBD-related disputes, without resorting to other forums such as World Trade Organisation (WTO) is also required.

Biological Diversity Act, 2002 Government of India has enacted this Act for the purpose of conservation of biological diversity, its sustainable use and fair and equitable sharing of benefits arising out of the use of Biological resources and associated knowledge. A National Biodiversity Authority has been set up at Chennai under the Act. The Act also provides for establishment of State level Boards and Local level Biodiversity Management Committees to deal with any matter concerning biodiversity conservation, its sustainable use and fair and equitable sharing of benefits arising out of the use of biological resources and associated knowledge. *See* biodiversity.

Biological Growth The natural growth process of a renewable resource, such as a species of fish or a forest. This process can be described as a mathematical function, with the natural growth at any point in time being determined by the existing level of the resource stock, and the carrying capacity of its habitat (Perman, 1999). *See also* ecological species-area relationship; interactive resources; maximum sustainable yield (MSY); renewable resources.

Biological Indices An index of ecosystem health or condition using biological or physical characteristics. *See* diversity index, index of biotic integrity.

Biological Minimum The theoretical, minimum population level of a species, which form the extinction threshold. It means if the population level goes below this level, then organism fails to survive.

Biological Rank The social rank of a species or genus. *See* Peck order.

Biological Resources 1. Biological resources mean plants, animals and micro-organisms or parts thereof, their genetic use or value, but does not include human genetic material. (The Biological Diversity Act, 2002). 2. These include genetic resources, organisms or parts thereof, populations, or any other biotic component of ecosystems with actual or potential use or value for humanity (Convention on Biological Diversity, Rio de Jeneiro, Brazil, June 3-14, 1992, http://www.biodiv.org/).

Biological Spectrum A term used by Raunkiaer to indicate the relative percentages of species of different forms of life in a given area. The term is not in vogue.

Biological Surplus The number of animals in excess of the carrying capacity during the "pinch period", i.e., the period of adverse factors, such as winter. *Note:* Hunting, fishing and trapping are biologically sound does not exceed the biological surplus.

Biology The science of life. A branch of knowledge dealing with living organisms and vital processes; this broadly includes zoology, botany, morphology, genetics, embryology and allied sciences, but commonly restricted to considerations of wide application to the origin, development structure, functions and distribution of living matter as represented by plants and animals and to be generally recurrent phenomena of life, namely growth, development, reproduction and death.

Biomagnification (Bioconcentration) 1.The accumulation of toxic materials, then passage to feeders in food chains. 2. The increasing concentration of a compound in the tissues of organisms as the compound moves from lower to higher tropic levels. *See* Bioaccumulation.

Biomass 1. The total weight (at a given time) of living organisms of one or more species per unit of space (species biomass), or of all the species in a community (community biomass). 2. The total weight of matter incorporated into all organisms (living and dead). 3. The total mass, at a given time, of living organisms of one or more species per unit area (species biomass) or of all the species in the community (community biomass). 4. The living or dead weight of organic matter in material units such as living or dead weight, wet or dry weight, ash-free weight, etc. 5. Organic material both above-ground and below-ground, and both living and dead, e.g., trees, crops, grasses, tree litter, roots etc. biomass includes the pool definition for above- and below-ground mass (IPCC, 2003). 6. Biomass is the total living biological material in a given area or of a community or group. Biomass is measured by weight, or by dry weight, per given area (usually measured per square metre or square kilometre). The entire earth contains about 75 billion tons of biomass. Humans comprise about 250 million tons (0.33%), domesticated animals about 700 million tons (1.0%), and crops about 2 billion tons or 2.7 per cent of the Earth's biomass. Biomass may also be a measure of the dried organic mass of an ecosystem. As the tropic level increases, the biomass of each tropic level decreases. That is, producers (grass, trees, scrubs, etc.) have a much higher biomass than animals that consume them. The level with the least biomass is the highest predators in the food chain (foxes, eagles, etc.). Biomass is also related to Net Primary Productivity (NPP). Factors which limit NPP and thus mean biomass accumulates only slowly, include: (a) low rainfall, (b) low temperaures, (c) little available nutrients, (d) short growing season, and (e) lack of supply of stock material. Factors which encourage (NPP) and thus tend to increase biomass are the converse of these.

Biomass, Above-Ground All living biomass above the soil including stem, stump, branches, bark, seeds and foliage (IPCC, 2003).

Biomass, Below-Ground All living biomass of live roots. Fine roots of less than 2 mm diameter are sometimes excluded becasuse these often cannot be distinguished empirically from soil organic matter or litter (IPCC, 2003).

Biomass, Dead Wood All non-living woody biomass not contained in the litter, either standing, lying on the ground, or in the soil. Dead wood includes wood lying on the surface, dead roots, and stumps larger than or equal to 10 cm in diameter or any other diameter used by the country (IPCC, 2003).

Biome. 1. Major biotic community composed of all the plants and animals and smaller biotic communities, including the successional stages of an area. The smaller communities in a biome possess certain similarities in gross external vegetation appearances (e.g., deciduous trees, coniferous trees, grasslands, and savanna/woodlands) and environmental conditions present (especially gross climatic conditions, e.g., desert, tropical, temperate, tundra). 2. A living community formed by all the organisms occurring together in a given habitat. Among the major forested biomes are: (1) rain forest (tropical and temperate), (2) taiga, (3) temperate hardwood forest, and (4) tropical dry forest.

Biometry 1. Application of statistical methods to the study and interpretation of living organism. 2. The study of the statistics of biological phenomena. 3. The application of mathematics and statistics to the study of living things.

Bionomics Study of the relation of an organism or population of organisms to its environment.

Biophysical All the naturally occurring objects and processes of an area on the assumption that all naturally occurring things can be classified as being either living (i.e., biotic) or non-living (physical or abiotic).

Biophysical Determinism A point of view in planning which advocates making resource allocation and use decisions primarily on the basis of the inherent ability of the resource to sustain use, i.e., an ecological carrying capacity concept of resource capability. Economic and social system needs and desires are viewed as being completely subordinated to this inherent capacity of the resource to meet any and all demands while maintaining its natural integrity, condition, and performance of other natural processes at a desirable level. Economic and social demands can only be satisfied within the ecological carrying capacity constraints. The terms "biological primacy," "physiographic determinism," and "ecological determinism," in their common usage, are equivalent to biophysical determinism—though "biophysical" more clearly implies concern for both physical and biological processes.

Biosafety, Protocol on *See* the Cartagena Protocol on Biosafety.

Biosecurity in Forestry The term 'biosecurity' as used by FAO encompases all policy and regulatory frameworks to manage risks, including relevant enviromental risks, which are associated with food and agriculture, fisheries and forestry. Increasingly used all over the World, the term describes a process and an objective, which is a key requirement for public welfare. A related term 'biosafety' is used in the Cartegena Biosafety Protocol, where it specifically refers to the release and crossboundary movements. *See* the Cartagena Protocol on Biosafety.

Biosphere 1. That part of the Earth's crust, waters, and surrounding air-layer which is inhabited by living organisms. 2. That part of the earth's envelope, comprising the lower atmosphere (aero-plankton), the seas and the land surface (mantle rock) in which living organisms exist in their natural state. 3. The biosphere is the outermost part of the planet's shell—including air, land, surface rocks and water within which life occurs, and which biotic processes in turn alter or transform. From the broadest geophysiological point of view, the biosphere is the global ecological system integrating all living beings and their relationships, including their interaction with the elements of the lithosphere (rocks), hydrosphere (water), and atmosphere (air). This biosphere is postulated to have evolved, beginning through a process of biogenesis or biopoesis, at least some 3.5 billion years ago. Biomass accounts for about 3.7 kg carbon per square metre of the earth's surface averaged over land and sea, making a total of about 1900 gigatonnes of carbon.The term "biosphere" was coined by geologist Eduard Suess in 1875, which he defined as: "The place in earth's surface where life dwels." The Second International Conference on Closed Life Systems defined biospherics as the science and technology of analogs and models of Earth's biosphere; i.e., artificial Earth-like biospheres. Others may include the creation of artificial non-Earth biospheres – for example, human-centred biospheres or a native Martian biosphere – in the field of biospherics. The concept that the biosphere is itself a living organism, either actually or metaphorically, is known as Gaia theory. *See also* Man and the Biosphere Programme; biosphere homogenization; biosphere reserve; Gaia hypothesis.

Biosphere Reserves Biosphere Reserves are areas of terrestrial and coastal ecosystems, which are internationally recognized within the framework of UNESCO's Man and Biosphere (MAB) Programme. These reserves are required to meet a minimal set of criteria and adhere to a minimal set of conditions before being admitted to the World Network of Biosphere Reserve designated by UNESCO for inclusion in the World Network of Biosphere Reserves. The world's major ecosystem types and landscapes are represented in this network, which is devoted to conserving biological diversity, promoting research and monitoring as well as seeking to provide models of sustainable development in the service of humankind. These reserves are rich in biological and cultural diversity and encompass unique features of exceptionally pristine nature. The goal is to facilitate conservation of representative landscapes and their immense biological diversity and cultural heritage, foster economic and human development which is culturally and ecologically sustainable and to provide support for research, monitoring, education and information exchange. The scheme is a pioneering effort at pursuing the increasingly difficult yet urgent task of conserving ecological diversity under mounting pressures. The thirteen Biosphere Reserves set up in the country so far not only aim to protect representative ecosystem, but also serve as laboratories for evolving alternative models of development. The Ministry of Forest and Environment, Government of India provided financial assistance to the respective State Governments for conservation and management of these Biosphere Reserves. Research and Development Projects are also supported. On the basis of the proposal submitted by the Ministry to the International Coordinating Council (ICC) of Man and Biosphere Reserve (MAB) Programme of UNESCO, three Biosphere Reserves – Sunderban (West Bengal), Mannar (Tamil Nadu) and Nilgiri (Tamil Nadu) have been included in the International Network of Biosphere Reserves. Inclusion of any site in the World Network of Biosphere Reserves facilitates International recognition and attracts additional funding for these reserves.

Biostatics The branch of physiology that deals with the relation of structure to function in plants and animals.

Bio-Survey and Bio-Utilisation Bio-survey and bio-utilization means survey and collection of species, subspecies, genes, components and extracts of biological resource for any purpose and includes characterization, inventorisation and bioassay (The Biological Diversity Act, 2002).

Biosystematics Taxonomic studies involving morphology, cytogenetics, ecology and phytogeography.

Biota The plants and animals of an area, taken collectively.

Biotechnology and Forestry Biotechnology encompasses a wide range of scientific techniques that use living organisms, or their parts, to make or modify products. Conventional plant biotechnology (plant breeding) has been used for thousands of years for the improvement of agricultural crops but its use for breeding and improvement of forest trees is more recent. Biotechnolgies are now commonly used for tree breeding and propagation and also for processing applications, such as pollution control and raw material breakdown. Modern biotechnologies currently used in forestry fall into three broad categories: (1) Biotechnologies based on molecular markers which can be used, *inter alia,* to (a) quantity genetic diversity among populations and individual trees; (b) identify genotypes in taxonomic studies, biological studies and genetic fingerprinting; and (c) locate genes affecting quantitative traits of economic importance. (2) Technologies that enhance vegetative propagation and support large-scale production of uniform materials. Tissue culture of plants under laboratory conditions can also be used to select traits such as disease resistance and tolerance of herbicides, metals, salts and low temperatures. Micropropagation is already used in crop and horticultural species and techniques exist for its application in a number forest tree species. High cost is currently an impediment to the direct use of micropropagated material in forestry programmes. (3) Genetic modification of forestry trees. The term Genetically Modified Organisms (GMO) generally refers to an organism into which genetic material from other organisms is incorporated.

Biotechnology The application of biological science and techniques to industrial process. This includes the genetic modification of food and the recycling of wastes.

Biotic All of the natural living organisms in a planning area and their life processes. A resource classification category which subdivides the natural resources and properties into either the biotic or the abiotic (non-living) entities and characteristics. Human activities are not usually grouped with either of these categories because they are not considered to be a part of a planning area's natural entities or characteristics. Nevertheless, native cultures have been actively influencing the course of biotic activity in some areas for centuries.

Biotic Climax 1. A climax community maintained in a stable condition by some biotic factor, e.g., grassland which is prevented by grazing from passing into woodland. 2. A community maintained by biotic factors and therefore, differing from any other climax community. One maintained by humans or livestock is termed disclimax; plagioclimax. *See* Climatic climax; Edaphic climax.

Biotic Control Check on the increase of population of an animal, insect or plant through disease-producing organisms, such as fungi, bacteria, insect parasites and predators, etc. *See* control.

Biotic Factor 1. Any environmental influence of living organisms, e.g. shading trees, trampling by heavy animals, fire caused by man, in contrast to inanimate, i.e. abiotic, particularly climatic and edaphic influences. 2. Any influence of living organisms, usually restricted to the influence of animals including man. 3. Influences for which living organisms are responsible as contrasted with climatic and edaphic factors. Usually restricted to the influence of animals, including man. The influence of man alone is termed anthropogenic. *See* edaphic factor.

Biotic Potential (Reproductive Potential) 1. The inherent ability of members of a population to grow in numbers within a given time and understated environmental conditions. This potential depends on the number of live, fertile offspring produced at each reproduction and, where sex is involved, the sex ratio, as well as the age classes distribution of the population. 2. The inherent capacity of an organism or species to reproduce and survive. This is expressed in terms of numbers that could be produced under optimum conditions and in the absence of environmental resistance. 3. The inherent power of an organism to multiply over a given period of time in the absence of control factors. *See* carrying capacity.

Biotic Province A geographical region characterized by the presence of one or more ecological associations that differ at least quantitatively from those of adjoining provinces and marked by a tendency to act as a centre of ecological dispersion.

Biotic 1. Pertaining to living organisms in their ecological rather than physiological relation. 2. Of environmental factors which are due to living organisms, as opposed to physical factors such as light and temperature. *See* abiotic and biotic factor.

Biotype 1. A genetically homogeneous population composed only of closely similar individuals. 2. A population with identical genetic constitution. 3. A genotypic race or group of organisms. 4. A region uniform in environmental conditions and in its population of animals and plants for which it is the habitat.

Bird of Prey Any of a number of flesh-eating birds as the eagle, the hawk, the owl, the vulture, etc.

Bird Any of a group of warm-blooded vertebrates with feathers and wings, belonging to the class Aves. The ornithology of India is not so rich in specimens of gorgeous or variegated plumage as that of other tropical regions. The peacock (*Pavo cristatus*) is the national bird of India. Out of the 8650 species in the World, India has as many as 1200, and so on a land surface of only

4 per cent, it has 16 per cent of the total number on earth. If subspecies are included there are 2061 forms in all, and out of these 1750 are residents and the rest are migrants. Ornithologists have classified birds into 27 Orders and 155 Families and India's status in ornithological terms can be judged from the fact that it has representatives from 20 Orders and 77 Families. Other than peacock, the parrots are also remarkable for beauty. Four vultures are found including the common scavengers, *Gyps indicus* and *Pseudugyps bengalensis*. Of falcons, there are the peregrine (*Falco peregrinus*), the *shareen* or royal falcon (*Falco peregrinator*), and the *lagar* (*F. jugger*) which are all trained for hawking. Among hawks, the *shikra* (*Astur badius*), the *goshawk* (*A. palumbarius*) and the sparrow hawk (*Accipiter nisus*) deserve mention. King-fishers and Herons of different kinds are sought for their plumage. The *mynah* (*Acridotheres tristis*), a member of the starling family, lives contentedly in a cage and talks well. Snipe, pigeons, partridges, quail, plover, duck, teal, sheldrake, wigeon—all of several varieties make up the list of small game.

Bison or Gaur (*Bos Gaurus*) Found in India is not a true bison at all; it is a wild ox, the largest of the bovines though in common parlance it is called "Indian bison". True bison is a bovine ruminant Bison bison, with high, well-haired shoulders, found in North America. The Gaur is the embodiment of vigour and strength as it has a huge head, deep massive body and sturdy limbs. Gaur are distributed in the hill forests of India, and appear to attain their finest development in the South Indian hill ranges and Assam.

Bit Map A pattern (i.e. on/off) on a grid stored in memory and used to generate an image on a raster scan display.

Bit The smallest unit of information that can be stored and processed in a computer. A bit may have two values — 0 or 1, i.e.; yes/no, true/false, on/off.

Bite (Fishing) Taking of bait by fish in bottom fishing.

Black Buck *See* Antelope.

Blank, Forest 1. An unstocked forest area where, for any reason, few or no trees are growing. 2. A forest area with few or no trees, usually covered with grass. 3. A gap in a plantation.

Blaze, to 1. To mark trees or logs with blazes. 2. To mark a tree, usually with paint or cutting into the bark. Often used along boundaries.

Blaze A shallow excision removing a portion of the bark with or without wood, from a tree or log, so as to leave a visible mark for indication. This is done for purposes of field identification, for putting hammer-mark, or for collection of exudation.

Blight An insect or fungus causing a sudden dying of shoots, foliage or blossoms; also the condition itself.

Block 1. A main territorial division of forest, generally bounded by natural features and bearing a local proper name. 2. A number of plots often, but not necessarily, contiguous, grouped together because they appear likely to be fairly homogeneous in respect of the variable to be studied, except for differences due to experimental treatment.

Blue Bull *See* Bull, blue; or Nilgai.

Blue Pine (*Pinus wallichiana*) The Blue Pine is a pine native to the Himalaya, Karakoram and Hindu Kush mountains, from eastern Afghanistan towards east across northern India up to Yunnan in south-west China. It grows at high altitudes in mountain valleys at altitudes of 1800-4300 m (rarely as low as 1200 m), and is a tree from 30-50 m in height. It grows in a temperate climate with dry winters and wet summers.This pine is also called the Himalayan White Pine. It is also often known as 'Bhutan Pine'. The leaves ("needles") are in fascicles (bundles) of five and are 12-18 cm long, and often droop gracefully. The cones are long and slender, 16-32 cm, yellow-buff when mature, with thin scales; the seeds are 5-6 mm long with a 20-30 mm wing. Typical habitats are mountain screes and glacier forelands, but it will also form old growth forests as the primary species or in mixed forests with Deodar Cedar, birch, spruce, and fir. In some places it reaches the tree line.The wood is moderately hard, durable and highly resinous. It is a good firewood but gives off a pungent resinous smoke. It is another commercial source of turpentine which is of superior quality than that of Chir Pine (*P. roxburghii*) but is not produced so freely. It is also a popular tree for planting in parks and large gardens, grown for its attractive foliage and large, decorative cones. It is also valued for its relatively high resistance to air pollution, tolerating this better than some other conifers.

Blue Sheep *See* Bharal or Blue sheep.

BMP (Best Management Practices) A series of guidelines or minimum standards for proper application of forestry operations, designed primarily to prevent soil erosion and water pollution, and to protect certain wildlife habitat values in riparian and wetland areas.

Boar, Indian Wild (*Sus Cristatus*) A species of wild swine, widely distributed in south and east Asia. It lives in grass or scanty bush jungle and sometimes in forest. It is very destructive to crops and in cultivated areas. The colour of the body is black mixed with grey, rusty-brown and white hairs.

Bole The main stem of a tree, sometimes used to refer to only the lower part of the stem up to a point where the main branches are given off, i.e., as a synonym for clear or clean bole or trunk.

Bole, Clear (or Clean) The part of a bole that is free of branches.

Bole, Commercial The length of bole that is ordinarily fit for utilization as timber. *See* timber, merchantable.

Bole, Standard Timber The length of the bole from ground level up to the point where the average diameter over bark is 8 inches (20 cms).

Boolean Algebra Operations based on logical combinations of objects (using and, not, or and x).

Boolean Arithmetic Analytical expression that uses a true or false condition. It usually contains logical expressions (e.g., Distance from edge > 50 m).

Boolean Operators Boolean operators (not, and, or) are used to combine logical expressions into a complex expression. These operators are based on logic which are used to query two or more sets of data. The operators allow inclusion, exclusion, intersection, and differences in the data to be determined.

Boolean Overlay A type of map overlay based on boolean algebra.

Boom A contrivance, usually of linked floating timbers, for arresting the passage of timber floated down a river from points on its upper reaches or in coastal depot, for preventing the escape of timber due to tidal currents.

Boreal Referring to northern latitudes.

Borer, Shoot or Twig A member of one of several families of coleoptere, lepidoptera or diptera, which bores into the wood or pith of twigs or shoots.

Boswellia It is a genus of trees known for their fragrant resin which has many pharmacological uses particularly as anti-inflammatories. The Biblical incense frankincense was probably an extract from the resin of the tree, *Boswellia sacra*. There are four main species of *Boswellia*. *Boswellia sacra* (syn. *B. carteri, B.*

thurifera) is the Arabian Frankincense, and the best quality comes from the Oman and the Yemen. *Boswellia serrata* is Indian frankincense or **Salai**. It is found in Rajasthan, Madhya Pradesh, Chhattisgarh and Andhra Pradesh in India. Its aroma is generally considered to be far inferior compared to *B. sacra* or *B. frereana*. *Boswellia papyrifera* is a species from Ethiopia, considered a superior version but is virtually unobtainable in the West. Boswellia has long been used in Ayurvedic medicine. Recently, the boswellic acids that are a component of the resin it produces have shown some promise as a treatment for asthma and various inflammatory conditions.

Botanical Area or Garden 1. An area which has been designated as containing specimens or group exhibits of plants, plant groups, and plant communities which are significant because of form, colour, occurrences, habitat, location, life history, arrangement, ecology, environment, rarity, and other features. 2. A garden, often with greenhouse, that is used for the culture and study of plants collected and grown for scientific and display purposes. *Note.* This aims at the conservation of plant species as living repositories of definite genetic constitution. It seeks to prevent the extinction of rare plant species. This is accomplished by growing them under suitable environmental condition. *See* arboretum.

Botanical Survey of India (BSI) Botanical Survey of India was established in 1890 with the basic objectives of carrying out floristic surveys. It was revived and reorganised in 1954. During the successive plan periods, its functions have been gradually expanded. The objectives and perspectives of Botanical Survey of India were thoroughly reviewed in 2002 by the subcommittee constituted by Programme Advisory Committee (PAC) for Botanical Survey of India and Zoological Survey of India. Primary objectives of BSI are: (1) exploration, inventorisation and documentation of phytodiversity in general and protected areas, hotspots, fragile ecosystems and sacred groves in particular; publication of National, State and District Floras; (2) monitoring phytodiversity to evaluate the qualitative changes in species rich and sensitive areas; *ex situ* conservation of critically threatened taxa in botanical gardens; (3) identification of species with traditional economic uses and preparation of protocols for their conservation and sustainable utilization; (4) to complete a national database of plant species, herbarium specimens, live specimens, illustrations, relatives of cultivated species and economically important species.

Botany The science that deals with plants, their life, their structure, growth and classification. It is a sub-division of biology concerned with plant life.

Branch Wood The woody portions of a tree exclusive of the bole and roots.

Breast Height Almost universally adopted as the standard height for measuring girth, diameter and basal area of standing trees. In India, Burma, America, Union of South Africa, Malaya and some other old British colonies, it is taken at 4 feet 6 inches (1.37 m) above ground level. Europe, UK and most other countries of the Commonwealth have it as 4 feet 3 inches (1.30 m) and this is recommended as a standard for International adherence by FAO. On slopes, breast height is taken on the uphill side.

Breeding Population A population within which free inter-breeding takes place and evolutionary change may appear and be preserved.

Breeding Potential The theoretical breeding rate, under ideal condition of an organism. It is low in large animals, but very high in many fishes and insects. Breeding potential is an index of the reproductive capacity of the species irrespective of survival to maturity. *See* biotic potential; environmental resistance.

Breeding Range The geographical area or region in which breeding is carried on by individual pairs of breeding populations of a particular type of animal.

Breeding Rate Natural inherent capacity to reproduce; numbers per unit time, usually expressed as a theoretical or attained rate.

Broad Assessment A synthesis of current scientific knowledge, including a description of uncertainties and assumptions, to provide a characterization and comprehensive description of ecological, social, and economic components within an assessment area critical for understanding past and present conditions and projecting future trends which provides a foundation for the identification of additional or necessary information for policy discussions or decisions.

Broad Leaved Trees or Species All trees classified botanically as Angiospermae. The species belonging to this group are generally broadleaved (e.g., oak – Quercus, beech – Fagus, maple – Acer, ebony – Diospyros, popular – Populus). They produce timber usually known as "hardwoods".

Brood Lac A twig of a lac host tree containing lac encrustation with larvae of the lac insect emerging or about to emerge from it; used in the propagation of lac.

Brood Tree, Lac A lac-infection host tree set apart for collecting brood lac for further infection.

Browse 1. That part of the current leaf and twig growth of potentially palatable shrubs, and trees available for animal consumption. It includes leaves. Bark of some trees is included. 2. The acts of consuming such growth.

Browsing Feeding on twigs or shoots, with or without attached leaves, of shrubs, trees or woody climbers. *See* grazing.

Brundtland Commission The World Commission on Environment and Development (WCED) (1984-87), the chairman of which was Dr. Gro Harlem Brundtland, former Prime Minister and Environment Minister of Norway.

Brush Matting Placing a mat of brushwood or grasses on land to conserve moisture and reduce wind erosion while a cover of trees or other vegetation is being established.

Brushwood 1. A growth of low shrubs and bushes. 2. Fallen or cut branches and twigs of trees.

Bryophytes Non-vascular plants including mosses, liverworts, and hornworts.

Buck, Black *See* Antelope.

Buffalo, Wild This occurs in the grass jungles of the Nepal Terai and the plains around the Ganga and the Brahmaputra in Asia. A few herds survive in parts of Udanti sanctuary in Raipur district of Chhattisgarh and Sunabaeda sanctuary in Kalahandi district of Orissa. Though it has a finer carriage, the wild buffalo differs little in general appearance from the tame one, except perhaps that it is a sleeker, heavier, and more robust looking animal; like the domestic buffalo, the wild buffalo is slaty black, the horns are flat and triangular in section, those of the cows are less massive and vary less in shape. Except for man, the tiger is the only enemy the wild buffalo has to fear, and against a vigorous bull even the tiger stands little chance.

Buffer 1. A designated land or water area, along the perimeter of some land use, the use of which is regulated so as to resist, absorb, or otherwise preclude unwanted development or other intrusions (visual, noise, recreational use) into areas beyond the strip of undisturbed vegetation that retards the flow of runoff water, causing deposition of transported material and thereby reducing sediment in receiving streams. 2. A vegetation strip maintained along a stream, lake, road, or different vegetative zone to mitigate the impact of actions on adjacent lands. Also called a buffer strip or zone. 3. An animal, that by serving as food for predators, cuts down the predation losses of another animal (as a game bird or animal) more desired in a community.

Buffer Action The ability of a soil to resist major alterations in its *p*H value under the influence of added dilute solutions of ionizable substances. A 'cushioning' effect produced by the colloidal material present in the soil.

Buffer Belts Areas of suitable width around or adjacent to sanctuaries/parks, within which no shooting other than that required for legitimate crop protection, will be permitted and within which no professional grassers will be allowed to establish cattle pens. Sometimes known as Buffer zones.

Buffer Species A non-game or comparatively undesirable animal species that is food for predators. Its consumption reduces predation (substituting for it) upon game or other desirable species. Managers attempt to increase buffer species to reduce predation harmful to their species objectives.

Buffer Stripping Establishing narrow strips of grass or other erosion-resisting vegetation below cultivation or above water diversions, usually on the contour, to resist erosion.

Buffer Zones These are zones between areas of intensive land use, such as logging or farming, and areas of strict conservation. They can help to reduce encroachment onto conservation areas if they offer employment opportunities that are more attractive than encroachment (Panayotou, 1993).

Buffering The creation of a zone of specified width around a point, line or area. The buffer is a new polygon which is used in queries to determine which entities occur within or outside the defined area. Generally used in GIS.

Bug An error in a computer programme or in a piece of electronic that causes it to function improperly.

Bull, Blue or Nilgai (*Boselaphus Tragocamelus*) A slate blue antelope of India. *See* Nilgai.

Bundle of Entitlements (or Rights) This refers to the rights and responsibilities of an owner over the use of a resource. There are generally several entitlements, including privileges (such as construction, exclusive use, or subsurface resôurce mining) and limitations (such as prohibited activities or obligation to sell to the Government in some circumstances). *See also* property rights.

Burning Controlled Any deliberate use of fire whereby burning is restricted to a predetermined area and intensity.

Burning, Early Controlled burning early in the dry season, before the leaves and undergrowth are completely dry or before the leaves are shed, as an insurance against later fire damage.

Burning, Late Controlled or uncontrolled burning late in the dry season, after leaf-fall where the trees are deciduous.

Burning, Patch Burning slash, grass, etc., in patches for the purpose of preparing sites for planting or sowing.

Burning, Strip A method of burning controlled practiced on slopes. The area is burnt in successive strips beginning on the uphill side.

Burr A woody outgrowth on the bole or branch of a tree, often caused by an accumulation of dormant buds.

Bush 1. A general term for all types of forest or woodland, usually referring to untended indigenous forest. 2. Shrub.

Bustards (*Otididae*) Large, chiefly terrestrial game birds (*Genus Otis*) of the Old World and Australia. They are related to the cranes and plovers. They are somewhat slow and stately on the ground, but are powerful fliers. They are first rate sporting birds and are excellent for eating. The Great Indian Bustard (*Choriotis nigriceps*) is found over a large part of peninsular India. As there is a danger of its extinction, it is given special protection throughout its habitat.

Butt The base of a tree or log.

Buttress An outgrowth from the base of the tree connecting it with the roots, especially common in tropical rain forest species. An exaggerated form of root swelling is called buttressing. *See* fluting.

Buzzard Any of various birds of prey of various species belonging to genus Buteo and allied genera. Buzzards found in India are:

COMMON BUZZARD (*Buteo buteo*). It is difficult to distinguish this from *B. ferox*. LONG-LEGGED BUZZARD (*Buteo ferox*). This is a heavy lumpish bird, with colour varying from pale buff-brown and white to almost black. It is a frequent visitor to the plains of the Punjab, Rajasthan and Uttar Pradesh in winter, arriving in February and leaving in March.

Byte A group of contiguous bites, usually 8, that represent a basic unit of information which is operated on as a unit, the number of bytes is used to measure the capacity of memory and storage units in a computer, e.g. 256 kbytes, 300 mbytes.

Cc

C++ A high-level programming language often used to write graphics programmes.

Cadastral Map A map showing the precise boundaries and size of land parcels.

Cadastral Survey Survey relating to land boundaries, made to create units suitable for title transfer or to define the limitations of title. Derived from "cadastre" meaning a register of land quantities, values, and ownership used levying taxes, the term may properly be applied to surveys of a similar nature outside the public lands. Such surveys are more commonly called "land surveys" or "property surveys".

Calcicole A plant that lives in soils rich in calcium.

Calcification A soil-forming process resulting in accumulation of calcium and magnesium carbonates in the soil horizons, and found largely in semi-arid and sub-humid desert and grassland regions and also in more humid forested regions.

Calcifuge A plant which tends to avoid calcareous soils.

Calliper (Caliper), Tree An instrument for measuring tree or log diameters by taking their rectilinear projections on a graduated scale. Girth calliper is a tree caliper (caliper) specially graduated to read off girth class directly.

Calliper, Girth A calliper (caliper), tree specially graduated to read off girth class directly.

Callus Tissue that develops after a plant is wounded and tends to cover the wound.

Cambium 1.The actively dividing layer of cells which lies between and gives rise to xylem and phloem, i.e., wood. 2. The layer of cells between the inner-bark and wood of a tree (where growth takes place).

Canadian Geographic Information System (CGIS) An early GIS using data collected for the land inventory system that was developed as a result of the requirements of the Canadian Agriculture and Development Act.

Canal An artificially created waterway to carry water.

Candle (Tree) The new bright green and tender growth of conifers in the spring.

Canker A definite, relatively localized, necrotic lesion primarily of the bark and cambium.

Canopy 1. The more or less continuous cover of branches and foliage formed collectively by the crown of a tree and the crowns of adjacent trees and other woody growth. Canopy closure may be the result of overhead tree cover. 2. The overhead or dominant trees in a forest. 3. The overhead branches and leaves of streamside vegetation.

Canopy Class One of the classes into which canopies found in a storeyed high forest are divided on the basis of their relative heights, e.g., top canopy, middle storey, etc.

Canopy, Closed A canopy in which the individual tree crowns generally touch one another.

Canopy Cover 1. The percentage of the ground covered by a vertical projection of the outermost perimeter of the natural spread of the foliage of plants. Same as crown cover (IPCC, 2003). Small openings within the canopy are included. Total canopy coverage may exceed 100 per cent due to layering of different vegetative strata.

Canopy Density Per cent area of land covered by the canopy of trees. It is expressed as a decimal coefficient, taking closed canopy as unity.

Capability 1. Capability refers to evaluations for usability based on the natural, intrinsic, or present state of the resource. The potential of an area of land to produce resources, supply goods and services, and allow resource uses under an assumed set of management practices and at a given level of management intensity. Capability depends on current conditions and site conditions such as climate, slope, landform, soils and geology, as well as the application of management practices, such as silviculture or protection from fires, insects, and disease. 2. Capability indicates "intrinsic ability" of land in general. It is the ability to produce some resource, crop, or use the intensity, and quality of land on a sustained basis (i.e. without significant resource deterioration over the time span of renewing biogeochemical cycles), unaltered by any level of potential, future human management activities or other type of alternation). It is sometimes confused with feasibility and suitability. "Feasibility" refers to usability; potential ratings based on an evaluation of offsite factors — such as accessibility, present and forecasted socio-economic conditions, technological developments, etc. Suitability is used for evaluations based on assumptions about potential usability or productivity if specified management alterations were to be made — such as drainage improvements, added irrigation and/ or fertilization.

Capital 1. One of the major factors of economic production consisting of property from which an income is derived, expressed in terms of money. The term is frequently used interchangeably with capital goods that are created by people. Capital goods are sometimes called "intermediate goods" because they serve consumers only indirectly in satisfying their wants. 2. Any asset that provides economic or social services over a period of time. The main types of capital used in environmental economics are human-made capital, human capital, natural capital and social capital. Human-made capital consists of assets, such as buildings, equipment, plants and machinery, and tools. Human capital is made up of the investment in education and training embodied in the workforce. Natural capital is made up of the stock of environmental assets such as soil and forests, wildlife and water, biological species, landscape, and wetlands. Social capital consists of the network of institutions and social relationships in society, which are the basis of the proper functioning of legal and economic systems. Capital is a particularly important concept in the analysis of sustainability and sustainable development, since an economy's capacity to ensure well-being for its citizens can be reduced over time if the aggregate capital stock is not maintained, or if there is insufficient investment in a certain type of capital. *See* capital for sustainable livelihoods.

Capital Asset Pricing The value of a resource stock can be expressed as the Net Present Value (NPV) of the stream of service flows it is expected to yield over the lifetime of the resource. Such a method for arriving at the price of a resource is referred to as the capital assets pricing method. Calculating NPV involves using the technique of discounting (Perman *et al.*, 1999).

Capacity Building The term often used in the sustainable development (SD) literature to denote the development of the ability of individuals, groups, organizations and institutions in a society to find and implement solutions to environmental issues as part of a wider effort to achieve the goal of sustainable development. This term encompasses more than simply formal training, and includes collaboration and partnership with overseas experts in improving the functions of civil society and local bureaucracies (OECD, 1995).

Capital for Sustainable Livelihoods Capital required for sustainable livelihoods can be categorised into five forms or types. They are: (1) natural capital: privately owned assets such as land, forests, water and pasture; (2) physical capital: privately owned assets that can be used to increase labour and land productivity (such as farm animals, tools and machinery) and publicly owned economic infrastructure (e.g. roads, electricity supply) and social infrastructure (e.g. schools, hospitals); (3) financial capital: cash (income and savings) which are readily convertible liquid capital; (4) human capital: health, nutritional levels, educational standard and skills; and (5) social capital: the set of social relationship on which people can draw to expand livelihoods options. The set of social relationship includes kinship, friendships, patron-client relations, reciprocal arrangements, membership of formal groups and membership of organizations that provide loans, grants and other forms of insurance (Carney, 1998).

Capital Investment An input to a system, typically of cash, that increases the stock of natural or human-made resources (assets) needed to maintain or increase the flow of outputs in the future. Benefits resulting from capital investments are normally recouped in excess of 1 year.

Caracal (*Felis Caracal Schmitzi*) This is a kind of lynx, found in North Africa and South West Asia, with reddish fur and black-tipped ears and tail. The pelt of the animal is valued. In India, it is found in the drier parts of the Punjab, Rajasthan, Uttar

Pradesh and Madhya Pradesh. An uncommon and elusive animal, it is fast approaching extinction and so requires special efforts for its preservation.

Carbon A non-metallic chemical element occurring in many inorganic compounds and all organic compounds. Diamonds and graphite are pure carbon; carbon is also present, with other substances, in air, coal, and charcoal.

Carbon Budget Approach An approach to framing an optimal climate change policy. An alternative to benefit-cost analysis (CBA) for global warming, this method ignores damage considerations and imposes an upper atmospheric concentration or warming limit, determined on the basis of ethical, political or precautionary considerations. Under the carbon budget approach, the costs of the constraint applied are reflected in the shadow value of emissions, and the shadow value will bear no relationship to the global warming damages occurring. The advantage of this technique is that no modelling of global warming damages is needed, although the question remains as to how stringent the carbon constraint should be. Fankhauser (1995) reports that the shadow prices from carbon budget models are often far greater than actual social cost estimates, at least in later time periods.

Carbon Cycle The biogeochemical cycle undergone by carbon that is utilized by organisms, later liberated upon the death and decomposition of the organisms, and returned to its original state to be reused by another organism. It includes the photosynthesis of carbohydrates by plant chlorophyll from atmospheric carbon dioxide and water. Plants and animals transform carbohydrates into the structures and energy for growth and life processes. Carbon dioxide is returned (aided by the action of bacteria and other microorganisms and by combustion) to the atmosphere by excreta and decay.

Carbon Dioxide (CO_2) A colourless, odourless, non-combustible gas. Humans and all other living organisms give off carbon dioxide in respiration and decomposition. Trees and other plants absorb it and use it during photosynthesis. Also emitted as a by-product of burning fossil fuels.

Carbon in Above-Ground Biomass Carbon in all living biomass above the soil, including stem, stump, branches, bark, seeds and foliage. Where the forest under-story is a relatively small component of the above ground biomass (carbon pool) it is acceptable to exclude it, provided this is done in a consistent manner throughout the inventory time series (FRA, 2005).

Carbon in Below-Ground Biomass Carbon in all living biomass of live roots. It includes below ground part of the stump. Fine roots of less than 2 mm diameter are excluded, because these often cannot be distinguished empirically from soil organic matter or litter (FRA, 2005).

Carbon in Dead Wood Biomass Carbon in all living woody biomass not contained in the litter, either standing, lying on the ground, or in the soil. Dead wood includes wood lying in the surface, dead roots, and stumps larger than or equal to 10 cm in diameter or any other diameter used by the country (FRA, 2005).

Carbon Sequestration The removal and storage of carbon from the atmosphere by green plants through the process of photosynthesis, in which carbon dioxide is combined with water to form carbohydrates that can be stored in plant tissues.

Carbon Sink An area where the rate of carbon uptake by living organisms exceeds the rate of carbon release, so that carbon is sequestered in organic or inorganic form. Young stand of forests is an example of carbon sink. *See* carbon stock.

Carbon Stock The quantity of carbon in a 'pool', meaning a reservoir or system which has the capacity to accumulate or release carbon. Examples of carbon pools are living biomass including above and below ground biomass; dead organic matter including dead wood and litter; soils (soil organic matter). The units are mass (IPCC, 2003). *See* carbon sink.

Carbon, Soil Organic carbon in mineral and organic soils (including peat) to a specified depth chosen by the country and applied consistently through the time series (FRA, 2005).

Carbon-Nitrogen Ratio The ratio of the weight of organic carbon to the weight of total nitrogen in a soil, or organic material.

Carnivora Group of placental mammals, mostly flesh-eating (cats, dogs, mongooses). Most have large incisor and canine teeth. Some carnivora (e.g., bears and giant panda) also feed on vegetation.

Carnivore 1. A flesh-eating animal. 2. Any of various predatory, flesh-eating mammals of the order Carnivora, including the dogs, cats, bears, weasels, and raccoons. Opposed to herbivore. *See* carnivora and omnivore.

Carp (*Cyprinus Carpio*) A fresh water fish inhabiting ponds and sluggish streams.

Carrying Capacity (Wildlife) The population (as of one species of animal), for which a given area (as of water or forest or pasture), can provide essentials (such as food and cover) and thus support the population without undergoing deterioration. It must be able to carry through the "pinch" period or period of greatest difficulty (such as winter). Regardless of other factors, the carrying capacity cannot exceed the saturation point. When herds of deer exceed the carrying capacity in a forest, permanent damage to growing stock or regeneration will result. In wildlife management, carrying capacity denotes the optimum density of game which a given environment is capable of sustaining permanently. The term can be used for cattle grazing in pastures or reserved forests also. For this the term "grazing capacity" will be more appropriate. The capacity in game range is exceeded when a species become so numerous as to destroy or reduce in vigour its food plants. Ranges over-browsed by deer may require as much as 10 to 15 years to recover. Game management is concerned with measuring carrying capacity accurately and with clues for early detection of over population.

Carrying Capacity 1. The number (or weight) of organisms of a given species and quality that can survive in, without deteriorating a given ecosystem through the least favourable environmental conditions that occur within a stated interval of time. 2. The maximum population density of a given species in an area beyond which no significant increase can occur without damage occurring to the resources upon which the population depends. 3. The quantity of biomass an environment is capable of carrying over a 12-months period or throughout the most critical period of the year or maintained indefinitely. 4. The maximum number or biomass of organisms of a given species that can be sustained or survived on a long term basis within an ecosystem, during a specific time period. 5. Carrying capacity is the threshold limit of any human activity beyond which physical capacity of the ecosystem is diminished and ecological capacity is degraded. The concept of carrying capacity has tremendous relevance to sustainability of resources. It is traditionally an ecological concept. It was basically developed to explain characteristic population growth forms in an ecosystem. It aims at explaining the upper limit of resource utilisation in an ecosystem. It is significant for scientific planning and management of natural resource use. Over the years, the concept has emerged as an effective tool of natural resource management. But difficulties in measuring the thresholds have restricted the concept to its use as only a planning tool. A blend of factors determining physical and ecological capacity, along with existing social realities, helps to determine the optimum carrying capacity for any resource. In human environment, carrying capacity is primarily influenced by the factors such as: (a) Lifestyle prevalent in the society; (b) Level of science and technology; (c) Institutional innovations in the society; (d) Increasing hopes and aspirations of the people for better standard of life. In any ecosystem, the carrying capacity depends on the available resources and the ability of the system to cope with the residual waste. The conceptual model of carrying capacity comprises: (a) Supportive capacity: this symbolises the ability of the ecosystem to allow withdrawal of resources like raw materials, water, etc. without causing permanent damage to the environment; (b) Assimilative capacity: this symbolises the ability to absorb certain amount of wastes without ill effects or without affecting the inbuilt assimilative capacity. Carrying capacity of a region from the point of aforesaid illustration is described as the number of persons that can be supported by a unit area of land while producing raw material and assimilating the wastes. The human population has shown manifold increase, which necessitated an ever-increasing demand on resources. The propensities of the societies to over-consume the natural resources lead to consume the natural capital, i.e. the base of productive resources itself. This phenomenon is synonymous with ecological equivalent of deficit financing. Likewise, the assimilative capacity can absorb wastes, to some extent but cannot regenerate the land productivity or recover the ecosystem functioning, or replenish the water regimes or restore the lost biodiversity beyond a limit. However, the carrying capacity is subject to change. The expansion of ecological boundaries of carrying capacity is possible in consequence to natural evolutionary forces transforming both physical resources and composition of life forms into an efficient structural and functional ecosystem. But the pace of evolutionary process is so slow and the forces acting on the ecosystem is so negative that it is unthinkable to expect a positive change in the carrying capacity of the system.

Carrying Capacity, Range The maximum number of individual animals (or equivalents) that can survive the greatest period of stress each year on a given land area. It does not refer to sustained yield. In range management, the term has become erroneously synonymous with grazing capacity.

Cartagena Protocol on Biosafety The Cartagena Protocol on Biosafety is the first international regulatory framework for safe transfer, handling and use of Living Modified Organisms (LMOs). It is a protocol under the aegis of the Convention on Biological Diversity. The Protocol seeks to protect biological diversity from the potential risks posed by living modified organisms resulting from modern biotechnology. It establishes an Advance Informed Agreement (AIA) procedure for ensuring that countries are provided with the information necessary to make informed decisions before agreeing to the import of such organisms into their territory. It further incorporates procedure for import of LMOs with respect to Food Feed and Product (FFP), Risk Assessment and Risk Management Framework and Capacity Building. The protocol contains reference to a precautionary approach. The protocol also establishes a Biosafety Clearing House to facilitate the exchange of information on living modified organisms and to assist countries in the implementation of the protocol. The protocol was adopted on 29th January, 2000. The protocol has been signed by 103 countries (except USA). India signed the Biosafety Protocol on 23rd January, 2001 and acceded to the Protocol on 17th January, 2003. The protocol has come into force on 11th September, 2003.

Cartesian Co-ordinates The system for locating a point by reference to its distance from axes intersecting at right angles, often represented as a grid on a map.

Cartograms Maps that show the location of objects relative to a non-euclidean variable such as population density or relative distance.

Cartographic Modelling A generic methodology for structuring a GIS analysis scheme.

Cartography 1.The art and science of drawing charts and maps. 2. The profession of map drawing. The term may be taken broadly as comprising all the steps needed to produce a map: planning, aerial photography, field surveys, photogrammetry, editing, colour separation, and multicolour printing. Mapmakers, however, tend to limited use of the term to the map-finishing operations, in which the master manuscript is edited and colour separation plates are prepared for lithographic printing.

Cartridge Tape A type of magnetic memory type enclosed in a plastic cartridge.

Casuarinae Equisitifolia It is a species from family casurinaceae. It is a large, evergreen tree with a straight stem and feathery foliage consisting of numerous long, slender, drooping, jointed, 6-9 angled leafless branchlets arising from rough, woody branches. The jointed branchlets, which are partly deciduous, are green and functions as leaves. In general appearance, casuarina resembles a feathery conifer. Wood is very hard and liable to crack and split. It is used for poles and rafters and chiefly for fuel for which it is excellent. It is cultivated throughout the greater part of India, mostly in costal belts. Plantation of casuarina is taken up as shelter belt in the sea shore. It is a strong 'light demander' suffering badly from suppression.

Cat Fish Any of various fishes of the suborder Siluraidea, mostly inhabiting lakes and streams, especially in the tropics. They attain large sizes and are important food fishes, though the flesh may not be of the highest quality.

Cat A small lithe, domesticated, soft-furred carnivorous quadruped, felis domesticus. The term is also applied to any of various flesh-eating mammals related to the domestic cat, as the lion, the tiger, the leopard, etc., and belonging to the genus Felis. Types of cats are: FISHING CAT. (*Felis viverrina*) common in North-East India. It does not appear to have ever been seen catching or eating fish. GOLDEN OR TEMMINCK'S CAT (*Felis temmincki* syn. *Profelis temmincki*): This is one of the rarest and most handsome of the wild cats. It grows to about 1.2 m in length and preys on sheep, goats as well as on birds and small mammals, found in Assam. It is also found in Nepal, Sikkim, Burma and South-East Asia generally, as far south as Sumatra.

INDIAN DESERT CATS (*Felis ornata* syn. *F. constantina*): This is easily distinguished by its sports in the Indian desert region, and in the dry zone of Central India where this is found along with the jungle cat. Westward the range extends to North-West India and Sind to North Africa and northwards to the steppes of Central Asia. INDIAN JUNGLE CAT (*Felis chaus*): This is the common grey-coloured animal found in jungle. LEOPARD CAT (*Felis bengalensis syn. Pronailurus bengalensis*): Handsome little animal with dark brown or black spots on a bright background. Very ferocious and difficult to tame. Distributed in the forest regions of India from Kashmir and the Himalayas to Cape Kanyakumari. MARBLED CAT (*Felis marmorata* syn. *Pardofelis marmorata Martin*): Found in Nepal, Sikkim and Assam, extending to Burma and Malaysia. RUSTY-SPOTTED CAT (*Felis rubiginosa* syn. *Prionailurus rubiginosus*): Found in Gujarat. A species related to the leopard cat, about half or three quarters of the size of the domestic cat. Said to be found also along the Western Ghats and elsewhere in Southern India.

Catch Crop A crop grown temporarily on land that will eventually carry a crop of different species, in order to maintain the productivity or prevent the erosion of the land prior to the establishment of the main crop.

Catchment Area 1. Catchment basin or a drainage area, especially of a reservoir or river. 2. The total area draining into a given waterway, lake or reservoir. 3. Drainage area or watershed.

Cattle Under the Indian Forest Act, 1927 the term includes elephants, camels, buffaloes, horses, mares, geldings, ponies, colts, fillies, mules, asses, pigs, rams, ewes, sheep, lambs, goats and kids.

Caves Caves constitute one of the unique habitats for wildlife. They provide shelter from extreme weather conditions. They also provide compatible condition such as varying degree of darkness, solitude and protection from predators. Many animals like birds, bats, and insects that love darkness occupy the caves for various activities. Preservation of unique habitats plays an important role in wildlife management. Unique habitats accompanied with the continuing plant communities provide enormous potentiality for existence of a wide spectrum of wildlife.

CD-ROM A compact disk, used as a read only memory device. A device for storing large volumes of data on optical disks.

Cell 1. A single unit in the raster GIS data model. 2. A location, containing area, defined by a line and column coordinate. 3. The basic element of spatial information in the raster/grid description of spatial entities. *See* pixel.

Census 1. A complete enumeration and classification of a population. The phrase "sample census" is sometimes used to describe the enumeration of a sample from which the probable results of a complete census can be estimated. 2. The collection of data about the entire population of a country or region. 3. A census is a survey whose domain displays the characteristics of an entire population. 4. A census is any study of the entire population of a particular set of 'objects'. There are a finite number of objects to study—although we may not know that number in advance and we may need to estimate that number.

Census (Wildlife) A count of mammals, birds, etc., taken to ascertain the number of each species present in a given area at particular seasons of the year, in order to observe increases and decreases in numbers and to determine the measure of protection or control required.

Census and Sampling A census is a survey whose domain is the characteristics of an entire population; a census is any study of the entire population for a particular set of 'objects'. In such study, there is a finite number of objects to study—although we may not know that number in advance. If we choose to collect, analyse or study only some members of a population, then we are carrying out a survey. If the total population is finite and known, or continuous (infinite) then what we are doing is defining some proportion of the total population to study; then we are creating a sample. A sample survey will usually offer greater scope than a census. This may mean, for example, that it is possible to study the population of a larger (geographical) area, or to find out more about the same population by asking a greater variety of questions, or to study the same area in greater depth.

Central Processing Unit (CPU) The part of the computer that controls the whole system.

Central Zoo Authority Central Zoo Authority (CZA) was established in 1992 under the provisions of Wildlife (Protection) Act, 1972. The Authority consists of 10 members and one whole-time member secretary and is chaired by the Minister, Environment and Forests, Government of India. Two committees, namely 'Administrative Committee' under the Chairmanship of Director General of Forests and Technical Committee under the Chairmanship of Additional Director General of Forests (Wildlife) have been constituted for carrying out the functions of the Central Zoo Authority. Main functions of the Central Zoo Authority are: specify minimum standards for housing, upkeep and veterinary care of the animals in the zoos, recognition of zoos on the basis of evaluation of their functioning, identify endangered species of wild animals for the purpose of captive breeding and assigning responsibility in this regard to zoos, coordinate the acquisition, exchange and loaning of animals for breeding, provide technical and other assistance to zoos for management and development on scientific lines. There are 165 recognized zoos in the country and out of it 44 zoos are major and rest minor ones.

Certification Certification is a tool for sustainable forest management. Certification, especially of forest product, has a lot of relevance to marketing and market access. The nature and extent to its contribution to sustainable forest management are still required to be unfolded in detail. Producer countries and trade groups have tended to highlight the trade-restrictive aspects of the practice, while consumer countries with strong environmental lobbies have stressed its potential benefits. One of the benefits highlighted is that exporting countries shall be compelled to manage their forests sustainably and importing countries shall be bound to purchase forest products from countries which are practicing sustainable forestry. One area of practicing certification is wood. Presently, there are different processes adopted in different countries. Many countries have developed their own criterion and indicators to provide a framework for certification. Two other areas of recent development are in the non-wood forest product and the pulp and paper sectors. Certification schemes have been developed to certify NWFPs. Regardless of the debate on relevance of certification to sustainable forest management, interest in certification has grown Worldwide over the years. Forest certification is a market-based instrument aimed at promoting sustainable forest management that takes into account environmental, economic and social issues. *See* forest certification.

Chain of Custody The process of monitoring the production and distribution of goods from the forest to the end-product, i.e., tracing the origin of the product. This is part of the certification process.

Chamaephyte A land plant whose buds or shoot apices, destined to survive the unfavourable season, are at or near (< 25cm) the ground surface. One of the (non-cryptophytic) life forms of Raunkiaer.

Change Matrix It represents a change in forest density/cover classes for a given area during a period of two consecutive assessments in matrix form by showing the changes of area from one class to another.

Channel A natural or artificial waterway of perceptible extent that periodically or continuously contains moving water, having a definite bed and banks which serve to confine the water.

Channelization The mechanical alteration of a stream which may include straightening or dredging of an existing channel, or creating a new channel to which the stream is diverted.

Chaos The erratic, non-repeating dynamics that are highly sensitive to initial conditions exhibited by a completely deterministic system.

Character An alphabetical, numerical, or special graphic symbol that is treated as a single unit of data.

Charge-Coupled Device (CCD) A device in which electron are stored at the surface of a semi-conductor.

Charts Special-purpose map designed for navigation or to present specific data or information. The term "chart" is applied chiefly to maps made primarily for nautical and aeronautical navigation, and to maps of the heavens, although the term is sometimes used to describe other special-purpose maps.

Chasmophytes Plants usually found in rock crevices.

Check Enumeration A re-enumeration of the whole or part of the growing stock in order to verify the results of a previous enumeration.

Check-Dam A small low dam constructed in a gully or other water-course to decrease the velocity of stream flow and thereby to minimize channel scour and promote deposition of eroded material.

Cheetah or Chetah Hunting leopard (*Acinonyx jubatus venaticus*). A leopard-like animal of Africa and South Asia, with a small head, long legs and a black-spotted tawny coat. It resembles the leopard, but has certain dog-like characteristics. It can be trained for hunting antelopes. Said to have been common in the olden days (Akbar kept 1000 animals in captivity for hunting). It is now extinct in India. It is now found only in Africa.

Chemical Oxygen Demand (COD) A measure of the amount of a dissolved oxygen supply in a body of water that would be used up in completely oxidizing added inorganic oxidizable compounds, e.g., in the oxidation of ammonia to nitrate. Biological Oxygen Demand (BOD) tests can only measure the biodegradable fraction of the total potential dissolved oxygen consumption by added wastes; COD tests may be used to measure the oxygen demand created by toxic organic or inorganic compounds as well as by biodegradable substances. A standard COD test, therefore, can be used to evaluate many industrial type wastes not readily analyzed for water quality factors by the sewage-oriented BOD test.

Chemosynthetic Activity The synthesis of organic matter from mineral substances, with the aid of chemical energy.

Chernozem A mature grassland soil of semi-arid climates, usually developed on loess, characterized by deep permeation of dark organic matter and a zone of accumulation of secondary $caco_3$ beneath. The surface soil, horizons usually has a good crumb structure. The name is derived from Russian meaning "black earth".

Chevrotain or Chevrotin Any of a number of related, small, hornless animals of Asia and Africa resembling the deer. They are the most primitive of known ruminants, found especially in India, Malay Peninsula and West Africa. The animal found in India is the Indian chevrotain or Mouse Deer (*Moschiolo memina*) which occurs in the forested areas of southern India at an elevation up to about 1800 m.

Chinkara Indian gazelle (*Gazella bennetti*). Gazelles are small, swift graceful antelopes of the genus Gazella and allied genera. Found in Africa, the Near East, and Asia, with spirally twisted backward pointing horns. They are remarkable for their graceful movements and lustrous eyes. The Indian Gazelle is found in the plains and low hills of North Western and Central India, extending through the open lands of the Deccan to a little south of the Krishna River. The usual haunts of the Chinkara are the waste land broken up by nallahs and ravines, scattered bush and thin jungle. A full grown male measures 65 cm at the shoulder, weigh 23 kg and has horns rarely exceeding 25-30 cm in length.

Chipko Movement This was a social and ecological movement that took place in Hindi belt of India. The word in Hindi means the same thing 'to hug'. The movement represented the popular sentiment and initiative aimed at preventing felling of the trees by adopting non-violent means such as hugging them. The Vishnoi community, from present day Rajasthan, used to cling to their trees whenever the agents of the local rulers came to cut the forest trees for their purposes. In modern India, the villagers in hill town of Gopeshwar in Chamoli district in Uttar Pradesh, tried the same method of clinging to their trees and thus gave birth to what came to be recognised as probably the world's most well known ecological movement. Chandi Prasad Bhatt from Gopeswar and Sunderlal Bahuguna from Tehri have provided the leadership to the movement, which continues to be strong in district Chamoli.

Chir Pine (*Pinus roxburghii*) The Chir Pine, named after William Roxburgh, is a pine native to the Himalaya. The range extends from northern Pakistan (North-West Frontier Province, Kashmir), across northern India (Jammu and Kashmir, Punjab, Himachal Pradesh, Uttarakhand, Sikkim) and Nepal to Bhutan. It generally occurs at lower altitudes than other pines in the Himalaya, from 500-2000 mt, occasionally up to 2300 mt. The other Himalayan pines are Blue Pine, Bhutan White Pine, Chinese White Pine, Chilgoza Pine and Sikang Pine. It is a large tree, reaching 30-50 mt tall and with a trunk diameter of up to 2 mt, exceptionally 3 mt. The bark is red-brown, thick and deeply fissured at the base of the trunk, thinner and flaky in the upper crown. The leaves are needle-like, in fascicles of three, very slender, 20-35 cm long, and distinctly yellowish green. The cones are ovoid conic, 12-24 cm long and 5-8 cm broad at the base when closed, green at first, ripening glossy chestnut-brown when 24 months old. They open slowly over the next year or so, or after being heated by a forest fire, to release the seeds, opening to 9-18 cm broad. The seeds are 8-9 mm long, with a 40 mm wing, and are wind-dispersed. Chir pine is widely planted for timber in its native area, being one of the most important trees in forestry in northern Pakistan, India and Nepal. It is also occasionally used as an ornamental tree, planted in parks and gardens in hot dry areas, where its heat and drought tolerance is valued. It is also tapped commercially for resin. On distillation, the resin yieds an essential oil, commonly known as turpentine, and non-volatile rosin. The proportion of rosin and turpentine oil in Chir Pine is 75 per cent and 22 per cent respectively with 3 per cent losses, etc.The turpentine is chiefly used as a solvent in pharmaceutical preparations, perfume industry, in manufacture of synthetic pine oil, disinfectants, insecticides and denaturants. It is one of the most important basic raw materials for the synthesis of terpene chemicals which are used in a wide variety of industries such as adhesives, paper and rubber, etc. Chir Pine rosin is principally used in paper, soap, cosmetics, paint, varnish, rubber and polish industries. Besides these, other uses include, manufacture of linoleum, explosives, insecticides and disinfectants, as a flux in soldering, in brewing and in mineral beneficiation as a frothing agent.

Chital or Spotted Deer (*Axis axis* Syn. *Cervus axis*). This is the most common deer of India and probably the most beautiful in the world. *See* deer.

Chlorophyll The green photosynthetic substance in plants which allows them to capture solar energy.

Chlorosis An unseasonable yellowing of foliage, symptomatic of a chlorophyll deficiency in the leaf tissues under normal light conditions.

Chomophyte A plant that grows in a fissure or crevice of a rock.

Chorochromatic Maps A map in which the area is divided into a series of zones which are each displayed using a single colour or shading.

Choropleth Map 1. A map consisting of a series of single valued, uniform area separated by abrupt boundaries. 2. A thematic map that displays a quantitative attribute using ordinal classes. Areas are shaded according to their value and a range of shading classes. 3. A map showing discrete areas, such as soil units and vegetation types. Uniform conditions are assured within each map unit.

Chresard That fraction of the total amount of water in the soil which is available for use by plants.

Chromosome One of a set of deeply staining nuclear bodies that become evident during cell division. They bear the genus or unit factors of heredity, and the number in any species is usually constant.

Civet Any of several varieties of cat-like, carnivorous mammals of Africa, India, Malaysia and southern China, with spotted yellowish fur. It is valued for its civet, a thick, yellowish, fatty secretion with a musk-like scent, obtained from glands in the pouch near the sexual organs. The secretion is much used in perfumery and commercial supplies come from the African civet (*Viverra civetta* Syn. *Civettictis civetta*). Types of civet cats found in India include: COMMON PALM CIVET or TODDY CAT (*Paradoxurus Hermaphroditus*): An arboreal, black-spotted or black-striped blackish brown civet with long coarse hair found in well-wooded regions, throughout India, excluding only the arid zone. *P. jerdoni*, PALM, the Brown Palm cat is found in the hill ranges of South India. LARGE INDIAN CIVET (*Viverra zibetha*): A solitary creature, sheltering in woods and bushes, found in Upper Bengal and Assam. SMALL INDIAN CIVET (*Viverricula indica*): A tawny grey or grayish-brown animal with streaks on back and spots in the flank. This is found from the Himalayan foothills southwards to Kanyakumari. Some are kept under domestication for the extraction or civet for the scent glands.

Clan 1. A small plant community of subordinate importance but of distinctive character, frequently the result of vegetative propagation. 2. A small but distinctive community of subordinate importance, composed of densely aggregated individuals of one or few species in climax vegetation; frequently the result of vegetative propagation.

Class A set of pixels in a GIS or image file that represent areas that have the same attribute or share the same condition.

Classification 1. Forming, sorting, apportioning, grouping, or dividing objects into classes to form an ordered arrangement of items having a defined range of characteristics, relationships, and distinctive differences. Classification systems may be taxonomic, mathematical, observed, or inferred, depending upon the purpose to be served. The purpose of classification is to describe the structure and relationships of objects to each other and to similar objects, and to simplify these relationships in such a way that general statements can be made about classes of objects, thereby achieving economy of memory and ease of manipulation. 2. Process of assigning individual pixels of an image to categories, generally on the basis of spectral reflectance characteristics. 3. The grouping of similar types according to criteria which are considered significant for this purpose.

Classification Scheme Hierarchical system of user-defined classes for the classification of imagery (remote sensing).

Classification (Plant or Animal Classification) Arrangement of animals and plants in a series of groups. The basic unit is the species, e.g., the peacock (*Pavo cristatus*). Species which are similar genera are grouped into families; families into orders, orders into classes, and classes into phyla, for animals or divisions for plants. *See also* binomial nomenclature.

Clay 1. The finest soil particles, under 0.002 mm in diameter. 2. Typically naturally occurring inorganic, crystalline mineral particles less than 0.002 millimetres in equivalent diameter. Composed of fragments of hydrous aluminum silicate minerals in soil and other earthy deposits. "Soil texture" consisting of 40 per cent or more clay-sized particles, less than 40 per cent silt-sized particles and less than 45 per cent sand-sized particles. Such soils have a high plasticity index, an expression of the amount of water that soil can hold without losing its plasticity.

Clay Loam or Clayey Loam A heavy soil intermediate in texture between clay and loamy. *See* soil class.

Clay Pan 1. In ordinary usage a dense, heavy subsoil more or less impenetrable to roots. 2. A dense and heavy soil, horizons underlying the upper part of the soil profile; hard when dry and stiff or plastic when wet. *See* pan.

Cleaning It is a tending operation. Generally this operation is done in a sapling stage, involving the removal or topping of inferior growth including individuals of the favoured species, climber, etc., especially when they are interfering with the better grown individuals of the favoured species. It merges with thinning as the saplings grow into poles.

Clearcut 1. A harvest operation removing an entire stand (regardless of size) in one cut. 2. A harvest operation removing an entire merchantable stand in one cut.

Clearcutting System or Clearfelling System 1. A nominal silvicultural system in which all the trees are cleared over a large area at one time in a brief period. Regeneration tactics are part of the operation and are generally artificial, but natural regeneration is sometimes possible by seeding from the air, from adjacent stands, or from seed, coppice, and/or advance growth already on the ground. One objective of this system is to establish even-aged stands. 2. It is a silvicultural system in which equal or equi-productive areas of mature crop are successfully clear-felled in one operation to be regenerated, most frequently artificially but sometimes naturally also. This system was adopted in India around 1842 for teak forests. Under this system, successive equal areas of forests were clear-felled and regenerated. This system suffers from maximum disadvantages from the point of ecological balance of the forests. The complete clearance of forest cover produces certain adverse condition such as desiccation, and general deterioration of soil fertility, primarily on account of erosion, laterization and destruction of humus. This sometimes results into failure of regeneration. The debris when left in the forest floor constitutes a fire hazard. Weeds also invade the cleared areas, which generally hamper establishment of main crop. From the point of environment conservation, this system is least beneficial. This system, however, envisages uniform crop of even aged gradation, ensuring an assured and sustained timber yield.

Clearing An open space in the forest, due to clearing of forest growth or naturally created blank.

Clients Clients are computers on a network that lets users access the server's information and resources. Client computers can range from diskless workstations to multimedia—enhanced, complete desktop systems.

Climate The average course or condition of the weather at a particular place over a period of many years as exhibited in absolute extremes, means, ranges and seasonal distribution of air temperature, wind velocity and direction, precipitation type, duration and amount, humidity and other weather elements. It is not synonymous with weather.

Climate Change 1. Climate change has become one of the most important areas of research in the field of environment. The impact of human emissions of greenhouse gases on, for example, the climate has been the subject of much research, particularly by the IPCC (2001). This concept is commonly known as global warming or the greenhouses effect, although in recent years 'climate change' has replaced these terms, owing to the diverse nature of the impacts. Greenhouse gases trap heat and lead to changes in the global average temperature. However, in a given country the temperature may be either increased or decreased depending on location, leading to shifts in weather patterns. The impacts of climate change include: potential sea-level rise; changes in weather patterns, including El Nino; increased incidence of severe weather conditions; desertification; and impacts on human health. Potential policy responses include mitigation and adaptation policies to reduce the impacts of climate change, either through reductions in emissions or through changes in behaviour or government spending patterns in response to the problems caused by climate change. 2. An alteration to measured quantities (e.g. precipitation, temperature, radiation, wind and cloudiness) within the climate system that departs significantly from previous average conditions and is seen to endure, bringing about corresponding changes to ecosystems and socio-economic activity. Associated with greenhouse gas, of which fossil fuel combustion and forest fires are contributors. Climate change is one of the most important global environmental problems. The average temperature of the earth's surface has risen by 0.6°C since the late 1800s. It is expected to increase by another 1.4°C to 5.8°C by the year 2100. Even if the minimum predicted increase takes place, it will be larger than any century long trend in the last 10,000 years. The sea level rose on an average by 10 to 20 cm during the 20th century and an additional increase of 9.88 cm is expected by the year 2100. There is new and stronger evidence that most of the warming over the last 50 years is attributable to human activities. Recognizing the threats posed by Climate Change, most countries joined an International Treaty, the United Nations Framework Convention on Climate Change (UNFCCC), to begin to consider what can be done to reduce global warming and cope with whatever temperature increase is inevitable. India became a party to the United Nations Framework Convention on Climate Change (UNFCCC) on 21st March, 1994 and adopted the convention.

Climate Change, Estimating Costs of The costs of climate change fall into three categories: the costs imposed on society by the impacts of climate change; the costs of reducing the gases that cause climate change (mitigation costs); and the costs of adapting to the change in the climate (adaptation costs). Climate change impact assessment has proved to be extremely difficult. The physical impacts are highly uncertain and human responses are also not easy to predict. Consequently, the range of damage estimates is very large. One particularly controversial variable is the value attached to the increased risk of death from the greater incidence of diseases such as malaria. If one bases this value on the willingness to pay (WTP), the figures for poor countries are much lower than those for rich countries. Allowing this disparity to become the basis of policy is considered by many to be unacceptable.

Climatic Factors Light, atmospheric temperature, pressure and humidity, winds and other features of climate — regional, local and seasonal — that influence vegetation.

Climatic Index A number which condenses climatic data into a simplified expression. (Transeau's ratio p/e is a climatic index.)

Climatic Zone Divisions of the earth bounded by imaginary circle parallel to the equator, having the same climate. Four chief zones are: polar, temperate, sub-tropical and tropical. A different classification recognizes five great divisions or zones of the earth's surface with respect to latitude and temperature. These are: Temperate zone — the region between the tropic of cancer and the arctic circle or between the tropic of Capricorn and Antarctic circle. Frigid zone — the region between the Arctic Circle and the North Pole or between the Antarctic Circle and the South Pole. Torrid zone — the belt of the earth between the tropics over which the sun is vertical at some period of the year and it lies between the tropic of cancer and the tropic of Capricorn.

Climax The culminating stage of plant succession for a given environment, the vegetation being conceived as having reached a highly stable condition. Some ecologists restrict the term to vegetation of mature sites and soils, which they presume to have a high degree of permanence. Others apply it to vegetation which they conceived to be stable only as long as the environment remains unchanged or to vegetation which changes only in response to changes in climate and/or soil substrate that are slow relative to the rate of plant succession.

Clements claimed that, for a given region, there was only one true climax — stable vegetation on mesic sites determined by climate, and hence climatic climax.

Climax (Ecology) 1. The final stage of a succession which continues to occupy an area as long as climate or soil conditions remain unchanged. At climax there is a stable plant community, which is able to reproduce itself. There is similarly a stable animal community. 2. The culmination stage in plant succession for a given environment used as an exact synonym of climatic climax by Clements and his school.

Climax (Vegetation) 1. The culminating stage in plant succession for a given environment; the vegetation being conceived as having reached over time a highly stable condition. 2. The plant covers on any area that will hereafter remain stable until climatic changes occur. *See* climax.

Climax, Edaphic 1. A community which differs from the climatic climax of the area owing to the influence of special soil factors. 2. A stable plant community maintained in any given area by the prevailing edaphic condition. Also a similarly stable animal community.

Climax Community (Climax) The final stable, self-perpetuating community in a developmental series under the prevailing climatic and soil conditions. A "climax" is determined in large measure by the nature of the topography or soil, e.g., a particular type of forest may be the "climax" on a north-facing slope while a grassland may be the "climax" on the south-facing slope of the same ridge. The main biotic components are not overthrown by invaders. No new species become dominant in the community. Climax is frequently used in the sense of species usually present (or at least common) only as members of a climax community.

Climax Forest A community that represents the "culminating" stage of a natural forest succession for its locality, i.e. for its environment.

Climax Units According to Clements, these units in descending order of complexity are: associate, faciation, lociation, society and clan.

Climax, Biotic A climax which differs from the climatic climax of the area owing to the action of biotic factors. Clements calls it disclimax.

Climax, Climatic 1. A stable plant community maintained in any given area by the prevailing climatic condition. Also a similarly stable animal community. 2. A climax which owes its distinctive characters to climatic factors in conjunction with only such biotic influences as plants and animals naturally occurring in the area bring about. *See* climax.

Climber Cutting A cultural operations or tending. Generally in such operation climbers are cut back.

Climber A herbaceous or woody plant that climbs up trees or other support by twining round them or by holding on to them by tendrils, hooks, aerial roots or other attachments. *See* creeper.

Cline 1. A pattern of genetical variation in which the differences of characters are graded in a definite direction in space. 2. A graded series of different forms of the same species, usually distributed along a spatial direction. 3. A gradual and continual change in a structural or functional character exhibited by a series of populations or throughout the range of a species, usually along a line of geographic or environmental gradient, in which individuals at the two extremes differ markedly. *See* ecotype.

Clique 1. A group of organisms in a food-web in which any pair of species shares at least one prey species. 2. Species groups that have similar diets but are different from other such groups.

Clone 1. A group of individuals derived from a common parent by asexual reproduction. 2. Plants derived vegetatively from one parent plant, so that each is genetically identical to each other and to the parent. This may occur naturally or artificially.

Cloning In biotechnology, obtaining a group of genetically identical cells from a single cell; making identical copies of a gene.

Close Season The period during which hunting, catching or killing any particular animal, bird or fish is prohibited by law.

Close, to To prohibit entry into a forest for exercising any right or privilege, such as grazing, felling, shooting, grass-cutting, minor forest produce collection, etc. Such closure may be for silvicultural, punitive or other reasons.

Closed (Wildlife) Restricted with reference to time and place for capturing, killing, shooting or poisoning game (e.g., blocks closed to hunting; a closed season for fishing). The breeding season for any species of wildlife is usually declared as a closed season.

Closed Area Any area closed to people or equipment for management purposes for certain types of use or treatment.

Closed Basin 1. A basin draining to some depression or pond within its area, from which water is lost only by evaporation or percolation. 2. A basin without a surface outlet for precipitation falling therein.

Closed Forest 1. Formation where trees in the various stories and the undergrowth cover a high proportion (> 40 per cent) of the ground and do not have a continuous dense grass layer. Typical examples of tropical closed forests includes tropical rainforest and mangrove forest. 2. Forest is called closed when the density is 1.0.

Closed System A system which exchanges neither energy nor matter with its environment. The Earth is a system which is closed with respect to materials. The matter on Earth is fixed in quantity so that material inputs to production originate from the Earth, and the residuals from the productive process remain on the Earth. However, with respect to energy, the Earth is an open system; it receives energy from the sun and loses energy to the surrounding system (Perman *et al.*, 1999). *See also* Second Law of Thermodynamics.

Closure, Crown The closing together of the crowns of trees, in a forest, as in the younger stages of a stand, or after thinning.

Club of Rome Set up by an International Group of Economists, Scientists, Technologists, Politicians and others in 1968, the organization's purpose is the study of the interactions between humans and the environment. These interactions include the economic, scientific, biological and social components of the human situation. The Club was established with the goal of eventually being able to predict the results of government policies and to formulate alternative policies where deemed necessary on environmental and survival grounds. The Limits to Growth and Beyond the Limits studies by Meadows *et al.* (1972, 1992) were supported by the Club of Rome.

Clump 1. The fusion of neighbouring cells, which are of the same class into larger units. 2. The aggregate of stems originating from the same root. Rhizome system or stool with particular reference to bamboo's and the larger grasses. Each clump in a bamboo forests may contain group of culms or single stems. 3. An isolated group of trees.

Cluster Analysis Techniques that group objects (e.g., pixels) into clusters according to user-defined rules. These techniques are used in digital interpretation of imageries.

Clustering The analysis of a set of measurements to detect their inherent tendency to form clusters in multi-spectral space. This technique is in vogue in interpretation of satellite imageries.

Clusters Natural groupings of objects created by cluster analysis in GIS. In a cluster, objects are mutually closer to each other than to objects in other.

Coarse Woody Debris Any piece of dead woody material.

Coast Land next to the sea.

Coastal Plain The flatter area, or plain, extending along the coast.

Coastline The shape or pattern of the coast.

Cobra (*Naja Tripudians*) A venomous snake found in India. When excited, it expands the skin of the neck into a broadhood with characteristic markings. The Indian Cobra (*Naja naja*) is found usually near habitation and dwellings. This is yellowish to dark brown, usually with spectacle-shaped black and white markings on the expandedhood. Also called Spectacled Cobra.

Cockchafer A melolonthid beetle.

Code A set of specific symbols and rules for representing data and programmes so that they can be understood by the computer.

Co-dominant 1. A tree receiving full sunlight from above but comparatively little from the sides. Such trees have medium-sized crowns. 2. Co-dominant is a dominant tree which falls a little below the general top level of the topmost canopy and is about 5/6th of the average height of the predominant tree. 3. A species that shares dominant character more or less equally with others. 4. Tree species in a forest that are about equally numerous and exert the greatest influence. 5. One of four main crown classes recognized on a basis of relative status and condition in the crop. The trees have their crowns in the upper canopy but are less free than the dominants. *See* tree class.

Co-efficient A constant factor of an equation or model as distinguished from a variable.

Cohort A group of individuals born during the same short period (often 1 year) of time.

Collar The portion of a plant, which marks the transition between stem and root, sometimes marked by a slight swelling. *See* root collar.

Colluvium 1. Deposit of rock fragments and soil material accumulated at the base of steep slopes by gravitational action. 2. Mixed deposits of soil material and rock fragments accumulated near the base of steep slopes through gravity, i.e., soil creep, landslides, and local surface runoff (but not stream flow).

Colonial Animals Animals, which live in-groups. Individuals are often attached to each other.

Colonist One of two or more species that invade new territory to form a colony.

Colonization The process of forming colonies.

Colony A new group of two or more species invading a new territory.

Comb-Duck Nukta (*Sarkidiornis Melanotos*) This is a large goose-like duck glossy black above, white below with a spotted head and neck. The male has a black, fleshy knob (the comb) on the top of the beak, which become greatly developed in the breeding season. The typical race is found throughout India except the northern and western Punjab. It is confined to the plains and appears to be a local migrant. It inhabits large marshy tanks and *jheels* with ready margins and plenty of trees in the vicinity. Breeding seasons June to September.

Command 1. An English-language specification issued by the user to a computer instructing it to perform some function. 2. An instruction sent from the keyboard or other control device to execute a computer programme.

Commensalism A relationship between two kinds of living organisms whereby one (the commensal) benefits and the other (the host) remains relatively or absolutely unaffected, and which is obligatory for the commensal. *See* symbiosis, parasitism.

Commercial Forest Forest land that is able to grow commercial timber within an acceptable time frame and is designated for such a purpose.

Commercial Timber The volume under bark of the bole having commercial value.

Commission on Sustainable Development (CSD) The United Nations Conference on Environment and Development (UNCED) held in 1992, adopted Agenda 21 — a blueprint for a global plan of action for achieving sustainable development. The Commission on Sustainable Development (CSD) was set up in 1993 under Economic and Social Council of the UN for the purpose of reviews of progress of implementation of the Agenda 21. *See* Agenda 21.

Commodity All resource products which are articles of commerce.

Community 1. An aggregation of living organisms, without reference to its ecological status. 2. An association of organism, living naturally in the same area and whose members are in varying degree interdependent, e.g., ants. 3. An assemblage of plants and animals living together and occupying a given area. With plants, a closed community is considered one whose components are so completely utilizing the site as to "exclude" (or give the appearance of excluding) further entrants. It is also important to note that classifying a community as "closed" is subjective and usually based on one-time measurements or observations.

Community (Association, Biotic Association, Ecological Community) A community is an assemblage of populations living in a stated area. It is a loosely organized unit to the extent that it has characteristics additional to its individual species and populations components. Communities have perceived functional unity, characteristic trophic structures, and patterns of energy flow. They also have taxonomic unity (in that there is a certain probability that certain species will occur together) and a relatively uniform appearance. Communities may be sharply defined. Very frequently, however, communities blend gradually into one another but they have the characteristic of being distinctively (statistically) different from adjacent units. The word is used with the simplest (e.g., an unrooted mat of algae) to the most complex ecosystem (e.g., a multistoried rain forest). Community units may be very large, like the continent-wide coniferous forest, or very small, like the community of invertebrates and fungi in a decaying log. The extent of a community is limited only by the requirement of a more or less uniform species composition. The composition and character of a community is an indicator of the type of environment that is present. Since "plant communities" and "animal communities" occur together in the same habitat and have many interrelations, the one can scarcely be considered independently of the other. Together they make up the "biotic community", a part of the general concept of community that also includes abiotic subsystems and factors.

Community Coefficient A measure of the similarity of the floras or faunas of two areas or of two communities. Several mathematically different forms have been devised but all are based on the ratio between the number of species common to the two populations and the total number of species in both populations.

Community Development Deliberate efforts to foster socio-cultural change on the human community level, change of a kind seen as valuable or progressive, usually including an improved quality of life through increases in resources, skills, facilities, technology, social competence, and social power.

Community Forests A forest area primarily designated to serve community needs.

Community, Biotic An assemblage of related population of plants and animals constituting a relatively self-sufficient ecological unit. Any assemblage of population living in a prescribed area. It is a unit to the extent that it has characteristics additional to its individual species and populations components. *See* community.

Community, Climax The final or relatively stable biotic community in a developmental series. It is self-perpetuating and in equilibrium with the physical, climatic, and edaphic conditions. The physiographic climax is a climax determined in large measure by the nature of the topography or soil, e.g., a forest climax may occur on a north-facing slope while grassland is the climax on the south-facing slope of the same ridge. The edaphic climax is a climax determined largely by the nature of the soil conditions, e.g., a saltgrass marsh in a poorly drained alkaline depression in grassland. A biotic climax is a climax caused by a permanent influence or combination of influences caused by one or more kinds of organisms, including people.

Commutation The process of transferring to the holders of rights over a property, the ownership of part of the property in compensation for extinguishing right over the remainders right.

Compaction Decrease in volume of soil and sediment as a result of compressive stress, continued deposition above them, but also from drying, use of heavy equipment, and other causes.

Compartment 1. A subdivision of forest area for purpose of orientation, administration, and management operations and usually defined by natural or artificial boundaries such as ridgelines, streams, or roads. 2. A territorial unit of a forest permanently defined for purposes of administration, description and record (preferably designated by Arabic numerals, 1, 2, 3, etc.). *See* block, coupe and sub-compartment. 3. It is also the basic unit of management.

Compartment History 1. A record of all events effecting the forestry of an individual compartment. 2. Compartment history is a written account or chronicle of past events pertaining to the compartment. In other words, it deals with a record of what has happened to the compartment since the inception of management. Compartment history details are kept in five formats. These formats are: (1) Format No. I – General description of the compartment. (2) Format No. II – Record of plantation and changes in growing stock. (3) Format No. III – Register of operation and outturn. (4) Format No. IV – Record of injuries. (5) Format No. V – Record of Observation. The working plan revision necessitates updating of information related to general description of the compartment. The information in the other formats are dealt and maintained by the concerned territorial forest division. All such information is supplied to working plan officer during the course of revision.

Compartment Line The boundary of a compartment.

Compatible Uses Land uses which can exist together, so that no one use detracts significantly from the quality, output, or value of another.

Competition 1. The struggle for the available food, light and moisture, which takes place among species and individuals in an assemblage of plants. 2. The effort of each organism to maximize fitness by both appropriating contested resources from a pool not sufficient for all, and adapting to the environment altered by all participants. Competition between the same species is termed intra-specific competition; competition between different species inter-specific competition.

Competition (Ecological) The general struggle for existence (and dominance) in which organisms compete for a limited supply of the necessities of life. It is the condition of rivalry between different organisms, usually closely related species (or within a species) which use the same resources and live in the same places, that exists when organisms are in short supply. If the resources are not in short supply, the condition that occurs when the organisms seeking and using that resource nevertheless harm one another in the process. Competition may be interspecific (i.e., between two or more different species), or intraspecific (i.e., between members of the same species).

Competitive Exclusion The elimination from a habitat of one species by another species through inter-specific competition. *See* competition.

Compilation of Map Preparation of a new or revised map or chart, or portion thereof, from existing maps, aerial photographs, field surveys, and other sources.

Complementary Uses Land uses, each of which is improved in quality or quantity by the other uses existing with it in the same area.

Component A functional part of an ecosystem. It can be a species, a part of a species, a life form, or any other functional group made up of other components (e.g., the component "grass" is constituted of many species in a given ecosystem, but it is defined by the ecosystem analyzer as a functional component based on an explicit rationale).

Composite Map A single maps created by joining together several maps that have been digitized separately.

Composition The various species which form a forest crop and their proportion in it.

Compost A mixture of vegetable materials, which has been allowed to rot, often with the addition of animal and/or mineral products; used as a soil improver.

Compounding of Offences The acceptance by a forest or other officer, legally empowered to do so, of a sum of money from a person against whom there is reasonable evidence that he has committed a forest offence, as compensation in lieu of prosecution in a court of law.

Comprehensive Plan (General Plan, Master Plan) An official document adopted by any authority or local Government or landowner setting forth its general policies regarding the long-term physical development of a city or other area. Such plans are broad enough to include all aspects of a development or redevelopment programme as distinguished from sporadic, isolated, or piecemeal planning. The process of designing futures not only of three dimensional accomplishments in space but also social mechanisms such as laws, regulations, policies, and forms of organization. Comprehensive plans typically include: (1) a land plan map which shows the location of all owned land, the interrelationship between all of the uses proposed on such land, the circulation system required to serve the uses existing or proposed, and the relationship between ownership within a reasonable area of influence; (2) land use policies related to the resources management, conservation and disposal of public lands; (3) land use policies related to the activities and the regulations as they affect portions of the land; (4) implementation schedules which establish priorities for programmes in management, mapping, engineering, and public works; (5) a programme for coordinating land use, intensity, and activity programmes with Central/federal, state, regional, other local agencies as well as with private applicants. Increasing emphasis is being laid on social, economic, and esthetic topics, moving plans beyond physical and land use documents.

Computer Assisted/Aided Cartography (CAC) 1. The use of computer hardware and specific software for making maps and charts. 2. Software designed to assist in the process of designing and drawing maps.

Computer Cartography The generation, storage and editing of maps using a computer.

Computer Graphics A general terms embracing any computing activity that results in graphic images.

Computer-Aided Cartography *See* 'computer cartography'.

Computer-Aided Design (CAD) Software designed to assist in the process of designing and drafting. This is normally used for architectural and engineering applications, but can also be used for drafting maps as an input to GIS.

Computing Environment The total range of hardware and software facilities provided by a computer and its operating system.

Concentration The amount of a substance occurring in a given amount of a medium — air, water, soil, tissue, etc. It may be expressed, e.g., as parts per million, grams per litre, or in other units.

Conceptual Data Model A model, usually attempts in verbal or graphical form, that attempts to describe in words or pictures quantitative and qualitative interactions between real-World features.

Conceptual Model The abstraction, representation, and ordering of phenomena using the mind.

Concretion Hardened local concentration of certain chemical compounds as calcium carbonate or iron oxides in the form of indurated grains or nodules of various sizes, shapes and colour.

Conductivity A measure of the ability of a solution to carry an electrical current dependent on the total concentration of ionized substances dissolved in water.

Configuration A particular combination of computer hardware and software for a certain class of application tasks.

Conflict Management It is about managing conflict in the areas of natural resources. Now it has become necessary to recognise the need to understand the causes and consequences of over ownerships, management and use of natural resources, including forests and trees, and to incorporate conflict management mechanisms into natural resource planning and management. Conflict management is based on dialogue leading to a mutually acceptable solution. This apart, it lays emphasis on capacity building, community empowerment and policy and legislative reform in support of this approach.

Confusion Index A measure of the relative dominance of the membership values assigned to an individual for two or more fuzzy classes. It is a term used in GIS and digital interpretation.

Conic Projections Map projections in which the surface of the globe is projected on to a cone (for example, Alber's equal area projection).

Conifer 1. Any of predominantly evergreen, cone-bearing trees with needle, awn, or scalelike leaves, e.g., pine, spruce, hemlock, cypress, larch, or fir (often called "softwoods"). 2. A tree belonging to the order coniferales of the botanical group, gymnospermae, bearing cones and generally needle-shaped or scale-like leaves usually evergreen and producing timber often known as softwoods", e.g., pine (Pinus), fir (Abies), spruce (Picea), larch (Larix).

Coniferales Conifers. Pinales. The most important order of the gymnospermae, comprising a wide range of trees, mostly evergreens, bearing cones (hence coniferous) and needle-shaped or scale-like leaves, and producing timber known commercially as softwood. Examples are: pine (Pinus), fir (Abies), spruce (Picea), larch (Larix).

Conservation 1. Protection of plant and animal habitat. 2. The management of a renewable natural resource with the objective of sustaining its productivity in perpetuity while providing for human use, compatible with sustainability of the resource. For a forest this may include periodic cutting and removal of trees, followed by management for regrowth of some form of the forest. 3. Conservation is defined as 'the management of human use of the biosphere so that it may yield the greatest sustainable benefit to present generations while maintaining its potential to meet the needs and aspirations of future generations' (IUCN *et al.*, 1980). 3. Planned management and wise use of natural resources, so as to prevent over exploitation, destruction or neglect, e.g., wildlife conservation. Originally the term was used to denote strict preservation, leading to locking up of resources and prevention of their use. This meaning has become antiquated. In a broader sense, conservation implies the field of knowledge concerned with the coordination and practical application of data from the science, with a view to increasing and sustaining the viability of natural resources. 4. The protection, improvement, and use of natural resources according to principles that will assure their highest economic and social service. A general word suggesting practices and customs of people that perpetuate resources and yields from some that are sustained. It usually includes preventing waste of non-renewable resources and recycling. Generally speaking, conservation of natural resource is "wise use without abuse". Conservation is a broad concept which involves not only the scientific but ethical, moral, economic and political aspects as well. It deals with judicious development and manner of use of natural resources of all kinds. A generalised definition of conservation is "the maximisation over time of the net social benefits in goods and services from resources". However, more precisely, conservation may be defined as the achievement of the highest sustainable quality of living for mankind by the rational utilisation of environment, protection of nature to enrich the life of man and control or elimination of environmental pollution in its many manifestations. It advocates practices that will perpetuate the resources of earth on which man depends. In other words, conservation involves perpetuation of the natural environment of man including the infinite resources of air, water, soil, and life forms. The World Conservation Strategy, prepared by International Union for

Conservation of Nature and Natural Resources (IUCN) in partnership with the United Nations Environment Programme (UNEP) and the World Wide Fund for Nature (WWF) and published in 1980, emphasises that the conservation of nature can only be carried out forward with development that meets human needs, and that development will not meet those needs unless it is soundly based on the conservation of the natural systems of the biosphere, which are the human life support mechanism, and also the source of food and other resources, on which we depend. In the 'caring for the earth' the latest world conservation strategy, it is stated that 'development must be people oriented, but it must be conservation based'. Conservation aims at (1) ensuring the preservation of environment in its normal state, (2) ensuring a continuous yield of goods and services by establishing a balanced cycle of harvest and renewal, and (3) sustainable utilisation of goods and services. It is achieved through different means of conservation measures. Some of the conservation measures are: Preservation and rational use of resources, sustained yield, restoration, protection, reutilization, substitution, allocation and integration. (a) Preservation and rational use of resources: Preservation serves an ecological purpose by maintaining the function of the total environment. But, not withstanding preservation, rational use implies the direct use of resources for their utility or product value. Thus harvesting a forest crop can be considered a legitimate component of rational use of natural resources, if they are carried out in such a way that the resource is perpetuated and not endangered; (b) Sustained yield: The concept implies that in any biological production system, the yield should not be more than the increment; (c) Restoration: The concept implies correction of past careless activities that have impaired the productivity of the resource base. The process of restoration is possible, only so long as species are protected and genetic diversity of life is maintained. When species become extinct, the restoration of past conditions become impossible; (d) Protection: It implies protection of natural resources from commercial exploitation to prolong generation of goods and services from the resource base; (e) Reutilization: It implies a process of recycling and reuse of waste materials in order to minimise pressure on the resource base as well as to maximise the material benefits; (f) Substitution: It is a concept, which encompasses two aspects. One is use of a common resource instead of a rare one when it can be used for the same purpose. Secondly, the use of a renewable rather than a non-renewable resource when condition permits; (g) Allocation: It implies a strategy of use to derive the maximum social benefits. For many produces and their products, the market decides the pattern of use, but in a matter of immense public importance, general welfare may dictate the use to which the resource is put; (h) Integration: The concept of integration aims at maximisation, over a period of time, of the sum of goods and services that can be produced from a complex resource base or system. This is in lieu of maximisation of certain benefits from a single resource at the expense of other benefits or other resources. Integration in a complex resource system is key to synergy and optimum performance of the system as a whole.

Conservation, Water The saving of water for beneficial use through (a) encouraging its absorption into the soil at or near the place on which it falls, (b) through impounding water which would otherwise be wasted, or (c) through reducing water losses from evaporation and transpiration.

Conservationist On who advocates conservation, especially of natural resources (as forests, wildlife).

Consistence The degree of cohesion of the soil mass and the resistance of the soil aggregates to disintegration under handling or other forms of pressure. The following terms are used for describing this property at three moisture contents: (a) consistence when dry — loose, slightly hard, hard, very hard and extremely hard; (b) consistence when moist — loose, very friable, friable, firm, very firm and extremely firm; (c) consistence when wet (stickiness) — non-sticky, slightly sticky, sticky and very sticky; (d) consistence when wet (plasticity) — non-plastic, slightly plastic, plastic, very plastic.

Consociation 1. Clements' term for a climax plant community characterized by the dominance of a single species. 2. A unit in an associate characterized by the prominence of a single species associate. *See* climax units.

Constancy 1. The percentage of a large number of plots in which a given species occurs. Usually expressed in 5 degrees each of 20 per cent range, degree 1 being 80-100 per cent. 2. The relative consistency of occurrence (and therefore degree of dispersal) of a species throughout a community or throughout different examples of a given community. Often expressed as the proportion of samples in which a species occurs. *See* frequency.

Constant A species that is present in almost every sample (generally accepted as in >80 per cent of a community).

Constitution 1. The distribution and representation of age and/or size classes in a crop stand structure. 2. The final legal declaration that a specified area has been given a specific status in law, e.g., as reserve.

Constraint A qualification of the minimum or maximum amount of an output or cost that could be produced or incurred in a given time period or with given factors or resources. A limiting or satisfying condition which must be met when setting objectives. "Ceiling" or "floor" may be used in the same manner.

Consumer In an ecosystem, a heterotrophic organism (one for which complex materials, especially organic foods, are the chief source of nutrition) which feeds on other organisms. A primary consumer, as a herbivore, obtains its nutrition directly from plants; a secondary consumer, as a carnivore, obtains its energy indirectly by feeding upon herbivores.

Containers, Plant Containers in which plants are raised from seed or into which they are transferred from seed bed for the purpose of planting out later. These may be of any easily available local material, e.g., leaf cups (*donas*), baskets, collapsible wooden frames, earthen pots, open tubes of bamboo, paper or thin metal sheeting and polythene bags.

Contiguous Tracts or any land units or legal subdivisions having a common boundary. Lands having only a common corner are not considered contiguous. *Contiguity* is the general condition and indices possibly expressing habitat or land use diversity.

Continuous Data Quantitative data that varies continuously throughout a raster layer.

Continuum An area over which the vegetation and/or animal population is continuous in composition, so that homogeneous communities cannot be distinguished in it.

Contour A line connecting points of equal elevation. A line on a topographic map connecting points of equal height and used to represent the shape of the earth's surface.

Contour Cropping The cultivation of crops in strips along the contours of a slope. *See* strip cropping.

Contour Furrow or Trench A furrow or trench constructed along the contours of a slope to check run-off and soil loss.

Contour Map An elevation map in which lines connect points of equal elevation.

Contour Stripping A type of strip mining that is practiced in areas of steep topography where the mineral seam outcrops or approaches the surface at approximately the same elevation along a hillside.

Contrast Enhancement Image-processing procedure that improves the contrast ratio of images. The original narrow range of digital values is expanded to utilize the full range of available digital values.

Contrast Filter A colour filter chosen to make a coloured subject which stands out sharply from surrounding objects.

Contrast Ratio On an image, the ratio of reflectances between the brightest and darkest parts of an image. The term is generally used in digital interpretation.

Contrast Stretching Expanding a measured range of digital numbers in an image to a larger range, to improve the contrast of the image and its component parts.

Control 1. The regulation of annual or periodic fellings. 2. The comparison of operation carried out in a forest with those prescribed by the working plan. *See* control area; control, basal area; control, volume; control, experimental; control forms.

Control (Entomology) Check on the increase of population of an insect, brought about by a single factor or a combination of factors. Control can be classed as natural control, i.e., the reduction in the reproductive rate of the species, caused by the natural factors of the environment; or as artificial control, i.e., the reduction in the reproductive rate of the species caused by the intervention of men. Various methods of insect control are: BIOLOGICAL: Control through utilization of parasites, predators, diseases, etc. BIOTIC: Control through disease-producing organisms, such as fungi, bacteria, insect parasites and predators, birds, lizards, etc. CHEMICAL: Control obtained thorough the use of insecticides, stomach-poisons, contact-poisons, repellants, attractants, and impregnation or other preservation treatments. CLIMATIC: Control exercised by meteorological factors, such as temperature, rainfall, atmospheric humidity, wind, sunshine, light, etc., and by topographical features and zoogeographical distribution. MECHANICAL: Control secured through barriers, screens, deterrents, traps, sun-heating, charring, etc. NUTRITIONAL: Control brought about by regulating quality of food-supply, alternative food plants, host resistance, quantity of food-supply, etc. SILVICULTURAL: Control secured through judicious silvicultural operations such as maintenance of natural forest, choice of silvicultural system, composition of mixed stands, thinning, etc. Climatic, nutritional and biotic controls come under natural control. The others constitute artificial control.

Control (Experimental) That part of an experimental series providing a standard of comparison for determining the effects of the treatments. A check on the increase of the population of an insect, animal or plant imposed by a single factor or a combination of factors. These may be natural (climate, nutritional factors, parasites or disease) or artificial (silviculture practices or direct intervention by biological, mechanical or chemical means).

Control (Pathology) The regulation and more especially the limitation of plant or virus population by one or more factors; these may be natural (e.g., climatic, nutritional, parasites) or artificial (i.e., through human agency) — indirectly by, e.g., silvicultural practices or directly by mechanical, chemical or biological means.

Control Area Regulation of the annual or periodic yield in an area over which fellings are prescribed. *See* yield regulation.

Control Forms Registers compiled with a view to checking the operations carried out against those prescribed in a working plan.

Control Line An inclusive term for all barriers, natural or constructed, that are used to control a fire.

Control Plot Untreated plot in an experimental design.

Control Point Any station in a horizontal and/or vertical control system that can be identified on a photograph and used for correlating the data shown on that photo.

Control Stations Point on the ground whose position (horizontal or vertical) is known and can be used as a base for additional survey work.

Control, Artificial (Entomology) Regulation of the numbers of a pest population to a level below which the damage done by it is financially unimportant, through the intervention of man. Biological, chemical, mechanical, and silvicultural control measures come under this category. *See* control.

Control, Basal Area Regulation of the annual or periodic yield by the basal area of trees prescribed for felling.

Control, Biological 1. Control of plants, diseases, and animal pests by the use of natural enemies. 2. The employment of the enemies and diseases of pest for the purpose of maintaining adequate control. The artificial application of biotic control.

Control, Biotic The natural control of the numbers of an insect, animal or plant by its enemies and diseases.

Control, Natural Nature's method of controlling plant and animal populations through the action of heat, cold, moisture, dryness, parasites, predators, disease, etc.

Control, Natural (Entomology) Nature's method of maintaining a biotic balance as in the reduction of pest populations, caused by the natural factors of the environment. Climatic, biotic and nutritional control methods come under this category. *See* control.

Control, Volume Regulation of the annual or periodic yield by the volume of felling prescribed. It is an yield regulation method by volume.

Controlled Burning or Prescribed Burning (Back Burning) It is a technique sometimes used in forest management, farming, or prairie restoration. Fire is a natural part of both forest and grassland ecology and controlled fire can be a tool for management. Controlled burning stimulates the germination of some desirable forest trees, thus renewing the forest. Some seeds, such as sequoia, remain dormant until fire breaks down the seed coating. In industrialized countries, controlled burning is usually overseen by fire control authorities for regulations and permits. The party responsible must delineate the intended time and place. Obtaining a permit may not limit liability if the fire burns out of control. In india also, this has remained as a subsidiary silvicultural pracitce as a art of preparation for artificial planting. However, the intended time, place and intensity is always well defined.

Convention on Biodiversity (CBD) Biodiversity is the variability among living organisms and the ecological complexes of which they are part, including diversity within and between species and ecosystems. Biodiversity has direct consumptive value in food, agriculture, medicine, and in industry. India is one of the 17 mega diverse countries which together possess 60 to 70 per cent of the world's Biodiversity. It may be worth mentioning that India ratified the International Convention on Biodiversity (CBD) on 18th February, 1994 and became party to the Convention in May 1994. The CBD is an international legal instrument for promoting conservation and sustainable use of Biological Diversity taking into account "the need to share cost and benefit between developed and developing countries and the ways and means to support innovation by local people".

Conversion A change from one silvicultural system or one (set of) species to another. *See* conversion system.

Conversion Cycle A cycle of energy transfer, from plant-eating animals which obtain their energy from plants, pass them on through meat-eaters to the top predators, who on decay supply organic matter for plant life, thus completing the cycle. *See* food chain.

Convolution The conversion of values from one grid to another, which is different in terms of size or orientation.

Coordinates Linear and (or) angular quantities that designate the position of a point in relation to a given reference frame.

Coordinate System Method of describing locations on earth by columns and rows, or x and y values.

Coot Any of certain sluggish slow-flying, slaty-black, swimming and diving birds, resembling ducks and belonging to the genus Felicia of the family fallidae. They have lobed toes; the upper mandible is prolonged on the forehead as a horny frontal shield. Common Coot (*F. atra*): Web-footed bird, inhabiting edges of lakes and still rivers, with base of bill extended to form a white plate on the forehead. In India, it is found wherever suitable water occurs. It ascends the Himalayas up to about 1800 or 2400 m. It is a resident species in many parts of India, but in winter its numbers are greatly increased by immigration.

Sportsmen do not usually trouble to shoot it, as it is easy to hit and the flesh is not very tasty; but native fishermen net it or catch it by hand for sale in the markets. PURLE COOT (*Porphyrio poliocephalus*): This is a large blue and purple bird with ungainly legs and feet. It is found in Kashmir as a resident bird.

Coppice A crop of coppice shoot.

Coppice History In the days of charcoal production, most forests in iron-making regions in Europe were managed as coppices. Such forests were usually being cut on a cycle of about 16 years. In this way, fuel could be provided for iron industry, in principle, for ever. This was regulated by a statute of Henry VIII, which required forests to be enclosed after cutting and twelve standards to be left in each acre to be grown into timber. The system of coppicing was known as Coppice-with-Standards. Here scattered individual stems were allowed to grow on through several coppice cycles (often 10 or more). This practice had been commonly used throughout the British Isles as a means of giving greater flexibility in the resulting product from any one area. The system not only gave rise to small material from the coppice but also a range of larger stuff from the standards for jobs like house building, bridge repair, cart making, and so on. The shoots (or "suckers") were used either in their young state for interweaving in wattle fencing as is the practice with willows, or the new shoots were allowed to grow and mature into large poles, as was often the custom with hardwood such as oaks or ashes. This practice created long, straight poles which were better for working than naturally grown trees which had bends and forks. Coppicing might also be practiced to encourage specific growth patterns, as with cinnamon trees which were grown for their bark. Coppiced timber/hardwoods were extensively used in carriage and shipbuilding, and they are still sometimes grown for making wooden buildings and furniture. In Southern Britain, coppice was traditionally hazel, grown amongst oak standards (large trees). This provided wood for many purposes, especially charcoal which before the availability of coal was economically significant in allowing smelting of metals. Some patches of these forests are still operated for coppice today, producing material for hurdle-making, thatching spars, local charcoal-burning or other crafts. The only remaining large-scale commercial coppice crop in the area is sweet chestnut which is grown in parts of East Sussex and Kent.

Coppice Shoot A shoot arising from an adventitious bud at the base of a woody plant that has been cut near the ground or burnt back. Sometimes (incorrectly) used to include root sucker. In American usage both are referred to as sprouts.

Coppice System It is a type of silvicultural system.In this system, the young crop originates from coppice shoots arising from the adventitious buds on the stumps of the felled trees or by other vegetative means. Here the rotation is usually short. This is ideally suited for those forests, which need to be managed for fuelwood and small timber. The forest should have the species that has the potentiality to reproduce by means of root suckers and coppice shoots. In the past, many dry deciduous forests in India were managed under this system. The single most demerit in the system lies in the fact that it exhausts the nutrients in the soil. However, over the period several modifications took place in this system in response to local needs and potentiality of forest. These modifications were incorporated into the main system to form a full-fledged system or sub-subsystem. These systems are known as "coppice-with-standard" and "coppice-with-reserve". They were widely adopted in dry deciduous forests of Central India. These systems are still in vogue in many parts of India.

Coppice, Seedling Coppice shoot arising from the base of seedling that have been cut or burnt back. The seedlings of many trees, of which sal is the best known, are able to produce new shoots (seedling coppice) from below ground (from dormant buds in the original hypocotyledonary region) if the original shoot is injured or checked in growth, and may do this annually for many years. Chir pines and other pines have this power too.

Coppicing or Coppice, to 1. To fell trees near ground level with a view to produce coppice shoots. 2. To produce coppice shoots. 3. Coppicing is a traditional method of forest management in which young and middle-aged tree stems are cut down to a low level. In subsequent growth years, many new shoots will emerge and after a number of years the cycle begins again and the coppiced tree, or stool, is ready to be harvested again. Typically a coppice forest is harvested in sections, on a rotation. In this way each year a crop is available. This has the side-effect of providing a rich variety of habitats, as the forests always has a range of different aged stools growing in it. The cycle length depends upon the species cut, the local custom, and the use to which the product is put. The power of producing new coppice shoots from the stump after the tree is felled depends on species as well as number of rotation. Teak and sal provide examples of good coppicing powers, whilest it is rare in conifers.

Coral Reefs Conservation Conservation of coral reefs is a national policy imperative. The country has corals in four areas, namely, Andaman & Nicobar Islands, Lakshadweep Islands, Gulf of Kutch and Gulf of Mannar. There is a national programme for intensive conservation and management of coral areas. The programme is continuing since 1987. Management Action Plans are under implementation in all the four areas through financial assistance extended by Government of India. *See* conservation.

Cormorant Any of various large, lustrous black, voracious sea birds of the genus Phalacrocorax (*Family Phalacrocoracidae*) that have a long neck, stiff wedge-shaped tail and slender hooked beak. They are found in most tropical and temperate sea-coasts of the world. The bird has a pouch of skin under the beak, into which it puts fish. It is a strong swimmer and diver, flies excellently and lives entirely on fish. In China and Japan cormorants have been trained to catch fish and bring them to their owners. LITTLE CORMORANT (*P. niger*). This is found throughout India excluding the Himalayas. It is the commonest species of cormorant and is often very abundant. It is fond of freshwater, preferring marshes and tanks to rivers. Out of water, its favourite perch is a low stump sticking out of water. It is a resident bird, breeding in July to September. LARGE CORMORANT (*Phalacrocorax corbo*). This is black and is of the size of the domestic duck. It is found in association with the little cormorant.

Correlation A relationship between two or more variables such that a change in the value of one is accompanied by some estimable change, direct or inverse, in the value of the other(s).

Correlation Coefficient A measure of liner correlation that can take values between + 1 and –1. A value near to + 1 indicates almost perfect positive association, high values of the other; a value near to -1 indicates almost perfect negative association; a value near to zero indicates absence of association.

Corticolous An organism inhabiting or growing on bark.

Counterfire, to An attempt to extinguish an advancing forest fire by deliberately burning the forest from the opposite direction.

Coupe 1. Forest area earmarked for felling in a predefined year. A felling area, usually one of an annual felling series unless otherwise stated. 2. Annual treatment area which may include felling or not. Such areas are part of treatment or felling series under the working circle. Coupes are laid to spread silvicultural operations such as felling, planting along a long time horizon. Preferably numbered with roman numerals, i, ii, iii, etc. Normally if felling cycle is 20 years, then XX annual coupes are laid. A part of the compartment or the full compartment or group of compartments can constitute the coupe. *See* compartment.

Covariance The sum of the products of two or more correlated variables from their means, divided by the number of degrees of freedom.

Covariance, Analysis of Analysis of variance applied to correlation problems. It compares any number of statistical groups simultaneously when each group is composed of two correlated variables.

Cove A small indentation or recess in the shoreline of a sea, lake or river; a sheltered area.

Cover 1. The proportion of the ground occupied by a perpendicular projection to the ground from the outline of the aerial parts of plants. 2. Canopy closure or the amount of overhead tree cover as measured using a spherical densiometer held at 1.5 m from the ground. 3. Plants and plant parts, living or dead, on the surface of the ground. Also the percentage of a named area that has such plants. 4. (Forage cover) The plants or other objects used by wild animals for nesting, rearing of young, resting, escape from predators, hiding from hunters, or protection from adverse environmental conditions.

Cover, Crown The horizontal projection on the ground of a tree crown.

Cover, Game Plants suitable for harbouring and feeding of game.

Cover, Ground The carpet of herbaceous plants and low shrubs, which covers the soil ground vegetation. Sometimes taken to include litter.

Cover Type A designation for plant species forming a plurality of composition across a given area (e.g., oak-hickory, northern hardwood, maple-birch, etc.).

Cover (Wildlife) 1. A place of natural shelter or vegetation which serves as shelter for birds, animals and fishes (especially when sought as game) from the adverse effects of excessive sunlight, drying and predators. Game birds have been successfully developed by suitable cover crops along field borders and forest edges. 2. The factors that provide natural shelter and protection for wild animals are: suitable arrangements of vegetation, dinning sites or rock formations, plants and their residues covering the ground and retarding run-off and erosion of soil, etc. 3. Anything that provides protection for aquatic or terrestrial animals from predators or ameliorates adverse conditions and/ or seasonal changes in metabolic costs. 4. Horizontal area occupied by vegetation or foliage. *Refer* Covert.

Coverage Geographic data set (in GIS) that represents a specific type of feature (e.g., vegetation coverage). Often simply called a layer. ARC/INFO also has a data format that is referred to as coverage.

Cover-Forage Ratio The ratio of the area in a habitat analysis unit providing good cover to that area providing good forage.

Covert A distinctive dense vegetation in which game or other species of interest are typically found, e.g., a corner in hedgerows.

Covey A small flock or a number of birds of the same kind, typically of partridges and certain related birds.

Crane A small flock or a number of birds of the family Gruidae (*Order Gurifomis*); superficially resembling herons, but usually larger. They have very long legs, neck and bill. COMMON CRANE (*Grus grus*): A winter visitor to India in large numbers (October to March). Considered very good for eating. DEMOISELLE CRANE (*Anthropoides virgo*): A winter visitor to India in enormous numbers (October to March). Considered good for eating. This bird is rather small in size with long flowing secondaries and breast feathers and white plumes behind the eyes. SARUS CRANE (*Grus antigone* Syn. *Antigone antigone* or *Megalornis antigone*): A huge bird with a reddish naked and long legs, found in pairs about marshy places. It is always bold in demeanour, always frequenting the same place. It is found throughout northern India. There are two forms. The typical form is seen in Uttar Pradesh, Upper Bengal and Punjab, south of the Chenab. The birds pair for life and are devoted and close companions. They are found in pairs in every *jheel* and tank of importance in India.

Creek A small stream of water which serves as the natural drainage course for a drainage basin of nominal or small size.

Creeper A plant, rarely with a woody stem, which grows mainly horizontally on or near the ground and puts out roots at intervals. It is a common misnomer for climber.

Crepuscular Relating to or like twilight. Applied to animals which appear or become active in twilight.

Criteria and Indicators Criteria are broad categories of conditions or processes by which the conservation and sustainable management of ecosystems and related resources may be assessed. Indicators are measurable outcomes for various aspects of a criterion.

Criteria & Indicators for SFM Practices Sustainable management practices necessitate periodical verification. For this it is necessary to have methods and frameworks for measuring and verifying sustainability practices. Criteria and indicators constitute such methods and frameworks necessary for periodic verification. Criterion describes a state or situation, which should be met to comply with sustainable forest management. Indicator is a quantitative, qualitative or descriptive attribute that, when periodically measured or monitored, indicates the direction of change. In other words, criteria can be attributes by which choice alternatives are evaluated or an aspect which is considered important by which sustainable forest management may be assessed. A criterion is accompanied by a set of indicators. Criteria and indicators for sustainable forest management are still in the process of their evolution. Presently, it is at a slower pace. It has began with economic criterion and slightly moved towards incorporating the ecological and social dimension of sustainability. Generally speaking, it is the social issues including participatory management, which are most difficult to grapple with. The measurement process throws many challenges. As the forest types changes, there will be a change in ecological criterion and indicators. Further, criterion and indicators which encompass both quantitative and qualitative aspects need to be context specific including social dimensions like equality, gender equality, women empowerment, etc. ITTO guidelines for the sustainable forest management of natural tropical forests (1992) have specified criteria and indicators for sustainable forest management. Seven criteria have been identified as essential elements of sustainable forest management. Seven criteria are: Criterion 1: Enabling conditions for sustainable forest management; Criterion 2: Forest resource security; Criterion 3: Forest ecosystem health and condition; Criterion 4: Flow of forest produce; Criterion 5: Biological diversity; Criterion 6: Soil and water conservation; Criterion 7: Economic, soil and cultural aspects. Different indicators have been identified and formulated under each criterion so that a change in any one of them would give information that is necessary to assess the progress towards sustainable forest management. However, these indicators are more of preliminary and indicative in nature rather than exhaustive. Again, looking at the changing needs of forest management practices, a different set of criteria and indicators, which are able to measure the effects of sustainable forest management, can be formulated. *See* environmental indicators.

Crocodile A large thick-skinned, long-bodied, aquatic reptile of tropical and sub-tropical waters, belonging to genus Crocodilus and related genera. Species found in India are *Crocodilus porosus* (which does not hesitate to attack man) and *C. palustris.*

Crop, Cover A subsidiary crop of low plants introduced in a plantation to afford soil cover between or below the main crop. It is also used to protect land from erosion.

Crop, Final The portion of the stand which is intended to be retained to the end of the rotation.

Crop, Forest The entire collection of trees (including bamboo's) growing on a given area. Forest crop may be classified in terms of their stages of development as seedling, thicket or sapling, pole, and tree stand, fully-stocked, and tree growth.

Crop, Main The stand left after thinning residual crop (or stand). Sometimes called major crop (or yield).

Crop, Nurse A crop of trees or shrub grown to foster the growth of another and more important tree crop in its early stages.

Crop, Pole A crop consisting of pole.

Crop, Pure A crop composed almost entirely of trees of one species, usually to the extent of not less than 80 per cent. *See* pure forest, pure stand, mixed forest.

Crop, Sapling A crop consisting of sapling.

Crop, Seedling 1. A crop consisting of seedling. 2. Also refers to a crop of trees, neither planted nor of coppice or root sucker origin, but originating *insitu* from seed. *See* forest, high.

Crop, Subsidiary That part of a stand which is removed in thinning.

Cross, to Fertilization of the female gamete of one individual by the male gametes of another, whether in nature or artificially. Often restricted to the crossing of individuals of unlike genetic constitution.

Cross-Hatching The technique of shading areas on a map, with a given pattern of lines or symbols.

Crossover Point The point at which there is a 50 per cent possibility that something belongs to particular fuzzy class.

Cross Validation A validation method in which observations are dropped one at a time from a simple size n, and n estimates are computed from the remaining (n – 1) observations. In geostatistics this is done using the kriging equations to check the variogram with respect to the sample data.

Crown The branches and foliage of a tree. The upper branchy portion of a tree above the bole. The shape of crown may vary on the basis of tree species and age.

Crown Class 1. In descending order of crown height and size, trees are classified into dominant, co-dominant, intermediate, and suppressed. 2. One of the classes into which the trees forming a stand are divided on the basis of the type of crown and its position with reference to the general canopy and to the crowns of neighbouring trees.

Crown Development The expansion of crown measured as crown length and crown width.

Crown Fire A fire that burns through the tops of living trees or brush.

Crown Height The height of crown as measured vertically from the ground level to the point half-way between the lowest green branch and the green branches forming green crown all round bole, clear (or clean). *See* crown length.

Crown Length The vertical measurement of the crown of a tree from the tip to the point half-way between the lowest green branches forming green crown all-round and the lowest green branch on the bole. *See* crown height.

Crown Per Cent or Ratio The ratio of the crown length to the total height of tree expressed either as a percentage or as a decimal fraction.

Crown Ratio The ratio of the length within a tree with leaves to the total tree height.

Crown Width The maximum spread of the crown expressed as its widest diameter.

Cruise 1. A survey of forest land to locate timber and estimate its quantity by species, size, quality, or other characteristics. 2. Surveying of forest land to locate merchantable timber and estimate its quantity by species, assortments, size, products, quality or other characteristics. 3. The estimate obtained in such a survey. *See* forest survey.

Cruising Radius The distance an animal may move from an initial point (as a den) in the course of a day. This is the maximum distance between locations at which an individual animal is found at different times of the day or at various seasons in the year. *See* Mobility.

Crumb A small aggregate of irregular shape and 1/8 inch or less in diameter, formed by the cohesion of a number of soil particles. *See* crumb structure.

Crumb Structure A condition in which the soil particles form water-stable crumb largely by the physical and physicochemical action of soil organic matter.

Crust A hard or brittle layer formed on the surface of many soils when dry.

Cryptic Colouration Colouration which conceals animals by resemblance to their natural surroundings, especially by the pattern or colouring of the animals.

Cryptophyte A plant whose buds or shoot apices, destined to survive the unfavourable season, are below the ground surface or in the soil under water.

Cull or Cull, to An inferior plant rejected from nursery stock; to reject such plants.

Culm The characteristic hollow and jointed stem of a bamboo or grass.

Cultivar Any clone, race, or product of breeding selected from a population of plants because it has desirable characteristics, and is cultivated and given a non-Latin name and designated by CV.

Cultivation, Shifting A method of cyclical cultivation, chiefly in vogue in the tropics, where cultivators cut the tree crop, burn it, and raise field crops for one or more years before moving on to another site and repeating the process. It is popularly known as *Taungya* (Burmese); *Kumri* (Tamil); *Punam* (Malayalam); *Podu* (Oriya); *Jhum* (Assamese and other local names).

Cultural Operations A general term for operations, as a rule not directly remunerative, undertaken to assist or complete existing regeneration to promote the proper development of the crop or to minimize the after effects of felling damage. It, therefore, includes subsidiary felling, weeding, cleaning, unremunerative improvement felling and thinning in groups of advance growth, girdling, or poisoning of unwanted growth, climber cutting and even piling felling debris and burning controlled, but usually not other ground operations, nor pruning. More often associated with silvicultural systems relying primarily on regeneration.

Culvert A conduit such as pipe through which surface water can flow under roads.

Cumulative Effects The additive, often uncoordinated, impacts when a number of unrelated, or related but discrete management activities take place in a given area.

Current Annual Increment (CAI) *See* increment, current annual.

Cursor A visible symbol guided by the keyboard, a joystick, a tracking ball, or a digitizer, usually in the form of a cross or a blinking symbol, that indicates a position on computer screen of VDU.

Customary Rights Rights which result from a long series of habitat or customary actions, constantly repeated, which have, by such repetition and uninterrupted acquiescence, acquired the force of a law within a geographical or sociological unit.

Cut, Allowable The amount of forest produce, howsoever measured, that can be cut in a given period under sustained yield management. *See* yield.

Cut Back, to To cut flush with the ground. Apart from its application to the cutting of weed and climber in tending, it is generally used for the cutting of a stool or any stem in the pole and seedling stage with the object of obtaining superior coppice growth.

Cut, Annual or Cut, Periodic The amount of forest produce cut or prescribed to be cut on a given forest area in a year or period. *See* yield.

Cutting 1. A short length of stem branch or root placed in the soil, or other medium, in order that it may develop into a plant. 2. American word used for felling.

Cutting Area, Annual The area of forest prescribed for felling each year. An annual coupe.

Cutting Cycle or Felling Cycle The planned interval between major harvest operations in a stand. In other words, it is the time period or cycle after which the stand is revisited for felling. A cycle of 20 years means that every 20 years a harvest would occur in a stand.

Cutting Section A subdivision of a felling series or felling coupes formed with the object of regulating fellings in some special manner. *See* coupes.

Cutting, Root and Shoot A young plant with a pruned tap-root and severed stem used for planting stump.

Cutworm The larva of species of the family nactuidae (moths) which in feeding cuts through the base of seedlings.

Cycle An interval of time during which one sequence of a regularly recurring succession of events or phenomena is completed. *See* Life cycle.

Cycle, Carbon The atmosphere contains a complex mixture of carbon compounds, in continuous state of creations, transformations and decomposition. Practically all organic matter originates in the process of photosynthesis. The plants use the radiant energy of the sun to convert carbon dioxide and water into carbohydrates by splitting water to derive hydrogen, and by drawing in carbon dioxide from the air. In the process the plants releases free oxygen (O_2) into the atmosphere. While plants absorbs carbon dioxide during photosynthesis, all living organisms respire and release carbon dioxide and decomposing bacteria do the same in regard to dead matter. But while respiration and decomposition go on all the time, photosynthesis takes place only during daytime. During daytime, carbon dioxide in the atmosphere comes down from an average of 320 parts per million to around 305 parts but at night it increases, going up to as much as 400 parts per million, near the ground level. Apart from the daily production and consumption of carbon (in the form of carbon dioxide), the earth has a vast stock of carbon in permanent form. This stock consists of inorganic deposits (mainly carbonates like calcium carbonates etc.) and organic fossils deposits (chiefly coal and oil). When we burn fossil fuels, we are merely adding more carbon dioxide to the atmosphere which has an excess supply already.

Cycle, Heat Heat is one of the prime requisites of life. This is supplied by solar radiation. It is calculated that the solar heat reaching the Earth's orbit (just above the atmosphere) amounts to about 2 calories for square centimetre per minute. But the Earth gets only less than half the radiation reaching the top of the atmosphere. About 29 per cent is absorbed by the ozone layer in the atmosphere. Atmospheric water vapour, carbon dioxide and dust particles absorb around 18 per cent. The cloud reflects back into space some 23 per cent. About 22 per cent is scattered by atmospheric dust. The earth receives only a balance of 38 per cent. Out of the 38 per cent solar radiation received, the earth re-radiates about 7 per cent by long wave radiation, thus reducing the stock terrestrial energy to 31 per cent. At the same time, out of the 22 per cent scattered by the atmosphere, 16 per cent ultimately reaches the Earth as diffuse radiation, the rest 6 per cent being irretrievably lost in space. Thus, on the whole the Earth receives about 47 per cent of the solar energy reaching the atmosphere. Meanwhile, the atmosphere acting as an intermediaries between the Sun and the surface of the Earth, retains about 5 per cent of the energy as sensible heat and about 24 per cent as latent heat in water vapour. It is essential that the absorption and radiation of heat should ultimately balance. Otherwise, the Earth would experience a net increase in heat or a net decrease according as a surplus or deficit of heat results from radiation. The balance between absorption and radiation is a mainly regulated by water vapour in the atmosphere. There is only very little amount of water in the atmosphere, about 0.001 per cent. This insignificant amount of atmospheric water exercises an influence on the climate of the Earth, out of all proportion to its total mass. Besides keeping the balance between the abortion and radiation of heat, it controls the water cycle and determines our climatic conditions.

Cycle, Oxygen Oxygen not only supports life but also plays a fundamental role as building block of practically all vital molecules accounting for about one-fourth of all the atoms in living matter. The most recent factors affecting the oxygen cycles of the biosphere and the oxygen budget of the Earth is man himself. He inhales oxygen and exhales carbon dioxide, thus reducing the stock of oxygen and increasing the supply of carbon dioxide. He goes further and burns fossil fuels, depleting the oxygen supply still further. He reduces photosynthetic activity by cutting down forests and replacing them with cities.

Cylindrical Projections Map projections in which the surface of the globe is projected onto a cylinder (for example, the Mercator projection).

Dd

Damp Wood A termite which enters wood directly from the air at the time of swarming and has no contact with the ground, but which requires abundance of moisture for its existence and consequently confines its activities largely to decaying wood.

Damping off The killing of young seedling by certain fungi that cause decay of the stem or roots. Damping off is particularly liable to occur in crowded seedling/beds of some species till the stems are lignified. In order to ward off this problem, watering in nurseries must be very sparing.

Dangling Arc A dead-end line or arc feature that is connected to other lines in the data layer at one end only. The term is used in GIS.

Data Observations made from monitoring the real world. Data are collected as facts or evidence, which may be processed to give them meaning and convert them into information.

Data Accuracy The extent to which an estimated data value approaches its true value.

Data Bias The systematic variation of data from reality.

Data Capture Collecting information for computer processing and analysis. Data may be captured automatically — for example, by a sensor that continuously monitors physical conditions such as temperature or manually; for example, by measuring girth of the tree or counting the standing trees in forests.

Data Communication Sending and receiving data *via* any communication medium, such as a telephone line or wireless system. The term usually implies that the data are digital (such as computer data) rather than analogue (such as voice messages). However, in the ISDN (Integrated Services Digital Network) system, all data including voices and video images — are transmitted digitally.

Data Conversion The process of converting data from one format to another. With many different GIS data formats available, this can be a difficult task requiring specialized software.

Data Editing The process of correcting errors in data input into a database system. This can be carried out manually or automatically.

Data Error The physical difference between the real world and a database or a GIS facsimile.

Data Input The process of converting data into a form that can be used by a database system or a GIS.

Data Link The communication lines and related hardware and software systems needed to send or communicate data between two or more computers over telephone lines, optical fibres, satellite networks, or cables.

Data Model The abstraction and representation of real world phenomena according to a formalized, conceptual schema, which is usually implemented using the geographical primitives of points, lines, and polygons, or discretized continuous fields.

Data Precision The recorded level of detail of the data.

Data Stream The process of progressing from raw data to integrated GIS database. This includes all stages of data input, transformation, re-projection, editing and manipulation.

Data Structure The organization of data in ways suitable for computer storage and manipulation.

Data Types The classification of different data according to their characteristics. For example, boolean (0/1), nominal, ordinal, integer, scalar (real), directional, or topological data are all types of data according to their function and degree of precision.

Database 1. A collection of interrelated information, usually stored on some form of mass-storage system such as magnetic tape or disk. A GIS database includes data about the position and the attributes of geographical features that have been coded as points, lines, areas, pixels, or grid cells. 2. A collection of data, usually stored as single or multiple files, associated with a single general category.

Database Management System (DBMS) A set of computer programmes for organizing the information in a database. Typically, a DBMS contains routines for data input, verification, storage, retrieval, and combination.

Datum In surveying, a reference system for computing or correlating the results of surveys. There are two principal types of datums — vertical and horizontal. A vertical datum is a level surface to which heights are referred. In the United States, the generally adopted vertical datum for levelling operations is the National Geodetic Vertical Datum of 1929. The horizontal datum is used as a reference for ground position. The North American Datum of 1927 is defined by the latitude and longitude of an initial point (Meade's Ranch in Kansas), the direction of a line between this point and a specified second point, and two dimensions that define the spheroid. The new North American Datum of 1983 is based on a newly defined spheroid (GRS80); it is an Earth-centred datum having no initial point or initial direction. The widely used datum is WGS84 of the United States.

DBH Abbreviation for Diameter of a Tree at Breast Height.

De Lecourt's Law In a fully stocked selection forest, the number of stems falls off from one diameter class to the next in geometric progression, which means that the percentage of reduction in stems number from one diameter class to another is constant. If the quotient of the series is known and the number of stems in any class is given, the whole series can be calculated and this gives proportionate distribution in an ideal selection forest or what is called as balanced composition.

Debt-for-Nature Swap Agreement under which a proportion of a country's debts are written off in exchange for a commitment by the debtor country to undertake projects for environmental protection. Debt-for-nature swaps were set up by environment groups in the 1980s in an attempt to reduce the debt problem of poor countries, while simultaneously promoting conservation. To date, most debt-for-nature swaps have concentrated on setting aside areas of land, especially tropical rain forest, for protection and have involved private conservation foundations.

Debug To remove errors from a programme or from hardware. Debugger is a programme that helps a programmer to remove programming errors.

Decalcification Removal of calcium carbonate ions from the soil by leaching.

Decay The decomposition of wood substance by fungi, chemicals or heat. Two stages of decay, the "incipient" and "advanced" are ordinarily recognized, though two supplemental ones, the "intermediate", and "final" stages are sometimes accepted.

Deciduous Applied to such perennial plants as are normally leafless for sometime during the year.

Deciduous and Evergreen Habits The most important variation in tree foliage is its deciduous or evergreen habit. It is related to climatic conditions whether associated with low temperature or dryness, and yet where evergreen and deciduous trees are mixed, the latter may be leafless at different times, just as in a mixed tree species differ in their individual sequence of leaf fall and coming into new leaf, although all experience the same climate and micro-climate. The leafless period in deciduous species varies considerably over its geographical range, being longer where the dry season is longer, and it also varies from year to year in the same way. Teak is virtually evergreen where rainfall is abundant and well distributed, whereas in the dry parts of its range it may be leafless for nearly half the year.

Deciduous Cover Vegetation classes where 75 per cent or more of the diagnostic vegetation is made up of tree or shrub species that shed foliage simultaneously in response to an "unfavourable" season.

Deciduous Forests 1. Forests dominantly having deciduous trees which shed foliage simultaneously in response to an "unfavourable" season or in any particular period of the season. They belong to the category of forests defined by Champion & Seth. There are two types of deciduous forests. One is dry deciduous and the another is moist deciduous forest.

Decision Support System (DSS) A system, usually computer based, dedicated to supporting decisions regarding a specific problem or set of problems. In other words, Decision Support Systems are a class of computer-based information system including knowledge based system that support decision making activities.

Decline The decrease in tree or forest resources caused by one or more biotic or abiotic factors.

Decomposition A large number of interrelated processes by which organic matter is broken down to smaller particles and soluble forms available for plant uptake.

Decreaser Plant Species Any plant species of the original vegetation that decreases in relative amounts, more particularly under continued over-use of a forage crop.

Deep Water Habitat Permanently flooded lands lying below the deepwater boundary of wetlands. This boundary is at a depth of 2 mt below the water level.

Deer Any animals of family Servidae comprising ruminant mammals with deciduous solid horns or antlers (usually in the male only). They have two large and two small hoofs on each foot. They are represented by numerous species and individuals in most regions except Africa and Australia. They form an important source of food for the larger carnivore. Types of Indian deer include: BARKING DEER or MUNTJAC (*Muntiacus muntjac*). *See* Muntjac. BROW-ANTLERED DEER (*Cervus eldi* Syn. *Panolia eldi*): The animal is so called because the brow tines of its antlers sweep forwards and the beams backwards in a continuous graceful curve. Found in swampy areas in the south-west corner of Logtak lake in Manipur. Two other sub-species are reported in Burma and Thailand.The animal is threatened with extinction and so is given special protection in its only habitat in Keibul Lamjao Sanctuary in Manipur. The race found in India is known as *Cervus eldi eldi*. Two other races are found in Burma and Thailand. CHITAL: SPOTTED DEER. (*Axis axis* Syn. *Cervus axis*). It is the most beautiful of all deer, with its coat of bright rufus fawn, profusely spotted with white at all ages and in all seasons. It is found in the forests at the base of the Himalayas, extending southwards to Kanya Kumari, wherever there is jungle combined with good grazing and plentiful supply of water. It is unknown in the arid zone of the Punjab and Rajasthan. A well-built stag stands 0.9 m. at the shoulder and weighs about 86 kilograms. CHEVROTAIN or MOUSE DEER. *See* chevrotain. HOG DEER (*Axis porcinus* Syn. *Cervus porcinus; Hyelaphus porcunus*): An animal, with a pig-like appearance and movements, closely related to the chital. It is found in the low alluvial grass plains of North India from Punjab to Assam. KASHMIR STAG: HANGUL (*Cervus hanglu*). *See* Hanglu. MUSK DEER (*Moschus moschiferus*): A small, hornless animal of Central Asia, the male of which secretes musk. The males carry no antlers, but have peculiar tusks, which are elongated upper canine teeth. The musk is secreted in a glandular sac under the skin of the abdomen of the male. It has a strong odour and is largely used in perfumery. The animal is much persecuted for its musk pod and is threatened with extinction. It therefore needs special protection.

In India it is found in Kashmir at high elevations (example, Upper Dachigam area). RAVINE or INDIAN GAZELLE: CHINKARA (*Gazella Bennetti*). *See* Chinkara. SAMBAR: SAMBUR: SAMBHAR: SAMBHUR. Plural Sambars, Sambar, etc. (*Rusa unicolour* Syn. *Cervus unicolour*): A medium to large deer with a mane and three-pointed antlers, found in South-Eastern Asia and many of the Indo-Australian Islands. The Indian race is *Rusa unicolour nigra*, and it is found in wooded districts of India. The Malay race *Rusa unicolor equinus* is found from Assam eastwards. SWAMP DEER: BARASINGHA (*Cervus duvaucelli* Syn. *Rucervus duvaucelli*): A brown or yellowish-brown deer, found only in India. A good stag measures 1.35m. at the shoulder, weighing about 175 kilograms. The horns have 10 to 14 tines, hence the name Barasingha. It is found in the Terai belt of Uttar Pradesh, Assam, Sunderbans and Madhya Pradesh. In Terai belts it lives in marshyland and is seldom out of water. In Madhya Pradesh it lives in grassy plain-land.

Defects Characteristics of a tree that reduce its quality, value and utilization potential. *See* "crook," "fork," "rot," "sweep," and "wolf tree."

Deficiency of Essential Nutrients Deficiency of essential nutrients brings about profound changes in the internal structure, e.g., formation of smaller cells, reduced cell division, and production of primary and secondary tissue, alteration in the shape of cells and other structures, accumulation of fats and sterols. *See* deficiency symptoms.

Deficiency Symptoms Deficiency of essential nutrients such as nitrogen, phosphorus, potassium, calcium, magnesium, iron, zinc, etc. often produce one to several visible symptoms which are on the whole characteristics of each element, though different species may show variations in this respect. Chlorosis, necrosis, dying up of leaf margins and tips, resetting, distortion in leaf shape, fusion, dying back of shoots, gummosis are examples of deficiency symptoms. *See* Deficiency of essential nutrients.

Deflation Removal of fine soil particles from soil by wind erosion.

Defoliation A reduction in the normal amount of foliage due to insect or fungal attack or other injury, may be partial or complete.

Deforestation 1. Clearing an area of forest for another long-term use. Technically, a semi-permanent depletion of tree crown cover to less than 10 per cent. 2. To deforest means to remove the tree crop from a piece of land without the intention of reforesting. Deforestation causes fertile soil to be blown away or washed into rivers, leading to soil erosion, drought, flooding, and loss of wildlife. 3. FAO has defined deforestation as the conversion of forest to another land use or the long-term reduction of the tree canopy cover below the minimum 10 per cent threshold. 4. Deforestation implies the long-term or permanent loss of forest cover and implies transformation into another land use. Such a loss can only be caused and maintained by a continued human-induced or natural perturbation. Deforestation includes areas of forest converted to agriculture, pasture, water reservoirs, and urban areas. The term specifically excludes areas where the trees have been removed as a result of harvesting or logging, and where the forest is expected to regenerate naturally or with the aid of silvicultural measures. Deforestation also includes areas where, for example, the impact of disturbance, overutilization or changing environmental conditions affects the forest to an extent that it cannot sustain a tree cover above the 10 per cent threshold (FAO, 2001).

Deforestation, Global Deforestation is the conversion of forest to another land use or the long-term reduction of the tree canopy cover below the minimum 10 per cent threshold. In general terms deforestation is loss of forests. Each year about 13 million hectares of the world's forests are lost due to deforestation, but the rate of net forest loss is slowing down, thanks to new planting and natural expansion of existing forests. From 1990 to 2000, the net forest loss was 8.9 million hectares per year. From 2000 to 2005, the net forest loss was 7.3 million hectares per year – an area the size of Sierra Leone or Panama and equivalent to 200 square km per day. Primary forests are lost or modified at a rate of 6 million hectares per year through deforestation or selective logging. Plantation forests are established at a rate of 2.8 million hectares per year. The ten countries with the largest net forest loss per year between 2000 and 2005 (Brazil, Indonesia, Sudan, Myanmar, Zambia, United Republic of Tanzania, Nigeria, Democratic Republic of the Congo, Zimbabwe, Venezuela (Bolivarian, Republic of) had a combined net forest loss of 8.2 million hectares per year. The ten countries with the largest net forest gain per year between 2000 and 2005 (China, Spain, Vietnam, United States of America, Italy, Chile, Cuba, Bulgaria, France and Portugal) had a combined net forest gain of 5.1 million hectares per year due to afforestation and natural expansion of forests. Thirty-seven countries and territories lost 1 per cent or more of their forest area each year between 2000 and 2005, while 20 countries gained more than 1 per cent per year due to natural expansion of forests and afforestation (FAO, FRA-2000).

Degrees of Freedom The number of independent comparisons; the number of deviations, or items, minus the number of constants, computed from the sample for fixing the points from which the deviations are measured. The term is used in statistics.

Delaunay Triangulation 1. Method of constructing a TIN model such that three points form the corners of a delaunay triangle only when the circle that passes through them contains no other points. 2. The graph obtained by joining pairs of points whose polyhedra are thiessen (voronoi/dirichlet) divisions of the plane. *See* Triangular Irregular Network (TIN).

Delta Flat plane of alluvial deposits between the branches at the mouth of a river, stream, or creek. It is a tract of land at a river's mouth, composed of silt deposited as the water slows down on entering the sea. Familiar examples of large deltas are those of the Nile, Ganges, Brahmaputra and Mahanadi.

DEM (Digital Elevation Model). A GIS raster layer representing elevation. This is a common GIS product created at a variety of scales.

Demarcate, to 1. The setting out and marking the limits of a forest in terms of a notification under the forest law. 2.To mark out on the ground the limits of boundaries of a forest, compartment, crop or coupe, or plot of land for any special purposes.

Demography The statistical science dealing with the birth and death processes of a population.

Den A retired place, such as a cave, serving as the habitation of a beast or as a place of shelter, concealment, etc.

Den Tree 1. A standing live tree with cavity/cavities in branches or in the bole, in use or having potential for use by wildlife (Sawarkar, 1991). 2. Large hollow trees which serve as dens for den-users like squirrels, wild cats, owls, etc. Den trees are of critical importance to some species of animals.

Dendrology The identification and systematic classification of trees.

Dendrometer Any instrument used for taking measurements of trees. The term is usually restricted to instruments that measure diameter growth or to optical instruments with which diameter measurements can be taken at various points up the stem.

Denitrification The breaking down of nitrates and nitrites in the soil by the action of certain bacterias in the absence of oxygen resulting in the evolution of free nitrogen.

Dense The forest is called dense when the crown density is between 0.7 and 1.0. *See* canopy density.

Density 1. As applied to wildlife, the number of individuals per unit of space (as area, or volume as a population of 100 per sq. km). The optimum density range is that within which an animal community is able to fluctuate without being subject to the ill effects of over - or under-crowding. 2. Number of Individuals per Unit Area. For an example, 280 trees per hectare indicates Tree Density.

Density Dependence Decrease in population growth rate with increasing population density and therefore, theoretically results in a sigmoid population.

Density of Stocking *See* density, crop and density, stand.

Density, Crop *See* density, stand.

Density, Canopy The relative completeness of canopy usually expressed as a decimal coefficient, taking canopy, closed as unity. The following classification of canopy density is in vogue: (1) closed when the density is 1.0; (2) dense when the density is between 0.75 and 1.0; (3) thin when the density is between 0.5 and 0.7; and (4) open when the density is under 0.5. *See* density, crop and density, stand.

Density, Stand Stand density is a measure of the relative completeness of the tree stocking expressed as decimal co-efficient, taking normal number of trees, basal area or volume as unity. In India it is synonymous with crop density, and density of stocking, though in America a distinction is often made between stand density and stocking.

Denude, to To lay bare, usually with respect to the soil, by the removal of its vegetation cover or organic layers.

Deodar (*Cedrus deodara*) The Deodar (also known as Himalayan Cedar, or Deodar cedar) is a species of cedar native to the western Himalaya in eastern Afghanistan, northern Pakistan, north-west and north-central India, south-western Tibet and western Nepal, occurring at 1500-3200 m altitude. It is a large evergreen coniferous tree reaching 40-50 m tall, exceptionally 60 m, with a trunk up to 3 m diameter. It has a conic crown with level branches and drooping branchlets.The leaves are needle-like, mostly 2.5-5 cm long, occasionally up to 7 cm long, slender (1 mm thick), borne singly on long shoots, and in dense clusters of 20-30 on short shoots; they vary from bright green to glaucous blue-green in colour. The female cones are barrel-shaped, 7-13 cm long and 5-8 cm broad, and disintegrate when mature (in 12 months) to release the winged seeds. The male cones are 4-6 cm long, and shed their pollen in autumn.The Deodar is a very elegant ornamental tree, much planted in parks and large gardens for its graceful drooping foliage. Deodar can only be grown where winters are mild, never falling below about –25°C. The most cold-tolerant trees originated in the north-west of the species' range in Kashmir and Paktia province of Afghanistan. The cultivars 'Kashmir' and 'Shalimar' are hardy. The specific name *deodara* is derived from a Latinisation of the Sanskrit name, 'deva daru', meaning timber of the Gods. It is the national tree of Pakistan.

Deposit Material left in new position by some natural transporting agent such as water, wind, ice, or gravity.

Deposition The settlement or accumulation of material out of the water column and onto the stream bank or bed. Occurs when the energy of flowing water is unable to support the load of suspended sediment.

Depot A site on which forest produce is collected, for an example timber depot, fuel depot or bamboo depot.

Dereserve, to To declare by law that an area of forest reserve shall cease to be a forest, reserved. Deservation of Reserve Forest or Protected Forests can be done by notifying under Indian Forest Act, 1927.

Derived Savanna Savanna vegetation existing on sites formerly supporting high forest, having developed from such forest through cutting and burning (e.g. through shifting cultivation) and being maintained as savanna by annual or frequent grass fires. Tree species in a derived savanna may differ from those of the original high forest.

Desert 1. Biome where the average amount of precipitation is erratic and less than 25 cm per annum, and evaporation exceeds precipitation. Such areas have sparse highly adapted vegetation, e.g. Cacti — a succulent, and spiny shrub. 2. It is an arid area without sufficient rainfall and consequently sparse vegetation to support human life. The term includes the ice area of the Himalayas and also polar regions (known as cold deserts). Almost 33 per cent of Earth's land surface is desert and this proportion is increasing. 3. A barren uninhabited land of large extent. It may be cold (e.g., the Arctic and the Antarctic) or hot (e.g., the Sahara). Cold deserts are due to low temperature appropriate to the latitude. Hot deserts are due to excess of evaporation over precipitation. Hot desert region in India can be divided into two parts – the great desert and the little desert. The great desert extends from Rann of Kutch beyond the Luni river northward. The whole of Rajastan-Sind Frontier runs through this. The little desert extends from the Luni between Jaisalmer and Jodhpur up to northern west.

Desert Crust A hard layer, containing calcium carbonate, gypsum, or other binding material exposed at the surface in desert regions.

Desertification 1. Degradation of land that ultimately leads to desert-like land features. 2. The change of arable land into a desert either because of natural causes or human activity. 3. Creation of deserts by changes in climate, or by human-aided processes. The processes leading to desertification includes overgrazing, destruction of forests, and exhaustion of the soil by intensive cultivation without restoration of fertility — all of which may be prompted by the pressures of an expanding population or by concentration in land ownership.

Desertification, UN Convention to Combat The decision to adopt the Convention to Combat Desertification (CCD) was taken at Rio in 1992, with the persistent demand of countries from Africa, where two-thirds of the land area is either desert or dry land. The main elements of the convention are: (1) establishment of a global legal framework; (2) creation of a system for exchanging information on ways to combat desertification; (3) principles that include a 'bottom-up' approach to ensure participation of local population in combating desertification; and (4) mobilisation of finances through bilateral and multilateral aid as well as the Global Environment Facility (GEF).

Design A method of arranging sample or experimental plots to minimize the effects of uncontrolled variations in fertility and other factors and to make it possible to estimate the magnitude of such effects in relation to those due to variations in treatment.

Designated Function (of Forest) The designated function refers to the function or purpose assigned to a piece of forest land by legal prescriptions or by decision of land owner/manager (FRA, 2005).

Dessication Dehydrating or drying up.

Deterministic Model A model for which there in only one possible answer for a given set of inputs. Used in GIS.

Deterministic A system that can be characterized exactly with no element of chance or probability. Used in GIS.

Detritivory The consumption of detritus, dead organic matter.

Detritus 1. Small pieces of dead and decomposing plants and animals. 2. Detached and broken-down organic fragments of structure. 3. Pertains to small organic particles like leaves, twigs, etc.

Deviation 1. A departure from the prescription of a working plan. 2. The difference between any particular observation in a set of observations and the arithmetic mean of the set.

Deviation, Mean The mean value of the deviation from the mean, taken irrespective of sign. *See* average standard deviation.

Deviation, Standard (SD) A measure of the dispersion about the mean of the population.

Device A piece of equipment external to the computer designed for a specific function such as data input, data storage, or data output.

Dew Point The temperature at which water vapour present in the atmosphere is sufficient to saturate it.

Diameter Class One of the intervals into which the range of stem diameters, e.g., of trees or logs, is divided for classification and use; also the trees, logs, etc. falling into such an interval.

Diameter Quotient The ratio of the diameter of a stem at any given height to its diameter at breast height. *See* form quotient, absolute.

Diameter, Breast Height (DBH) The diameter of a stem measured at breast height; it is generally taken over bark for trees. (D.b.h. O.b.)

Diameter, Crop The diameter corresponding to the mean basal area of a uniform, generally pure crop.

Diameter, Exploitable The minimum diameter at breast height at which trees are considered suitable for exploitation. *See* girth, exploitable.

Diameter, Mean The diameter corresponding to the mean basal area of a group of trees or a stand; sometimes used for the mean, arithmetic of the summated crop diameters.

Diameter, Mid The diameter of a log or a stem measured halfway along its length.

Diameter, Top The diameter corresponding to the mean basal area of the biggest trees in a uniform, generally pure crop, taking into consideration the 100 biggest diameters per acre or 250 biggest diameters per hectare. *See* age, crop and height, top.

Diapause A period of spontaneous dormancy interrupting developmental activity in larva or pupa, or arresting reproductive activity in an adult insect. This state is independent of environmental conditions. *See* hibernation.

Dibble, to To sow seeds in shallow holes made with a suitable instrument.

Dieback 1. The progressive dying, usually backwards from the tip of any portion of a plant. 2. The death of the shoot, the root remaining alive. There are some species which show phenomenon of dying back. The sal species is one among them. Here the seedling usually remains a number of years without making much above ground growth. Growth on the original shoot more or less stops, and in the next season thin whippy new shoots little or no bigger grow up from ground level or deeper; the process continuing even 20 years without the development of a permanent leader; gradual growth of the root stock does take place, and eventually a stage may be reached when a single erect shoot grows up and develops into a tree. Similar behaviour is met with in *Pterocarpus santalinus*, also in *Terminalia tomentosa* (Champion and Seth, 1968).

Differential GPS (DGPS) The process of using two GPS receivers to obtain highly accurate and precise position fixes. It is said that using DGPS gives a result of sub-metred accuracy.

Diffuse-Porous Woods Hardwoods in which the pores (vessels) are scattered or diffused throughout the growth rings without any abrupt diminution in size from the spring wood to the summer wood. *See* ring-porous woods.

Diffusion The spatio-temporal process concerned with the movement of objects from one area to another through time. Examples include forest fire development, the movement of pollutants through any medium, and the spread of a disease through any medium, and the spread of a disease through a population.

Digital The representation of data in discrete, quantized units or digits.

Digital Elevation Model (DEM) 1. A quantitative model of a part of the earth's surface in digital form. Also known as digital terrain model (DTM). 2. A digital model of height (elevation or altitude) represented as regularly or irregularly spaced point height values.

Digital Image An image where the property being measured has been converted from a continuous range of analogue values to a range expressed by a finite number of integers, usually recorded as binary codes from 0 to 255, or as one byte. The image is taken from a scanner fitted in a satellite or an aeroplane or a camera.

Digital Image Processing Computer manipulation of the digital-number values of an image. It is a process by which imagery is converted to a land use map. A forest cover map or forest density map is an output resulted from digital image processing. *See* digital image.

Digital Mapping *See* 'computer cartography'.

Digital Number (DN) Value assigned to a pixel in a digital image. The value varies from 0 to 255.

Digital Terrain Model (DTM) A digital model of a topographic surface using information on height, slope, aspect and other topographic features.

Digitization Process of converting an analog display into a digital display.

Digitize An act or process of using a pair of x, y co-ordinates to encode map co-ordinates in digital form. Digitizing is the process of converting data from analogue to digital format.

Digitizer A device for entering the spatial co-ordinates of mapped features from a map or document to the computer. A pointer device, a cursor, puck, or mouse is used to locate key points. A piece of computer hardware used to convert analogue data into digital format. *See* 'digitizing table', 'scanner' and 'laser line follower'.

Digitizing Process and operations for encoding graphic data into some numeric system (e.g., X, Y Co-ordinates) and storing it on a computer.

Digitizing Table A table underlain by a fine mesh of wires and connected to a computer that allows the user to record the location of features on a map using an electronic cursor. These are used to digitize maps and other graphical analogue data sources manually.

Dilution Reduction in the concentration, or strength, of a substance in water.

Dimorphism 1. The occurrence of two different forms of flowers, leaves, etc., on the same plant or on distinct plants of the some species. 2. The occurrence of two forms distinct in structure, colouration, etc. Among animals of the same species.

Dioecious Applied to flowering plants having unisexual (male or female) flowers on separate individuals. *See* monoecious.

Diploid Having the usual two chromosome sets; individual so constituted, the normal condition for vegetative tissues of higher plants. *See* haploid; meiosis; polyploid.

Dipterocarpus It is a genus of flowering plants from the family – *Dipterocarpaceae*. The genus has about 70 species, occurring in Southeast Asia. It is an important component of dipterocarp forests. Its generic name comes from Greek and means "two-winged fruits". The genus is of considerable importance as timber trees, although not as important as *Shorea*.

Direct Valuation This is a class of methods for placing an economic value on an environmental asset such as a lake or a forest, or environmental improvements such as improved air or water quality standards. These methods measure the money value of such goods directly, either by creating hypothetical markets in which individuals are asked to state their value of the good (the contingent valuation method, CVM), or by looking at the markets for goods which are related to the environmental food.

Disafforest, to Often used as a synonym for dereserve, to; it also covers corresponding action in the case of protected forest.

Discharge Volume of water flowing in a given stream at a given place and within a given period of time, usually expressed as cubic metres per second or cubic feet per second.

Disclimax Abbreviated as disturbance climax. Any proclimax that originates from and is maintained due to disturbance by man or domestic animals. *See* climax, biotic.

Discounting Discounting is the practice of placing progressively lower numerical values on future benefits or costs the further into the future they occur. The practice of discounting arises because individuals attach less weight to a benefit or costs in the future than they do to a benefit or cost now.

Discretization The process of dividing an area into a series of self-contained units.

Disjunct The distribution of a species with geographically separated populations.

Disk A storage medium consisting of spinning disk coated with magnetic material for recording digital information.

Diskette *See* floppy disk.

Dispersal The spread, on any time scale, of plants or animals from any point of origin (drift) or from one place to another (migration).

Dispersion The range of variation of the values in a set of observations of a character common to the individuals of a population.

Dissolved Organic Matter (DOM) or Dissolved Organic Carbon (DOC) Organic material having a dimension smaller than 0.45 microns and passes through a 0.45 micron filter.

Dissolved Oxygen The concentration of oxygen dissolved in water, expressed in mg/l or as per cent saturation, where saturation is the maximum amount of oxygen that can theoretically be dissolved in water at a given altitude and temperature.

Dissolved Solids Total of disintegrated organic and inorganic material contained in water.

Distortion On an image, changes in shape and position of objects with respect to their true shape and position.

Disturbance 1. Any relatively discrete event in time that disrupts ecosystem, community, or population structure and changes resources, substrate availability, or the physical environment. 2. A disturbance is defined as an environmental fluctuation and destructive event that disturb forest health, structure, and/or change resources or physical environment at any given spatial or temporal scale. Disturbances that affect health and vitality include biotic agents such as insects and diseases and abiotic agents such as fire, pollution and extreme weather conditions (White and Pickett, 1985).

Diversity 1. The variety of plant and animal taxa, including genes, amino acids, flowers, species, or populations. 2. The variety of plant and animal communities, forest types, stand conditions, age classes and landscape components.

Diversity Index A numerical value derived from the number of individuals per taxon (abundance) and the number of taxa present (richness).

DOB Abbreviation for diameter over or outside bark.

Dog Dogs are carnivorous quadrupeds of the genus Canis, found wild in various parts of the world and domesticated in all countries, in numerous races or breeds, varying greatly in shape, size, and colour. The Indian wild dog (*Cuon alpinus*) is a predator of several kinds of deer and helps in keeping the balance of nature.

Dominance 1. In general, the influence of a dominant species. 2. The extent to which a given species or life form predominates in a community because of its size, abundance or cover, and affects the fitness of associated species. *Note*: Dominance is interpreted in two different ways for vegetation classification purposes: (1) where one or more vegetation strata (life forms) covers greater than 25 per cent, the life form greater than 25 per cent which constitutes the uppermost canopy is referred to as the dominant life form; (2) where no vegetation life form covers greater than 25 per cent, the life form with the highest per cent canopy cover is referred to as the dominant life form. In the case of a 'tie', the upper canopy will be referred to as the dominant life form.

Dominant 1. A tree forming part of the dominant tree class. 2. That constituent of plant community which exerts the greatest influence on its character. 3. A species of the upper canopy. 4. That component of a community, typically a species, which exerts the greatest influence on its character because of its life-form and/or great abundance. 5. Dominant trees in an even-aged forests form the uppermost canopy and include predominants, the tallest trees determining the general top level, and the rather shorter codominants. *See* tree classification.

Dominant Character One that is fully developed whether the gene is present in one or both members of the chromosome pair, or the individual is heterozygous or homozygous.

Dominated 1. Applied to a tree that has its crown somewhat below the level reached by its dominant neighbours. 2. Applied to all forms of plants occupying a subordinate position with reference to dominant plants in the same community.

Dormancy, Seed A condition of mature viable seed in which germination is considerably delayed even though external conditions favour germination.

Dormant (or Latent) Bud A bud that remains inactive for an indefinite period until stimulated into growth.

Dot-Matrix Plotter A plotter of which the printing head consists of many, closely spaced wire points that can write dots (100-200 per inch) on the paper to make a write-up or map. Also known as an electrostatic plotter or matrix plotter.

Dove Any of numerous birds of the family Columbidae. *See* Pigeon. INDIAN RING DOVE (*Streptopelia decaocto*): This is a pale gray and brown dove with a plain black collar or ring round the base of the neck. This is the commonest dove of India, found everywhere in the country. It ascends the Himalayas up to 3300mt. While mainly a resident species, it is locally a migrant. SPOTTED DOVE (*S. chinesis*). This is recognised by the brown and gray upper parts, conspicuously spotted. It is found throughout the greater part of India. Several forms are known. It is a resident bird with slight local movements. EMERALD DOVE (*Chalcophaps indica*): Slightly larger than a *mynah*. Found in Western Ghats, sub-Himalayan tracts from Kumaon to Assam, Chhattisgarh and Eastern Ghats. LITTLE BROWN DOVE (*S. senegalensis*): Found in parts of peninsular India. A resident species. RED TURTLE DOVE (*Oenopopelia tranquebarica*): The only Indian dove in which the sexes appear different. Widely distributed in India. A resident species. RUFUS-TURTLE DOVE (*S. orientalis*): A large vinous-brown dove with conspicuous rufus scale markings. Two forms are found in India. One form is resident while the other migrates from the hills to the plains in winter.

Down Log Trunks and limbs of trees or fashioned/unfashioned logs in various stages of decomposition on the forest floor. (Hoover and Wills, 1984).

Dpi (Dots per inch) A measurement of the density of dots used to print or scan an area with larger values representing more detail and a finer resolution.

Drag-Hole A hole cut at one end of a log to facilitate the attachment of gear for dragging.

Drainage Area *See* catchment area.

Drift 1. Unconsolidated geological material that has been moved from the site of weathering. 2. Voluntary or accidental dislodgement of aquatic invertebrates from the stream bottom into the water column where they move or float with the current. 3. Any detritus material transported in the water current. 4. Something washed ashore. 5. A mass of water deposited ashore by wind or water currents.

Drift-Wood Timber that is a drift, beached, stranded or sunk (in a river, lake or sea).

Drill 1. A line impressed on a seedbed for receiving seed. 2. Any implement used for making such impressed lines.

Drive In hunting to chase (game) from thickets into the clear or into nets, traps, etc. *See* Hunting (BEATING).

Drum Scanner A scanning device for converting maps to digital form, in which the y-axis movements are governed by the rotations of the drum.

Dry Wood A termite which is exclusively wood inhabiting, never entering the ground and requiring but little moisture for its existence.

DUB Abbreviated for Diameter Under Bark.

Duck Any of the various swimming birds of the family Anatidae (order Anseres), which have short neck, short legs, webbed feet, and a depressed and expanded beak. The sexes are almost always different from each other in plumage. These characteristics and their small size distinguish them from swans and geese which also belong to the same family. They are more or less aquatic and most are powerful flyers. They are found all over the world, living mostly in fresh-water (rivers and *jheels*), but to a lesser extent in brackish waters. Thirty-eight species of wild duck (including teals) are recorded in India. Twenty-nine are winter visitors and nine are resident species. Most common species abundantly caught for food are the following. They constitute the sportsman's favourites.

COMMON TEAL (*Anas crecca*): A very small duck, distinguished from other Indian species by the conspicuous emerald green and black speculum and the pale cinnamon bar on the coverts. Found all over India in winter. GARGANEY or BLUE-WINGED TEAL (*Anas guerquedula*): It is found throughout India in winter. It is most commonly and abundantly netted for food. WHITE-EYED POCHARD. *See* Pochard. COMMON POCHARD. *See* Pochard. PINTAIL (*Anas acuta*). *See* Pintail. GADWALL (*Anas strepera*): A large duck. Most abundant winter visitor from October to April in Northern India. WIGEON (WIDGEON): A duck with a relatively small beak, widest at the base. *Genus Anas*. *See* Wigeon. SHOVELLER: A widely distributed duck *Spatula clypeata* of the northern hemisphere. It derives its name from the greatly broadened beak. In winter it is found throughout India (October-April), common in the north, scarcer in the south. SPOTBILL DUCK (*Anas poecilorhyncha*): This is a duck distinguished by the bright red spots at the base of the beak. It occurs in most parts of India, usually keeping to itself and not associating with other ducks. It is a resident bird, though locally migratory in places. It is a good bird for the table, though from the sporting point of view, it is less interesting than many other ducks.

Dune Moving hillock formed by shifting sand.

Durability The resistance offered by wood against disease, decay and insect attack.

Duramen *See* heartwood.

Dxf A file format used for the exchange of GIS data.

Dynamic Model A model in which time is the key variable while all other input variables remain constant. Outputs from the model vary as time progresses.

Dysgenic Tending towards racial deterioration, in particular towards loss of vigour and productiveness. *See* eugenic.

Dystrophic Habitats low in nutrients and toxic.

Ee

Eagle Any of a number of large, strong, flesh-eating birds of prey, (*Genus Aquila*) belonging to the falcon family *Falconidae,* noted for their strong hooked beaks, large curved claws, sharp vision and powerful wings equipped for speedy flight. TAWNY EAGLE (*Aquila rapax*): A large brown or blackish brown bird of rather fierce appearance. It sits heavily on tops of trees or soars in great circles. The form found in India is the Oriental race of *Aquila rapax* called *Aquila rapax vindhiana*. It is found throughout India except in the Malabar Coast. In the Himalayas it is found up to 1200 m. It is a resident species.

Earth Summit Plus (1997) A five year review of Earth Summit that took place in 1997. The summit was called Earth Summit Plus Five (ESPF). The objective of this summit was to assess the impacts of the Earth Summit held in 1992. Heads of Governments from 42 countries participated and representatives from other countries attended the conference. The outcome of the summit was a resolution passed at the end of the summit. It required countries to take steps for the implementation of Agenda 21 as well as some of the other declarations like (1) Copenhagen Declaration on Social Development, (2) the International Conference on Population and Development, (3) the Beijing Platform Actions regarding Women Participation, (4) the UN Conference on Human Settlements' (Habitat II) recommendation on Sustainable Human Settlements, and (5) the report of the Ad Hoc Intergovernmental Panel on Forests (IPF). The summit did not bring desired results.

Earth System Science An integrated approach to the study of the Earth that stresses investigations of the interactions among the

Earth's components in order to explain Earth dynamics, evolution, and global change.

Earth, Tropical Red A uniform, friable and porous red soil which may contain a laterite horizon.

Ecesis The whole process whereby a plant establishes itself in a new area, from germination to its equivalent (e.g. the rooting of some detached portion) to reproduction, whether sexual or asexual.

Echard That fraction of the total amount of water in the soil which is not available for use by plants.

Eco-Climate Climate operating as an ecological factor. The sum of the meteorological factors within a habitat.

Ecocline A cline correlated with ecological factors.

Eco-Development It is a process which emphasises strengthening of the ecosystem as well as ensuring an accelerated rate of socio-economic development in the society. The essential feature of eco-development is its sustainability. Eco-development is a process of change, in which exploitation of resources, the direction of investment, the orientation of technological development and institutional changes stand in harmony to each other and enhance both current and future potentials to meet human needs and aspirations. Eco-development focuses on core principle like conservation of natural resources. Conservation encompasses not only preservation but also the rational management of natural resources so that they can yield the greatest sustainable benefit to the present generation while enriching or at least maintaining their potentials to meet the needs of the future generations. Apparently, conservation appears incompatible to development, but in reality, they are compatible. This is vindicated from the fact that while development aims at achieving human goals largely through the current utilisation of natural resources, conservation aims at ensuring the endless continuance of such utilisation. Conservation, especially with reference to living resources, has objectives such as: (a) Maintaining essential ecological processes and life support systems; (b) Preserving biodiversity, especially genetic diversity. Eco-development strategy necessitates a pragmatic scheme of prioritisation of resource use. The basis of prioritisation should be the degree of expendability of the resource. From the perspective of eco-development, natural resources are classified into four types on the basis of renewability, exhaustibility and cyclicality. This is a four-way classification system instead of traditional two-way classification. A rational resource use policy in the context of eco-development should be based on the principle that moves on to a lower order in the scale only after exploring the possibility of utilising the natural resources in the higher order. Eco-development approach, which has many shortcomings, emerged after the concept of biophysical sustainability failed. It focused on the satisfaction of basic human needs while maintaining ecological health (Sachs, 1979; Glaeser and Vyasulu, 1984). In contrast to the biophysical sustainable approach, eco-development concentrated on need fulfilment at the local level. It remained marginal to the development debate as it limited itself to development at the local scale and neglected larger issues of national economic management (Adams, 1990). However, the 'basic need approach' of eco-development remains instrumental in shaping present thinking on sustainable development.

Eco-Efficiency This term describes patterns of production, which exploits the positive *correlation* between economic efficiency and ecological efficiency. Obtaining eco-efficiency involves continuing to produce goods and services which satisfy customer needs at competitive prices, while reducing over time the environmental resources used in, and environmental damage caused by, their production. Government policies to improve eco-efficiency includes taxing natural inputs and the emissions of toxic wastes.

Ecograph A graphic presentation of the requirements of a species for, and/or its adaptation to, two or more environmental factors simultaneously.

Eco-Label Eco-labels, green labels or environmental lebels are easily identifiable seals on product packaging. They inform consumers about the effects that the production, consumption and waste of products and services have on the environment. They have two objectives. The first is to provide consumers with information about the environmental effects of their consumption with a view to encouraging more environmentally friendly consumption patterns. The second is to encourage Governments, firms and other agents to raise environmental standards in general. Eco-lebels are granted by a public or private body on the basis of criteria, which establish a product to be less destructive to the environment than similar competitive products.

Eco-Labelling A two-step process used to determine when a product can display a special seal or mark signifying that it is less harmful to the environment than most other similar products. The two steps are: establishment of criteria and certification that a product meets the criteria.

Ecological Consumerism Consumerism is sensitive to the environmental impacts of its consumption. Besides considering a product's quality and price, the ecological consumer considers its impact on health and environment, not only at home but across the world.

Ecological Economics This is the transdisciplinary approach to economics, which emphasizes the relationships between economic and ecological systems. Humans are considered to be major component of the overall economic ecological system, rather than being the dominant and central component. Ecological economics accounts not only for the financial constraints on consumption, as in conventional economics, but also for the natural constraints implied by the limited ability of the environment of the environment to provide natural resources. These constraints are relevant to sustainability and sustainable development.

Ecological Fallacy A problem associated with the 'modifiable aerial unit problem' that occurs when it is inferred that data for areas under study can be applied to individuals in those areas.

Ecological Footprints Each person has a certain ecological impact due to the products and services used to produce the goods and services which they consume and due to the waste products of such consumption. The term 'ecological footprint' is a figurative term used to describe the amount of land needed to provide the ecological services corresponding to the consumption of each social unit, from the individual to the country. A comparison of a country's ecological footprint with its available biological capacity provides a measure of its ecological deficit (O'Riordan, 1997).

Ecological Land Classification A process of delineating and classifying ecologically distinctive areas based on geologic, landform, soil, vegetative, climatic, wildlife, water and human factors. This holistic approach to land classification can be applied incrementally, from site-specific ecosystems to very broad ecosystems.

Ecological Services Ecological functions which are currently perceived to support and protect the human activities of production and consumption or affect overall well-being in some way.

Ecological Stability The ability of an ecological system to maintain a relatively constant level, or equilibrium, of biodiversity, biomes or productivity, in response to normal functions and cycles in the surrounding environment (Pearce *et al.*, 1989).

Ecological Systems 'A dynamic complex of plant, animal and micro organism communities and their non-living environment interacting as a functional unit.'(Convention on Biological Diversity, Rio de Janeiro, Brazil, June 3-14, 1992). Ecological systems or ecosystems can also be defined as systems in which species live and evolve. The process of natural selection means that any species, which proves to be ill suited to the ecological system is eliminated while better-suited species survive. An ecological system is in equilibrium when the different species achieve balance in which no species is growing or declining over time (Tietenberg, 1994). *See* Ecosystem; Biodiversity.

Ecology 1. The study of plants and/or animals in relation to their environment. 2. A branch of science concerned with the interrelationship of organisms and their environment, especially as manifested by natural cycles, and rhythms, community development and structure, interaction between different kinds of organisms, geographic distribution, and population alteration. *See* autecology; synecology.

ECO-MARK It is a scheme for labelling environmentally friendly consumer products which meet certain environmental criteria along with quality requirements of Bureau of Indian Standard (BIS). The scheme was launched by Ministry of Environment and Forests, Government of India in 1991.

Economic Depletion Depletion of any natural resources to the point where extraction costs equal market price. At the point of economic depletion, there may be remaining stock, but it is not profitable to extract because the cost of extraction exceeds the market price of the resource. This contrasts with the notion of physical depletion, which means that the stock of the resource is exhausted.

Economic Sustainability Economic sustainability can be defined as a situation in which the capital stocks which generate an economy's flow of well-being are not depleted overtime. The different classes of capital stock usually considered in an analysis of economic sustainability are: human-made capital, environmental or natural capital, human capital and social capital. There are two major categories of economic sustainability. They are: (1) weak sustainability, which requires the aggregate value of the total capital stock should be non-decreasing and (2) strong sustainability, which requires that each of the different classes of capital stock should be maintained in its own right, at least above safe minimum standard. *See* sustainable development; sustainability.

Economically Viable A project or programme is said to be economically viable if it yields more benefits than it costs after a benefit-cost analysis has been carried out. While making an analysis, the benefit-cost-analysis should also include project's opportunity costs and the values of any externalities, positive or negative, generated by the project.

Economies of Scale This refers to the increase in output, which results from all its inputs being increased in the same proportion. If output increases by the same proportion as the inputs, this represents constant returns to scale.

Ecoregion A part of an ecozone characterized by distinctive regional ecological factors, including climate, physical geography, vegetation, soil, water, fauna and land use.

Ecosystem An ecosystem, a contraction of "ecological" and "system", refers to the collection of biotic and abiotic components and processes that comprise, and govern the behaviour of some defined subset of the biosphere. There are many definitions of ecosystem. They are: 1. All the interacting parts of the physical and biological worlds in time and space. 2. Any system containing a living organism or a complex of living organisms that "we isolate mentally for purposes of study". 3. A community of different organisms interdependent on each other together with their non-living environment, which is relatively self-contained in terms of energy flow, and is distinct from neighbouring communities. 4. A dynamic and interrelated community of biological organisms and the surrounding environment linked through nutrient cycling and energy flows. Elements of an ecosystem may include flora, fauna, lower life forms, water and soil. Introduction of new elements, whether abiotic or biotic, into an ecosystem tends to have a disruptive effect. In some cases, this can lead to ecological collapse or "trophic cascading" and the death of many species belonging to the ecosystem in question. Under this deterministic vision, the abstract notion of ecological health attempts to measure the robustness and recovery capacity for an ecosystem; that is, how far the ecosystem is away from its steady state. Ecosystems have become particularly important politically, since the Convention on Biological Diversity (CBD) — ratified by more than 175 countries — defines "the protection of ecosystems, natural habitats and the maintenance of viable populations of species in natural surroundings" as one of the binding commitments of the ratifying countries. This has created the political necessity to spatially identify ecosystems and somehow distinguish among them. The CBD defines an "ecosystem" as a "dynamic complex of plant, animal and microorganism communities and their non-living environment interacting as a functional unit". *See* landscape; ecosystem health; ecosystem management.

Ecosystem Based Forest Management Management guided by monitoring of ecological interactions and processes necessary to sustain ecosystem composition, structure, and function over the long run (Silva Term Multilingual Terminology Database, IUFRO).

Ecosystem Health Ecosystem health is a measure of the ability of an ecosystem to maintain its structure and functions over time. It is difficult to provide a general definition of ecosystem health, since the criteria with which health can be judged vary according to the characteristics of the system. However, in general it refers to resilience of a system to shocks, its stability and its productivity. An ecological system is healthy and free from "distress syndrome" if it is stable and sustainable — that is, if it is active and maintains its organisation and autonomy over time and is resilient to stress. The sustainability of an ecosystem means that its structure is stable, and that it maintains over time its ability to perform ecological functions. In nutshell, an ecological system is called healthy if it is stable and sustainable, maintaining its organizational structure and autonomy over time, performing its ecological functions on sustained basis and resilient to stress. *See* ecosystem management.

Ecosystem Integrity The quality of a natural unmanaged or managed ecosystem in which the natural ecological processes sustain the function, composition and structure of the system.

Ecosystem Management 1. The management of an area defined by the ecosystem's condition, rather than jurisdictional boundaries, in a manner that maintains or improves the structure and function (or condition) of an individual ecosystem as a whole rather than modifying the abundance of one or a few species. 2. The production of goods and services from an ecosystem for people in such a way as to minimize, reduce, or eliminate soil, air, and water pollution and seek to integrate production with protection. 3. Management driven by explicit goals, executed policies, protocols, and practices, and made adaptable by monitoring and research, based on our best understanding of the ecological interactions and processes necessary to sustain ecosystem composition, structure, and function. Functionally, the ecosystem constitutes the six critical components. They are (1) energy flows; (2) food chains; (3) diversity pattern in time and space; (4) nutrient cycles, (5) development and evolution and (6) control. The concept of managing ecosystem emphasises on managing the mutual relationship and interdependence among structural and functional components of the ecosystem. The objective and practices of ecosystem management are consistent not only with the necessities of ecology and the individual landscape units but also with imperatives of the forest management. It is also concerned with pattern and rate of harvest of renewable natural resources, and their impact on the environment. It aims at maintaining not only the physical and functional component of the ecosystem but also the productive efficiency of the system. However, our understanding of ecosystem function is always subject to change. Therefore, management decisions should be science-based, incorporating the importance of human needs with the capacity of our earth to meet those needs in perpetuity. Presently the important ecological aspects behind ecosystem management are limiting factors, homeostasis, dynamism, resilience and carrying capacity. There are two laws, which explain the organism's response to these environmental changes. They are: (1) the law of minimum and (2) the law of tolerance. These two laws are popularly known as 'laws of limiting factors'.

Ecosystem Services Biosphere is the vast repository of living resources. It provides immense resources to humanity in the form of 'goods' and 'services'. Such living resources are called as primary resources because of the fact that they primarily constitute the building block of the society. What is more significant is the fact that biosphere, having a web of interrelated ecosystems, acts as source of services which are of immense use to mankind. Mainly there are two kinds of services the ecosystems of the biosphere provide to mankind. One is the life supporting services of the ecosystem. This is the service by which the ecosystem is perpetuated indefinitely. Some of the important services under this category are maintenance of gaseous balance, regulation of earth's temperature, maintenance of weather pattern all over the globe and soil and water conservation. These services are basic to earth's biosphere. The second is cleansing services of the ecosystem. This is the service by which wastes created by the economic system adopted by man are cleansed to a great extent. However, functioning of the ecosystem depends, to a critical extent, upon non-renewable resources like minerals in rocks and soil. Therefore, the biosphere provides, on one hand, all primary goods and services necessary for the economic activities in the society, and on the other, life supporting services for perpetuation of the very biological productive system in the biosphere.

Ecotone 1. The transition zone (or tension belt) between two adjoining community irrespective of their ecological status. 2. The transition zone between two adjoining communities. 3. An edge habitat. 4. A junction of two or more vegetation types. It is a transition area between two adjacent ecological communities (as forest and grass land). There is competition between animals common to both.

Ecotourism Simplistically, the term indicates a type of tourism that focuses on nature-related experiences (e.g., whale watching, bird watching). The World Tourism Travel Environment Research Center (WTTERC) has defined ecotourism as: 'implying a building of environmental considerations into all tourism and travel products and consumption'. This would suggest that sustainable tourism development is a level of activity at or below the level which will not result in environmental or social-cultural deterioration or be perceived by tourists as depreciating their enjoyment and appreciation of the area.' There are various types of ecotourism, including nature-based tourism, such as walking and hiking in rural areas; agro-tourism, which involves staying in rural farm houses and eating home grown produce; bird watching; and other low impact sports.

Ecotype 1. A genetically differentiated subpopulation that is restricted to a specific habitat. 2. An element of Linnaean species, separable as being associated with particular habitat factors. 3. A biotype resulting from natural selection by the special conditions of a particular habitat. Ecotypes are generally subdivided into many subtypes on the basis of soil or climate such as edaphic ecotypes, climatic ecotypes.

Ecozone An area of the Earth's surface that is representative of a broad-scale ecological unit characterized by particular abiotic (non-living) and biotic (living) factors.

Ectendomycorrhiza A mycorrhiza combining the features of ectomycorrhiza and endomycorrhiza. *See* ectomycorrhiza and endomycorrhiza.

Ectodynamorphic Soils whose properties are influenced mainly by factors other than parent material. *See* Endodynamorphic.

Ectomycorrhiza A mycorrhiza in which the fungal hyphae form a closely woven envelope (sometimes referred to as a mantle) covering the root apex and penetrating to a limited extent between the cells of the cortex.

Ectoparasite A parasite that lives on the outer surface of an animal, opposed to endoparasite.

Edaphic 1. Ecological formations resulting from or influenced by factors inherent in the soil (as salinity, alkalinity, drainage, etc.), as opposed to climatic. 2. Pertaining to the soil in its ecological relationships. *See* edaphic factors; edaphic climax.

Edaphic Factor 1. Any characteristic or condition of the soil, generally physical or chemical, that influences organisms. 2. Ecological influences characteristic of the soil, brought about by its physical and chemical characteristics.

Edaphology The scientific study of the relationships between soils and living things, including man's use of the land.

Eddy A circular current of water, sometimes quite strong, diverging from and initially flowing contrary to the main current. It is usually formed at a point at which the flow passes some obstruction on the inside of river bends. Often forms backwater pools, or pocket water in rapids and cascades.

Edge Effect 1. An edge effect is the effect of the juxtaposition of contrasting environments on an ecosystem. This term is commonly used in conjunction with the boundary between natural habitats, especially forests, and disturbed or developed land. Edge effects are especially pronounced in small habitat fragments where they may extend throughout the patch. When an edge is created to any natural ecosystem, and the area outside the boundary is a disturbed or unnatural system, the natural ecosystem in the edge is seriously affected. In the case of a forest when the adjacent land has been cut, it creates an openland/forest boundary, sunlight and wind penetrate into such area to a much greater extent. Air temperature, vapour pressure deficit, soil moisture, light intensity and levels of photosynthetically active radiation (PAR) all change at edges. It has been estimated that the amount of Amazonian area modified by edge effects exceeded the area that had been cleared. Forest fires incidences are more common near the edges and they result an increased desiccation at edges and increased understory growth due to increased light availability. Increased fire frequency since the 1990s are among the edge effects which are slowly transforming Amazonian forests. 2. The result of presence of two adjoining plant communities (as in an Ecotone), on the numbers and kinds of animals present in the immediate vicinity. Wildlife uses interior of the forest less than the margins, where maximum wildlife utilization occurs. Small openings increase the edge effect.

Edge Enhancement Image-processing technique that emphasizes the appearance of edges and lines in an image.

Edge Habitat A loosely defined type of habitat that occurs at the boundary between two different habitat types. Typically, edge habitats share characteristics with both adjacent habitat types and have particular transitional characteristics that are important to wildlife. *See* edge.

Edge Matching The process of joining data digitized from adjacent map sheets to ensure a seamless joint. The term is used in GIS.

Edible Game Birds Strictly speaking, all birds are edible since there are none with poisonous flesh. Birds which feed on carrion are not usually eaten. *See* game birds.

Edit To remove errors from or modify a computer file of a programme, a digitized map, or a file containing attribute data.

Efflux That which flows out. Used in wildlife sciences. Generally applied to game which moves out of an area. It is synonymous with outflow.

Egret Any of various herons (*genus Egretta*), that bear long, white beautiful plumes on the lower back known as aigrettes, during the breeding season and commonly have pure white plumage. Synonymous with Lesser white heron. *See* Snowy Egret. It was once threatened with extinction, but is now adequately protected. Egrets found in India include: LITTLE EGRET (*Egretta garzetta*): This is a long-necked, long-legged white bird found in parties about the neighbourhood of water. It is distinguished easily by the black beak at all seasons and the two long crest plumes in breeding plumage. It is found throughout the plains of India. CATTLE EGRET (*Bubulcus ibis*): Parties usually attend on grazing cattle. Found throughout India.

El Niño 1. A warming of the surface waters of the eastern equatorial Pacific that occurs at irregular intervals of 2-7 years, usually lasting 1-2 years. Along the west coast of South America, southerly winds promote the upwelling of cold, nutrient-rich water that sustains large fish populations, and abundant sea birds, whose droppings support the fertilizer industry. Near the end of each calendar year, a warm current of nutrient-pool of tropical water replaces the cold, nutrient-rich surface water. Because this condition often occurs around Christmas, it was named El Niño (Spanish for boy child, referring to the Christ child). In most years the warming lasts only a few weeks or a month, after which the weather patterns return to normal and fishing improves. However, when El Niño conditions last for many months, more extensive ocean warming occurs and economic results can be disastrous. El Niño has been linked to wetter, colder winters in the United States; drier, hotter summers in South America and Europe and drought in Africa. 2. It is also called the Southern Oscillation, or ENSO (El Niño Southern Oscillation) which is the largest climatic fluctuation observed on earth. A periodic, short-term climate change due to warmer currents (as high as 14 degree centigrade warmer) in the pacific ocean creating significant changes or reversals in barometric pressures in the pacific and Indian oceans (southern oscillation). Together these warmer currents and changed barometric pressures are referred to as ENSO. The effects of ENSO are global, producing heavy rainfall or snowfall in some areas while drought in other areas and therefore, significantly affecting plant and animal life. *See* ENSO.

Electromagnetic Radiation (EMR) 1. Energy propagated in the form of an advancing interaction between electric and magnetic fields. All electromagnetic radiation moves at the speed of light. 2. Energy propagated as time-varying electric and magnetic fields. These two fields are inextricably linked as a single entity since time-varying electric fields produce time-varying magnetic fields and *vice versa*. Light and radar are examples of electromagnetic radiation differing only in their wavelengths (or frequency). Electric and magnetic fields propagate through space at the speed of light.

Electromagnetic Spectrum 1. The entire range of radiant energies or wave frequencies from the longest to the shortest wavelengths — the categorization of solar radiation. Satellite sensors collect this energy, but what the detectors capture is only a small portion of the entire electromagnetic spectrum. The spectrum usually is divided into seven sections: radio, microwave, infrared, visible, ultraviolet, *x*-ray, and gamma-ray radiation. 2. Continuous sequence of electromagnetic energy arranged according to wavelength or frequency. 3. Range of electromagnetic waves or radiation that is the result of energy emitted by hot objects (e.g., the sun).

Electromagnetic Wave Method of travel for radiant energy (all energy is both particles and waves), so called because radiant energy has both magnetic and electrical properties. Electromagnetic waves are produced when electric charges change their motion. Whether the frequency is high or low, all electromagnetic waves travel at 300,000,000 metres per second.

Electronic Distance Metering (EDM) A Theodolite combined with an optical range finder for accurate distance measurements.

Element 1. A fundamental geographical unit of information, such as a point, line, area, or pixel. May also be known as an entity.

2. The smallest definable object of interest in the survey; it is a single item in a collection, population, or sample.

Elephant Huge, four-footed, thick-skinned, five-toed mammal, with long curving ivory tusks and a long prehensile trunk or proboscis, belonging to the family Elephantidae. Only two species now exist: the Indian elephant (*Elephas indicus* Syn. *E. maximus*) with comparatively small ears and the African elephant (*Loxoanta africanus*) with large flapping ears. The former is, now at any rate, an inhabitant of the hills, in the forests of Tamil Nadu, Kerala, Mysore, Orissa and in the terai forest of Uttar Pradesh, West Bengal, Jharkhand and Assam. The maximum height is 3.6 m (12 feet). Laws regulate its protection. The killing of rogue elephants has to be specifically licensed.

Elephant, Project *See* Project Elephant.

Elfin Forest Forest of small, often fantastically-shaped trees, generally covered with lichens or mosses (byrophytes); characteristically found in high mountain elevations.

Ellipsoid Mathematical model for the shape of the earth, taking account of flattening at the poles.

Elliptical Orbits Bodies in space orbit in elliptical rather than circular orbits because of factors such as gravity and drag. The point where the orbiting satellite is closest to Earth is the perigee. The point where the satellite is farthest from Earth is called apogee. A line drawn from perigee to apogee is the line-of-apsides, sometimes called the major axis of the ellipse. It is simply a line drawn through the ellipse the long way.

Eluviation Removal of soil material from the upper to the lower soil, horizons in solution or in colloidal suspension.

Embankment A bank, mound, dike, or the like erected along or across a wetted area designed to hold back water or carry a roadway.

Empirical Based on observation or experiment rather than hypothesis or theory.

Enclave 1. A patch of territory completely surrounded by a larger area from which it differs in some essential respect, e.g., an area within but not forming part of a forest reserve. 2. A small, often relic community of one kind of plant in an opening of a larger plant community.

Endangered Species Species that are threatened with imminent extinction; includes species whose numbers or habitats have been reduced to critical levels.

Endemic 1. Confined in its indigenous occurrence to a particular region. 2. The normal population level of a potentially destructive species. 3. Endemic species are those whose distribution is restricted to a particular area or region. 4. Peculiar to a locality or region — often used of a disease that is constantly present to a greater or less extent in a particular place.

Endogenous Produced within another body.

Endomycorrhiza A mycorrhiza in which the fungal hyphae are entirely within the host organism.

Endowment The act of giving or allocating resources and goods to individuals or group of individuals or nations.

Energy Budget. A quantitative description of the energy exchange for a physical or ecological system. The budget includes terms for radiation, conduction, convection, latent heat, and for sources and sinks of energy.

Energy Period The duration in days of the rest for germinative energy, usually the time during which germination occurs rapidly and continuously. Also the time from the inception of the test to a distinct flattening of the cumulative germination per cent curve.

Energy Security Forests constitute a source of energy to a majority of people in the world. Two billion people in developing countries still depend on traditional fuels like fuelwood as their principal source of energy. Bio-mass constitutes about 15 per cent of the world's total energy consumption and represents half of the world wood consumption. Fuelwood is used for 58 per cent of all the energy used in Africa, 15 per cent in Latin America, and 11 per cent in Asia (WCMC / IUCN / WWF, 1991). Fuelwood, when used sustainably and wisely, offers potentially renewable source of energy for future generation.

Enhancement 1. Process of altering the appearance of an image so that the interpreter can extract more information from imagery. 2. Techniques used to make a remote sensing image more interpretable.

ENSO (El Niño-Southern Oscillation) Interacting parts of a single global system of climate fluctuations. ENSO is the most prominent known source of inter-annual variability in weather and climate around the world, though not all areas are affected. The Southern Oscillation (SO) is a global-scale seesaw in atmospheric pressure between Indonesia/North Australia, and the southeast Pacific. In major warm events El Niño warming extends over much of the tropical Pacific and becomes clearly linked to the SO pattern. Many of the countries most affected by ENSO events are developing countries with economies that are largely dependent upon their agricultural and fishery sectors as a major source of food supply, employment, and foreign exchange. New capabilities to predict the onset of ENSO event can have a global impact. While ENSO is a natural part of the Earth's climate, whether its intensity or frequency may change as a result of global warming is an important concern.

Entities Distinct units of a real world phenomenon.

Entomophily A pollination by insects.

Entropy A measure of disorder in the system. The lower the entropy in system, the more order there is and the more energy is available. For instance, compare a piece of wood and ashes and dispersed heat, which remains after it is burned. From the First Law of Thermodynamics, the matter and energy in existence after the burning are exactly the same as they were before. However, the entropy has increased; the order and amount of available energy have both decreased.

Enumeration The counting, singly or together, of individuals of one or more species in a forest crop and their classification by species, size, condition, etc. Enumeration may be complete (total) or partial (sample); a partial enumeration may be carried out on separate sample plots or in strips or lines. *See* survey; forest inventory; stock cruise, to; survey, forest.

Envelope Polygon The external polygon of a vector map inside which all other features are contained.

Environment 1. The surrounding conditions, influences, or forces that affect or modify the whole complex of climatic, edaphic and biotic factors that act upon an organism or an ecological community and ultimately determine its form and survival. 2. All the biotic factors and abiotic factors of a site 3. Refers to the quantity and quality of natural resources, both renewable and non-renewable. It includes the ambient environment, which consist of landscape, water, air and the atmosphere, and is crucial determinant of human quality of life, as well as supporting human life. This state of the environment is a critical determinant of the quantity, quality and sustainability of human activities (Panayotou,1993). *See* habitat.

Environmental (Protection) Act, The The Environmental (Protection) Act was passed by Indian Parliament on 23rd May, 1986. The Act refers to the Stockholm Conference of 1972 and is based on Article 253 of the Constitution. By virtue of this Act, the Government of India has armed itself with considerable powers deemed necessary for the prevention, control and abatement of environmental pollution. The power includes, coordination of action by states, planning and execution of nation wide programmes, laying down environmental quality standards, specially those governing emission or discharge of environmental pollutants, placing restrictions on the location of industries and so on. The powers claimed are indeed comprehensive; the coverage includes handling of hazardous substances, prevention of environmental accidents, research, inspection of polluting units, establishment of laboratories, dissemination of information, etc.

Environmental Accounting The systematic description of interaction between environment and economy by means of an accounting framework. This framework is intended to provide information on the effects of the economy on the environment, and the contribution of the environment to economic output, both within a given time period and overtime. The standard System of National Accounts (SNA) measures Gross Domestic Product (GDP), the most widely used indicator for economic performance and economic growth. The SNA framework has three majors with respect to the environment — the neglect of the depletion of natural resources; the inadequate treatment of defensive expenditure; and the failure to account for the degradation of environmental quality and its effects on human health and welfare. No consensus has yet been reached on the appropriate substitute for an adjusted Gross National Product (GNP) — a 'green' national product (Markandya and Pavan,1999).

Environmental Agreement, Multilateral There are many multilateral environmental agreements in vogue. These are: Convention on Wetlands for international Importance, especially as waterfowl habitat; Vienna Convention for the Protection of the Ozone Layer; Montreal Protocol on substances that deplete the Ozone Layer; Conventions on Biological Diversity; UN Framework Convention on Climate Change; Kyoto Protocol; the Basal Convention on Transboundary Movement of Hazardous Substances, Convention to Combat Desertification; Stockholm Convention on Persistent Organic Pollutants (MOEF, 2006).

Environmental Assessment Accurate and scientifically defensible assessment of the impacts of proposed human actions on the environment and on human health and safety.

Environmental Audit It is an independent assessment of a company's environmental performance with respect to environmental standards. Environmental audits are increasingly used alongside financial accounts to assess the performance of companies. They are extended to measure a company's overall environmental performance, so that additional information on the extent to which it exceeds environmental standards would be provided. Environmental audits are used as part of the Environmental Impact Assessment (EIA) of projects. This can be used to compare the ex-post environmental impacts of a project with the impacts which were projected and, on the basis of scientific evidence, both measure the discrepancy and analyse its causes (Ledgerwood *et al.*, 1992). In other words, environmental audit is a management tool and provides a structured and comprehensive mechanism for ensuring that the activities and products of an enterprise do not cause unacceptable effects on the environment. In India, submission of an Environmental Statement by polluting units seeking consent either under the Water (Prevention and Control of Pollution) Act, 1974 or the Air (Prevention and Control of Pollution) Act, 1981 or both and the Authorization under the Hazardous Wastes (Management and Handling) Rules, 1989 has been made mandatory through a Gazette Notification of April 1993 under the Environment (Protection) Act, 1986. The Environmental Statement enables the units to undertake a comprehensive look at their industrial operations and facilities, understanding of material flows and focus on areas where waste reduction and consequently savings in input cost is possible. The primary benefit of environmental audit is that it ensures cost effective compliance of laws, standards, regulations and company policies etc.

Environmental Economics This branch of economics brings scarce environmental resources into mainstream economic analysis. It addresses issues of pollution control, the efficient setting of emission standards, waste management and recycling, the industrial activity of environmental externalities, the conservation of natural resources, the valuation of natural resources and so on. The objective of environmental economics is to identify policies, which will move the economic system towards an efficient allocation of natural resources.

Environmental Ethics The set of moral principles that we apply to our actions with respect to the environment. Environmental ethics can be described as the ethical foundation of environmental economics.

Environmental Factors The whole complex of climatic, edaphic and biotic factors that act upon an organism or an ecological community and ultimately determine its growth and survival. These can be classified as: (1) decimating factors such as accidents, starvation, enemies, etc. which tends to destroy a population and (2) welfare factors such as abundant food supply, shelter, etc. which tends to benefit the species. Absence of a welfare factor usually means the presence of a decimating factor, as when shortage of food supply threatens death by starvation.

Environmental Impact Assessment (EIA) A process designed to identify actual and potential environmental effects of operations in order to plan how to minimise or avoid adverse effects and maximise positive effects. An Environmental Impact Assessment (EIA) aims to look at forest management and identify actual and potential impacts on the environment as a result of operations and plan to minimise or avoid negative environmental impacts and maximise positive environmental impacts. EIA is undertaken at the earliest stage of an activity, ideally at the planning stage, and the outcome of an EIA usually takes the form of an environmental impact statement. It provides the means of conveying to the decision makers the nature, magnitude and significance of proposed activity's environmental impacts. The information is provided at a point in time when it can materially affect the decision made; that, at a stage when plans can still be altered, or mitigation measures incorporated into the design. EIA is one of the proven management tools for incorporating environmental concerns in development process and also in improved decision making. The programme of EIA, in vogue in India for the last two decades, was initiated with the appraisal of River Valley Projects. The scope of appraisal was subsequently enlarged to cover other sectors like industrial projects, thermal power plants, mining schemes and infrastructure projects. To give legislative status to the procedure of impact assessment, EIA was made mandatory since January 1994 for thirty categories of development activities.

Environmental Impact Assessment (EIA), Objective of All developmental activities use natural resources as raw material and the wastes generated are disposed into different environmental media. The signs of stress on the scarce natural resources are evident from the deteriorating air quality, soil degradation, polluted rivers and streams and in the general status of environment in various regions. It is now well recognized that, for sustainable development and optimal use of natural resources, environmental considerations are required to be integrated in planning, designing and implementation of development projects. The envisaged benefits from development projects cannot be fully realized unless they are environmentally and socially sound and sustainable. EIA is one of the proven management tools for incorporating environmental concerns in development process and also in improved decision making. *See* environmental impact assessment.

Environmental Indicators Environmental indicators both quantify and simplify complex environmental information so that its significance is clearer and thus easier to communicate. The World Bank categorizes issues into: source indicators (agriculture, forest, marine resources, water and sub-soil assets); sink or pollution indicators (climate change, acidification, eutrophication, toxification); life-support indicators (biodiversity, oceans, special lands such as wetlands); human impact indicators (health, dependence on water, and air quality as well as occupational exposure, food security and quality housing, waste and natural disasters) (Hammond *et al.*, 1995). *See also* Criteria and Indicators.

Environmental Management Plans (EMPs) The growing awareness, over the years, on environmental protection and sustainable development has further given emphasis on sound environmental management practices through preparation of Environmental Management Plans (EMPs) for minimising the impacts from developmental activities. EMPs are part of Environmental Impact assessment.

Environmental Management Control in the use of natural resources and the implementation of measures to ensure their conservation, the protection of habitats and control of hazards.

Environmental Planning, Spatial Spatial planning is primarily location or site specific planning. It is used for land use plans, city planning, and is recently extended to regional planning as well. In the conventional town and country planning, environmental issues were not addressed to the desired level, which has resulted in environmental degradation and deterioration of the urban areas. Hence, spatial environmental planning has been introduced as a technique for conservation of the environmental resources and for achieving developmental targets in an environmentally sound manner. *See* Spatial Environmental Planning.

Environmental Resistance 1. The sum of the environmental factors (as drought, mineral deficiencies, competition) that tend to restrict the biotic potential of an organism or kind of organism and impose a limit on numerical increase. 2. The sum of the factors limiting the numbers of an organism in a specific environment. 3. The combined action of all locality factors tending to limit the bio-mass (population pressure) in any habitat.

Environmental Statement Environmental statement is required under Environment Act. It is a part of process of environmental audit. Environmental audit is a management tool that provides a structured and comprehensive mechanism for ensuring that the activities and products of an enterprise do not cause unacceptable effects on the environment. Submission of an environmental statement by polluting units seeking consent either under the Water (Prevention and Control of Pollution) Act, 1974 or the Air (Prevention and Control of Pollution) Act, 1981 or both and the Authorization under the Hazardous Wastes (Management and Handling) Rules, 1989 has been made mandatory since April 1993 under the Environment (Protection) Act, 1986. The environmental statement enables the units to undertake a comprehensive look at their industrial operations and facilities, understanding of material flows and focus on are as where waste reduction and consequently savings in input cost is possible.

Environmental Sustainability Environmental sustainability can be defined as sustainability of the ecological services on which humans depend, directly and indirectly. These services include the provision of food and other raw materials, and the ecological services required to support agricultural production including hydrological regulation, production and protection of soils and regulation of climate. Environmental sustainability connotes different meanings at different scales. A local scale, the conversion of a forest to agriculture may be economically and environmentally sustainable, if ecosystem services required to support the agriculture are maintained. However, if these services are not maintained, for instance if too many ecosystem are depleted in an area prone to soil erosion, then the agricultural conversion may be environmentally and therefore, economically unsustainable. Environmental sustainability at a global scale includes maintaining the ecological stability of the global ecosystem, for instance by limiting the emissions of greenhouse gases to levels which will not lead to catastrophic changes in the climate (Markandya *et al.*, 2002). *See* sustainability; sustainable development.

Environmental Taxation The use of economic, and in particular fiscal, instruments for environmental protection. Taxes are compulsory payments to government or government bodies. As defined in OECD (1997) a tax falls into the environmental category 'if the tax base is a physical unit (or a proxy for it) of something which has a proven specific negative impact on the environment, when used or released.' This definition addresses the way the tax functions, rather than the reasons for introducing or increasing the tax. A distinction must be made between environmental taxes and environmental charges. Charges are payments made for specific environmental services. The major advantage of environmental taxation is the fact that it leads to internalization of externalities into the prices of goods and services which are detrimental to the environment, leading to a correction of market failure and shift in consumer behaviour. Environmental taxation has gained increasing support and a number of practical experiments have taken place in OECD and some developing countries (Ekins, 1999; Seroa da Motta *et al.*, 1999).

Environmental Toxicology The study of the movement of toxic compounds through ecosystems and their impacts.

Ephemeral Short-lived or transitory.

Epicormic Branch (or Shoot) Branches originating in clusters from a dormant (or latent) bud or adventitious bud on the trunk of a tree or on an older branch, when exposed to some adverse influence in the form of shock, such as excessive light, fire, drought, frost and sudden exposure to defoliation. It is undoubtedly often caused by a deficient water supply being associated with more or less stag-headedness, but any lack of balance of roots-crown seems sufficient to cause it, including that caused by overcrowding or under-thinning. Sal and teak both readily develop epicormic shoots from the causes mentioned (Champion and Seth, 1968).

Epidemic A marked and generally rapid increase in the population of a pest or agent of disease.

Epiphyllous Of an organism growing on living leaves. *See* corticulous.

Epiphyte A plant growing on, but not nourished by, another plant. A plant that begins life as an epiphyte but later sends roots into the soil, is termed a hemiphyte. *See* parasite.

Epizootic 1.Living on animals from the outside or on their surface, i.e. ecotparasitic or commensal. 2. Of a population of animals that builds up to abnormal levels. *See* epidemic.

Epsilon Modelling A method of estimating the effects of positional error in GIS overlay operations. Epsilon modelling is based on the use of buffer zones to account for digitizing error around point, line and area features.

Equation, Regression A mathematical expression of the best fitting line or curve describing the relationship between two or more variables.

Equator An imaginary circle around the Earth that is everywhere equally distant (90 degrees) from the North Pole and the South Pole. The equator is a great circle and defines latitude in degree.

Equilibrium 1. A state, often theoretical in which inanimate and animate lives are balanced in nature. 2. A state where all populations in a community remain of constant in size. 3. A state where all abiotic conditions are stable. *See* balance of nature.

Equitability A measure of relative species distribution calculated as a diversity index.

Equity In broad terms this refers to justice or fairness. This concept can be applied both in the present, and over time, where it has particular relevance for the analysis of sustainable development. In current terms, equity can be thought of as, for example, fair access to natural resources or a trading system, which does not systematically discriminate against a particular group. For the purpose of defining sustainable development, equity refers to fairness in the allocation of resources and opportunities between present and future generations.

Eremophyte A plant characteristic of the desert environment.

Erode Wearing away of material by wind, water, or glacial ice.

Erosion, Gully Erosion caused by water, in which gullies are produced.

Erosion, Rill Erosion caused by water, in which numerous very small and more or less straight channels are produced; the channels get obliterated by ordinary use.

Erosion, Sheet Erosion of a fairly uniform layer of material from the land surface; often scarcely perceptible, especially when caused by wind.

Erosion The process by which the surface of the earth is worn away by the action of water, glaciers, winds, waves, etc. The land surface becomes lowered as a result of weathering, corrosion and transportation, under the influence of gravity, wind, running water, action of sea, etc. Soil erosion may result from external factors such as bad agricultural practices, deforestation, overgrazing. Various types of erosion are distinguished — Accelerated erosion: Abnormal or rapid erosion in an environment disturbed by animal life chiefly man, and due to primarily such disturbance. Gully erosion: A form of erosion, caused by water, in which gullies are produced. Rill erosion: A form of erosion, caused by water in which very small, numerous, more or less straight channels of an impermanent nature are produced. Sheet erosion: Erosion of a fairly uniform layer of material from a land surface, often scarcely perceptible, especially when caused by wind.

Erosion Cycle The successive stages though which a newly uplifted land mass must pass before it is worn down to a surface near sea level including (a) juvenile stages, (b) mature stages, and (c) old-age stages wherein the land is worn down in such a way that the streams meander sluggishly across a lowland.

Erosion, Accelerated Abnormally rapid erosion in an environment disturbed by animal life, chiefly man, and due to primarily to such disturbance.

Erosion, Gully A form of erosion caused by water, in which gullies are produced.

Erosion, Normal The removal of soil and rock material by water, wind and gravity, in a manner and at a rate characteristic of the land surface in its natural environment; sometimes referred to as geological erosion.

Erosion, Pavement A layer of more resistant material left exposed by the erosion of soil overlying it.

Erosion, Splash Erosion preceded by the destruction of the crumb structure by rain-drops of drip.

Error Propagation The generation of errors in a GIS database at various stages of the data stream and during subsequent analyses.

Error, Experimental The variations between plot or other experimental units, due to causes other than the treatments that have been applied. It may refer to a variance of a standard error. It does not imply a mistake, but limitations of material and method.

Error, Non-Sampling Non-sampling errors are those errors which arise because of reasons like error in laying of sampling unit, errors in measurement and recording of trees, biases of the enumerators, instrumental errors etc. Such errors cumulatively contribute to total errors in the estimate.The non-sampling errors are basically man made. Therefore, such errors can be corrected by taking effective and appropriate measures.

Error, Sampling Sampling errors are those errors, which result from the fact that only a very small area of the forest or population is enumerated and its results are applied to interpret the whole population. In a forest inventory, it is not possible to compute the true value of sampling error. It is desirable to keep sampling errors within prescribed limits. This is possible only by making proper choice of the size of sampling units, their numbers and distribution in the population.

Error, Standard (SE) A measure of the extent to which repeated determinations of a quantity of a mean, sample or of a comparison between the means, would vary among themselves. The standard error can be obtained by dividing the standard deviation by the square root of the number of observations.

Escape 1. A plant originally cultivated, now found wild. 2. An exotic plant or animal later found in the wild.

Escape-Covert A covert serving as refuge from predator attack, by reason of density or mechanical protection.

Escarpment A geologic term for a long, precipitous, cliff-like ridge (observed above or belowground) commonly formed by faulting or fracturing.

Establishment Period The period between the initiation of natural regeneration or the formation of a plantation and its being considered establishment.

Establishment Development of a new, crop, naturally or assisted, to a stage where the young regeneration, natural or artificial, is considered safe from normal adverse influences such as frost, drought or weeds, and no longer needs special protection or tending operations other than cleaning, thinning and pruning.

Estivation (Aestivation) The process of passing a summer, a hot season or a period of prolonged drought in a torpid condition. *See* hibernation.

Estuarine Zone An environmental zone or system consisting of an estuary and those transitional areas which are consistently influenced or affected by water from an estuary such as, but not limited to, salt marshes, coastal and intertidal areas, bays, harbours, lagoons, inshore waters, and channels. *See* estuary.

Estuary 1. The lowest broadening part of a river where salt-and-fresh-water mix, often indicating area of potentialities for good fishing. 2. The portion of a coastal stream influenced by the tide of the body of water into which it flows. 3. A bay, at the mouth of a river, where the tide meets the river current. 4. An area where fresh and marine waters mix. For an example Mahanadi estuary.

Ethnobotany The research into the traditional medicines of indigenous peoples.

Eucalyptus It is a evergreen, glabrous tree, attaining a gigantic size, usually secreating aromatic resinous gum. Oil glands are found in its leaves. Leaves of the adult tree as a rule alternate, petiolate and vertical. Flowers in umbels or heads, usually pedunculate. Seeds numerous but a large proportion abortive, these usually larger than the fertile seeds. Species about 140, all Australian, excepting a few in New Guinea and Indian Archipelago. Many species cultivated in India, chiefly on account of their fast growing behaviour, producing an extraordinary quantity of hard heavy wood, such as 105 tonnes per hector per year. Of these, the species such as *E. globules* (blue gum), *E. tereticornis*, are mention worthy. Eucalyptus appears to have attracted attention in their home in the early part of 19th century. Then for the most part of the blue gum were planted in Europe for ornament. Then their economic value was realized and plantations were formed extensively in the Mediterranean countries, California, Florida, Hawai and several other parts of the western hemisphere, in and other sun tropical and warm temperature regions throughout the globe. In India it was probably introduced in the year 1843 as a source of fuelwood. Regular plantations chiefly of *E.globules*, were commenced in 1956 and have since been extended on large scale. Numerous species of the genus have since been tried in all parts of India, on the hills and the plains. In India it is known as 'Nilgiri' since this species has been planted in Nilgiri hills of Tamil Nadu. As a rule it is heavy light demander and intolerant of shade. Many species coppice well, the most vigorous probably being *E.globules*. Generally windfirm, but many species are liable to become bent, snarled and stunted in exposed situations. Most if not all eucalyptus grow best on deep fresh soil with a fair amount of subsoil moisture. Many, however, accommodate themselves to unfavourable conditions and in such cases their growth is affected. Now-a-days, numerous clonal varieties of eucalyptus has been developed for cultivation to increase the yield in agroforestry and plantation model.

Euclidean Distance 1. Distance between objects or values that is computed as a straight line. 2. A straight-line distance measured as a function of Euclidean geometric space. Term used in GIS.

Eugenic Tending towards racial improvement. *See* dysgenic.

Euphotic Zone The lighted region of a body of water that extends vertically from the surface to the depth at which light is insufficient to maintain light requiring biological processes.

Eurythermous Of animals able to tolerate a wide range of environmental temperature.

Eutrophic Habitats rich in nutrients and organic materials and are highly productive.

Eutrophication Eutrophication is a natural process in bodies of freshwater. The process involves enrichment of water with nutrients, especially nitrogen and phosphorus, leading to increased production of organic matter. Eutrophication in freshwater bodies can be hastened by the introduction of man-made inputs. Eutrophic bodies of water are those, which have a high nutrient content, and therefore, a high biological productivity. This increases the uptake of oxygen, reducing the oxygen content of the water. By-products of high levels of biological activity include animal waste and dead bodies; these accumulate in the water, reducing its depth and promoting the invasion of the water by reeds and shrubs. The process of eutrophication is accelerated by the introduction of nutrients into water by humans. The main processes by which humans introduce nutrients to water are in the disposal of sewage and the leaching of animal slurry and chemical fertilizers from agricultural land. Levels of eutrophication can be reduced by treating domestic sewage, reducing the levels of phosphates in cleaning products, and by reducing the use of inorganic fertilizers.

Evaluation Evaluation is "an activity" for finding out the value or results of something (Carlsson, Kohlin and Ekleem, 1994). Evaluation can be conducted either by personnel engaged in project, programme or plan or independent persons or organization. Evaluation means, "assessing the value of". One undertakes this common exercise in all spheres of life, in formal way or informal way. The objective of evaluation is to determine the effect of some action, or event or programme. Evaluation, as a management function, is carried out in case of planned and organized development work. Evaluation may be undertaken during the implementation of the plan or programme or after it has been completed.

Evaluation and Appraisal. Both these words are not synonymous. Both have different management connotation. Appraisal deals with economic viability, technical feasibility and social desirability of project that is under consideration. Therefore, appraisal is a part of planning process. Appraisal is carried out before the launching of the project. Whereas, evaluation is carried out after the launching of the project. Besides, it has completely different management functions. Therefore, it is not a part of planning, though it aids planning. *See* evaluation.

Evaporimeter An instrument used to measure the rate of evaporation of water.

Even-Aged Applied to a stand consisting of trees of approximately the same age. Differences up to 25 per cent of the rotation age may be allowed in cases where a stand is not harvested for 100 or more years.

Evenness The even distribution of individuals among species. Maximum evenness is said to occur when individuals are spaced equally among species. *See* richness.

Evergreen Never entirely without green foliage, leaves persisting until a new set of leaves has appeared. *See* deciduous.

Evolution 1. The process of gradual change—generally development but also degeneration—in the attributes of organisms through successive generations. 2. Genetic theory seeks to explain evolution in terms of changes in the gene frequencies of populations brought about by variation in reproductive habits, mutation, recombination, selection, migration, and genetic drift.

Exacting Making high demands as regards soil and other factors. *See* tolerance.

Exchangeable Cation Percentage This term indicates the degree of saturation of the soil exchange complex with a cation and is [defined as: ecp = exchangeable cation (me.per 100 g. soil) / cation-exchange capacity (me per 100 g.)] × 100.

Existence Value This is a type of non-use value. The argument behind existence value is that people care about the environment not only because they, or their heirs, can get some benefit by using or preserving environmental assets. The motivation behind this which may be sympathy for animals and nature or moral conviction. There is, therefore, an intrinsic value.

Exogenous Produced on the outside of another body. *See* endogenous.

Exotic A plant or animal of foreign origin, introduced in a region but not fully naturalized or acclimatized. Not native or indigenous.

Exotic Species All species of plants and animals not native to an area or naturally occurring historically in any ecosystem. The phrase "naturalized exotics" can also be used. *See* naturalized.

Exotic Not native to the area in question. *See* indigenous.

Exploit To remove and utilize a resource.

Exposure The relation of a site to weather conditions, especially sun and wind aspect.

Externalities An externality arises when the actions of an individual, firm or community affect the welfare of other individuals, firms or communities. For this effect to be defined as an externality, the agent responsible must not take account of the effect that it has on the other party. Externalities reflect the fact that social and private costs and benefits often do not coincide, so that an action which benefits an individual or firm, may harm society in general. Externalities may be positive or negative. Environmental pollution is a classic case of a negative public externality, which affects a variety of economic activities as well as general quality of life. An example of positive externality is the pleasure which neighbours derive from looking at a well maintained home garden.

Extinction Co-efficient The degree of light attenuation in water. The availability of light with increasing depth as a negative exponential.

Extinction Threshold The minimum number in a population of a particular species of animals, below which the population numbers are too few for rebuilding the species and so extinction results. *See* exitinction.

Extinction The death of the last surviving individual of a species, group, or gene, globally or locally. Generally extinction occurs when the population of a species falls below the level that is viable for reproduction, and the species ceases to exist. Species loss happens naturally, as more successful species take over the habitat of, or hunt to extinction, less successful ones. However, natural levels of species loss are a natural process for which we need not be very much concerned. What is disturbing is the fact that extinction occurs due to human activities? Human causes species loss in two major ways. The first is hunting or poaching. The second is the loss of habitat, i.e., conversion of species rich land such as forest or wetland, to agriculture or urban land.

Extinguish, to 1. The putting out a fire completely. 2. A term applied to the process of legally terminating forest right.

Extrapolation The estimation of the values of an attribute at unsampled points outside an area covered by existing measurements.

Ff

F Symbol 'f' is used in genetics for a generation; f1 the first generation of a hybrid; f2 the second; and so on.

False Colour Image or F-Colour Composite (FCC) A colour image where parts of the non-visible EM spectrum are expressed as one or more of the red, green, and blue components, so that the colours produced by the Earth's surface do not correspond to normal visual experience. Also called a false-colour composite (FCC). The most commonly seen False-Colour images display the very-near infrared as red, red as green, and green as blue.

Feature The word has several meanings, depending on context: (a) overall appearance; (b) a set of measurable properties diagnostic of a class or material; (c) referring to geometric or geomorphic entities, such as a hill, stream, on anything found on a natural or manmade surface.

Filtering In analysis of imagery, the removal of certain spectral or spatial frequencies to highlight features in the remaining image.

Flight Path Line on the ground directly beneath a remote sensing aircraft or space craft. Also called flight line.

Focal Length In cameras, the distance from the optical centre of the lens to the plane at which the image of a very distant object is brought into focus.

Faciation A subdivision of an plant association characterized by a particular group of dominant species and determined by minor climatic differences. *See* climax units.

Facies The seral equivalent of faciation.

Factor 1. One of the forces reducing the numbers (decimating factors) or affecting the increase rate (welfare factors) of game. 2. A circumstance that affected the result of an observation or experiment. Used especially of a set related treatments in an experiment; each treatment of the set is a different state or level of the same plant species, different level of application of a fertilizer, or different methods of cultivation.

Factorial Experiment A statistical experiment in which the treatments to be compared are the combinations of state, strengths or grades of two or more factors applied singly and in combination in order to determine whether any of them interact.

Facultative A species with the ability to live under different environmental conditions. Usually used in reference to species occurrence in a wetland or upland habitat. If the species is most likely (67-99 per cent frequency) found in a wetland, it is called a facultative wetland species. If the species is most likely (67-99 per cent frequency) found in an upland, it is called a facultative upland species. If the species is sometimes found in a wetland (34-66 per cent frequency), it is called a facultative species. *See* obligate.

Falcon A small diurnal bird of prey related to hawks and eagle, with short, curved beak and powerful hook-shaped claws, found throughout the world. Especially one trained to pursuit of other birds or game; usually the peregrine (*Falco pergrinus*), which is widely used for catching game and other birds, is not found in India. LAGGAR FALCON (*Falco jugger*) is the bird found in India from about 750m of the Himalayas southwards up to southern Tamil Nadu. It is a strictly resident species.

Falconry (Hawking) The art of training falcons to pursue and to attack wild fowl or game birds. It is a sport practiced in India to a certain extent.

Family 1. A developmental unit, usually small, in the early stage of sere, consisting of a group of individuals belonging to a single species. This group may, but not necessarily so, spring from a single parent. 2. Grouping of related genera used in classification of plants and animals. Names of plant families usual end in aceae, e.g. *Rubiaceae.* Animal families end in idae, e.g., *Homididae.*

Fast Growing Species As a thumb rule, a fast growing species is one, which yields a minimum yield of 10 cubic metres per hectare per year. In case of younger plantations, the height increment should not be less than 60 cm per annum. However, these criteria to define a fast growing species are not complete by themselves, unless they are qualified in other respect.

Fauna 1. A general term for all forms of animal life characteristic of a region, period or special environment. 2. The animals of a given region or period, taken collectively (as distinguished from the plants or flora). The Indian Board for Wildlife had, in 1952, issued a list of thirteen rare fauna, which are threatened with extinction and which should therefore be given special protection. These are: Indian lion; snow leopard; clouded leopard; cheetah; rhinoceros; Indian wild ass; Kashmir stag; musk deer; brow-antlered deer; pygmy hog; great Indian bustard; pink-headed duck; and white-winged wood duck. After promulgation of Wild Life Act, 1972, rare fauna and flora were notified and revision of such list is also being notified as and when required.

Featured-Species Management A type of wildlife management that does not attempt to manage for all species, but selects a few species of particular concern or interest (e.g., big game species or endangered species) and aims management programmes at them. With respect to habitat, it is generally assumed that providing habitat for these species provides habitat for other species as well.

Features see 'spatial entities'.

Fecundity The number of eggs, or seeds, or generally offspring in the first stage of the life cycle, produced by an individual.

Felling The cutting of a standing tree.

Felling, Seeding Opening the canopy of a mature stand to provide conditions for securing regeneration from the seed of trees retained for that purpose. It is the first stage of regeneration felling under a shelterwood system. A greater proportion of the overwood is removed, leaving a small specified number of seed bearers which are removed latter when regeneration is adequate in terms of quantity and height growth, as the final felling. *See* final felling.

Felling, Intermediate In a shelterwood system, the overwood may be removed in only two fellings; first the main seeding felling, in which the greater proportion of the overwood, leaving a small specified number of seed-bearers which are removed later when the regeneration is adequate in terms of quantity and height growth, as the final felling. However, all parts of the regeneration area do not become ready for final fellings at the same time so that operation may have to be carried out in two or more stages. Therefore, in some species, it is found preferable to remove the overwood over the area as a whole in two or even three stages making one or two intermediate fellings before final felling. *See* felling, secondary.

Felling, Irregular Illicit felling and felling neither prescribed nor expressly permitted by a working plan. *See* felling, unregulated.

Felling, Main The felling(s) from which the final yield is derived. The yield may either be obtained from a single felling, i.e. clear felling or a series of regeneration fellings. *See* principal felling.

Felling, Order of The predetermined sequence of felling for successive year over a period.

Felling, Preparatory A felling made under a high forest system usually towards the end of the rotation with the object of creating conditions favourable to seed production and natural regeneration. *See* felling, increment. *See* felling, seeding; felling regeneration.

Felling, Regeneration A felling made with a view to encouraging or promoting or assisting regeneration under a shelterwood or selection system. It includes seeding felling, secondary and final felling.

Felling, Salvage The removal of tree for the purpose of utilizing merchantable timber before it becomes worthless of trees killed or damaged by fire, wind, snow, insects, fungi or other harmful agencies.

Felling, Secondary A felling regeneration carried out between the seeding felling and the final felling under a shelterwood system in order gradually to remove the shelter and admit increasing light to the regenerated crop. *See* felling, intermediate.

Felling, Selection The annual or periodic removal of exploitable trees individually or in small groups in an unevenaged forest in order to realize the yield and establish a new crop irregular in its composition and constitution. The improvement of the forest is a primary consideration of selection felling. Periodic removal is the general practice in Indian forestry. The length of the period generally varies from 20 to 30 years. In practice the rotation length of the crop is divided into four or five periods, which are known as felling cycle.

Felling, Selective A term used to indicate the removal only of certain species of high value or trees above a certain size and of certain species, without full regard to silvicultural requirements. The basis of selection may be market demand, biodiversity need, ecological requirement, etc.

Felling, Strip A method of felling whereby the crop is removed in strip in one or more operations usually for the purpose of promoting regeneration.

Felling Cycle The time that elapses between successive main fellings on the same area. Main fellings may be periodic nature. Periodic removal is the general practice in Indian forestry. The length of the period generally varies from 20 to 30 years. In practice the rotation length of the crop is divided into four or five periods, which are known as felling cycle. Felling cycle is the revisit period for felling in a coupe. *See* cutting cycle.

Felling Series. Felling series constitute a forest area which forms the whole or part of a working circle. In practice the working circle area is divided into more than one felling series. The division of working circle area is always done with an objective to make felling and regenartion suitable to local conditions and to maintain or create a normal age class distribution in the crop. The yield is calculated either separately for each felling series or for the entire working circle area. Calculating yield for each felling series used to be the practice in the past but with the change in forest management after National Forest Policy, 1988, this practice is almost stopped in many states.

Felling, Severance A cleared strip of varying width cut through a stand of forests to develop a wind firm edge at a place where regular fellings particularly shelterwood strip felling are to commence at a later date.

Felling, Shelterwood Any felling in a more or less evenaged and mature crop made with the object of encouraging regeneration under the shelter of the seed trees.

Felling, Subsidiary An operation done in a coupe following the main felling. It includes the removal, girdling and poisoning of marked trees left unfelled, cutting back, malformed and ill-developed advance growth and unsaleable and damaged stems and thinning in group of poles. *See* cultural operations.

Felling, Advance A felling in advance of working plan prescriptions.

Felling, Clear Strictly the felling of the whole standing crop in one operation.

Felling, Exploitation Similar to a selective felling but yield, intermediate of marketable produce is the primary consideration. *See* selective felling.

Felling, Final The removal of the last seed or shelter trees after regeneration has been effected under a shelter-wood system. It is the final stage in regeneration felling.

Felling, Improvement 1. The removal or destruction of less valuable trees in a crop in the interest of better growth of the more valuable individuals. It is usually applied to a mixed forest. It may include thinning of closely stocked groups along with clearing and promotion of young growth of valuable species. Improvement felling is not a silvicultural system in pure sense. It does not aim at regenerating the crop or producing a crop of distinct characteristics. Trevor (1946) has suggested that in view of the fact that large areas of degraded and poor forests in India are likely to remain under improvement felling to prepare them for eventual management under a more intensive system, and that as the treatment, which aims at bringing these forests to the normal state, implies and entails encouragement of regeneration, it should be treated as an accessory system (Ram Prakash and L.S. Khanna, 1979). 2. Improvement felling is a set of operation aimed at improving forest crop. Unlike that of other silvicultural systems, it does not aim at initiating a regeneration process. It is a method of treatment, which involves essentially the removal of inferior growing stock in the interest of better growth of the more valuable species and individuals. It is usually applied to mixed uneven-aged forests. The treatment comprises the operations such as: (a) felling of dead, dying and diseased trees, (b) felling of unsound mature trees if they are silviculturally available, (c) thinning of congested group of poles, (d) cutting back of badly-shaped saplings and advance growth expected to give better coppice shoots, and (e) removal of undesirable undergrowth or trees of inferior trees which are likely to prevent regeneration. *See* thinning.

Felling, Increment A heavy opening of the canopy towards the end of the rotation, designed to stimulate increment of the individual trees left to form the final crop. This may provide a significant price increment. It may also bring the advantages of improved crown development, establishment of advance growth where it is required and a more rapid decomposition of excess humus if present. These types of fellings are not related with regeneration operations. Again, it may lead to some loss of total increment. However, considerable advantages are claimed for increment fellings by some European foresters, both as regards of total increment and price increment. *See* increment, light.

Felling, Unregulated 1. Any felling under prescriptions that give no definite yield either by area or by volume. 2. Any felling that is not controlled by silviculture prescriptions.

Ferrallite Well-drained soils formed from basic igneous rocks, consisting mainly of hydrated oxide of iron and aluminium with low silica content. Referred to as laterite in much of the literature.

Fertility Gradient The variation in natural fertility in any direction across an area of ground or tract.

Fertilizer Any organic or inorganic material of natural origin which is added to a soil in an attempt to provide plant nutrients.

Fidelity The constancy with which certain species are found in plant communities. The numbers 1 to 5 are generally used to indicate whether a plant is rare, seldom present, often present, mostly present or constantly present in the communities dealt with.

Fiducial Limits Those value of the variable in a set of values provided by a sample between which, with a certain agreed probability, the mean, population or true is expected to lie.

Field 1. A type or class of data. 2. Within a database, a set of records containing information. *See* tuple.

Field Layer or Festratum The herbs, grasses and low shrubs forming the soil cover below taller vegetation. Mosses etc., may be included but are usually separated as the ground flora.

Field Moisture Capacity The amount of water, expressed in percentage of dry weight, that a soil can retain against the pull of gravity, i.e., after saturation and allowing excess water to drain away. *See* field capacity.

File A collection of related information in a computer that can be accessed by a unique name. Files may be stored on tapes or disks.

Filler A tree or species of inferior value retained in thinning or cleaning in the absence of any more valuable stem.

Filter 1. In raster graphics, a mathematically defined operation for removing long-range (high-pass) or short-range (low-pass) variation. Used for removing unwanted components from a signal or spatial pattern. 2. A cell matrix of varying shape and size used to modify the cell values in a raster map layer through a variety of mathematical procedures such as mean, sum, maximum and minimum. A filter is often used to smooth noisy data.

Fine Sand Particles between .02 and 0.2 mm.

Fire Belt A strip open or planted with trees maintained to check the spread of fire.

Fire Behaviour, Factors of Fire depends on fuels more than any other factor. Apart from this, climatic factors such as temperature, moisture and atmospheric stability influence the probability of an ignition and the rate at which fuels are consumed by fire. Generally speaking, increasing temperature, decreasing moisture levels and increasing wind velocities favour the intensity and rate of spread of fires. Topography can significantly influence fire behaviour. Steep slopes favour the spread of fire; a fire moving up a steep slope often resembles a fire spreading before a strong wind (Brown and Davis, 1973).

Fire Break An existing barrier natural or otherwise or one prepared before a fire occurs from which all or most of the inflammable materials have been removed. It is designed to stop light ground or surface fires and to serve as a line from which to work and to counterfire, if necessary also to facilitate the movement of men and equipment during the course of fighting.

Fire Climax A community maintained by regular fires and therefore, differing from any other climax community. *See* pyrophyte.

Fire, Creeping A fire spreading slowly over the ground, usually with low flame.

Fire Danger A general term expressing the sum of the factors — risk, hazard, inflammability, liability and safety — which determine whether fire will start, spread or damage and whether and to what extent they can be controlled. *See* fire hazard.

Fire Dependent A community requiring one or more fires of varying frequency, timing, intensity, and size, in order to achieve optimal conditions for population survival and/or growth.

Fire, Ground 1. A forest fire that burns the ground cover only. 2. In other countries, it refers to any fire that consumes the organic materials of the forest floor and also burns into the underlying soil itself. A peat fire is an example of ground fire.

Fire Line A cleared permanent fire break intended to prevent fires crossing from one area into another.

Fire Management, Forest Fire management encompasses three activities which are required to protect forest from fire. They are: prevention, pre-suppression and suppression. Fire management also includes the use of prescribed fire to meet land management objectives (FAO, 1986; USDA Forest Service, 1990). *See* forest fire; fire prevention; fire presuppression; fire suppression.

Fire Prevention Fire Prevention includes two general areas; activities directed at people — the major cause of fire, and activities directed at mitigating the flammability of the forests.The former includes public information campaign and fire prevention messages. The later includes fuel management to reduce fire risk (e.g. prescribed burning, thinning, brush removal). Legislation must complement fire prevention by establishing the setting of incendiary fires as a crime and penalizing offenders in portion to the damage caused. Prevention also benefits from regulations defining the conditions under which intentional burning can be undertaken. Prescribed burning is an effective fuel management tool in forests of fire-tolerant species and benefits include reduced hazardous fuels, disposal of logging debris, site preparation for seeding and planting, improved wildlife habitat and management of competing vegetation.

Fire Patrol (Fire-Watcher) A person employed to aid in fire protection.

Fire Protection All activities concerned with protection of a forest from damage by fire. The activities include: fire prevention, fire detection, fire presuppression, and fire suppression. *See* fire management, forest.

Fire Risk The relative change or probability of fire starting, determined by the presence or absence of causative agencies. A component factor of the fire danger in an area. *See* hazard.

Fire Scar A healing or healed-over injury caused by fire, on the trunk or other large member of a tree or on a forest tract. *See* fire wound.

Fire Season 1. The period of year during which forest fires are likely to occur and become dangerous. 2. The period or period of the year during which the use of fire in a forest is subject to legal restriction. *See* close season.

Fire Sub-climax A stable community of vegetation, consisting of fire hardy species, established in an area where fires are annual or common. May be a sub-climax or a sere-climax.

Fire Pre-suppression Fire pre-suppression encompases all fire management activities planned and accomplished in advance of ignition. They are designed to ensure effective suppression and include fire planning, detection, dispatching, fire danger rating or risk profiling, fire weather monitoring and suppression training.

Fire Suppression Fire suppression includes all the work of extinguishing a fire following its detection. It is always with minimum cost consistent with land and resource management objectives. There are three methods of bringing forest fire under control. A direct attack on the burning edge of the fire is the first method and this is used when the fires are small. A parallel attack on the fire is the second method which involves the construction of a fire line parallel but close to the edge of the fire. An indirect attack on fire is the third method which is used when the fire is too intense for other means of attack and entails the construction of fire lines some distance from the fire edge and burning out of all intervening fuels (Candler, *et. al.*, 1983),

Fire, Surface 1. A forest fire which burns not merely the ground cover, but also the undergrowth. 2. Surface fire refers to any fire that runs over the forest floor and burns only the surface litter, the loose debris and smaller vegetation. *See* ground fire.

Fire Trace A cleared (often burnt) line used as a base from which to counterfire.

Fire Wound A fresh or healing injury to the cambium caused by fire. *See* fire scar.

Fire, Crown A fire spreading though the crowns of trees and consuming all or part of the upper branches and foliage.

Fire, Forest Any fire not employed as an indirect means of forest protection or management and which occurs on forest land. According to a Forest Survey of India Report (1999), about 50 per cent of forest areas in the country are fire prone (ranging from 50 per cent in some states to 90 per cent in the others). About 6 per cent of the forests are prone to severe fire damage. Various regions of the country have different normal and peak fire seasons, which normally vary from January to June. In the plains of northern and central India, most of the forest fires occur between February and June. In the hills of northern India fire season starts later and most of the fires are reported between April and June. In the southern part of the country, fire season extends from January to May. In the Himalayan region, fires are common in May and June. During the 1990s, several forest fires occurred in the hills of Uttar Pradesh and Himachal Pradesh. From 1995 to 1999, fire hazards in these two states assumed dangerous dimensions. An area of 677, 700 hectares was affected by these fires. The estimated timber loss from these hazards was US $ 43 million. Other losses due to these fires included loss of soil fertility, soil erosion, loss of employment, drying up of water resources, and loss of bio-diversity. These fires brought a major change in the microclimate of the region in the form of soil moisture balance and increased evaporation. The dense smoke from the fires affected visibility up to 14,000 feet.

Fish A class of vertebrate, cold-blooded, strictly aquatic animals having gills throughout life and with limbs modified into fins. They are important to man, especially as a source of food, fertilizers, oils etc. Angling is a favourite sport. Among the edible fishes of India the carp (*Cyprinidae*) and the catfish (*Siluroidae*) are most important. From the angler's point of view, by far the finest fish is the mahseer (*Barbus mosal*), a species of Barbel. This is found in most hill streams from the Punjab to Assam and in South India. One of the richest and most delicious of Indian dishes is the hilsa (*Clupea ilisha*).

Fitness The relative competitive ability of a genotype (survivorship × fecundity) expressed as the average number of surviving progeny of the genotype compared to the average number of surviving progeny of the competing genotypes.

Fixation The process of stabilizing soil, particularly shifting against erosion.

Flamingo (Plural Flamingos or Flamingoes) Any of the various aquatic birds of the family Phoenicopteridae that have remarkably long legs and neck, webbed feet, a broad bill resembling that of a duck but abruptly bent downward. Usually it has rosy-white plumage. It is gregarious, breeding in colonies in swamps and shallow lagoons. The common flamingo of India, *Phoenicopterus roseus* is found capriciously throughout India. It is common in the Great Rann of Kutch.

Flatbed Plotter A device for drawing maps whereby the information is drawn by the plotting head being moved in both the x and y directions over a flat, fixed surface. Draws with a pen, light beam, or scribing device.

Flats Areas that have shallow water or are periodically exposed, having very even elevation. If these shallow areas are not vegetated they are sometimes termed shoals.

Flight Limit The maximum distance a bird can traverse at one continuous flight.

Flight Shooting Shooting wild fowl during the morning and evening flights to and from their feeding or resting ground.

Float Device for carrying shouted tackle to where fish are expected to signal bite.

Flocculation 1. The aggregation of fine suspended material into flock-like masses. 2. A condition in a soil where the individual fine particles are aggregated into comparatively loose floccules. This makes the soil relatively crumbly and pervious on drying, unlike defoliation which makes it relatively hard, compact and impervious.

Flood Plain 1. Area adjoining a body of water that may become inundated during periods of maximum water levels. 2. That land outside a stream channel described by the perimeter of the maximum probability of flood. 3. A strip of relatively smooth land bordering a stream, built of sediment carried by the stream and dropped in the slack water beyond the influence of the swiftest current. 4. Land bordering a stream, built of sediments from the stream and subject to flooding in times of high water unless protected artificially.

Flood Any water flow that exceeds the bank capacity (greater than bank discharge) of a stream or channel and flows out onto the flood plain.

Floppy Disk A cheap, low-capacity storage medium, usually measuring 3.5 inches in diameter, capable of storing up to 2.0 mbytes of data. Also known as a diskette or floppy.

Flora A general term for all forms of plant life characteristic of a region, period or special environment.

Florican, Lesser (*Sypheotides Indica*) This is a small long-legged bustard, found chiefly in grassy plains, with a curious habit of jumping into the air. It is confined to India. Its habitat lies on the drier portions of the peninsula lying west of the Western Ghats and east of the Godavari.

Flow 1. The movement of a stream of water and/or other mobile substances from place to place. 2. The movement of water, and the moving water itself. The volume of water passing a given point per unit of time. Base flow is the portion of stream discharge that is derived from natural storage. Subsurface flow is that portion of the groundwater moving horizontally through and below the stream bed. Surface flow is that part of water in a channel flowing on the surface of the substrate.

Flush A site around a streamlet or spring that is kept wet or moist ("flushed") by moving water.

Fluting The tendency to show irregular involutions and swellings on the bole just above the basal swell characteristic of some species, e.g., teak. It is often unrelated to buttress formation. *See* buttress; root swelling.

Fluvial Pertaining to streams or produced by stream action.

Flyway A geographic course along which birds customarily migrate between breeding and wintering area. Generally, such a migration route together with the breeding and wintering areas that it connects.

Font Symbolism used for drawing a line, or the name of a typeface used for displaying text.

Food Chain 1. A series of organisms (such as animals) in a community interrelated in their feeding habits, the smallest being fed upon by a larger one, which in turn feeds a still larger one, and so on. The chain is based on herbivorous species. Plants form the ultimate basis of the chain. The term furnishes a convenient method of denoting food relationship in a natural community. 2. A food chain is the flow of energy from one organism to the next. There is one organism per trophic level, and trophic levels are therefore easily defined. They usually start with a primary producer and end with a top predator. Here is an example of a food chain: phytoplankton→copepod→fish→ squid→ seal→ orca. This "chain" can be described as follows: Orca (also known as "killer whales") feed upon seals, that feed upon squid, that eat small fish, that feed on copepods, that feed on microscopic algae. In this example, algae—autotrophs by virtue of their ability to photosynthesize—are the base of the food chain. It is always the case that number or at least biomass decreases from the base of the chain to the top. In other words, the number and mass of phytoplankton cells are much greater than the number and mass of copepods being supported by the phytoplankton. It can be viewed in another way too. To support one orca requires many seals, large numbers of squid, huge numbers of fish, and so on down the chain (see energy pyramid). This is because, with each transfer, some of the energy is lost to the environment. On average, only 10 per cent of the organism's energy is passed on to its predator. Food chains are overly simplistic as representatives of what typically happens in nature. The food chain shows only one pathway of energy and material transfer. Most consumers feed on multiple species and are, in turn, fed upon by multiple other species. The relations of detritivores and parasites are seldom adequately characterized in such chains as well. *See* food web.

Food Conservation The rate at which an animal converts food into tissue, usually expressed as kilograms of food consumed per kilogram of live weight gained.

Food Cycle A group of food chains constituting all or a significant part of the food relations that enable survival of the population of a community.

Food Security Poor people often live precariously with no cushion against adversity. Forests and forestry operations play an important role as a safety net, providing both subsistence and income in time of crop failure, shortfall, unemployment or other emerging hardship. They provide foods, which are most extensively used to help meet dietary shortfall during particular seasons in the year. Energy rich forest foods such as roots, tubers, rhizomes and nuts play an important role in the time of famine. Forest contributes to food security of poor community by providing accessibility to food as well as a wide range of foodstuffs to augment their subsistence farming. It contributes to agricultural productivity by maintaining soil fertility, conserving moisture, providing fodder for livelihood. It also protects the watersheds and regulates water flow and quality.

Food Species Food species are those species of plants and animals that are edible by humans. There are thousands of plant species that are deemed edible and that could form part of the human diet. However, the vast majority of the world's food is now produced by only 20 of these species, on which humans have thus become reliant for their sustenance.

Food Web 1. The interlocking pattern of feeding relationships in a community. 2. A food web or food network extends food chain concept from a simple linear pathway to a complex network of interactions. This "web" makes it possible to show much bigger animals (like a whale) eating very small organisms (like plankton). Food sources of most species in an ecosystem are much more diverse. In this figure, the grouping of Phytoplankton → Herbivorous zooplankton → Carnivorous zooplankton → Arctic char → Capelin on the far right is a food chain; the whole complex network is a food web/network.

Food-Gatherer A person who lives upon food procured by hunting, fishing and gathering rather than through agriculture or animal husbandry.

Foot, Cubic A unit of true measure equivalent to a cube of 1 foot side.

Foot, Cubic, Staked A unit of gross volume of stacked material.

Foot, Running An expression of measure for timber sawn, poles, etc., in terms of length, the other dimensions and often also the minimum acceptable length of the individual piece specified. Acceptable length of the individual piece being specified.

Forage In range management, unharvested plant material of any kind available for animal consumption. It may either be used for grazing or be cut for feeding. When cut it becomes feed. *See* grazing.

Forest 1. An area set aside for the production of timber and other forest produce, or maintained under woody vegetation for certain indirect benefits which it provides, e.g., climatic or protective. 2. A plant community predominantly of trees and other woody vegetation, usually with a canopy, closed. 3. An area of land proclaimed to be a forest under a forest law. 4. Forest symbolizes an ecosystem characterized by a more or less dense and extensive tree cover. 5. Communities characterized by a predominance of woody vegetation growing more or less closely together, whether 'closed' or 'open' in canopy, and whether fully intact ecologically or modified, fragmented or planted by humankind. Technically forests are defined as ecosystems with a minimum of 10 per cent tree canopy cover. 6. A forest is an area with a high density of trees (or, historically, a wooded area set aside for hunting). 7. It was held in T.N. Godavarman Thirumulkpad *v.* Union of India & Others [(1997) 2 SCC 267] that the word "forest land" would include any area recorded as forest in the Government record irrespective of the ownership. 8. As per FAO definition, land spanning more than

0.5 hectares with trees higher than 5 metre and a canopy cover of more than 10 per cent, trees able to reach these thresholds *in situ*. It does not include land that is predominantly under agricultural or urban land use. Forest is determined both by the presence of trees and the absence of other predominant land uses. The trees should be able to reach a minimum height of 5 metre *in situ*. Areas under reforestation that have not yet reached but are expected to reach a canopy cover of 10 per cent and a tree height of 5 m are included, as are temporarily unstocked areas, resulting from human intervention or natural causes, which are expected to regenerate. Forest includes areas with bamboo and palms provided that height and canopy cover criteria are met. It includes forest roads, fire breaks and other small open areas. It includes forest in national parks, nature reserves and other protected areas such as those of specific scientific, historical, cultural and spiritual interests. It includes windbreaks, shelterbelts and corridors of trees with an area of more than 0.5 ha and width of more than 20 mt. It includes plantations primarily used for forestry or protection purposes, such as rubber-wood plantations and cork oak stands. It excludes trees stands in agricultural production systems, for example, fruit plantations and agroforestry systems. The term also excludes trees in urban parks and gardens (FRA, 2005).

Forest Area, Global Forest area in the world extends about 4 billion hectares (3952 million hectares or about 40 million km^2) or 30.3 per cent of total land area of the globe. Forest area per capita is 0.62 hectares. More than half of the world's forest area is found in the Russian Federation, Brazil, Canada, USA and China, combined. Ten countries account for two-thirds of the global forest cover. Sixty-four countries have less than 10 per cent of their total land area forested, mostly in North Africa, West Asia and small islands. American Samoa, Federated States of Micronesia, French Guiana, Gabon, Guyana, Palau, Pitcairn, Seychelles, Solomon Islands, Suriname and Turks and Caicos Islands all have more than three quarters of their total land area forested. Forty-five countries have more than 50 per cent of their total land area forested (FAO-RRA, 2000).

Forest Capital A weighted measure of the extent and integrity of forest resources in a given region (say a country). Primary forests may be deemed to have greater integrity than other types of forests, and therefore, be given more weight than modified fragmented or planted forests.

Forest Certification Forest certification is a market-based instrument aimed at promoting sustainable forest management that takes into account environmental, economic and social issues. It involves the independent assessment of forest management according to internationally (or nationally) accepted standards, and the tracking and monitoring of the supply of forest products to the marketplace. If the forest management is in compliance with a set of specified standards, and the timber from this forest has been tracked and accounted for through all stages of the production process, then it can be given a label which is recognized in the market place. *See* Certification.

Forest Circle *See* circle.

Forest Concession *See* forest privilege.

Forest Conservation The management of forest resources with the objective of sustaining its productivity in perpetuity while providing for human use, compatible with sustainability of the resource. It may include periodic cutting and removal of trees, followed by management for regrowth of some form of the forest. Forest conservation is a broad concept, which involves not only the scientific but ethical, moral, economic and political aspects as well. It deals with judicious development and manner of use of forest resources of all kinds. Modern forest conservation in India has its foundations in the creation of large forest reserves in the late 19th and early 20th centuries, to protect timber, soil and water resources. The country protected area network presently encompasses more than 80 national parks and 450 sanctuaries covering more than 1,50,000 square kilometres. Around 19 per cent of India's forest are inside the protected areas network. The network is not, however, fully representative of the country's bio-geographical zones and efforts are being made to establish protected areas in underrepresented zones, especially on the Indo-Gangetic plain and in the Western Ghat region. There remains a slew of problems to establish national parks and sanctuaries because many restrictions are imposed on the use of land and natural resources. Other challenges include insufficient powers for wildlife staff to deal with poachers, difficulties of communication in remote areas and lack of trained manpower at lower levels. The focus of National Forest Policy,1988 is to increase the country's area under forest and tree cover and to rehabilitate degraded forest areas. While an emphasis is on the production of fodder and fuel-wood, the protection of soil and water resources, and the prevention of desertification in dry zones remain important goals of the afforestation and rehabilitation programmes.

Forest Cover 1. All trees and other plants occupying the ground in a forest, i.e. including any ground cover. 2. All woody growth occupying the ground in a forest, as distinct from the ground cover. 3. A category of forest site, including all the interchangeable phases of vegetation that it supports, defined mainly by the general nature of the ground cover.

Forest Cover Assessment It is about assessment of the extent of forest trees and other plants occupying the ground in forests. Generally such assessment is done by interpreting satellite imageries. In India forest cover assessment is done by Forest Survey of India (FSI), Dehradun. FSI assesses forest cover of the country on a two-year cycle and publish the information in the form of "State of Forest Report" (SFR). Its first assessment was published as SFR 1987. The latest tenth assessment in the series was published as SFR 2005. While in the first assessment, resolution of data used was 80m × 80m and scale of interpretation was 1:1 million. The same in the eighth assessment was 23.5 × 23.5 and 1:50,000, respectively. Taking advantage of advancement in remote sensing technology and wealth of data accumulated by Forest Survey of India, the SFR 2003 provides much more comprehensive status of forest and tree cover in the country.

Forest Crop *See* crop, forest.

Forest Decline A blanket term encompassing deforestation (conversion of forests into other uses) and forest degradation (deterioration in health and quality).

Forest Degradation 1. A reduction in the biomass, productivity or biodiversity of a forest, and alterations in ecological functions such as habitat, climate regulation and soil and water protection. Sometimes also referred to as a lowering in the quality or integrity of a forest ecosystem. One example is a change in forest composition, which negatively affects the growing stock. 2. FAO has defined forest degradation as changes within the forest, which negatively affect the structure or function of the stand or site, and thereby lower the capacity to supply products and/or services (FAO, 2001).

Forest Division or District An executive unit under a divisional or district forest officer. A forest division or district is manned by an officer of the rank of Deputy Conservator of Forests.

Forest Economics Those aspects of forestry that deal with the forest as a productive asset, subject to economics laws.

Forest Economy A forest economy consists of the management of the forest for wood, Non-Wood Forest Products (NWFPs), grazing of animals, and regulation of forest services either for consumption or sale. A sustainable forest economy is one in which the forest and all of its components are conserved, and are not exploited at a rate faster than at which they are regenerated.

Forest Estate An area, whatever its ownership, dedicated to forest purposes.

Forest Finance The finance side of forest economics.

Forest Fires Any fire on forest land which is not being used as a tool in forest protection or management in accordance with an working or management plan. Forest fires are caused by natural as well as man-made causes. Many forest fires start from natural causes such as lightning which set trees on fire. However, rain extinguishes such fires without causing any damage. High atmospheric temperatures and dryness (low humidity) offer favourable circumstances for fire to start. Fires on account of such natural causes are rare. Fire on account of man-made causes are very common. Generally forest fire is caused when there is live source of fire such as material with naked flame, ignited beedi or burning in the agricultural field adjoining to forests. There are two types of forest fires. They are: (1) Surface fire: It is a type of fire which burns primarily on the forest floor level, spreading along ground as the surface litter (senescent leaves and twigs and dry grasses, etc.) catches fire and the forest floor is engulfed by the spreading flames; (2) Crown fire: It is a type of forest fire in which the crown of trees burnts. The fire spreads at the crown level. A crown fire is particularly dangerous in coniferous forest because resinous material burnts furiously. On hill slopes, if the fire starts downhill, it spreads up fast as hot air adjacent to a slope tends to flow up the slope spreading flames upwards. If the fire starts uphill, then there is less likelihood of its spreading downwards. According to Forest Survey of India (1999) about 50 per cent of forest areas in the country are fire prone and about 6 per cent of the forests are prone to severe fire damage. Again Forest Survey of India in 1995 estimated that 1.45 million hectares of forests are affected by fire annually. According to an assessment made by the Ministry of Environment and Forests, Government of India, 3.73 million hectares of forests are affected by fire, annually in India. There are very few cases of fire due to natural causes in India. The majority of forest fires are manmade.

Forest Floor 1. A general term for the surface of the ground under a tree canopy. 2. The dead vegetative matter on the ground in the forest, including litter (forest and the less decomposed humus). 3. The accumulated organic matter at the soil surface.

Forest Fragmentation The splitting of forest land into smaller, detached areas as a result of cultivation, road, urban development and other activities. This can isolate wildlife populations and may result in forested areas too small to meet the habitat requirement of some species. Development of corridors helps to rectify this situation to some extent.

Forest Health The condition of a forested ecosystem that sustains its complexity while providing for human needs.

Forest Improvement Changes within the forest which positively affect the structure or function of the stand or site, and thereby increase the capacity to supply products and/or services (FAO, 2001).

Forest Influences All effects upon health, climate, soil and water-supply resulting from the presence of forests.

Forest Inventory *See* enumeration; inventory; inventory, forest.

Forest Management 1. The practical application of the scientific, technical and economic principles of forestry. 2. The process of planning and implementing practices for the stewardship and use of forests and other wooded land aimed at achieving specific environmental, economic, social and/or cultural objectives. It includes management at all scales such as normative, strategic, tactical and operational level management (FAO, 2001). 3. Formal or informal process of planning and implementing practices aimed at fulfilling relevant environmental, economic, social and/or cultural functions of the forest and meeting defined objectives (Terminology Database Silva Term, IUFRO). 4. The application of technical forestry principles and practices and business techniques to management of forests.

Forest Management, Intensive A regime of forest management, where silvicultural practices define the structure and composition of forest stands. A formal or informal forest management plan exists. A forest is not under intensive management, if mainly natural ecological processes define the structure and composition of stands. (FRA, 2005)

Forest Management, Issues and Concerns of Population and poverty are the root causes of destructive pressures on Indian forests. Despite ongoing and significant efforts to improve the management of India's forests, intensive human pressures continue to contribute to an overriding trend towards depletion of forest resources. Therefore, they constitute the major issues and concerns for forest management in India. Other management issues and concern are afforestation, lack of natural regeneration, forest protection, grazing, encroachment, premature harvesting, diversion of forest land to non-forestry use, insufficient knowledge, policy failures, lack of financial support to forestry sector, paucity of practical research in forestry, etc. Afforestation efforts on non-forest public lands and village commons have yet to meet expectations and requirements. Many planting sites have been encroached upon for grazing, premature harvesting of wood or been diverted for other developmental works. Insufficient knowledge, poor quality planting stock, lack of financial support and inadequate extension efforts also hinder afforestation efforts. Forest research efforts need to be strengthened to support development and provide solutions to field problems. Sociological research efforts need to be strengthened to support development and provide solutions to field problems. Such efforts need to be carried out in parallel with addressing technical and economic challenges. Planning processes need to be further revised to ensure that project planning fully embraces participatory principles and undertake adequate consultation with communities.

Forest Management, History of Nature conservation has a long history in India. The earliest recorded measures can be traced to 3rd century BC when provisions for the establishment of protected areas, including rules for the administration and management of forests, were codified in the *Arthasashtra Indica*. Traditional forest management also incorporated the establishment of sacred groves, untouched by human interference, as means of expressing reverence of nature. Community use of village groves for domestic purposes was permitted, with hunting being reserved for the kings. Extensive clearing of forests accompanied the advance of agricultural and pastoral societies, but an awareness of the need for ecological prudence was retained. The origin of scientific forest management in the tropics was found in India. Dating from the mid-19th century, these are the bases of classical tropical forest management, particularly the principles developed as part of the Brandis System of scientific management of forests. Population pressures eventually disrupted this strictly eco-logical management and poverty-driven pressures had to be accommodated, leading to the rise of community forestry programmes as a partial solution. More recently, India has encouraged participatory approaches to forest management through Joint Forest Management (JFM) initiative.

Forest Management Unit (FMU) An area of forest under a single or common system of forest management. There is always a single management plan or working plan for each FMU. Generally each forest division constitutes a FMU and for each forest division, there is a separate working plan.

Forest Mensuration The determination of the dimensions, form, volume, age and increment of logs, single trees, stands or whole woods.

Forest Offence Any act punishable under a forest law or rules made under it.

Forest Organization The systematic subdivision and arrangement for the purpose of administration and management of forest resources. Sometimes extended to include provision of staff, plant, etc.

Forest Outlier An area of forest separated from the main occurrence of its type, its presence being due generally to some local variation in ecological conditions or to past migration of vegetation associated with major climatic changes. In tropical Africa, this term is applied typically to an isolated area of high forest surrounded by savanna. It is almost always associated with a stream and increased soil moisture.

Forest Pathology The science that deals with diseases of forest trees, crops and products.

Forest per cent The rate of discount used in computation in forest finance, e.g., estimates of soil expectation value. It is more accurately expressed the rate per cent in compound interest at which the forest capital is actually working as indicated by the increase in value between two periods.

Forest Plantation Forest stands established by planting or/and seeding in the process of afforestation or reforestation. They are either of introduced species (all planted stands), or intensively managed stands of indigenous species, which meet all the following criteria: one or two species at plantation, even age class, regular spacing (FAO, 2001).

Forest Policy The general principles determined according to social and economic objects adopted for the creation and/or maintenance of forests and their use.

Forest Privilege A temporary (or terminable) and defined facility involving the use of the forest or forest land or forest produce, sanctioned by the owner of forest to individuals or communities. *See* forest concession; forest right.

Forest Produce All material yielded by a forest estate. Generally defined in forest acts, regulations, etc., and may include earth, stone, gravel and minerals. Classified as (1) Major forest produce — timber, small-wood and firewood and (2) Minor forest produce — all forest produce, other than major forest produce, including grass, fruit, leaves, animal products, soil and minerals. The Fourth World Forestry Congress has recommended that minor forest produce should be called 'forest produce other than wood'.

Forest Protection The activities directed towards the prevention and control of damage to forests by man, animals, fire, insect, disease, or other injurious and destructive agencies.

Forest Range An executive territorial unit, usually the charge of a forest ranger.

Forest Resource(s) Management (FRM) Planning administration and management of forest resources to provide environmental and economic benefits for society. It involves the study of recreation and utilization of natural resources, including wood, wildlife, special forest products and water (Silva Term Multilingual Terminology Database, IUFRO).

Forest Resources Forest resources include those found in forests and other wood land and as tree outside forests. *See* forests; resources.

Forest Right A legally recognized claim, possessed by a person, community or property, to share in the enjoyment of some or all of the benefits of the forest property of another easement. These rights include: (1) territorial rights; (2) ownership of trees and other resources, such as NWFPs, minerals, grazing; (3) rights of access, use and control (for specific purposes and times); and (4) intellectual property rights. *See* forest privilege.

Forest Services Protection (against soil erosion by air or water, avalanches, mud and rock slides, flooding, air pollution, noise, etc). Social and economic values (e.g. hunting and fishing, other leisure activities, including recreation, sport and tourism). Aesthetic, cultural, historical, spiritual or scientific values (including landscape and amenity) (FAO-FRA – Terms & Definitions).

Forest Settlement The legal determination of the limits of a forest estate and the definition of the rights admitted within it.

Forest Settlement Officer The officer appointed to carry out forest settlement.

Forest Stewardship Environmentally and socially responsible use, management and development of forest resources in order to maintain and enhance the value of the forest for present and future generation.

Forest Survey of India Forest Survey of India (FSI), an organization of MOEF is engaged in generating information and database on forest cover and forest resources in the country besides providing training, research and extension. Forest Survey of India was created with effect from June 1, 1981 as a successor to "Pre-investment Survey of Forest Resources" (PISFR), a project initiated in 1965 by Government of India and sponsored by FAO and UNDP. The main objective of PISFR was to ascertain the availability of raw material for establishment of wood based industries in selected areas of the country. Further, the National Commission on Agriculture (NCA), in its report in 1976, recommended the creation of a National Forest Survey Organisation for collection of data on scientific lines through country-wide comprehensive forest resources survey at regular intervals. Consequently, PISFR was reorganized into FSI. After a critical review of activities undertaken by FSI, Government of India, in 1986, redefined its mandate in order to make it more purposeful and relevant to the needs of the country. The present mandate of FSI is as follows: (1) To prepare a comprehensive State of Forest Report (SFR) including National Vegetation Map (NVM) once every two years. FSI will also prepare thematic maps through use of remote sensing data with minimum essential ground truth verification (most ground truth verification would be done by the respective state governments) on a ten-year cycle; (2) To collect, store and retrieve necessary forestry and forestry-related data for national and state level planning and to create a computer based National Basic Forestry Inventory System (NBFIS); (3) To design methodologies relating to forest surveys and subsequent updating. This would include methodologies for vegetation mapping including thematic maps through use of satellite imageries/aerial photographs, ground-truth verification, growing stock and volume assessment; (4) To undertake work in regard to preparation of forest inventory in selected States / UTs on agency basis till the establishment of their own resources survey units; (5) To impart training in modern forest survey techniques to foresters at various levels of responsibilities in the States/UTs/Government of India; (6) To support and oversee techniques/inventory work undertaken by State/UT Forest Departments (MOEF, 2005).

Forest Type Forests can be classified in different ways and to different degrees of specificity. They are: (1) A category of forest defined generally with reference to its geographical location, climatic and edaphic features, composition and condition. (2) One such way of classifying forests is in terms of the "biome" in which they exist combined with leaf longevity of the dominant species (whether they are evergreen or deciduous). (3) Another way of classifying forests is in terms of whether the forests composed predominantly of broadleaf trees, coniferous (needle-leaved) trees, or mixed. (4) Forests can be classified in different ways on the basis of their geographical position too. One such way is in terms of (a) boreal forests occupy the sub-arctic zone and are generally evergreen and coniferous, (b) temperate zones support both broadleaf deciduous forests (e.g., temperate deciduous forest) and evergreen coniferous forests (e.g., Temperate coniferous forests and Temperate rainforests). Warm temperate zones support broadleaf evergreen forests, including laurel forests, (c) tropical and sub-tropical forests include tropical and sub-tropical moist forests, tropical and sub-tropical dry forests, and tropical and sub-tropical coniferous forests. (5) Physiognomy classifies forests based on their overall physical structure or developmental stage (e.g. old growth *vs.* second growth), (6) Forests can also be classified more specifically based on the climate and the dominant tree species present, resulting in numerous different forest types (e.g., ponderosa pine/Douglas-fir forest). 7. Champion and Seth defined forests type as a vegetation unit which possesses (broad) characteristics in physiognomy and structure sufficiently pronounced to permit of its differentiation from other such units.

Forest Types, Basis of Champion and Seth defined forests type as a vegetation unit, which possesses (broad) characteristics in physiognomy and structure sufficiently pronounced to permit of its differentiation from other such units. The possible bases for classification are at least of seven, viz. (1) Physiognomy, (2) Structure, (3) Function, (4) Floristics, (5) Dynamics, (6) Environment, and (7) History (Champion and Seth, 1968).

Forest Types Based on Eco-system This system of classification gives sufficient weightage to both vegetation and climate. Champion's (1936) classification of forests of India into different forest types was an important initiative under this category. Puri (1960) suggested the classification of forest types of India taking into considerable ecological status and climate. Champion and Seth (1968) finally evolved a system of classifying forests of India. Forests of India have been divided into five major groups, namely tropical forests, montane sub-tropical forests, montane temperate forests, sub-alpine forests and alpine scrub. The type groups have been further subdivide into sixteen forest types. The tropical forests have been divided into following seven forest types: (1) Wet evergreen forests, (2) Semi-evergreen forests, (3) Moist deciduous forests,

(4) Littoral and swamp forests, (5) Dry deciduous forests, (6) Thorn forests, and (7) Dry evergreen forests. The group of montane sub-tropical forests have been divided into three following types: (1) Sub-tropical broad leaved hill forests, (2) Sub-tropical pine forests, and (3) Sub-tropical dry evergreen forests. The group of montane temperate forests have been divided into following three types: (1) Montane wet temperate forests, (2) Himalayan moist temperate forests, and (3) Himalayan dry temperate forests. The sub-alpine forest contains only one type of forests called sub-alpine forests. The group of alpine scrub has been divided into two following forest types: (1) Moist alpine scrub and (2) Dry alpine scrub.

Forest Types Based on Crop Composition Forest Survey of India has standardized different compositions for classifying forest into different forest types. Dominance of any species in a composition is the basis for forest types classification. What is noteworthy here is that the basis of classification of forest is not ecological but crop composition. The objective of such a classification is generally management. Here the predominant species means occurrence of that species at least 25 per cent and more than any other species.

FSI's Classification of Forest based on Crop Composition

Sl. No.	*Crop composition (Forest type)*	*Description*
1.	Fir	When Fir is predominant species and constitute more than 25%
2.	Spruce	Where Spruce is predominant species and constitute more than 25%
3.	Fir-Spruce	Where Fir and Spruce both taken together are predominant species and constitute more than 25%
4.	Blue-pine (Kail)	Where Blue pine is predominant species and constitute more than 25%
5.	Deodar	Where Deodar is predominant species and constitute more than 25%
6.	Chir-pine	Where Chir-pine is predominant species and constitute more than 25%

Sl. No.	*Crop composition (Forest type)*	*Description*
7.	Mixed conifers	Where no single species is predominant and all conifers taken together constitute more than 50%
8.	Oak-Rhododendron Forest	Where Oak and Rhododendron constitute 50% of the crop with at least 15% of minimum of each
9.	Up-land hardwoods	Broad leaved species constitute more than 50% in the Upper/Chir zone above 1500 metre altitude
10.	Teak	Where teak is predominant species and constitute more than 50%
11.	Sal	Where Sal is predominant species and constitute more than 50%
12.	Bamboo forest	Where bamboo is predominant and constitute more than 50%
13.	Mangrove	Mangrove forests
14.	Garjan forest (*Dipterocarpus tuibinatus*)	Where Garjan is predominant species and constitute more than 50% in the top canopy
15.	Garjan with Miscellaneous	Where Garjan constitutes at least 25% along with miscellaneous species
16.	Khasi pine	Where Khasi pine is predominant species and constitute more than 25%
17.	Khair forest	Where Khair trees are predominant and constitute more than 25%
18.	Salai forest	Where Salai is predominant species and constitute more than 25%
19.	Alpine pastures/ Alpine scrub	Alpine pastures/Alpine scrub
20.	Teak with Miscellaneous	Occurrence of Teak over 25% and less than 50%
21.	Sal with Miscellaneous	Occurrence of Sal over 25% and less than 50%
22.	Mixed Bamboo	Bamboo predominant and not less than 25%

Sl. No.	Crop composition (Forest type)	Description
23.	Teak mixed with Bamboo	Teak and Bamboo together constitute over 50% with each constituting at least 15%
24.	Salai with Miscellaneous	Salai 20-50%
25.	Kardhai (*Anogeissus Pendula*)	Where Anogeissus is predominant species and forms more than 25% of the crop
26.	Teak mixed with Sal	Together they constitute more than 50% with at least 15% of each
27.	Conifers mixed with hardwoods	Where the conifers constitute at least 50% and no single species is predominant
28.	Khair and Sisham	Both constituting over 50% with at least 15% of each
29.	Oaks	Where Oak/Kharsu Oak/Ban Oak individually or together constitute more than 50% of the crop
30.	Low Land Hardwood	Where low land hard woods, i.e. miscellaneous broad leaved spp. constitute more than 50% of the crop (At altitudes below 1500 mts)
31.	Miscellaneous forest	Forest which could not be classified in any of the above classes
32.	Eucalyptus	Where Eucalyptus is predominant species and constitute more than 50% of the crop
33.	Eucalyptus with Miscellaneous	Occurrence of Eucalyptus over 25% and less than 50% of the crop

Forest Utilization The branch of forestry concerned with the harvesting, conversion, disposal and use of forest produce.

Forest Valuation The branch of forest economics concerned with the valuation of forest estates, forest crops and their components.

Forest Village A village community established inside a reserved forest or protected forest, usually for the supply of labour for the execution of forest works.

Forest, Abnormal A forest in which, as compared to an acceptable standard, the quantity of material in the growing stock is in deficit or in excess or in which the relative proportions of the age or size classes are defective.

Forest, Beach A littoral forest found on the sandy shore above the high tide mark of tidal forest.

Forest, Ecological Benefits of Forest covers large areas of the globe and functions as animal habitats, hydrologic flow modulators, and soil conservers. It constitutes one of the most important aspects of the Earth's biosphere. It acts as a repository of biodiversity. Although often thought of as carbon dioxide sinks, mature forests are approximately carbon neutral with only young forests acting as carbon sinks. Nonetheless, mature forests do play an important role in the global carbon cycle as stable carbon pools, and clearance of forests leads to an increase of atmospheric carbon dioxide levels.

Forest, Capital The value represented by land, growing stock and physical infrastructure such as roads, buildings, etc. and all that which makes up a forest property.

Forest, Climax A forest which is the culminating stage of the natural succession in a locality. *See* climax.

Forest, Closed 1. Forest with a closed canopy. 2. Forest in which specified acts such as hunting or burning under Forest Acts and Rules are prohibited.

Forest, Communal A forest owned and generally managed by a community such as a village, town, tribal authority or local government, the members of which share in the produce or proceeds. Community forest, Panchayat forest, Village forest are the examples of communal forest.

Forest, Coppice A forest consisting of trees derived mainly from coppice shoot or root sucker.

Forest, High 1. A crop or crops of trees, normally with a closed and high canopy and usually of seedling origin. 2. A forest which originated from seed falling from the standing forest trees. Also known as seedling forest. 3. Sometimes used for a closed forest of tall trees in contrast to savannah woodland or scrub.

Forest, Irregular 1. A forest composed of trees of markedly different ages. Also known as uneven-aged forest. 2. Sometimes used for a patchily stocked forest.

Forest, Littoral A forest growing at or near the sea-shore. Beach forest, and tidal forest are types of littoral forest.

Forest, Mixed A forest composed of trees of two or more species intermingled in the same canopy; in practice, and by convention, at least 20 per cent of the principal one. The species composing the mixture may be distinguished as principal, accessory and auxiliary. *See* mixed crop; pure forest and forest types.

Forest, Normal A forest which, for a given site and given objects of management, is ideally constituted as regards growing stock, age class distribution and increment and form which the annual or periodic removal of produce equal to the increment can be continued indefinitely without endangering future yields. A forest which by reason of its normalcy in these respects serves as a standard of comparison for sustained yield. *See* Normal forest also.

Forest, Old Growth The term "old" varies by the species or group of species in a stand. Some individuals believe an old growth forest to be an uncut, virgin forest with very little man-made disturbance, while other individuals believe an old growth forest can be created by limiting future disturbance and creating certain characteristics evident in uncut virgin stands and thus termed a managed old growth forest.

Forest, Panchayat Any forest whose management is vested in a village Panchayat, i.e., a body of men elected by the villagers from among themselves for specific administrative, management or other purposes pertaining to the village forest.

Forest, Production A forest managed primarily for its forest produce. *See* forest produce.

Forest, Protected A legal term for an area subject to limited degree of protection under the provisions of chapter IV of the Indian Forest Act, 1927.

Forest, Protection of An area wholly or partly covered with woody growth, managed primarily to regulate stream flow, prevent erosion, hold shifting sand, or to exert any other beneficial influence forest, production; forest, protected.

Forest, Regular A forest composed of evenaged forest. *See* even-aged.

Forest, Reserved An area so constituted under the Indian Forest Act or any other forest law.

Forest, Riparian Tree growth that owes its existence or condition to its proximity to a water course, lake, swamp or spring.

Forest, Riverain (*Riverine*) Forest growing along rivers or in Islands in river beds.

Forest, Sclerophyllous A type of forest developed in a climate with relatively wet-cold and dry-hot seasons. Characterized by trees and shrubs having leathery, usually small, leaves capable of withstanding the dry summer and functioning during the moist winter. *See* sclerophyte.

Forest, Seasonal Forest showing well-marked seasonal changes in appearance. The term is mainly used with reference to the tropics.

Forest, Secondary Forest growth that has come up naturally after partial or complete removal of a crop because of reasons such as clear felling, fire or other causes. It is frequently different in composition and character from the growth it replaces. *See* secondary growth.

Forest, Selection 1. Crop containing many, theoretically all-age classes or gradations. *See* all-aged. 2. A forest managed under the selection system.

Forest, Storeyed High A crop of trees in which the canopy can be differentiated into two or more strata. The dominant species are usually different in each stratum. For an example two-storeyed and multi-storeyed high forest.

Forest, Thorn A forest in which the dominants are chiefly small thorny trees and shrub.

Forest, Tidal A type of littoral forest found on the sea shore below the high-tide mark, and so subject to tidal influence.

Forest, Unclassed Forest land owned by government but not constituted into a reserved forest or protected forest as per the Indian Forest Act, 1927.

Forest, Uniform An even-aged or regular forest.

Forest, Village 1. A state forest assigned to a village-community under the provisions of the Indian Forest Act. 2. A forest established and managed for the supply of forest produce to a village.

Forest, Virgin Natural forest essentially uninfluenced by human activity over a very long period.

Forestation Establishing forests naturally or artificially on areas where it is now absent or insufficient.

Forester 1. Primarily a person engaged in the profession of forestry. 2. A subordinate forest officer superior to a forest guard in-charge of a protection of a beat or a group of beats or in direct charge of forest works.

Forestry 1. The theory and practice of all that constitutes the creation, conservation and scientific management of forest and utilization of their resources. 2. The system of managing and using for human benefits the natural resources that occur on and in association with land with trees. 3. Forestry is the science, business and art of managing and conserving forests and associated lands for continuing economic, social and environmental benefits. It involves the balanced management of forest resources for optimum yields of wood products, abundant wildlife, plentiful supplies of pure water, attractive scenic and recreational environments in wild, rural and urban settings, and a variety of other services and products. Forestry draws on knowledge and experience from many disciplines and other professions (Science Council of Canada, 1973).

Forestry Congress, the World It is a gathering to serve as forum for Governments, universities, civil society and the private sector to exchange views and experiences and to formulate recommendations for implementation at national, regional and global levels. The Congress also provides an opportunity for the sector to produce an overview of the state of forests and forestry in order to discern trends, adapt policies and raise awareness of issues among decision-makers, the public and other parties concerned. Its functions are advisory and not executive. The outcomes are brought to the attention of FAO conference which may consider endorsing, through a resolution, any declaration emanating from the Congress. The Congress: (1) Brings together knowledge and experience to give guidance on the formulation and implementation of forest policy; (2) Expresses view which may help research organisations to identify future areas of study and international organisations to plan future work; promotes the elaboration and world-wide acceptance of technical standards such as an international forestry terminology, a uniform classification of forestry literature, and consistent research methods. Till date twelve

World Forestry Congresses have been held in different countries. The First World Forestry Congress was held in the year 1926 and the last Congress was held in Canada in 2003. In the year 1954, India did host the World Forestry Congress.

Forestry Practices Any activity that is carried out on forest land in connection with management of forest resources. Timber harvesting, road construction, silvicultural management, plantation, controlled grazing, cleaning, thinning, recreation, pest control, wildlife management and forest fire management are some of the examples of forestry practices.

Forestry, Aesthetic The practice of forestry with the object of developing or maintaining a forest for high scenic value.

Forestry, Commercial The practice of forestry with the object of producing timber and other forest products as a business enterprise.

Forestry, Extensive The practice of forestry on the basis of low operating and investment costs per hectare.

Forestry, Farm The practice of forestry in all its aspects on farm or village lands, generally integrated with other farm operation.

Forestry, Industrial The practice of forestry to sustain a given industrial enterprise, such as a saw mill, pulp mill, chemical plant, mining or a combination of these.

Forestry, Intensive The practice of forestry with the object of obtaining the maximum in volume and quality of products per unit area through the application of the modern technology in the field of silviculture, management, information technology, geo-science, cartography, biotechnology, etc.

Forestry, Multiple-use The simultaneous use of a forest resources or forest area for two or more purposes. The example of managing a piece of forest for timber as well as non-wood forest products is a case in point. However, often in some cases such as production of wood with wildlife conservation, the objective and approach conflict each other.

Forestry, Protection The practice of forestry with the primary object of (1) protecting lands whether those upon which the forest is situated or those at a distance from it, against wind and water erosion; (2) conserving water supplies for human consumption, fish culture, etc.; (3) reducing hazards from flood damage to human life and property; and (4) amelioration of adverse climatic effects.

Forests, Distribution of Forests can be found in all regions capable of sustaining tree growth, at altitudes upto the tree-line, except where natural fire frequency is too high, or where the environment has been impaired by natural processes or by human activities. As a general rule, forests dominated by angiosperms (broadleaf forests) are more species-rich than those dominated by gymnosperms (conifer, montane, or needle leaf forests), although exceptions exist (for example, species-poor aspen and birch stands in northern latitudes). Forests sometimes contain many tree species within a small area (as in tropical rain and temperate deciduous forests), or relatively few species over large areas (e.g., taiga and arid montane coniferous forests). Forests are often home to many animal and plant species, and bio-mass per unit area is high compared to other vegetation communities. Much of this bio-mass occurs below-ground in the root systems and as partially decomposed plant detritus. The woody component of a forest contains lignin, which is relatively slow to decompose compared with other organic materials such as cellulose or carbohydrate. Forests are differentiated from woodlands by the extent of canopy coverage. In a forest the branches and foliage of separate trees often meet or interlock, although there can be gaps of varying sizes within an area referred to as forest. A woodland has a more continuously open canopy, with trees spaced further apart, which allows more sunlight to penetrate to the ground between them.

Forests and Environment Forests ensure environmental functions such as biodiversity, water and soil conservation, water supply and climate regulation. Mismanagement of woodlands in humid and sub-humid tropical countries significantly contributes to soil losses equivalent to a 10 per cent loss of agricultural Gross Domestic Product (GDP) per year. Deforestation accounts for up to 20 per cent of the global greenhouse gas emissions that contribute to global warming. In arid environments, forests are crucial to food security in dry seasons and years. Forests provide habitats to about two-thirds of all species on earth. Deforestation of closed tropical rainforests could account for the loss of as many as 100 species a day (World Bank, 2004).

Form 1. The rate of taper of a log or stem. 2. Less precisely the shape of the whole or part of a tree. 3. Sometimes used in the sense of life form. 4. Officially, the category subordinate in rank to that of variety within the hierarchy of plants. 5. More generally, a sporadic variant distinguished by a single or very few correlated characters, without a distinct distribution area, e.g. flower colour, the variations from type being less, and considered of less importance, than those shown by varieties. They may be phenotypes or genotypes.

Form Class 1. Any of the intervals into which the range of absolute form quotient of trees or logs is divided for classification and use; also the trees or logs falling into such an interval. 2. A general classification of trees according to taper.

Form Factor The ratio of the volume of tree or its parts to the product of its basal area and height. Depending on the height measurement of basal area and on the parts of the tree considered, the following classes of form factor are distinguished: (1) Artificial form factor, when the basal area is measured at any convenient height, usually breast height and the above and below the point of measurement; (2) Absolute form factor, when the basal area is measured at any convenient height, and the volume refers only to that part of the tree above the point of measurement; (3) Normal (or true) form factor, when the basal area is measured at a constant proportion of the total height of the tree, e.g., 1/10th, 1/20th, etc. Here the total height and the volume refers to the whole tree above ground. Unless otherwise stated, form factor implies artificial form factor taken at 1.37 metre above ground.

Form Height The product of form factor and height (tree).

Form Point A point in the crown of a tree estimated to be the centre of wind pressure, or the geometrical centre of the crown.

Form Point Height (or Ratio) The relationship, usually expressed as a percentage, of the height of the form point above ground level to the total height of the tree.

Form Quotient, Absolute The ratio of the diameter or girth of a stem at one-half its height above the breast height to the diameter or girth.

Form Quotient, Normal The ratio of the mid-diameter or mid-girth of a tree to its diameter or girth.

Form Quotient Volume Table A volume table based on form absolute quotient as well as diameter and heights.

Form, Life The characteristic vegetative form of a species. Different systems of life forms have been postulated by different ecologists.

Format The way in which data are systematically arranged for transmission between computers, or between a computer and a device. Standard format systems are used for many purposes.

Formation 1. Includes all the operations contributing to the creation of a new crop up to the point where it is considered established. 2. The major unit of vegetation comprising the climax communities of an area uniform in its major physiognomic features. 3. In the oldest and widest sense, a major unit of vegetation comprising all plant communities that resemble each other in appearance and in major features of the environment, e.g. tropical rain forest.

Formation, Closed One in which the individuals are so close as to be in contact with one another above the ground.

Fortran (Formula Translation) A high-level programming language, much used in computer graphics. Recent improvements, embodied in Fortran 77, have made structured programming and interactive data input much easier.

Fourier Analysis A method of dissociating time series or spatial data into sets of sine and cosine waves.

Fowl Any of several domesticated or wild gallinaceous birds. Red Jungle Fowl (*Gallus gallus*): A resident species, found in North India, almost everywhere in hills and jungles. Grey Jungle Fowl (*G. sonneratti*): This has a strong resemblance in both sexes to domestic fowls. The grey streaked plumage of the male combined with the glossy black tail is distinctive. It is purely an Indian species found in Western and Southern India in hilly and jungle ground. It is a resident species found up to the summit of the hills, extending southwards to Cape Kanya Kumari. In Northern India it is replaced by *Gallus gallus*, considered as the ancestor of domestic fowls.

Fox Any of certain carnivores of the dog family (*Canidae*), especially those constituting the genus Vulpes. They are smaller than the wolves and are characterised by elongated pointed muzzle, erect ears, red fur and long bushy tail. They are proverbial for cunning and are preserved in England and elsewhere as beasts of chase, Fox-hunting is an acknowledged sport. INDIAN FOX (*Vulpes bengalensis*): This is the common fox of the plains, slightly smaller than the red fox, with a distinctive black tip to its tail. It is found throughout India. RED FOX (*Vulpes vulpes*): This is a richly coloured fox with long silky fur and a superb brush. Length of head and body is 66 cm Tail with hairs. It is found in Ladakh region of Jammu & Kashmir.

Fractal An object having a fractional dimension; one which has variation that is self-similar at all scales, in which the final level of detail is never reached and can never be reached by increasing the scale at which observations are made.

Fragmentation *See* forest fragmentation.

Framework Convention on Climate Change (FCCC) This convention went into force on 21st March, 1994. Reducing carbon dioxide emissions to 1990 levels by the end of the decade was specified as a voluntary target within the Convention. The Convention identified a set of nations committed to achieving a stabilization of CO_2 emissions by 2000. Other nations have subscribed to the general principles of the framework conventions, but are not on the list of nations committed to meeting the stabilization target.

Frequency 1. A measure of the abundance of a species present in a mixed community. Six grades are usually differentiated by occular estimate or more precise methods, viz., very abundant (v.a.); abundant (a); frequent (f); occasional (o); local (l); rare (r) and very rare (v.r.). 2. The number of individuals in a community. 3. The proportion of samples in which a species occurs. 4. The number of observations assigned to any of the arbitrary set of classes is known as class frequency.

Frequency Distribution A graphical, tabular or mathematical representation of the manner in which frequency of variable is distributed over the range of its possible values. When the variate has a fractional value (e.g., the height of trees) the frequency distribution is termed 'continuous'; when the possible values of a variate differ by definite steps (e.g., the number of seedlings in a quadrat) it is termed "discrete".

Frequency Distribution, Normal A continuous frequency distribution symmetrical about the variable having the greatest frequency and conforming to a particular mathematical formula.

This distribution appears to be good approximation to many (but by no means all) naturally occurring distributions and is the basis of many methods of statistical analysis.

Fresh Water Supply, Decline in This is an area fast emerging as a major challenge in the growing demand of fresh water supply. Fresh water for irrigation is increasingly limited in many regions of the world. Withdrawal of water for industrial and irrigation of cropland is increasing. The environmental impacts of excessive withdrawal of fresh water are amply demonstrated in many instances in the world. The demand for water went up six-fold in the last century. The increasing demand for fresh water is the most pressing concern of the new millennium. Excessive withdrawal of fresh water has the potential to threaten future food production system and deprive people of the basic living standards. Apart, this human activities are sending massive quantities of pollutants into aquifers, irreversibly damaging the freshwater supplies that provide drinking water to almost one-third of the planet's people. It has been found in many studies that 50 per cent of the drinking water is lost through leaks and 40 per cent of water withdrawn for intensive irrigation goes waste. There is also a huge difference in the quantity of water used by each person in underdeveloped countries and urban areas of industrialized nations.

Friability A property of soil that enables it to break down fairly easily into crumb. *See* consistence.

Frilling 1. Killing of trees 2. A method of killing trees by inflicting a series of cuts around a stem and applying a herbicide to the wounds. Frilling or girdling of trees is used to reduce stand density or kill individual undesirable trees.

Frost Cracks Fissures in trees caused by frost which close later and are covered with callus growth. They usually occur at the base of old trees.

Frost Level The height above ground upto which frost injury is liable to extend in a given locality.

Frost Locality An area in which frost is more frequent and more intense. Examples of frost locality are frost spot, frost hole, frost hollow and frost pocket.

Frost, Advective A frost produced by cold air brought from elsewhere.

Frost, Glazed The freezing of super cooled rain or moisture into a smooth coat of ice on terrestrial objects.

Frost, Ground Freezing confined to ground level such as ice crystals forming on surface objects, soil or ground vegetation.

Frost, Lifting Lifting of seedling or small plants above their normal soil level as a result of the expansion of the mass, following the freezing of the soil water.

Frost, Pool The accumulation to a considerable depth of heavy cold air flowing down into natural depressions from the adjoining areas. This has a more deleterious effect on vegetation than ground frost, as the freezing effect extends to a considerable height. *See* advective frost; radiation frost.

Frost, Radiation Frost occurring on nights with a clear sky, produced by loss of heat by radiation. *See* ground frost, advective frost, pool frost.

Frost-Free Season The period between the last injurious frost in the spring and the first injurious frost in the autumn.

Fume Damage Injury by fumes or gases; often not distinguished from smoke damage.

Fuzzy Set A set of objects in which the membership of the set is expressed in terms of continuous membership function having values between 0 and 1. Unlike boolean sets, fuzzy sets can have overlapping sets to different degrees.

Gg

Gadwall (*Anas Strepera*) A greyish-brown dabbling duck of about the same size as a mallard. It is a winter visitor and one of the commonest and locally abundant migratory wild fowls.

Gaia Hypothesis The Gaia hypothesis, named after the Greek for 'Earth Goddess', is the notion that the world is a self-equilibrating organism with an internal feedback system that will correct deviations from the optimal ecological state.

Gall A pronounced, localized swelling with greatly modified tissue structure, evoked on plants as a response to irritation, by a foreign organism. A plant tumour.

Gallery A passage, burrow, or mine excavated by an insect in plant tissues for feeding, eviposition or exit.

Game Those species of animals, birds etc., which are hunted or shot, either for trophies, or for their meat or for sport, or for a combination of any of these. Two types are usually distinguished—BIG GAME: Large animals (e.g. tiger, panther, deer) sought or taken during hunting for pleasure and sport. SMALL GAME: Game birds and mammals not classified as big game such as hares, rabbits, foxes. This practice used to be there in India in the past.

Game Animal An animal, which is a legitimate quarry by State or other law.

Game Birds Those birds which are legitimate quarries by State or other law. True game birds are recognised as those belonging to the order Galinae, but the term in ordinary usage includes many others, such as pigeons, sandgrouse, hemipodes and also some water-birds. All of them conform to the sportsman's standard that "they are good to eat and difficult to shoot". In North America the term 'game birds' includes the so-called upland game birds (Gallinaceous or chicken like birds) such as quail, pheasant, grouse and partridge; aquatic game birds such as ducks, geese and swans; and the shore birds — woodcock, snipe and plover. In Great Britain the term is said to apply only to the grouse, pheasant and partridge. *See* bird.

Game Fish An edible fish, capable of affording sport to the angler in its capture.

Game Laws Laws enacted for preservation of game. Species and the size and sex of animals that can be taken are defined by law, as also the manner of taking; periods of close season are established to provide protection during the reproductive period. The open season is restricted and regulated in a suitable way so as to ensure adequate replacement of game.

Game Management Game management is the art of making the forests land produce wildlife game in sufficient numbers to permit harvest for recreational purpose.

Game Forms of wildlife hunted for sport, food, fur etc.

Gamete A male of female reproductive cell, typically the produce of meiosis, capable of uniting in the process of fertilization with one of the opposite sex. *See* zygote.

Gamma Diversity Landscape-level or regional diversity.

Gantt Charts Graphical time charts used to assist project management.

Gap The distance between two graphic entities (usually lines) on a digitized map. Gaps may arise through errors made while digitizing or scanning the lines on a map.

Gap Dynamics The change in space and time in the pattern, frequency, size, and successional processes of forest canopy gaps caused by the fall or death of one.

GCP (Ground Control Point) A geographic feature of known location that is recognizable on an image and can be used to determine geometrical corrections.

GDP *See* Gross Domestic Product.

GDP and Forests *See* Gross Domestic Product and Forests.

Gene A unit factor of heredity, which is normally associated with a fixed position on a chromosome, is transmitted in the gamete from parent to offspring, and governs the transmission and development of a hereditary factor. Genes determine the particular characteristics of a given organism, including the functions that it performs. They contain the information that is used in the reproductive process to produce a new organism. Genes are one level on which biodiversity can be measured. The larger the variety of genes in a given ecosystem, the greater the diversity of species and the functions that they perform. This, other things being equal, will tend to make an ecosystem more stable (Swanson, 1994).

Gene Flow The consequence of cross-fertilization between members of a species which results in the spread of alleles across and between populations.

General System Theory A theory based on the idea that to understand the complexity of the real world, we must attempt to model this complexity.

Generalization The process of reducing detail on a map as a consequence of reducing the map scale. The process can be semi-automated for certain kinds of data, such as topographical features, but requires more insight for thematic maps. The process by which information is selectively removed from a map in order to simplify pattern without distortion of overall content.

Generation All those individuals of an organism which are separated from a common parent of ancestor by an equal number of reproductive cycles.

Genetic Engineering A process of inserting new genetic information into existing cells in order to modify a specific organism for the purpose of changing one of its characteristics.

Genetic Modification The scientific process of taking genes that represent desirable characteristics from one organism and introducing them into the genetic make-up of another organism in order to make a new product. The desirable characteristics introduced to plants using this technique include resistance to pesticides and herbicides and delayed ripening or early ripening to suit the market requirement. In the case of animals, the characteristics include the introduction of genes, which cause animal flesh to be leaner and genes, which cause animals to develop and mature more quickly. The process of genetic modification is controversial for a number of reasons. Genetically Modified Crops (GMOs) are often developed to be sterile, meaning that farmers are obliged to buy their seed each year.

Genetics The science of heredity.

Genotype 1. The entire genetic constitution, expressed or latent, of an organism. It can also be used for the genetic constitution of an individual with respect to any limited number of gene under examination. 2. A group of organisms having the same genetic constitution phenotype. 3. From the point of taxonomy, the genotype is the species selected as the type of a genus. 4. All members of a species sharing the same genetic constitution.

Geocoded Data Image that has been rectified to a map projection and cell sizes, and has been radiometrically corrected.

Geocoding 1. The activity of defining the position of geo-graphical objects relative to a standard reference grid. Geographic referencing or coding of the location of data items. Used in GIS.

Geodesy Science concerned with the measurement and mathematical description of the size and shape of the earth and its gravitational fields. Geodesy also includes the large-scale, extended surveys for determining positions and elevations of points, in which the size and shape of the earth must be taken into account.

Geodetical Surveying The determination of the position of points on the earth's surface accounting for its curvature rotation and gravitational field.

Geographical Analysis Any form of analysis using geographical data.

Geographical Data Model Formalized scheme for representing data which has both location and characteristic.

Geographical Information System (GIS) A set of computer tools for collecting, storing, retrieving at will, transforming and displaying spatial data from the real for a particular set of purposes.

Geoid 1. The figure or shape of the Earth as generalized by extending mean sea level continuously through the continents. 2. Figure of the Earth visualized as a mean sea level surface extended continuously through the continents. It is a theoretically continuous surface that is perpendicular at every point to the direction of gravity (the plumbline).

Geometric Correction Image-processing procedure that corrects spatial distortions in an image.

Geomorphology The study of the Earth's surface and the physical processes acting on it.

Georeferencing Assigning map coordinates to an image. Usually involves resampling of pixels to extrapolate the values for the new pixels.

Geostationary Orbit An orbit at 41,000 km in the direction of the Earth's rotation, which matches speed so that a satellite remains over a fixed point on the Earth's surface.

Geotropism The influence of gravity on the direction of growth of plant organs. The influence is positive where growth is towards the centre of the gravity of the earth and negative when away from it. *See* heliotropism.

Germination per cent A general term for the percentage, by number, of seeds in a given sample that actually germinate. Sometimes loosely used as a germinative capacity (or power). *See* plant per cent.

Germination Test A statistical test in which the germinative capacity of seeds and the effects on germination of various treatments applied to the seeds are examined.

Germination 1. Germination is the resumption of growth of a seed. The process begins with swelling, which is followed by splitting of the coat and emergence of the hypocotyl and radicle but for practical purposes definite and full resumption of active growth is essential before a seed is accepted as having germinated. The physiological process involved are absorption of water, cell enlargement and division, increase in enzyme activity, and utilization of stored food material and its transfer to growing regions, increase in respiration and assimilation, increase in cell division and differentiation (Champion and Seth, 1968). 2. The development of a normal seedling from a seed.

Germination, Field The percentage, by number, of seeds in a given sample that germinates and appears above the soil surface in the field or nursery, irrespective of their survival or plant per cent.

Germinative Capacity (or Power) 1. The percentage resumption of growth of a seed or spore. Usually recognized by rupture of, by number, of seeds in a given sample that actually germinate, irrespective of time (here germination per cent); or that germinate within twice the energy period. 2. The total number of seeds that germinate in a germinator plus the number of sound seed remaining at the end of the rest, expressed as a percentage of the total sample. *See* terminative power; plant per cent.

Germinative Energy 1. The percentage, by number, of seeds that germinate within a given period, e.g. seven or fourteen days, under optimum condition. 2. The percentage by number, of seeds in a given sample that have germinated up to the time when the rate of germination (number of seeds germinating per day) reaches its peak.

Girdling 1. Girdling is a method of killing unwanted trees by making continuous incisions, through the bark and underlying living tissues, completely around the tree stem. Girdling "starves" roots by depriving them of sugars produced in the leaves. 2. Girdling is to cut through the bark and outer living layers of wood in a continuous incision all-round the bole of a tree ring or ring bark. 3. Destruction of the living tissues in a ring around the stem, branch or root, by agents such as fungi or insects.

Girth Class One of the intervals into which the range of girth of trees or logs is divided for classification or use; also the trees or logs falling into such an interval.

Girth Limit 1. The limit of a girth class. 2. The prescribed girth below which a tree may not be felled. *See* minimum girth and exploitable girth.

Girth Quotient The ratio of the girth of a stem at any given height to its girth.

Girth, Breast Height (g.b.h.) The girth of a stem measured usually over bark at breast height.

Girth, Exploitable The minimum girth at breast height at which trees are considered suitable for harvesting or felling or exploitation. *See* diameter, exploitable and size, exploitable.

Girth, Mean 1. The girth corresponding to the mean basal area of a group of trees or a stand. 2. Sometimes used for mean, arithmetic of the summated girths of the trees in question.

Girth, Mid The girth of a log, bole or tree, measured half-way along its length or height.

Girth, Minimum Usually a prescribed girth below which a tree may not be felled. It indicates a qualified limit for marking of trees during main felling or an absolute limit for the protection of a species.

Girth, Quarter The girth of a tree or log divided by four. A measure commonly used in countries where volumes are reckoned by Hoppus feet.

Glacial Drift A general term for the rock debris that has been transported by glaciers and is deposited, either directly from the ice or from the melt water, or on melting, of the glacier.

Global Commons Natural resources that are shared as common property by all nations. Examples of assets that comprise the global commons are the Earth's atmosphere, the stratosphere and the world's oceans. *See* tragedy of commons.

Global Environmental Facility (GEF) The Global Environmental Facility (GEF) is a global financial body, funded jointly by UNDP, UNEP and the World Bank, that provides grants to support projects in developing countries which help to address environmental problems of a global nature. GEF supports to address crucial threats to the global environment by building capacity in the recipient countries especially developing countries and economies in transition. GEF is also the designated financing mechanism for the three international environment conventions, namely the Conventions on Biological Diversity, United Nations Conventions on Climate Change, Convention to Combat Desertification, besides Stockholm Convention on Persistent Organic Pollutants (POPs). The four main global environmental problems towards which GEF is targeted are: biodiversity loss, global climate change, pollution of international waters and depletion of ozone layer.

Global Warming Predicted increase in temperature worldwide due to increasing levels of 'greenhouse gases' in the atmosphere, especially carbon dioxide. Global warming brings changes in the climatic system, which result in significant, often adverse, impacts on many ecological systems and socio-economic sectors. This constitutes one of the greatest threats of human induced climatic change. Insular and coastal pollution would be the first affected by rise in sea level. The problem could rapidly spill over to inner areas if the volume of water in the oceans increases substantially. Most scientists agree that the rate of recent rise in sea level is two millimetre a year. It is scientifically predicted that global warming will result in changes in the extent of sea ice, increased thawing of permafrost and melting of polar ice masses, with the possibility of causing profound societal impacts around the globe. According to the study conducted by World Wildlife Fund (WWF), rising temperatures will cause wooded areas to advance steadily northwards, replacing the current Tundra that hosts millions of birds and many unique species.

A loss between 40 to 57 per cent of Tundra between 2070 and 2099 would mean the destruction of a habitat currently supporting around four to five million geese and 7.5 million waders. The study further added that the very first effects of arctic warming will probably be felt within 10 years and may well cause the extinction of several species. Disequilibrium in the hydrological cycle is also an offshoot of global warming. The atmosphere contributes carbon dioxide to the oceans, where it mixes with the top layers of seawater. Some mineral ions also become nutrients for vast marine life. The ocean yields sulphur to the atmosphere to the extent of 39 million t/year, mostly in the form of Dimethyl Sulphide (DMS). This is produced by marine phyto-plankton and enters the atmosphere in aerosol form. It then acts as a source of condensation nuclei for water vapour and initiates cloud formation and precipitation downward. Creation of cloudier conditions makes the sea cooler and this leads to decreased production of DMS — a negative feedback effect for further cloud formation. In this way, an equilibrium is being maintained. This apart, ocean also exerts long-range controls over precipitation through El Niño phenomenon (NOAA, USA, 1994).

GLONASSs (Global Navigation Satellite Systems) It is the Russian equivalent of the United States GPS system.

GMT (Greenwich Mean Time) This is the international 24-hour system used to designate the time at which satellite images are acquired.

Goose Any of numerous large, swimming birds forming a distinct sub-family Anserinae of the family Anatidae. They are somewhat of the intermediate between swan and ducks. They differ from ducks in that the sexes are alike in plumage and the male assists the female in hatching the egg. They are monogamous and mate for life. They have compressed bills, legs of moderate length and usually larger and longer necks than ducks. Geese are excellent game birds and good food. Out of seven migratory species found in India, two are important, being largely netted for sale. They are: GREY LAG GOOSE (*Anser anser rubrirostris*): It keeps mostly to the larger *jheels* in northern and north-western India. BAR-HEADED GOOSE (*Anser indicus*): A typical goose, grey-brown and white in colour. It breeds in Central Asia and during winter it moves to South India in October and leaves in March.

Goral Any Asiatic animal like the chamois of Europe related to the goat and the antelopes. Scientific name *Nemorhadus goral*, also spelt *Nemorhadus goral*. It has small horns, shorter than the distance apart at the base. Three species or perhaps mere races of goral are found in India. These are: BROWN GORAL (*Nemorhadus hodgsoni* Syn. *N. goral hodgsoni*): This is found in Nepal and Sikkim. BURMESE GORAL (*N. griseus*): This is found in Assam, Burma, Tibet and eastern China. GREY HIMALAYAN GORAL (*N. goral goral*): Found in Kashmir and the Western Himalayas.

Governance Failure and Forest Degradation Governance relates to the systems and process, the legal frameworks and the institutions through which decisions are made in a society, the ways in which these interrelate and their relevance and relationship to the various constituent parts of the nations (WCFCD, 1999). Therefore, society should establish a governance system that has pronounced elements of community participation and conflict resolutions. This acts as an incentive to sustainable forest management practices. Absence or erosion of governance system leads to abuse of authority by those who are positioned in the higher echelons of society. As a result, there emerges a social insecurity and inequitable distribution of the benefits from the use of forest resources.The symptoms of social insecurity are reflected in the following dimensions of governance in a society: (1) The character of land ownership and land tenure, (2) The distribution of the benefits accrued from the exploitation of forest resources, (3) The inequality between males and females and the displacement of communities and indigenous groups. When there is erosion of governance in a society, then environment becomes the first casualty. Therefore, evolving right governance structure is a prerequisite for tackling problems related to forest conservation (Bebarta, 2006). *See* Government failure.

Government Failure There are two main types of Government failure. The first occurs when a Government tries to correct a distortion, which arises due to market failure such as environmental externalities but fails. The second occurs when the actions of a Government have a distortionary effect in themselves. An example of this is the widespread provision of subsidies for the exploitation of natural resources such as timber, bamboo etc. A failure in policy is said to occur when the policy interventions necessary to correct market failures are not taken.

It also arises when Government decisions or policies are themselves responsible for worsening market failures.

GPS (Global Positioning System) 1. A set of satellites in geostationary earth orbits used to help determine geographic location anywhere on the earth by means of portable electronic receivers. 2. A system of orbiting satellites used for navigational purposes and capable of giving highly accurate geographic co-ordinates using hand-held receivers. 3. A receiver that calculates its absolute geographic position by determining its relative position to a set of at least three satellites.

Gradient Analysis The analysis of species composition along a gradient of environmental conditions.

Gradoni Small terracing (about 1 metre wide and not necessarily continuous) made along the contours of a slope with a tilt inwards to the slope.

Graft Hybrid A graft in which the genetically distinct tissues of stock and scion are intermingled in the organs developing from the point of union chimaeras.

Graft, Natural A natural vegetative fusion of the tissues of contiguous parts of different members of the same individual root graft.

Grafting Placing a portion of the scion of one plant in close cambial contact with the cambial layer of another plant or another part of the same plant (generally rooted), with the object of securing vegetative union between the two, the scion being detached from its parent plant either before or after the operation. Both the site of union and the composite individual are termed grafts. The genotype, but not necessarily the phenotype of the rootstock and the scion, remains unchanged after grafting. Vegetative union occurring naturally is termed a natural graft; commonest between roots (root graft).

Granular Applied to a type of soil structure in which the soil aggregates are more or less sub-angular or rounded in shape of size up to 1/4 inch ir diameter.

Graphical User Interface (GUI) Computer interface, such as MS Windows, that is used to provide a user-friendly interface between a user and the computer.

Grass Savanna Savanna with shrubs and widely, irregularly scattered trees. *See* savanna.

Grassland 1. A community in which grasses predominate; trees are either altogether absent or present in relatively small number.

2. An area in which the natural vegetation consists almost entirely of perennial grasses, whereas trees are either limited to stream courses or are widely distributed. This type of land is characteristic of sub-humid and semi-arid climates.

Grassland Climax A climax community consisting of grassland.

Graticule Network of parallels and meridians on a map or chart.

Graticule, Geographic System of coordinates of latitude and longitude used to define the position of a point on the surface of the Earth with respect to the reference spheroid.

Gravel Soil particles over 2.0 mm. Also applied to soils composed largely of such particles. *See* soil texture.

Gray Scale A sequence of gray tones ranging from black to white.

Grazing 1. The eating of any kind of standing vegetation by domestic livestock or wild animals. Sometimes limited to the eating of herbage in contrast with browsing. 2. Used sometimes as a synonym of forage.

Grazing and Forests Overgrazing in forests of the tropical regions is always carried out beyond their carrying capacity. This is basically the principal reason for the forest degradation. The situation is alarming in most of the countries in the tropical belt of the globe. Managing grazing in forests within the ambit of carrying capacity has remained a challenge. The case of India is an eye opener for forest policy maker all over world. Forests have been an important source of grazing and fodder in the absence of adequate productive pasture land and a viable policy for fodder development. It is estimated that over half of the livestock population of India, some 270 million, grazes in forests. Additionally, grazers collect an estimated 175 to 200 million tonnes of green fodder annually. This results in over-grazing and over-extraction of green fodder, leading to forest degradation through damage to regeneration and compaction of soil. A sample survey by Forest Survey of India (FSI) estimates that impact of grazing affects approximately 78 per cent of India's forests, of which some 18 per cent suffers high incidence and 31 per cent medium incidence (FSI, 1999).

Grazing Capacity The amount of grazing that an area can support under controlled grazing expressed as number of animals or equivalent cow units per hectare. *See* optimal grazing incidence.

Grazing Ground An area used for grazing.

Grazing Incidence The amount of grazing in an area expressed as number of animal or equivalent cow units per hactare grazing intensity.

Grazing, Conservative A grazing incidence that results in an approximately proper utilization of the grazing area in all but the most severe drought years, and causes little or no soil disturbance. *See* grazing, controlled.

Grazing, Controlled Grazing, conservative through controlling the period and incidence by the movement of livestock in different parts of the area in prescribed sequence.

Grazing, Deferred Postponing the time of grazing from the start of growth until after a definite stage of forage plant development or forage plants have ripened. *See* grazing, seasonal.

Grazing, Rotational The use of different parts of the grazing area or pasture in orderly sequence .The use of this term is sometimes restricted to grazing involving short rotational closures of a week or a month or more at different seasons in the year, grazing involving closures of a year or more at a time, being called periodic grazing.

Grazing, Seasonal The grazing of an area only during a certain period or periods of the year, roughly corresponding to one or more of the seasons. *See* deferred grazing.

Grazing, Selective The preferential and sometimes excessive grazing of certain plants in mixed pasture.

Grazing, Uniform The obtaining of uniform production of forage over a range or pasture by special aids and facilities such as cross fencing, mowing upgraded portions, salting etc.

Great Circle A circle with the same diameter as the earth. This is used to describe the shortest route between any two points on the earth's surface.

Green Belt An area of land between a city or town and the countryside, which is designed to limit the encroachment of urban areas onto rural land. A green belt is designed by the local planning authority, to act as buffer zone between an urban area and the countryside.

Green Manuring Turning a crop under, while green or soon after maturity, for the purpose of soil improvement.

Greenhouse Effect The warming of the Earth's atmosphere caused by increasing levels of carbon dioxide and other gases in the air, which trap the sun's heat within the atmosphere.

Greenhouse Gas Sinks Any process, activity or mechanism that removes greenhouse gases or their precursors from the atmosphere.

Greenhouse Gas Source Any process or activity (e.g. forest fires or conversion of forest land to agricultural or urban uses) that releases greenhouse gases or precursors of those gases into the atmosphere. As trees and forest products decompose or burn, they release carbon in the form of carbon dioxide.

Greenhouse Gases Those gases, such as water vapour, carbon dioxide, tropospheric ozone, nitrous oxide, and methane, that are transparent to solar radiation but opaque to longwave radiation. Their action is similar to that of glass in a greenhouse. *See also* greenhouse effect.

Gregarious Flowering The general flowering, within one or a few years and over considerable area, of all or most of the individuals of certain species that do not flower annually; in some cases followed by the death of the plant, e.g. Bamboos and strobilanthes. *See* sporadic.

Gregarious Habitually living and/or reproducing in more of less pure groups or communities, as opposed to individuals in a mixed crop. *See* sporadic.

Gregariousness The quality of being gregarious. Many animals show instinctive or temperamental preference for a social rather than a solitary existence. Borrowing rodents, wild dogs, ground squirrels are examples of gregariousness. Flocking habits reflect gregariousness in birds.

Grey Scales Levels of brightness or darkness for displaying information on monochrome display devices.

Grid Map A map in which the information is carried in the form of regular squares. Also called a raster.

Grid 1. A set of regularly spaced sample points. 2. A tessellation by squares. 3. In cartography, an exact set of reference lines over the earth's surface. 4. Network of uniformly spaced parallel lines intersecting at right angles. When superimposed on a map, it usually carries the name of the projection used for the map, that is, Lambert grid, Transverse Mercator grid, Universal Transverse Mercator grid. 5. In utility mapping, the distribution network of line utility resources, e.g. electricity or telephone lines.

Gross Domestic Product (GDP) The total output, or value added, from economic activity within a country's boarders, whether or not it is undertaken by nationals of that country but excluding production by citizens working abroad. Gross Domestic Product (GDP) is thus a gross measure of economic activity and does not account for the extent to which capital assets depreciate. GDP is distinct from Gross National Product (GNP), which is total value added by economic activity of citizens of the country in question, whether the activity takes place within the country's borders or not.

Gross Domestic Product (GDP) and Forests The gross value added by forestry sector in year 2000 (including forestry, logging and related activities, the manufacturing of wood, wood products, paper and paper products) is estimated at about 1.2 per cent of GDP. Between 1990 and 2000, the gross value added by the sector registered a modest growth of about 1.4 per cent, while the global economy grew by about 30 per cent because of gains in other sectors, especially manufacturing and services. As a result, the share of forest sector in GDP declined from about 1.6 to 1.2 per cent. Within the sector, the contribution of forestry *per se* remains low and appears to be declining. The overall decline of importance of the forest sector is consistent with that of most primary sectors, especially agriculture (FAO, 2005).

Gross National Product (GNP) A country's GNP is the total output, or value added, by economic activity of the citizens of that country, whether the activity takes place within the country or not. GNP is a gross measure of economic activity. GNP is distinct from Gross Domestic Product (GDP), which measures the value added by economic activity within a country's borders.

Ground Control Point (GCP) A geographic feature of known location that is recognizable on images and can be used to determine geometric corrections.

Ground Cover Herbaceous plants (including grasses and ferns) and the lowest shrubs occupying an area. Bryophytes and lower forms of vegetation may be distinguished as the ground layer — ground flora. *See* forest cover.

Ground Flora (Layer) The lowest stratum of a many-layered plant community consisting of herbs, grasses, low shrub and bryophytes.

Ground Receiving Station Facility that records data transmitted by a satellite.

Ground-Truth Data Data about a feature collected in the field.

Ground Truthing Acquiring data about features of interest in remote sensing by collecting ground-truth data in the field, inspecting aerial photography, additional maps, other ancillary data.

Groundwater Budget The summation of the movement of water into and out of a groundwater reservoir during a specified period of time.

Groundwater Discharge Flow of water from the groundwater reservoir onto the earth's surface.

Groundwater Percolation The process by which water from the soil enters the underlying geology by slow downward movement.

Groundwater Recharge Flow of water from the earth's surface into the groundwater reservoir.

Groundwater Water located in interstitial areas below the earth's surface. Groundwater is recharged by infiltration, and enters streams through seepage.

Group-Selection Method A method of regenerating uneven-aged stands in which trees are removed in small groups. It is an important silvicultural system.

Growing Stock Estimation Estimation of growing stock is important for assessing the status of forests as well as for determination of sustained yield. Growing stock is the sum total of the bio-mass of trees standing in a forest. It is in other word, the total volume of woody trees in forests. However, according to the prevailing practice in forestry, only those trees, which have a girth more than 20 cm. at breast height (Over Bark) are considered for calculation of growing stock. In other words, those very young pole crop having girth less than 20 cm are not counted towards volume calculation. This is the practice in Madhya Pradesh and Chhattisgarh and also in many other states. However, in some states, trees having girth more than 30 cm or diameter more than 10 cm are considered for growing stock estimation.

Growing Stock, Commercial The part of the growing stock that is considered as commercial under current market conditions (and with a diameter at breast height of Z cm or more). It is necessary to indicate the minimum diameter at breast height (Z cm) applied for considering a tree as being commercial.

Growing Stock, Normal The total volume of trees in a fully-stocked forest with a age normal class distribution for a given normal rotation.

Growing Stock 1. Sum (by number or volume) of all the tree growing in the forest or a specified part of it. 2. Volume over bark of all living trees more than X cm in diameter at breast height. It includes the stem from ground level or stump height up to a top diameter or Y cm, and may also include branches to a minimum diameter of W cm. It is necessary to indicate the three thresholds (X, Y, W in cm) and the parts of the tree that are not included in the volume. It is also necessary to mention whether the reported figures refer to volume above ground or above stump. It also includes wind fallen live trees (FRA, 2005). *See* forest crop and growing stock estimation.

Growth Form The characteristic general appearance—shape, posture and mode of growth, rather than size or colour of an organism.

Growth Rings Layers of wood produced around a tree's stem and branches during each growing season; also called annual rings. The number of annual rings indicates a tree's age, while the thickness of rings provides an estimate of a tree's growth rate. Rings are frequently visible when a tree is cut, or can be examined with the help of an increment borer.

Guano Natural manure composed chiefly of the excrement of sea birds, found especially on the islands near the Peruvian coast. It is rich in phosphates and nitrogenous matter and hence used as a fertilizer.

Guild A functional category used for combining species that overlap significantly in their utilization of a particular resource. (French, 1977)

Gully A large intermittent water course with steep sides. It is an obstacle to agricultural machinery.

Gully Control Control of erosion in gullied areas by means of structures, e.g. check dams, grading, establishment of suitable vegetation, or by diverting water away from gullies to controlled areas.

Gully Plugging Construction of check dam in gullies caused by accelerated erosion.

Gum Ducts Intercellular canals in dicotyledons, especially of the dipterocarpaceae family. The ducts contain different substances such as gum, resin, oil etc.

Gum Veins Shield-like tangential plates of varying size, or even complete rings of gum impregnated wood, found in many hardwoods, particularly eucalyptus.

Gum, Wound A dark amorphous substance produced in the wood of hardwoods and some conifers in response to injury, infection or other irritation.

Gummosis 1. In wood anatomy, partial or complete destruction of cells, the resulting mass being transformed into gum which occludes the newly-formed cavity and occasionally the cells adjacent to it. 2. In forest pathology, a disease process in hardwoods tree, characterized by gum exudation.

Gymnospermae (Gymnosperms) The botanical name for the group of vascular flowering plants that produce seeds not enclosed in an ovary, the most important division is coniferophyta which contains most conifers and their allies.

Hh

Habit The shape, general appearance and mode of growth common to the individuals of a species or other systematic group.

Habitat 1. The sum of effective environmental conditions under which an organism lives. 2. Often used for the natural range of distribution of a species. An association may have several dominants, either mixed together or occurring in different places. 3. The kind of place in which a plant or animal lives, such as forest habitat, grassland habitat, warm seas, mountain tops, fresh-waters, tropical jungles, etc. 4. The unit area of environment. 5. The abode, natural or otherwise, of a plant or animal, considered particularly in relation to all the environmental influences affecting it. 6. The place where a plant and/or animal population lives and its surroundings, both living and non-living. It includes the provision of life requirements such as food and shelter. 7. The environment where a plant or animal will naturally be found. 8. A major subdivision of formation, restricted to (the presumed) climax communities. 9. The locality, site and particular type of local environment occupied by an organism. *See* environment.

Habitat Component A simple part or a relatively complex entity regarded as a part, of an area or type or environment in which an organism or bio-logical population normally lives or occurs (Thomas, 1979).

Habitat Diversity The variety of wildlife habitat features and types in a specific area. Habitat diversity takes many forms: (1) The variety of plants and animals on a site; (2) Structural diversity or the vertical arrangement of vegetation from canopy to forest floor; (3) Horizontal diversity or the distribution of habitat types across the landscape; and (4) Temporal diversity or habitat changes over time. Generally, areas with substantial habitat diversity will support more wildlife species than areas with less habitat diversity. *See* habitat.

Habitat Quality The overall rating of the quality or quantity of plant or animal habitat. It is also called as suitability indices.

Habitat Type A land or aquatic unit, consisting of an aggregation of habitats having equivalent structure, function, and responses to disturbance.

Hachure Any series of lines used on a map to indicate the general direction and steepness of slopes. The lines are short, heavy and close together for steep slopes; longer, lighter, and more widely spaced for gentle slopes.

Halophyte A plant that is more or less restricted to saline soil or to sites that are influenced by salt water.

Halosere A sere which has its commencement in salt water.

Hammer-Mark, to To mark timber, standing or felled, with a marking hammer.

Hangul or Kashmir Stag (*Cervus elaphus hanglu*) The Red Deer of Europe typifies a group of large deer consisting of several species and races distributed over Europe, north of the Himalayas in Asia, North Africa and North America. Two or three species are found in India. Of these the Hangul is the commonest and best known. This is found in the north side of the Valley of Kashmir and in some of the adjacent valleys. It is a forest animal found singly or in small parties. Its coat ranges from light to dark brown, fading to dingy white on the lips, chin, under-parts and buttocks. Fawns are spotted. The fine spreading antlers assume great variety in form. Normal heads have fine points on each antler. Reputed to number about 2000 in 1947, there were hardly 175 in August 1962. It is one of the rare animals of India, on the verge of extinction. It is protected in Dachigam sanctuary in Jammu & Kashmir.

Haploid Having one chromosome set only; the individual so constituted. This is the characteristic condition of sexual cells. *See* diploid and meiosis.

Harassment Interference by predators with the normal movements, activities and actions of game.

Hard Data 1. Data obtained by direct measurement. 2. It is the physical components of a GIS — the computer, plotters, printers, VDUS, and so on.

Hard System Analysis A set of theory and methods for modelling the complexity of the real world.

Hardcopy A copy of a graphics or map image or paper or other stable material.

Hardening Off 1. Preparing seedlings in a nursery for planting out by gradually reducing watering, shade, and/or shelter resulting in a hardening of the plant. 2. The natural process whereby plants become adapted to drought, cold or heat.

Hardwood A conventional term for the timber of broad-leaved trees, and the trees themselves, belonging to the botanical group angiospermae. Hardwoods are almost invariably distinguished from softwoods by the presence of vessels in their timbers, irrespective of physical hardness or softness in either case. In countries where coniferous species are of little commercial significance, the terms hardwood and softwood are commonly used in their literal significance, i.e. hardwood, and softwood. The hardwoods have been differentiated into the naturally durable "primary" hardwoods and "secondary" hardwoods, both of which are physically hard and strong enough for heavy constructional purposes but the latter requiring preservative treatment if used in exposed positions. In India and elsewhere, the lighter hardwoods have often been termed "light or soft" wood.

Hare Any of a large group of swift animals (genus Lepus: family Leporidae) of the rodent family with long ears, soft fur, a cleft upper lip, a short tail and long powerful hind legs, adapted for leaping. It resembles a rabbit but is larger. Common Hare (*Lepus nigricollis ruficaudatus*): Found from the Himalayas downwards to the Godavari river, except in the desert zone. Desert Hare (*Lepus nigricollis dayanus*): Found in the arid zone of the Punjab, Rajasthan and Kathiawar. Black-Naped Hare (*Lepus nigricollis nigricollis*): This is distinctive in having a dark brown or black patch on the back of its neck from its ears to shoulders. It is found in South India extending northwards up to Khandesh in the west and the Godavari river in the east.

Hawk Any of a family of diurnal birds of prey (family Falconidae) characterised by short, rounded wings, a long tail and legs, a hooked beak and large, curved claws. Hawks include the falcons, buzzards, kites. Very large Hawks are known as eagles and vultures. Formerly used in falconry. Zoologically restricted to a bird of the sub-family Accipitrinae which includes the sparrow hawk and the goshawk, with rounded and shortest wings and low flight. Indian species are: SHIKRA (*Accipiter badius* Syn. *Astur badius*): A small Indian hawk found throughout the Indian Union and up to 1500 m in the Himalayas. It is a favourite bird in falcony as it is easily trained. SPARROW HAWK (*Accipiter nisus*): Distributed almost throughout India.

Hazard 1. A measure of that part of the fire danger, which is dependent on the materials available for burning, and its relative amount, class character, moisture content and condition. 2. Inflammable material constituting a threat of special suppression or of likelihood of ignition because of location. 3. Concerns inflammable material only.

Hazard Reduction Any treatment of inflammable material, other than accidental burning, that results in diminishing the chances of fire starting or spreading in them.

Headwaters The upper tributaries of a drainage basin.

Heart The central core of a tree or log; usually the pith with a small portion surrounding it. *See* pith.

Heartwood The inner layers of wood, which in the growing tree, have ceased to contain living cells. It is generally darker in colour than sapwood though not always clearly differentiated from it.

Heath 1. An open, uncultivated tract of land with a sandy or gravelly soil supporting low vegetation and occasionally scattered tree growth, particularly pine. 2. Vegetation developing on poor, usually acid, sandy or gravelly soils in lowlands and dominated by heathers.

Hectare Area measure in the metric system, equal to 10,000 square metres or 2.471 acres.

Hedgehog An insectivorous mammal of genus Erinaceous and related genera, frequenting hedges and gardens and having spiny hairs on the back and sides. It has a pig-like snout, hence its name. It is armed with very many spines and is able to roll itself into a ball, with this brisling in every direction. This should not be confused with the porcupine. Indian species are: HARDWICKE'S HEDGEHOG (*Hemiechinus collaris*): Found in the dry desert zone of Kutch, Rajasthan and Western Punjab, and the neighbouring tracts. PALE HEDGEHOG: (*Paraechinus micropus*) This is also found in the dry desert zone.

Hedonic Pricing Hedonic pricing is a market-based valuation method that is used to value non-market, often environmental, assets. The method can be used to infer the value of non-marketed goods by analyzing the practices of marketed goods to which the non-marketed goods are related.

Heel in, to To store young plants prior to planting by placing them in a trench and covering the roots or rooting portions with soil.

Height (Tree) The straight line distance between ground level and the extreme top of a tree, usually measured on slopes on the uphill side of the tree.

Height Class One of the intervals into which the range of tree heights is divided for classification and use; also the trees falling into such an interval.

Height, Crop A term used in sample plot work and yield table in India, and refers to the average height of a crop, as determined by Lorry's formula. The mean value derived from the formula is not of great significance as it does not adequately express the quality class.

Height, Dominant *See* height, top.

Height Growth Increment in height.

Height, Mean The height corresponding to the mean crop diameter.

Height, Merchantable The height of a tree to which it is saleable. *See* bole, commercial.

Height, Stump The height of the top of a stump above ground.

Height, Timber 1. Sometimes loosely used for merchantable height. 2. The height of the tree to a point where its girth or diameter falls to a specified minimum or the point where the main stem branches out into the crown, whichever is lower. It may be reckoned from ground level or stump height.

Height, Top 1. In general terms, it is the average height of the dominants in a stand. This height primarily depends on the site quality. Therefore, top height is used as measure of site quality. 2. Used in India in sample plot work and yield table and it refers to the height corresponding to the mean diameter (calculated from basal area) of the 250 biggest diameters per hectare as read from the height/diameter curve. When the number of trees falls below 125 per hectare, top height becomes synonymous with crop height. *See* height, crop.

Heliotropism The response in growth or position of plant organs to the direction of light. The response is positive when growth is towards the light, and is negative when away from it. *See* phototropism and geotropism.

Helophyte A cryptophyte that exclusively, or mainly grows in soil saturated with water or in the water itself, and from which leaf and flower bearing shoots emerge. Helophytes do not include all the plants ordinarily known as marsh plants.

Herbaceous A class of vegetation dominated by non-woody plants known as herbs (graminoids, forbs and ferns). Herbs generally form at least 25 per cent ground vegetal cover. Trees, shrub and dwarf shrub generally have less than 25 per cent cover. In rare cases, herbaceous cover exceeds the combined cover of trees, shrubs, dwarf shrubs, and non-vascular plants and is less than 25 per cent cover. Height classes for the graminoids are short (< 0.5 m), medium-tall (0.5-1 m) and tall (>1 m). Height classes for the forbs are low (<1 m) and tall (>1 m). For both graminoids and forbs, the height classes are measured when the inflorescences are fully developed. *See* herbs.

Herbage A growth of herbs, that is, plants with no persistent stem above ground.

Herbarium Collection of dried, pressed plants used as an aid to identification of unknown plants and by taxonomists in the classification of plants. The plant specimens are accompanied by information, such as the date and place of collection, by whom collected, details of habitat, flower colour and local names. Herbaria range from small collections containing plants of limited region, to the large national herbaria containing millions of specimens from all parts of the world.

Herbivory The consumption of living plant material.

Herbs Non-woody vascular plants such as grasses, grass-like plants, and forbs. *See* herbaceous.

Herd Any large aggregation, or detached unit, of hoofed mammals.

Heredity The transmission from parent to offspring of certain characteristics. For this reason there is a tendency for offspring to resemble parents and ancestors.

Heron or Hern Any of various wading birds of the genus Ardea (family Ardeidae) with a long neck and long legs, long tapering bill with a sharp point and sharp cutting edges, large wings and soft plumage. They live in the vicinity of marshes and river banks, feeding mostly on aquatic animals and fish. They nest in trees, often in communities. Heron found in India are: COMMON OR GREY HERON (*Ardea cinerea*): A tall grey bird marked with black and white, recognised in flight by the slow flapping of the wings and the long legs projecting behind. In India it is a resident bird in the plains and the hills up to 1500 m. It is essentially a solitary bird though gregarious in the nesting season. NIGHT HERON (*Nycticorax nycticorax*): Various nocturnal and crepuscular herons of Nycticorax and related genera found in temperate and tropical genera found in temperate and tropical regions. *N. nycticorax* is a small heavy heron, sleeping by day in thick trees.Typically it is found in Europe, Africa and parts of Asia. In India it is very general, being found throughout the plains and in the North West Himalayas up to 1500 or 1800 m. It is mainly a resident species though locally migratory. POND HERON: PADDY-Bird (*Ardeola grayii*) commonest of its family in India. It is small and is found in every piece of water, escaping notice by its dungy colouration. It ascends the hills up to 1200 m. It is chiefly a resident species, though locally migratory. PURPLE HERON (*Ardea purpurea*): Chiefly greyish with black crown and maroon breast. *See* Egret.

Heterogamy 1. The condition of having gamete differing in size and/or constitution. 2. That of having flowers of two or more sexual types in the same inflorescence. 3. That of a parthenogenesis generation, which alternates with a truly sexual one.

Heterosis The manifestation in a hybrid of a degree of vigour superior to that exhibited by either of its parents hybrid vigour.

Heterotic Characterized by heterosis.

Heterotrophic Plants Those which cannot live without organic food, obtained more or less readymade from bodies or other organisms. *See* autotrophic plants.

Heterozygous An individual is said to be heterozygous in respect of a particular character when the pair of gene carrying that character are dissimilar homozygous.

Hibernation 1. Dormancy or period of suspended activity during winter, common among mammals, reptiles and many vertebrates of temperate and arctic climates. 2. Passing the winter or cold season in a dormant condition, reflecting greatly reduced metabolic activity. 3. Passing the winter or cold season in an inactive state. Short of aestivation which is a sleep like condition of suspended activity for passing dry periods. *See* aestivation.

Hierarchical Database Structure A method of arranging computer files or other information so that the units of data storage are connected by a hierarchically defined pathway. From above to below, relations are one-to-many.

High (N) The peak of a cycle. A period of abundance.

High Moor A type of bog in which both the vegetation and the peat have low nutrient status, the vegetation having developed either on basin sites receiving run-off water poor in minerals and in sites developed from coarse or siliceous soils or in sites in a cool humid climate (as in higher latitudes) where heavy precipitation has leached most of the nutrients from the soil and caused water-logging for much of the year, creating a blanket bog or blanket peat. Sphagnum species and ericaceous shrubs are typical of high moor vegetation in the northern temperate zone. The raised bog is a special form of high moor, in which the peat accumulation in the centre of the bog is greater than at its edges, giving rise to a cross-section like an inverted saucer's. The central portion is thus raised above the natural ground-water level, becomes solely dependent upon precipitation, and is therefore exceedingly low in plant nutrients.

High-level Language A computer programming language using command statements, symbols, and words that resemble English-language statements. Examples are Fortran, Pascal, C^{++}, pl/i, Cobol, Basic.

High-Pass Filter A spatial filter which selectively enhances contrast variations with high spatial frequencies in an image. It improves the sharpness of images and is a method of edge enhancement.

Histogram 1. A diagram representing the frequency of the values of a variable between specified limits by means of rectangles of equal width whose areas are proportional to the frequencies. 2. A diagram showing the number of samples that fall in each contiguously defined size class of the attribute studied. 3. A means of expressing the frequency of occurrence of values in a data set within a series of equal ranges or bins, the height of each bin representing the frequency at which values in the data set fall within the chosen range. A cumulative histogram expresses the frequency of all values falling within a bin and lower in the range. A smooth curve derived mathematically from a histogram is termed the probability density function (PDF).

Hog An omnivorous non-ruminant mammal of the family Suidae, sub-order Artiodactyla of the order Ungulata. The pygmy hog, *Sus salvanius,* said to have been once found all along the base of the Himalayan foothills, is now feared to be nearly extinct. It is one of the animals which requires special protection. It is similar to its larger cousin. It needs protection even though adult never grow bigger than 25 cm high at the shoulder.

Holard The total water content of the soil.

Hole, Bore 1. A hole formed in a cell wall by the dissolving action of an advancing hypha of a wood inhabiting fungus. It is also known as hyphal hole. 2. A hole in plant tissues, e.g. bark or a wood surface, made by a boring organism.

Hole, Emergence A hole made through the outer bark, wood surface, or fruit for the emergence of insects.

Hole, Ventilation A hole made by adult bark beetles from their egg galleries to the surface for the purpose of ventilating these galleries, disposing of excess boring dust and for turning round ventilation tunnel.

Holism The thesis that wholes are more than the sum of their parts. It suggests that wholes have characteristics that cannot be explained in terms of their constituent parts or emergent qualities. The freezing point of water, for example, cannot be predicted from our knowledge of hydrogen and oxygen. The adjective is holistic.

Hollow A small depression on a level surface. Also termed pit.

Home Range The area to which an animal confines its activities. It wanders in this area without excluding others. Deer, rabbit and many rodents exhibit home range tendency. *See* territory.

Homeostasis Ecosystem is a dynamic system. It has many components which are operationally inseparable. They interact with each other on a continuous basis to form a functional unit. This gives rise to a vital process of production, consumption and decomposition in a functional unit. There is inherent functional and structural harmony among all the components in the ecosystem. Apart from harmony, each ecosystem has the capacity for self-maintenance and self-regulation. In other words, the ecosystem has an inbuilt system of internal control. But, with the rise in demand for more goods and services from the ecosystem, the degree of human intervention in the resource use system has increased manifold. In many instances the interventions lead to disruption of the natural control system. But, every biological system, to a great extent, resists such interventional changes and tries to remain in a state of equilibrium or homeostasis. Homeostasis means inherent capacity of a system to revert back to its normal state after a period of perturbation. A homeostatic mechanism exists at different levels of biological organisation. Besides, there is an equilibrium between living and non-living components of the environment also. This homeostatic mechanism has the propensity to resist any change to a great extent, in the system as a whole. These mechanisms at structural and functional levels of ecosystem symbolise the principle of 'balance of nature'. But over the years, it has been found by the ecologists that instead of 'balance of nature', there is 'flux of nature' in the ecosystem functioning. The new concept of 'flux of nature' indicates that the equilibrium is not static but dynamic. That means the ecosystem allows a number of changes to interact with and evolves itself into a dynamic system. However, if certain thresholds are not maintained, the homeostatic mechanism or dynamic equilibrium system collapses. Violent interventions of man into the 'nature's system of production, consumption and decomposition leads to transgression of all such thresholds'. The thresholds which are required to be maintained in an ecosystem management practices are the physiological limits under which organisms can continue to survive and function without stress. Within such limits, the biological processes do permit some degree of adaptations in response to marginal random disturbances, induced anthropologically or otherwise. The time required for such adaptation responses is critical. If a naturally (literally) determined time-lag is not allowed, the outcome is an unsustainably continued perturbation of the ecosystem leading to non-linearities, irreversibilities and consequent surprises (Rao, 2000).

Homogamy 1. Inbreeding due to isolation heterogamy. 2. The condition of having flowers of the same sex, viz. male, female, and hermaphrodite heterogamy. 3. Having stamens and pistils maturing in a flower at the same time.

Homozygous An individual is said to be homozygous in respect of a particular character when the pair of gene carrying that character are similar. *See* heterozygous.

Hook Order Pattern of social organization found in a herd of cattle, similar to peck order found among birds. Any member of herd has the right to hook (or make an attack with the horns) one of lower status without fear of retaliation and its tame submission to hooking by one of higher rank. *See* peck order.

Host An organism on or within which another organism feeds and develops.

Host Computer The primary or controlling computer in a data network.

Host, Alternate A second host species essential for the completion of the life history of a parasitic organism.

Host, Alternative A second host species which may form the food of a parasitic organism, but is not essential for the completion of its life history.

Hot Spots Specific small areas within a landscape exhibiting significantly higher levels of plant/animals diversity or unique composition of plants/animals (Sawarkar, 1995).

Human Capital A form of capital stock that consists of human skills and knowledge. This can be thought of as a form of capital since it increases the productive power of the individuals who possess the skills and knowledge. Another characteristic of human capital is that, in common with other forms of capital, investment in the capital stock (i.e. in education and training) is necessary to maintain or increase the stock, while without investment the stock will depreciate (Perman *et al.*, 1999).

Human Development Index (HDI) The United Nations Development Programme (UNDP) in its Human Development Report has included the Human Development Index (HDI) as a measure of human development since its inception in 1990. The index is intended to be a relatively simple, broad indicator of human development. It is made up of quantitative measures of each country's standards of living, and the longevity, and educational opportunities of its citizens. These factors are measured by adjusted income, life expectancy at birth, and educational attainment.

Human Rights Human rights represent the minimum social, economic and political standards that are generally considered to be acceptable. The advancement of human rights and their protection law is often thought of as one of the requirements of human development. The Universal Declaration of Human Rights, adopted by the United Nations General Assembly on 10th December, 1948, was the first multinational declaration to refer to human rights. The declaration calls for the prohibition of slavery, torture, other cruel and degrading treatment, arbitrary arrest, detention, and exile and also states that everyone has the right to life, liberty and security. It calls for an end to all forms of discrimination, for fair trials and reasonable punishment, and the universal protection of the law. It calls for freedom of thought, conscience, opinion, expression, association and religion. Economic provisions include the rights to social security, work and just conditions of work and to join trade unions.

Humidity, Absolute The amount of water vapour per unit volume of space.

Humidity, Relative The ratio, generally expressed as a percentage of the amount of water vapours present in the air to the amount required for saturation at the same temperature.

Humification The decomposition of plant and animal matter into amorphous, relatively insoluble organic compounds, usually dark in colour.

Hummock A small, mounded rise of organic matter and vegetation on a level surface. Also termed mound.

Humus 1. The more or less decomposed organic matter of the soil, which may form a separate layer or be intimately mixed with the mineral particles (intimate humus). 2. Black organic material of complex composition, which is the end product of microbial breakdown of plant and animal residues at the soil surface. 3. The dark or dark-brown organic material present in soil, produced by the decomposition of vegetable or animal matter, essential to fertility and favourable water supply. The organic matter is decomposed to such an extent that it has lost all signs of its original texture. It is usually colloidal.

Humus Layers 1. The group of organic and organic-enriched mineral horizons at the soil surface. 2. A group of soil horizons located at or near the surface of a pedon, which have formed from organic residues, either separate from or intermixed with, mineral materials.

Hunting The term denotes the seeking, pursing and taking of game and wild animals for subsistence, profit or sport. In Great Britain and Western Europe hunting for sport is defined as the taking of any wild animal by the aid of hounds that hunt by nose.

Elsewhere hunting refers to the field sport of shooting small and large game. Big game hunting has always exercised great fascination for mankind. In India hunting was a widespread practice. However with the introduction of Wildlife Act, 1972, this practice has come to a halt in India unless done illegally or with due permission from Chief Wildlife Warden in special cases. Therefore, the hunting practice here is explained with reference to past only. In India the principal game fields were found in: (i) The sub-Himalayan tract extending eastwards from the Yamuna river to Assam, which holds the tiger, elephant, rhino, sloth bear, black (Himalayan) bear, sambhar, cheetah, etc., (ii) The forests of Central India (including parts of Madhya Pradesh, Chhattisgarh and Andhra Pradesh), which abound in tiger, bison and sambhar; (iii) The dense forests of Tamil Nadu, Kerala and Karnataka where tiger, elephant, bison and deer are found; (iv) The Nilgiri hills where the ibex is found. The different methods of hunting were: (1) STAKING: This is a common method of hunting. In open country free from trees, game can be viewed from a distance. Under these conditions a slow and stealthy approach is necessary. Therefore, use beirg made of every bush, rock mound, or tree as a means of concealment. Attention should also be paid to the direction of wind. (2) STILL-HUNTING: In dense bush or scrub it is impossible to see more than a few metres. One comes upon game suddenly and the best chance of getting a shot is to walk slowly and cautiously, ever on the alert. (3) TRACKING: Big animals that herd together (e.g. elephant and deer) cannot be stalked or still-hunted. They leave well-defined tracks on soft ground. A skilful hunter can follow their track even on hard ground. (4) BEATING DRIVING: Some animals inhabit in or retire to a patch of dense jungle in which it is impossible for a man to advance silently within shooting distance. The only way to hunt such animals is to drive them out into the open or along some path where the sportsman is waiting. This is done with the help of a number of men with drums who form a line and advance into the jungle making a loud noise with the drums. When the animals come out of its hiding place, the hunter has a chance of shooting it. (5) SITTING UP IN A MACHAN: In the case of beasts of prey a half-eaten kill is dragged to a suitable place where the hunter can hide and await the arrival of the animal. (6) CALLING: This form of hunting is practiced in pursuit of deer.

It consists of waiting in hiding and making noise in imitation of the call of a female during the rutting season. In such a case a male is likely to answer and come right up to the hunter.

Hunting Ground Place or area used for hunting, specifically a region in which game is hunted.

Husk, to The strip off the external integument or covering of fruits or seeds.

Hyaena or Hyena Any of a group of wolf-like, nocturnal carnivores of Africa and Asia, of the family Hyaenidae. They have a bristly mane, short hind legs, powerful jaws, neck and shoulders, but low and comparatively poorly developed hind quarters. They have a characteristic shrill cry. They feed chiefly on carrion and are considered cowardly. The common hyaena found in India. Hyaena striata (Syn. *H. hyaena*), the striped or laughing hyaena, is about the size of a large dog. It is found wherever the wolf is absent and is equally destructive.

Hybrid 1. Offspring of organisms of dissimilar genotype, often the offspring of a cross between different species. 2. Any cross-bred animal or plant. 3. The product of a cross between individuals of unlike genetic constitution.

Hydrarch Succession Succession beginning in water or very wet land as in ponds, lakes, marshes, etc. *See* hydrosere xerarch succession.

Hydraulic Gradient 1. The slope of the water. 2. The drop in pressure head per length in the direction of stream flow.

Hydraulic Head The height of the free surface of a body of water above a given point beneath the surface, or the height of the water level at an upstream point compared to the height of the water surface at a given location downstream.

Hydric 1. Applied to a habitat that is wet. 2. Having an abundant supply of moisture.

Hydrologic Budget A compilation of the total water inputs and outputs to and from a lake.

Hydrologic Cycle 1. A complex sequence of conditions through which water naturally passes from water vapour in the atmosphere, though precipitation upon land or water surfaces and ultimately back into the atmosphere as a result of evaporation and transpiration. 2. A dynamic natural system concerned with the circulation of water through the atmosphere, biosphere and geosphere.

Hydromorphic Soils Soils developed in the presence of excess water.

Hydrophil Of organisms inhabiting water or wet land.

Hydrophilous Inhabiting wet land or water.

Hydrophyte 1. A plant which has evolved with adaptations to live in aquatic or very wet habitats, e.g., cattail, water lily, water tupelo. 2. A cryptophyte which survives the unfavourable season by means of buds that live at the bottom of the water; the vegetative shoots remain submerged, only the flowers and inflorescences rising above the surface. 3. A plant which grows wholly or partly immersed in water. 4. A class of Raunkiaer's form, life comprising plants with perennating buds lying in water.

Hydrosere The different stages in hydrarch succession.

Hygric 1. Of sites or habitats characterized by decidedly moist or humid conditions. 2. Species tolerating or well adapted to humid conditions.

Hygrometer An instrument or apparatus for measuring the humidity, relative of the atmosphere.

Hygrophil Of organisms inhabiting moist sites.

Hygrophilous Inhabiting moist sites.

Hygrophyte A plant that is more or less restricted to moist sites.

Hygroscopicity The power to absorb moisture from the atmosphere and retain it.

Hygrothermograph An instrument that records automatically and continuously both temperature and relative humidity, absolute on a single chart.

Hyperparasite An organism parasitic upon another parasite.

Hyper parasitization Parasitization of a parasite, i.e. by a hyperparasite.

Hyperspectral The use of many narrow sections of the electromagnetic spectrum in remote sensing.

Hypha One of the thread-like elements which forms the mycelium of a fungus.

Hypsometer An instrument for determining the height of standing trees from observations taken at some distance from the tree.

Hypsometry The measurement of the elevation of the earth's surface with respect to sea level.

Hz Cycles per second, i.e. unit for frequency.

Ii

Ibex (Plural Ibexes, Ibises) Any of several species of wild goats (genus Capra) of Europe, Asia or Africa. The male has large, backward, curved horns, like scimatars. Capra ibex of the Alps, is now rare there, being found now only in Mongolia and Abyssinia. Two species are found in India. ASIATIC OR HIMALAYAN IBEX (*Capra ibex sibirica*): Found at elevations above 3600 m in the Himalayas, especially in Kashmir. About 1.07m high at the shoulder. NILGIRI IBEX (*Hemitragus hylocrius*): Found in the more rocky hills of the Nilgiris and the high ranges of Kerala at elevations of about 2500 m.

Ibis (*Plural Ibis or Ibises*) Any of several long legged, wadding birds related to the herons and consisting the family Threskiornithidae. They inhabit warm regions, feedings on aquatic amphibian animals. They are distinguished by a long, slender downwardly curved bill. The sacred ibis of the Nile is well known. WHITE IBIS (*Threskiornis melanocephalus*): This is found throughout India as a resident species. It is found in inland waters, preferring large marshes and *jheels*. BLACK IBIS (*Pseudibis papillosa*): This is a large black bird, identified by the bare head and long curved beak. It perches on trees and feeds on the ground. It is found in the plains of India. It is a resident species.

Illuviation The process of deposition of soil material removed from one horizon to another horizon of the soil, usually from an upper horizon to a lower horizon in the profile.

Image Pictorial representation of a scene recorded by a remote sensing system. Although image is a general term, it is commonly restricted to representations acquired by non-photographic methods. In remote sensing and GIS as a term that describes digital representations of earth features.

Image Enhancement Any of a group of operations (e.g., contrast stretch, spatial filtering) that improve the detectability and presentation of targets or categories in an image.

Image Processing Manipulation of an image to improve or change some quality of the image. Image processing encompasses all the various operations that can be applied to producing the final photographic or computer-based image rendition.

Imagery Visible representation of objects and (or) phenomena as sensed or detected by cameras, infrared and multi-spectral scanners, radar, and photometers. Recording may be on photographic emulsion (directly as in a camera or indirectly after being first recorded on magnetic tape as an electrical signal) or on magnetic tape for subsequent conversion and display on a cathode ray tube.

Immobilization The conversion of an element from inorganic to organic combination in microbial or plant tissues. This has the effect of rendering unavailable (and usually not readily soluble) an element that previously was directly available to plants.

Impact Assessment, Environmental and Social An Environmental and Social Impact Assessment (ESIA) is a combination of Environmental Impact Assessment and Social Impact Assessment. An Environmental Impact Assessment (EIA) is an exercise to (1) Identify actual and potential impacts on the environment as a result of various industrial or mining activities or forest operations, (2) Plan to minimize or avoid negative environmental impacts and maximize positive environmental impacts. Similarly a social impact assessment aims at (i) Identifying actual and potential impacts on people as a result of operations, and (ii) Planning how to minimize actual or avoid negative impacts and maximize positive impacts on stake holders and others. Therefore, a social impact assessment involves collecting information about stakeholders and their interests, and then considering their actual, or possible, impacts of industrial or mining activities or forest operations on these interests in order to propose mitigation measures. Because environmental and social impacts often overlap, a social impact assessment is often undertaken along with Environmental Impact Assessment (EIA). In such cases the exercise is known as Environmental and Social Impact Assessment (ESIA). It examines industrial or mining or forest management in terms of the effect it has on both the environment and people. It is indispensable on the part of forest organization to adapt it as a means of identifying its positive and negative impacts, both currents and potential on environment and people. It acts as a guide to the forest organization for setting its objectives and targets and provides a basis for management planning process. The assessment is also used as a base line study to monitor actual impacts of operations against potential impacts predicted by ESIA. Environment and social impact assessment should be carried out before any field operations began. Where operations are being carried out, an ESIA should be undertaken for all existing and future operations. Such practices are in vogue in few countries. But such practices are yet to begin in many counties. Apart from this, another study called as Ecological Impact Assessment (EIS) is generally conducted along with Environmental Impact Assessment (EIA). This study is commonly concerned with impacts on the natural environment, fauna and flora and ecological processes. It aims at determining sensitivity of fauna, flora, habitats and ecosystem to physical or chemical impacts (Spellerberg Ian, F., 1992). Based on degree of assessment, there are two types of assessments. They are: (1) In-depth Environmental and Social Impact Assessment of the physical, biological and social implications of a proposed operation or management regime; and (2) On-site Environmental and Social Impact Assessment carried out mostly by the internal officer/managers of the organization. This is a rapid assessment of possible impacts to ensure that planned actions minimize negative impacts. This helps to develop an aptitude among officers/managers for considering environmental and social impacts before that. Consequently, it helps to minimize the chances of any negative effects. A Social Impact Assessment exercise requires extensive consultation with stakeholders. It therefore provides opportunity to develop consultation and promote participation amongst stakeholders. SIA exercise consists of the processes such as: (a) Identification of stakeholders and their interests, (b) Identification and evaluation of potentially significant social impacts, (c) Consideration of options for avoiding or mitigating negative impacts and for optimizing positive impacts, (d) Exploring the options for optimizing positive impacts, (e) Prioritization of activities required to address negative impacts, (f) Prioritization of activities required to address impacts, and (g) Incorporation of activities into the management planning process.

Impeded Drainage Condition in which downward movement of gravitational water is hindered.

Impermeable A soil, which does not readily permit the passage of water through it.

Importance Value 1. An index of the relative abundance of a species in a given community. 2. The sum of relative density, relative frequency, and relative dominance. Anyone of these three parameters could also be considered an importance value.

Impoverishment (of soil) The deterioration of the inherent fertility of the soil. *See* soil, degraded.

Inbreeding 1. Crossing between a succession of parents derived from a single origin, or from the self, to of a single parent. *See* out breeding. 2. The interbreeding of closely related individuals occurring naturally (as in a closed population) as a result of social or religious custom (as in some royal families) or as a deliberately chosen system of breeding (as of cattle or poultry). This serves to fix desirable characters of and eliminate unfavourable characters from a suitably selected stock, but tends to effect an unwanted decline (as in size, vigour or fertility) through the fixation of undesirable and often recessive characters when the initial stock is in anyway defective. Distinguished from outbreeding.

Incompatibility 1. Inability of the gamete of two organisms to unite and reproduce sexually; applied in particular to pollen intersterility. 2. Inability of the tissues of stock and scion to form a permanent union. 3. Inability of one substance to mix with another without undesirable reaction; used with reference to insecticides where incompatibility involves loss of efficiency on mixing. 4. A difference in the physiology of a parasite and its host which limits or stops the development of the former.

Increase, Natural The actual increase in numbers of an organism as determined by its biotic potential and the controlling effects of biotic factor and climatic factors.

Increment 1. The increase in girth class, diameter, basal area, height, volume, quality, site, price or value of individual trees or crops during a given period. 2. The rate at which a tree or a crop increases with age.

Increment Borer An auger-like instrument with a hollow bit used to extract cores or cylinders of wood from trees with annual ring, growth for increment and age determination, e.g., Pressler's borer.

Increment Boring Increment boring is defined as the boring of a tree stem with Pressler's increment borer or any other borer to determine increment of trees with annual rings.The principal objective of this exercise is to determine age and diameter increment of trees having conspicuous growth rings. Determination of age and diameter increment helps in finding out the age required by the trees to reach a particular exploitation diameter.

Increment per cent The average annual growth in volume (or basal area) over a specified period, expressed as a percentage of the volume (or basal area) either at the beginning, or more usually half-way through the period.

Increment, Annual The increment of volumes of trees during one year.

Increment, Current Annual Strictly the increment in a specific year or the current year.

Increment, Final Mean Annual The mean annual increment determined after or before final felling.

Increment, Light The rapid diameter increment of trees due to light stimulus following increment felling.

Increment, Mean Annual The total increment upto a given age divided by the age. The mean of all CAI, i.e. total increment up to any specific age divided by that age. *See* MAI.

Increment, Normal 1. The increment attainable by a fully stocked stand, or by a series arranged in a normal age class distribution, under specified management for the locality. 2. The maximum growth put on by each age gradation, given a certain species, locality and rotation, and optimum condition of growth.

Increment, Periodic Annual The average annual increment for any short period. Sometimes referred to as the "periodic mean annual increment".

Incrementalism This denotes the failure to account for the cumulative effects of decisions taken on a project-by-project basis. For example, consider the loss of biodiversity and carbon sequestration services caused by creating an arrays of farm land or urban development projects. The environmental costs of each individual projects are minimal, but the aggregate effect of such decisions may threaten environmental sustainability of the area.

Index of Biotic Integrity (IBI) A measure of the degree to which water, site quality or forest resource quality of an area deviates from that expected on relatively undisturbed sites of similar type.

Index Plant A plant indicating the whereabouts of game or the suitability of a range for game.

Index Species A plant or animals species so highly adapted to a particular kind of environment that its presence is sufficient indication that a habitat under investigation belongs to the kind to which the species is adapted.

Indexed Files Files of data records in which pointers based on a particular ordering such as alphabetic, are used to quicken accessing and searching instructions.

Indian Darter or Snake Bird (*Anhinga rufa* Syn. *A. melanogaster*) These have long and slender S-shaped necks, narrow heads and dragged-like bills, which streamline the birds to enable them to swim underwater and spear their fishy prey. They feed their young in the same manner, as do pelicans and cormorants. They swim, dive and fly well and perch on trees. They are resident species in India, being found in suitable localities. They do not ascend the hills. They frequent fresh-water (rivers, lakes, and *jheels*).

Indicating per cent The increment in value of a forest during a year expressed as a percentage of the capital value of the forest at the beginning of the year.

Indicator 1. An organism or kind of organisms (as a species) or an ecological community that is so strictly associated with particular environmental conditions that its presence is indicative of the existence of these conditions in a particular environment. It is a condition which is visible and which denotes some other condition, which is invisible. 2. Species or community which, with reference to a site, indicates generally the presence in it of certain conditions, processes and uses and sometimes specifically the species that would grow in it. 3. A quantitative, qualitative or descriptive attribute that, when periodically measured or monitored, indicates the direction of change.

Indicator Line A fixed line in an experimental area along which periodic observations are made, usually in quadrats laid out on either side, for the assessment of regeneration.

Indicator Plant 1. Any plant that, by its presence, its frequency or its vigour, indicates any particular property of the site—particularly but by no means exclusively, of the soil. 2. Any plant which by its presence, increase or decrease, indicates the quality of the site.

Indicator Plot A small plot kept under detailed observation within a larger experimental area, e.g., when testing regeneration methods.

Indicator Species 1. A selected species presumed to indicate the welfare of other species or that, which represents a specific habitat condition (Thomas, 1979). 2. An organism that occurs only in areas with specific environmental conditions. Because of their narrow ecological tolerance, the presence or absence of these species on a site is a good indicator of environmental conditions. Foresters often use the distribution of indicator under-story plants to get a quick estimate of site conditions, for example, drainage and fertility. Biologists may use indicator species to evaluate the health of an ecosystem.

Indigenous Native to a specified area or region not introduced.

Indigenous Peoples The existing descendants of the peoples who inhabited the present territory of a country wholly or partially at the time when persons of a different culture or ethnic origin arrived there from other parts of the world, overcame them and by conquest, settlement, or other means reduced them to a non-dominant or colonial situation, who today live more in conformity with their particular social, economic and cultural customs and traditions than with the institutions of the country of which incorporates mainly the national, social and cultural characteristics of their segments of the population which are predominant' (Working definition adopted by the UN Working Group on Indigenous Peoples).

Indirect Use Value One of the types of value that make up the total economic value of an environmental resource. Its definition lies between those of use value and non-use value, and can be used to refer to two main types of situation. The first occurs when a person makes direct use of an environmental resource, for example, an aquaculture, but where that activity benefits from the services of another environmental resources such as freshwater collected in the water body inside a forest. The nature and extent of this type of indirect use value is clearly very uncertain. The second situation in which indirect use values accrue when a resource is used in way that does not involve depleting the resource, for example recreation.

Infection, Lac The process of tying brood lac on to a host tree to raise a lac crop to it. Sometimes called "inoculation ".

Infestation The occurrence of any pest unusual abundance over a limited area. Applied to single trees or stands.

Infiltration 1.The process by which liquid water enters the surface soil or zone of aeration. It includes both wetting to the field moisture capacity and the subsequent progressive downward movement of free water by gravity flow. 2. The process by which water moves from a surface body into the groundwater system. *See* percolation and seepage.

Infiltration Capacity The rate of penetration of still, clear water downwards into a soil.

Infiltration Rate The rate at which surface runoff and precipitation soaks into the ground surface.

Infiltration Velocity The volume of water moving downward into the soil surface per unit of area per unit of time. The local instantaneous volume is the limit approached as the area and time interval are made small. The maximum infiltration velocity is the infiltration rate.

Inflammability The relative susceptibility of materials to ignition, i.e., the case with which materials ignite regardless of their quantity. A part of the fire danger on any area.

Infrared It pertains to Electro Magnetic Radiation (EMR) in the 0.7 to 100 μm region of the spectrum.

Injection, Tree The introduction, often with pressure of a chemical — usually a water-soluble salt in solution — into the sap stream of a living tree, to kill it or protect it from disease, or to kill a parasite such as mistletoe; or into a freshly killed tree, to destroy bark-beetle or wood beetle broods.

Innovation The use of a new idea, material or technology to produce new goods or services or to change the way in which goods or services are produced or distributed. Innovation can include improved managerial systems, new production techniques, new technology, the results of research and development or the application of information technologies.

Inoculation Deliberate introduction of living or killed organisms, usually micro-organisms, into a new environment such as soils, culture media or the living body of a higher organism, animal or plant. *See* infection, lac.

Input Device A hardware component for data entry. *See* digitized, keyboard, scanner, tape drive.

Input The data entered to a computer system. Input as a verb is the process of entering data into a computer.

Insect, Primary A species of insect which can attack and injure trees that are living and in normal vigour. Some species are "primary" under certain conditions and "secondary" under others.

Insect, Secondary A species of insect which can attack only trees that are already weakened, dying or dead. *See* primary insect.

Insectary A place where insects are bred and studied.

Insolation 1. Solar radiation, as received by the earth; also the rate of delivery of such radiation per unit of horizontal surface. 2. The effect of excessive sunlight on trees or other plant growth previously grown under more shaded conditions.

Institutional Failure A situation in which the existing institutions are inadequate to deal with environmental and other problems, or in which the institutions required to deal with an environmental problem are not in place. *See* government failure.

Intangible Benefits Benefits that cannot be valued in monetary terms. This can be due to lack of data on the benefit in question; for instance, availability of fresh air inside a forests.

Integer A number without a decimal component. A means of handling such numbers in the computer which requires less space and proceeds more quickly than with numbers having information after the decimal point (real numbers).

Inter-Relationship Mutual relationship between different forms of animal and plant life to each other and to their environment.

Interaction The extent to which the effect of one factor (or treatment) varies with changes in the strength, grade or level of other factors in an experiment.

Interactive A GIS system in which the operator can initiate or modify programme execution *via* an input device and can receive information from the computer about the progress of the job.

Interbreed 1. To breed together as in cross-breed. 2. To breed within a closed population as in inbreed.

Interface A hardware and software link that allows two computer systems or a computer and its peripherals to be connected together for data communication.

Intermittent Working Managing a forest without aiming at continuous production. *See* yield, intermittent.

International Tropical Timber Organisation (ITTO) ITTO is an inter-governmental organisation based in Japan. It is made up of representatives of tropical timber producer and consumer countries. By the end of 1996, there were 53 members, accounting for 75 per cent of the world's tropical rain forests and more than 90 per cent of international trade in tropical timbers. All ITTO member countries are committed to the year 2000 objective—that by the year 2000, all internally traded tropical timber should be sourced from sustainably managed forests. ITTO guidelines have reasonably wide acceptance with government, industry and NGOs worldwide as the basis for sustainable management of tropical forests. These guidelines are relevant to operational management as well as to national policy, monitoring and reporting.

International Union for the Conservation of Nature (IUCN) After the formation of United Nations as a world body, a series of international environmental agreements and framework of international environmental organisations began to emerge. This eventually evolved into the International Union for the Protection of Nature (IUPN), established in 1949. It became International Union for the Conservation of Nature (IUCN) in 1956.This organisation played an important role in developing the modern concept of sustainability. World Wildlife Fund (WWF) was set up in 1961 as a fund raising organisation to support IUCN. But, with the passage of time, this organisation emerged as a powerful player in natural conservation in its own. Initially IUCN focused on nature protection, but afterwards, it embarked on major environmental programme. By the end of the 1960s, IUCN had begun to show a greater concern for economic development and holistic approach to conservation. IUCN, along with UNEP established after Stockholm conference, prepared the World Conservation Strategy. UNEP and WWF not only contributed to development of basic themes of conservation and development but also provided financial support to translate such themes into action.

Internet The global network of computers, originally set up as a means of secure communications for military and intelligence purposes.

Interplant To plant saplings or young trees among existing forest growth, planted or natural.

Interpolation The estimation the values of an attribute at unsampled points from measurements made at surrounding sites.

Interpretation The process in which a person extracts information from an image.

Interpretation Key Characteristic or combination of characteristics that enable an interpreter to identify an object on an image.

Interrupt the Cover, to To form gaps or openings in the canopy by the removal of trees.

Intersect Overlay Polygon-on-polygon overlay corresponding to the boolean and overlay. The output map will contain only those polygons that cover areas common to both sets of input polygons.

Intersection 1. In terms of geometric, it is the crossing of lines or polygons to form new units. 2. In terms of logic, it is the combination of data from two boolean sets using the 'and' operator.

Interspersion 1. The intermingling of different kinds of organisms (species of plants or animals) within an ecological community (such as a forest, or a wildlife population). 2. The intermixing of plant species and plant communities that provides habitat for animals in a defined area (Thomas, 1979).

Intrinsic Value An aspect of the value of an asset, for example, an ecosystem or a species, which is separate from its role as an instrument in providing well-being to humans. Intrinsic value refers to the value of the objects in and of itself, and has been used to justify the conservation of, for example, biodiversity.

Introduced Species Established plants and animals not native to the ecosystem.

Introductions, Benign They are defined in the IUCN Guidelines for Re-introductions (IUCN, 1998) as '...an attempt to establish a species, for the purpose of conservation, outside its recorded distribution, but within an appropriate habitat and eco-geographical area. This is a feasible conservation tool only when there is no remaining area left within a species 'historic range'.

Invasion The movement of one or more plants from one area into another and their establishment in the latter. It comprises migration, ecesis and competition as its essential parts. It may populate a bare area or produce new developmental stages.

Invasive Species The term invasive species refers to a subset of those species defined as introduced species or non-indigenous species. Invasive species can alter ecological relationships among native species and can affect ecosystem function, economic value of ecosystems, and human health. A species is regarded as invasive if it has been introduced by human action to a location, area, or region where it did not previously occur naturally (i.e., invasive), becomes capable of establishing a breeding population in the new location without further intervention by humans, and spreads widely throughout the new location. Natural range extensions are common in many species, but the rate and magnitude of human-mediated extensions in these species tend to be much larger than natural extensions, and the distances that species can travel to colonize are also often much greater with human agency. Invasive plants and animals may pose a risk to a particular species, habitat or ecosystem. However, the majority of introduced species do not cause significant ecological change or environmental harm because they exist primarily in habitats already subjected to intensive human alteration; such species may not be considered 'invasive'.

Inventory, Forest As used in FAO, the term "forest inventory" includes information regarding the extent and classification of forest areas, the distribution of different forms of ownership, estimates of volumes of standing timber, and comparison of annual growth in the forest with annual drain due to natural causes and fellings. However, different meanings have been assigned to the word 'inventory' in different regions of the globe. For example, it has been found that in one country the term 'forest inventory' may include forest areas, timber volumes and annual growth, while in another it may be used in more limited sense and refers solely to annual growth, while in another it may be used in a more limited sense and refers solely to the measurement of standing timber. The main objective of forest inventory is to collect qualitative and quantitative information about the forest resources within the prescribed precision limits. In India, forestry inventory helps in describing the forest area, estimating volume of standing trees and their growth, primarily timber within a specified area. The data generated are used for planning forest management practices and preparing reports on potentiality of forest resources. In the good old days, forest inventory was synonymous with timber estimate. Forest department under every state government prepares forest inventory before revising the forest working plan. This apart, Forest Survey of India (FSI) prepares inventory too. As per the methodology adopted by FSI, the country has been stratified into 14 physiographic zones according to tree species composition and other physiographic and ecological parameters. In strata, districts are considered first sampling units and grids of size 1¼′ × 1¼′ as secondary sampling units. Ten per cent of districts are being inventoried every year. *See* Forest Survey of India.

IR 1. Infrared region of the electromagnetic spectrum that includes wavelengths from 0.7 μm to 1 mm. 2. Short wavelength portion (0.7 to 0.9 μm) of the IR (Infrared) band that is detectable by IR colour film or IR black-and-white film.

Irreversibility This refers to the effects of actions that cannot be undone. This is the second critical concept that characterizes nature of renewable resources. If the forest ecosystem is used beyond its carrying capacity, then irreversible changes take place in the structure and function of the ecosystem. Consequently, such changes finally drive the ecosystem to a different state with the loss or extinction of species. Economically, irreversibility leads to uncertainty in resource allocation in an ecosystem. As a result, it affects efficiency and productivity of the ecosystem.

Irruption A large, sudden, non-periodic increase in density of a natural population often accompanied by an extension into hitherto unoccupied range. Irruption is due to favourable alteration of the environment.

Island A tract of land completely surrounded by water or by another distinctive vegetation cover, dissimilar from the specific tract.

Island Biogeography The study of theories relating to the rates of colonization.

Isolate, to To give a tree or trees a permanently free position by removing surrounding trees.

Isoline A line which joins points of equal value.

Isopleth Map A map displaying the distribution of an attribute in terms of lines connecting points of equal value; see contour, contrast with choropleth map.

Isotropic An adjective to describe something that has the same physical actions in all directions.

IUCN Categories The IUCN Categories are: EXTINCT (EX): A taxon is 'Extinct' when there is no reasonable doubt that the last individual has died. A taxon is presumed extinct when exhaustive surveys in known and/or expected habitat, at appropriate times (diurnal, seasonal, annual), throughout its historic range have failed to record an individual. Surveys should be over a timeframe appropriate to the taxon's life cycle and life form. EXTINCT IN THE WILD (EW): A taxon is 'Extinct in the Wild' when it is known only to survive in cultivation, in captivity or as a naturalized population (or populations) well outside the past range. A taxon is presumed 'Extinct in the Wild' when exhaustive surveys in known and/or expected habitat, at appropriate times (diurnal, seasonal, annual), throughout its historic range have failed to record an individual. Surveys should be over a time frame appropriate to the taxon's life cycle and life form. CRITICALLY ENDANGERED (CR): A taxon is 'Critically Endangered' when the best available evidence indicates that it meets any of the criteria A to E for Critically Endangered and it is therefore considered to be facing an extremely high risk of extinction in the wild. ENDANGERED (EN): A taxon is 'Endangered' when the best available evidence indicates that it meets any of the criteria A to E for Endangered, and it is therefore considered to be facing a very high risk of extinction in the wild. VULNERABLE (VU): A taxon is 'Vulnerable' when the best available evidence indicates that it meets any of the criteria A to E for Vulnerable and it is therefore considered to be facing a high risk of extinction in the wild. NEAR THREATENED (NT): A taxon is 'Near Threatened' when it has been evaluated against the criteria but does not qualify for Critically Endangered, Endangered or Vulnerable now, but is close to qualifying for or is likely to qualify for a threatened category in the near future. LEAST CONCERN (LC): A taxon is 'Least Concern' when it has been evaluated against the criteria and does not qualify for Critically Endangered, Endangered, Vulnerable or Near Threatened. Widespread and abundant taxa are included in this category. DATA DEFICIENT (DD): A taxon is 'Data Deficient' when there is inadequate information to make a direct, or indirect, assessment of its risk of extinction based on its distribution and/or population status. A taxon in this category may be well studied, and its biology well known, but appropriate data on abundance and/or distribution are lacking. Data Deficient is therefore not a category of threat. Listing of taxa in this category indicates that more information is required and acknowledges the possibility that future research will show that threatened classification is appropriate. It is important to make positive use of whatever data are available. In many cases great care should be exercised in choosing between DD and a threatened status. If the range of a taxon is suspected to be relatively circumscribed, and a considerable period of time has elapsed since the last record of the taxon, threatened status may well be justified. NOT EVALUATED (NE): A taxon is 'Not Evaluated' when it has not yet been evaluated against the criteria. (For criteria A to E, refer IUCN Red List Categories and Criteria). *See* IUCN Red List.

IUCN Red List World Conservation Union, through its Species Survival Commission (SSC) has for more than four decades been assessing the conservation status of species, sub-species, varieties and even selected sub-populations on a global scale in order to highlight taxa threatened with extinction, and therefore, promote their conservation. The SSC remains firmly committed to providing the world with the most objective, scientifically-based information on the current status of globally threatened biodiversity. The taxa assessed for the IUCN Red List are the bearers of genetic diversity and the building blocks of ecosystems, and information on their conservation status and distribution provides the foundation for making informed decisions about conserving biodiversity from local to global levels. The IUCN Red List of Threatened Species provides taxonomic, conservation status and distribution information on taxa that have been globally evaluated using the IUCN Red List Categories and Criteria. This system is designed to determine the relative risk of extinction, and the main purpose of the IUCN Red List is to catalogue and highlight those taxa that are facing a higher risk of global extinction (i.e. those listed as Critically Endangered, Endangered and Vulnerable). The IUCN Red List also includes information on taxa that are categorized as Extinct or Extinct in the Wild; on taxa that cannot be evaluated because of insufficient information (i.e. are Data Deficient); and on taxa that are either close to meeting the threatened thresholds or that would be threatened were it not for an ongoing taxon-specific conservation programme (i.e. are Near Threatened).Taxa that have been evaluated to have a low risk of extinction are classified as Least Concern. The Least Concern assessments did not appear on IUCN Red Lists produced before 2003 (except for 225 cases in 1996) because the main focus has been on threatened species. Taxa not included on the IUCN Red List are those that went extinct before 1500 AD, Least Concern species that have not yet been data based, and species that have not yet been assessed (i.e., they are in the Not Evaluated category). The only taxonomic groups, that have been comprehensively assessed, are the amphibians, birds, mammals, conifers and cycads. The vast majority of plant taxa listed in the 1997 IUCN Red List of Threatened Plants have not yet been evaluated against the revised Red List Criteria.

Jj

Jackal Any of several races of wild dog of the genus Canis. *Canis aureus* is a yellowish-grey, meat-eating dog of Asia, and northern Africa, smaller than the wolf. It runs in packs and hunts its prey at night. It eats carrion and small animals, which are easy to kill, such as poultry and the sticky young of deer. Their warning note of the presence of a tiger or leopard is characteristic.

Jungle The general Indian term for forest.

Jungle Wood A loose term for timber of miscellaneous inferior species.

Justice Justice in an economic context, means that the economic actions and outcomes of economic systems, especially the distribution of benefits, which are ethically acceptable.

Juxtaposition The act of arranging stands in space (Thomas, 1979). Applies to all types of vegetation.

Kk

Key Areas Areas that offer key habitat functions for a species such as breeding, fawning, roosting, nesting or those that have obligate species; biological or geomorphic in nature (Sawarkar, 1995).

Key File In some CAD/CAM systems, a file containing the codes defining the operation of certain keyboard functions or menu commands. In DBMS, a file containing information about search paths or indexes used to access data.

Key Species In order of priority, generally a small number of species identified as species of conservation importance and might include endangered, endemic, rare or threatened species of plants and animals (Sawarkar, 1995).

Keyboard The device used for typing information into the computer.

Keyboard Entry A method of entering small volumes of data at the computer keyboard.

Keystone Species 1. Animals or plants which by virtue of their presence or absence, alter the structure of a community. 2. A species that increases or decreases the diversity of a system. These species are competitively superior species. They are the species without which an ecosystem would collapse or change to a different state, performing different ecological functions or ecological services. A change in the ecological functions of a system may affect the ecological stability of surrounding areas. An example of a keystone species is the elephant. It is responsible for creating paths through forests, which are essential for many of the other animals living in forests. This concept can be used to assign priority to the protection of species and habitats (Barbier, 1993).

Kheddah A stockade or an enclosure, usually constructed with the use of stout round logs, with an entrance gate, into which wild elephants are driven for the purpose of capture. The gate is dropped down after the entry of elephants. *See* pit method for capturing elephants.

Kill An animal or bird shot during hunting. Collectively the animals or birds shot in a hunt, during a season or in a particular period.

Kill-Ratio The proportion or per cent of the game population which can be killed yearly without diminishing subsequent crops. The ratio or the yield to the population.

Kingfisher Any of numerous non-passerine birds of family Alcedinidae. They are usually crested and bright-coloured, with a short tail, stout sharp bill, and weak syndactyl feet. Birds found in India are: BLACK CAPPED KINGFISHER (*Halcyon pileata*): Found along the coast-line of India, south of Bombay. BROWN-HEADED STORK-BILLED KINGFISHER (*Ramphalcyon capensis*): Practically found throughout India except the arid zone. COMMON KINGFISHER (*Alcedo atthis*): Found throughout India. PIED KINGFISHER (*Ceryle rudis*): Found throughout India. Above 750 m in the Himalayas, Ceryle, lugubris replaces this. WHITE-BREASTED KINGFISHER (*Halcyon smyrnensis*): Found in plains and lower hills throughout India.

Kite Any of various hawks of the family Accipitridae with long, narrow, pointed wings, a deeply forked tail, a weak bill, and feet adapted for taking such prey as insects and reptiles. They are noted for graceful sustained flight. BRAHMINY KITE (*Haliastur indus*): This is a bright chestnut bird of prey with black wing tips and white head and breast found near water. It is a resident bird throughout India including the Himalayas up to 1800 m, avoiding only deserts and thick forests. It is locally migratory. It derives its name from its traditional association with Vishnu, the god in the Hindu Trinity. It resembles the ordinary Pariah kite in flight and habits but differs from it ins always found frequenting in the neighbourhood of water. PARIAH KITE (*Milvus migrans*): It is one of the most familiar birds of India. It is a large brown bird, soaring high in flight and scavenging about every bazar and house. The forked tails identifies it at once. It is found throughout India, including the Himalayas up to 2400 m. Though mainly resident, it is locally migratory. It is a fearless scavenger.

Knot A portion of a branch embedded in the wood by the natural growth of the trees. The knot is "loose" or "tight" depending on whether the branch was dead or living at the time it was embedded.

Knowledge Management Knowledge management encompasses identifying and mapping intellectual assets within the organisation, generating new knowledge through analysis and synthesis of competitive advantage within the organisation, making vast amounts of corporate information accessible, sharing best practices and technology that enables all the above. (Silva Term Multilingual Terminology Database, IUFRO.)

Krait A highly venomous nocturnal snake of the genus Bungarus native to Asia. It frequents cultivated lands and human dwellings, feeding on other snakes. The krait found in India is *Bungarus coeruleus*.

Kriging Name for a suite of interpolation techniques that use regionalized variable theory to incorporate information about the stochastic aspects of spatial variation when estimating interpolation weights.

Krummholz The shrubby, multi-stemmed form assumed by trees near tree line.

K-Selection Selection of life-history traits that promote an ability to make a large proportionate contribution to a population which stays close to its carrying capacity.

Kumri *See* cultivation, shifting; taungya.

Kyoto Protocol (1997) The Kyoto Protocol, 1997 was a landmark convention in the history of world. This made the role of the forests prominent in mitigating global climatic change. The deliberation at the fourth conference of the Parties in Buenos Aires, Argentina in November 1998 laid emphasis on forests. The Kyoto Protocol establishes legally binding commitments for reduced emissions of greenhouse gases from industrialised countries and permits the use of limited activities in the land use and forest sector to meet these commitments. The protocol provides to industrialised countries incentives to invest, in their own as well as in other countries, in forestry activities which increase carbon sequestration and/or reduce carbon emissions. The FCCC recognised that countries had 'common but differentiated responsibilities'. The Convention decided that industrialised countries, with larger historical and current 'Greenhouse Gasses (CHGs)' emissions, would be the first to reduce GHG emissions and allow developing countries to promote industrialisation. Under the resulting Kyoto Protocol, industrialised countries agreed to reduce their emission in the 2008-2012 period by 5.2 per cent compared to 1990 level. Though many details of the Kyoto Protocol remain to be clarified, the treaty if ratified should offer possibilities for many rich countries to arrange investment in forestry. Till 2002, 84 countries have already signed it but it is not yet in force. *See* UNFCCC and climate change.

Ll

Lac Resinous exudation secreted by the lac, insect in the form of incrustation over it and from which shellac is made.

Lac, Insect Tachardia (laccifer) lacca (coccidae), which produces lac as a resinous incrustation on the twigs of certain trees and plants (hosts).

Lactotype A specimen chosen as type of a species if the author of the classification fails to designate a type.

Lacustrine Relating to lakes and standing bodies of water.

Lagoon 1. A small, pond like body of water usually connected to a larger body of water. 2. An area of shallow water separated from the sea by a low bank. 3. A settling pond for treatment of wastewater.

Lake A body of fresh or saline water of considerable size completely surrounded by land.

LAN A Local Area Network (LAN) is a local network of computers, usually within the same building, which may be used, for instance, to connect a fileserver to a number of access terminals. *See* network, local area.

Land Cover Map Map of ground features that can be differentiated on a scene (e.g., urban areas, bare land, pasture, forest areas, etc.).

Land Management It is using a given area of land wisely to the best advantage both economically and ethically. The use aims at conservation of water, protection of soil from erosion, restoration and increase of fertility and productivity.

Land, Marginal Land whose capacity, under a specified form of management and given economic conditions, to produce an income in excess of the costs of such management is doubtful. It is usually with reference to agricultural land.

Land, Submarginal 1. Land, which is incapable of sustaining a certain use or ownership status without economic loss. 2. Land which cannot be profitably used for agriculture subsistence land.

Landing Net Net for lifting fish out of water, used when fish are hooked and played on tackle not strong enough to lift them.

Landsat A series of earth resource scanning satellites launched by the United States of America. Landsat is an orbiting satellite giving regular repeat coverage of the whole of the earth's surface.

Landsat MSS Landsat Multispectral Scanner. Earth observation satellite with 4 bands at 80m spatial resolution.

Landsat TM Landsat Thematic Mapper. Earth observation satellite with seven bands at 30m spatial resolution.

Landscape Management It is managing an area or region by integrating a variety of values associated with land that may be ecological, social, cultural or economic.

Landscape 1. The spatial mosaic of several ecosystems (patches, corridors and matrix) across a defined area. 2. Heterogeneous land area composed of a cluster of interacting ecosystems that is repeated in similar form throughout. 3. The geographical and ecological integrity and resilience of a particular land areas, not mainly its aesthetic qualities. Landscape is not just a geographical concept, but includes human, cultural, and traditional values that are associated with the land. 4. Large ecological units which function as integrated bioregions, containing national parks, sanctuaries, all or some combination of legal and functional categories of forests, village systems, lands under various ownership and landuse categories and wastelands (Holthausen, Sawarkar, Darden, 1991).

Landslide 1. Fall or slide of soil, debris or rock, on or from a steep slope. 2. The sudden sliding of masses of rock soil or other superficial deposits on steep slopes.

Landslip A small landslide.

Langur Any of certain large, slender, long-limbed, long-tailed Asiatic monkeys of the sub-family Colobinae. The entelius *Semnopithecus entellus* (Syn. *Presbytis entellus*) is held sacred by many Hindus and worshipped as Hanuman. Four species are found in India. CAPPED LANGUR (*Trachypithecus pileatus*): This is distinguished by a cap or crown of erect, long, coarse hairs directed backwards from the forehead. It is found in Assam. It is also seen in East Pakistan and Burma. COMMON LANGUR

(*Presbytis entellus* Syn. *Semnopithecus entellus*): Found practically throughout India from the Himalayas to Cape Kanya Kumari, except the western desert regions. Some 14 or fewer races are distinguished. GOLDEN LANGUR (*Presbytis geei*): Found on the banks of the Sankosh river, near Jamduar close to the India-Bhutan border. NILGIRI LANGUR (*Presbytis johni* Syn. *Kasi johni*). Found in the Western Ghats at high elevations.

Laser Line Follower An automatic digitizer that uses a laser beam to follow and digitize lines on a map.

Laser Printer A printer in which the information is written onto light-sensitive drum or material using a laser.

Laterite A soil, horizons indurated with hydrated iron and aluminium oxides, formed in humid tropical climates; generally brickred or yellowish brown in colour and having a cellular structure. Pisolitic laterites consist of fairly small ironstone nodules and are often called "murram". Vesicular laterites have a more uniformly indurated layer penetrated by many channels. The pisolitic type lies over the vesicular.

Laterization The process by which igneous rocks, usually of basic composition, weather in tropical climates under certain conditions of temperature and rainfall leading to the abstraction of silica from the silicates and accumulation of hydrated oxides of iron and aluminium.

Lath, Sowing (Seeding) Device used to secure an even distribution of seed in the drills of a seed bed.

Latitude 1. Angular measurement north and south of the equator. Represented on the globe as parallel lines circling the globe perpendicular to the lines of longitude. 2. Lines of latitude, or parallels, are drawn around the earth parallel to the equator. Positions of latitude are given in degrees north or south of the equator. In contrast, lines of longitude, or meridians, are imaginary lines drawn around the Earth from North Pole to the South Pole. Positions of longitude are given in degrees east or west of the prime meridian, which passes through Greenwich, England.

Latosol A highly coloured tropical soil with no sharp horizons.

Layer 1. A logical separation of mapped information according to theme. Many geographic information systems and CAD/CAM systems allow the user to choose and work on a single layer or any combination of layers at a time. 2. An undetached branch lying on or partially buried in the soil, which strikes root and is capable of independent growth after separation from mother plant. 3. It is a distinct map theme in GIS. Usually a separate GIS file.

Layer, Annual *See* ring, growth.

Layer, to To reproduce, either artificially or naturally, by layer.

Layer-Based Approach An approach to organizing spatial data into thematic map layers, wherein each map layer contains information about a particular subject and is stored as a separate file (or series of files) for ease of management and use.

Leaching The removal of soluble substances, e.g., from soil or timber, by percolation.

Leader The terminal shoot of a tree or plant leading shoot.

Leader, Multiple Forked growth resulting from the development of more than one leader, usually due to injury.

Leaf Area Index (LAI) Summation of all the upper leaf surface areas projected downward to a unit area of ground beneath the canopy. Specific leaf area is the upper surface leaf area per unit leaf weight.

Leaf Mould 1. A loose term for more or less decomposed litter (forest with little or no admixture of mineral soil; sometimes identified with the soil horizons. 2. The decomposition products of leaves other than those of conifers, having the appearance of fine earth.

Leaf Spot A leaf disease characterized by numerous, usually distinct, circular or angular lesion.

Legend 1. The part of a map explaining the meaning of the symbols used to code the depicted geographical elements. 2. The list of classification types that are portrayed on a map. A legend can contain only a subset of the total classes in the overall.

Legislative and Regulatory Measures for Environmental Conservation Preservation, conservation and protection of the environment necessitates stringent legislative and regulatory measures. In India these objectives are supported by a set of legislative and regulatory measures. Some of them are The Water (Prevention and Control of Pollution) Act, 1974, The Air (Prevention and Control of Pollution) Act, 1981, The Environment (Protection) Act, The Indian Forest Act, 1927 (16 of 1927), 1986, The Public Liability Insurance Act, 1991, The National Environment Tribunal Act, 1995, The National Environment Appellate Authority Act, 1997, The Wildlife

Protection Act, 1972 and The Forests (Conservation) Act, 1980. Apart from this, the main legislations relating to protection of animals is The Prevention of Cruelty to Animals Act, 1960. Besides the legislative measures, a National Conservation Strategy and Policy Statement on Environment and Development, 1992, National Forest Policy, 1988, and a Policy Statement on Abatement of Pollution, 1992 have also been enunciated.

Lentic 1. Still water. 2. Organisms living in a swamp, pond, lake or any other standing water.

Leopard or Panther (*Panthera Pardus*) A large, ferocious spotted, nocturnal carnivore, of the cat family, with a long tail. It is found in Africa and South Asia. It is a much smaller animal than the lion or tiger. The coat is greyish or whitish buff with characteristic black spots and rosettes. It lives in scrub jungle and rocky places with bushes and caves for shelter. Its maximum length is 2.25m. Three races are known: *Panthera pardus pernigra; Panthera pardus millardi; Panthera pardus fusca*. The last is the common Indian leopard, found in almost all forests. The race pernigra probably occurs in Kumaon and Garhwal. The races millardi is found in Kashmir at high latitudes. Leopards are hunted for their valuable skins. Types of leopards include: BLACK LEOPARD: Variety found in south India. It is as beautiful as it is rare. It is found in Java and the black colour is due to melanism. CLOUDED LEOPARD (*Neofelis nebulosa macrosceloides*): This is found in the forests of Assam, Sikkim and also Nepal, and Bhutan. It is nocturnal in habit and is rarely seen. The coat has a ground colour of brown or yellowish brown with dark blotches on the sides forming a clouded pattern. It is one of the rare animals of India, threatened with extinction. HUNTING LEOPARD: CHEETAH (*Acinonyx jubatus venaticus*): The general body colour is tawny to pale buff with a black stripe from the eye to the mouth and solid spots on the rest of the body. It loves open country and being an easy target, has been hunted almost to extinction. SNOW LEOPARD: OUNCE (*Panthera uncia* Syn. *Uncia uncia*): This is found in the Himalayas from Kashmir to Sikkim at altitudes of 3500 to 4000 m, near the snow line. It is slightly smaller than the ordinary leopard but with a relatively longer tail. The animal has a ground coat of grey tinged with buff with distinct spots on the head, neck and lower parts. It is valued for its fur and is trapped in pits. It is one of the rare animals of India, threatened with extinction.

Lesion A circumscribed diseased area.

Lichen A composite organism formed from the symbiotic association of a true fungi and an alga.

Life Cycle 1. The various stages or changes in form and functional activity through which an organism passes between successive recurrence of a specified primary stage, such as from fertilized ovum of one generation to the fertilized ovum of the next generation. 2. The period of time between fertilization of the egg and the death of the individual that develops from it.

Life Form 1. A Raunkiaer term for one of his selectively morphological categories, which are based mainly on the position and nature of the resting buds that survive any period(s) unfavourable to growth, e.g. A cold or a dry season. 2. More generally, one of a series of classes based on the characteristic vegetative shape and appearance of a taxon.

Life History A history of the stages or changes through which an organism passes in its development from the egg, spore or other primary stage until its natural death. The continuous history of the activities and duration of each stage in the complete life cycle of a species during one generation or annual series of generations. *See* life cycle.

Life Support Functions The functions performed by some ecological systems, without which human life would not be possible. They include the provision of food and shelter and the maintenance of a habitable atmosphere and climate. The ecological systems that perform these functions are also known as critical natural capital.

Life Table A summary of the age or life stage related to the survivorship of individuals in a population.

Life Zone A biogeographic zone. A term mainly used in North America for zones in which animal and plant life vary according to altitudinal rather than to geographical factors.

Lift, to To loosen and remove a plant from the ground as in transplanting.

Light Electromagnetic radiation ranging from 0.4 to 0.7μm in wavelength that is detectable by the human eye.

Light Demander A species that requires abundant light for its best development. The term indicates increase in photosynthetic activity with increasing light upto full intensity. In tropical moist deciduous forests, *Shorea robusta, Tectona grandis, Adina cordifolia, Terminalia* species are the examples of light demanders. *See* shade-bearer and shade demander.

Light Requirement The amount of light necessary for the satisfactory development of a species tolerance.

Lime Concretion An aggregate cemented by precipitation of $CaCO_3$.

Lime Requirement The quantity of limestone or other specified liming material required to raise the *p*H value of a unit area of an acid soil to any desired value under field conditions.

Limiting Factor 1. The environmental factor that is of predominating importance in restricting the size of a population (e.g. lack of winter browse is a limiting factor for many deer herds). Applied to game management, the factor that outweighs all others in limiting productivity. 2. The environmental influence through which the toleration limit of an organism is first reached, which acts, therefore, as the immediate restriction in one or more of its functions or activities or in its geographic distribution (Hanson, 1962). 3. In an ecosystem, various environmental factors like light, temperature, humidity, wind speed, availability of food, nutrients etc., play an important role in their functioning. They also keep on changing quantitatively as well as qualitatively. These changes affect the well-being and survival of the organism in an ecosystem as they can thrive only if all factors essential for life are available. The essential factors, which become scarce act as limiting factors for the plant's growth and survival. There are two laws, which explain the organism's response to these environmental changes. They are: (1) The law of minimum: This law states that the growth and well-being of an organism is ultimately regulated by that essential resources that is in its lowest supply relative to what is required. The most deficient resource is, therefore, called the limiting factor. (2) The law of tolerance: This law states that for each physical factors in the environment, a minimum and maximum limit exists. This limit is called tolerance limit, beyond which the organism does not thrive or survive. In other words, either too little or too much of any required factor like food, energy, heat, vitamins, minerals, water or oxygen threatens the survival of organisms and even the entire species.

Limits to Growth The title of a book by Meadows *et al.* (1972), which has given its name in turn to the position that economic growth is ultimately constrained by its availability of natural resources. 'Limits to growth' theory takes the view that environmental resources are ultimately finite, as is the residual carrying capacity of the environment. The theory suggests that economic growth cannot be indefinitely sustainable, since there are limits to the availability of environmental resources and the ability of the environment to assimilate waste.

Limnetic The open water region of a body of water, specifically in areas too deep to support rooted aquatic vegetation.

Limnology The scientific study of physical, chemical meteorological and biological conditions in free-waters, especially of ponds and lakes.

Line 1. A one dimensional connection between two points expressed in terms of length. 2. One of the basic geographical primitives, defined by at least two pairs of xy coordinates. 3. Entity type used to represent linear features using an ordered set of (x,y) co-ordinate points or a chain of grid cells. 4. The thread used for angling. It may be of silk, nylon or terylene.

Line Breeding A form of mild inbreeding directed towards keeping the offspring closely related to a highly admired ancestor.

Line of True Scale Line on a map along which distances are not distorted due to the effects of the map projection method used.

Line Out, to To transplant to seedling from seedbed to rows in a nursery.

Line Printer A printer that prints a line of characters at a time.

Line Threading A method of spatial interpolation reliant on estimating isolines through a series of observation carried out on it.

Lineage The record of a data set's origin and all the operations carried out on it.

Line-in-Polygon Overlay The process of overlaying a line map over a polygon map to determine which lines cross which polygons.

Linkage The tendency of some Mendelian factors to remain associated during inheritance.

Linked Display Method of dynamically linking map and non-map output such as charts and data plots such that changes in one are reflected by changes in the other. Such displays are used to aid exploratory data analysis.

Lion A large member of the cat family. It is a powerful tawny carnivore; with tufted tail and (in the male) a mane. The Indian lion is *Panthera leo persica* while the African lion is *Panthera leo leo*. Except for slight differences in appearance they are similar in habits. The Indian lion is now confined to the Gir Forest. Average length from nose to tip of tail is 2.80 m; largest specimen on record 3.23 m. Lions inhabit sandy plains and rocky places with thorny thickets. Now the lion is strictly protected, as it is an animal threatened with extinction, in the Gir National Park in Gujarat.

Lithosequence A sequence of soils whose properties are functionally related to differences in the parent rock as a soil formation factor.

Lithosere Xylem which originates on a rock surface.

Lithosols In a zonal group of soils having an incomplete solum splola or no clearly expressed soil morphology and consisting of a freshly and imperfectly weathered mass of hard rock or hard rock fragments.

Litter The uppermost layer of organic debris (dead vegetable matter) on a forest floor, freshly fallen or only slightly decomposed, and consisting chiefly of leaves but also including bark fragments, twigs, etc. *See* soil, horizons; also humus.

Littoral 1. Growing at or near the seashore. 2. Also applied to a species growing in a littoral forest. 3. The onshore area of body of water, extending from the shore to the limits of rooted aquatic plants.

Loafing Cover A place offering shade in summer, or sun and wind protection in winter, for idling.

Loam A soil composed of sand, silt and clay in such proportions that properties of the soil are not dominated by any one of them.

Loam, Tropical Red A uniform red plastic loam without distinct horizons.

Loamy Includes all sandy loams, clay loams, loam, silt and silt-loam textures. Sometimes subdivided into moderately course textured, medium textured and moderately fine textured groups.

Local Area Network (LAN) A local network of computers, usually within the same building, which may be used, for instance, to connect a fileserver to a number of access terminals. *See* network, local area.

Locality, Factors of The effective biotic, climatic and edaphic conditions of a site. *See* environment.

Location-Allocation Modelling The use of network analysis to allocate the location of resources through the modelling of supply and demand through a network.

Lociation A subdivision of faciation characterized by a specific local abundance and grouping of two or more dominants of the faciation. *See* climax units.

Loess Deposits of wind-blown fine sand, silt or rarely clay.

Log The stem of tree or a length of stem or branch after felling and trimming.

Log Trap A log left to attract insects and facilitate their destruction tree.

Log, Butt The lowest log in the tree, i.e., the one next to the stump.

Log, to 1. To fell and extract timber over a forest tract. 2. To convert felled trees into logs to cross cut. 3. To cut off one or more branches from a tree, i.e. to prune.

Log, Top The uppermost log from the bole of a tree.

Logging Logging means wood harvesting, which includes all operations in harvesting a forest crop, from the stage of planning to harvesting it till the produce reaches market. In other words, it could be taken as a chain of operations starting with marking of trees and ending in delivery of the wood in the market or at the threshold of the industry.

Longitude Lines of longitude, or meridians, are imaginary lines drawn around the Earth from North Pole to the South Pole. Positions of longitude are given in degrees east or west of the prime meridian, which passes through Greenwich, England. In contrast, lines of latitude, or parallels, are drawn around the earth parallel to the equator. Positions of latitude are given in degrees north or south of the equator.

Lookup Table An array of data values that can be quickly accessed by a computer programme to convert data from one form to another.

Look-up Table (LUT) A mathematical formula used to convert one distribution of data to another, most conveniently remembered as a conversion graph.

Lop and Top The branches and top cut from a tree, generally one felled or fallen.

Lotic 1. Flowing water. 2. Living in a brook, stream, or river.

Lynx (*Felis lynx isabellina* Syn. *Felis lynx*) Any of a group of wild cats found throughout the northern hemisphere and characterized by a ruff on each side of the face, long legs, a short tail, long tufted ears, and keen vision. In India it is found in Ladakh (J&K) only and in adjoining Tibet. This is a race of lynx of Northern Europe and Asia with a distinctive sandy grey or isabelline colouring, hence the racial name isabellina.

Mm

Machine Language Instructions coded so that the computer can recognize and execute them.

Macro A text file containing a series of frequently used operations that can be executed by a single command. Can also refer to a simple high-level programming language with which the user can manipulate the commands in a GIS.

Macronutrients Chemical elements (not including carbon, hydrogen, or oxygen).

Maggot Legless larva, usually of diptera, found in decomposing organic matter.

Magic Sites They are micro sites found in riparian zones. They appear as an independent unit within macro habitat of riparian zone. Such sites have adequate moistures and deep soil. Vegetation in such magic sites is completely different from the general composition and structure of the surrounding forests. They are extremely significant from the point of varied ecological activities. They have rich biodiversity. Over the years, such sites are receiving tremendous pressure on account of increasing anthropogenic activities around them.

Magnetic Media Tape or disks coated with a magnetic surface used for storing electronic data.

Mahseer (Mahi) (*Barbus Mosal*) A large Indian fresh water food and sport fish, of family Cyprinidae.

Maiden Young seedling plant in a coppice crop.

Mainframe A large computer supporting many users.

Mallard (*Anas Platyrhynchos*) A common and widely distributed wild duck which is the source of the domestic ducks. It breeds in great numbers in Kashmir. It is found in winter in Punjab and Uttar Pradesh and part of Madhya Pradesh and Maharashtra.

Mammal An animal belonging to the highest class of vertebrata (*Mammalia*) comprising man and all other animals that nourish their young with milk, that have mammary glands, a brain, a muscular diaphragm separating heart and lungs from the abdominal cavity, and that reproduce viviparously. Most mammals live on land but some are found in the sea (such as whales, sea lions, walruses, and dugongs).

Man and the Biosphere Programme Programme established by UNESCO, which aims to encourage the rational use and conservation of resources in the biosphere. Under this programme, 357 biosphere reserves have been established around the world. *See* biosphere.

Management The term connotes the wise and skilful use of resources, such as land, manpower, forest, wildlife, etc., after a careful survey, planning, organization and coordination. *See* scientific forest management.

Managed Forest /Other Wooded Land Forest and other wooded land that is managed in accordance with a formal or an informal plan applied regularly over a sufficiently long period (five years or more) (FAO, 2001). 2. All categories of forests excluding protected area managed for multiple use (Thomas, 1979).

Management, Ecosystem Resource management systems designed to produce essential commodities and other values to meet human needs and desires, and to maintain or enhance soil productivity, gene conservation, biodiversity, landscape patterns, and the array of ecological processes common to healthy ecosystems.

Management, Indicator Species Managing indicator species under category as follows: endangered, threatened, endemic or rare species on national listing; species with special habitat needs that might be influenced by management; a species whose population changes are believed to indicate effects of management or resource use pressures on other species of a major biological community, habitat structure, composition or condition, or water quality (Hoover and Wills, 1984). *See* indicator species and indicator plant.

Management Plan, Functions of Wildlife It is now accepted as a basic principle of protected area management, that every protected area should have a management plan (Makinnon *et. al.*, 1986). The management plan guides and controls the management of protected area resources, the uses of the area and development of facilities needed to support that management and use. It facilitates all development activities and all management actions in an area. It has the following functions: (1) It reveals the resource status; (2) It reveals the trends of resource use; (3) It lays bare the objectives of resource management; (4) It expresses the problems and constraints; (5) It provides an array of management options; (6) It helps in evolving the optimal strategy; and (7) It helps in monitoring the resource use and accomplishment of objectives.

Management Plan, Objectives of Goals and objectives are central to the management plan. They constitute the framework for determining what action to take when they will be taken and the budget and personnel required for implementing it. A management plan is a valuable tool for assessing the resource strength, identifying management needs, setting objectives and priorities and organising resources to achieve the goal. The management plan helps the manager to allocate and make best use of resources available at hand. The plan can also be used to assess the requirement of financial resources. A management plan can also serve as a communication tool to gain understanding and support from both the public and relevant government agencies. Such two-way communication helps in gaining the co-operation of local communities and the political goodwill. The planning process initiated helps the management personnel to comprehend the full spectrum of management needs. This ultimately provides a rational base for administration and implementation.

Management Plan, Wildlife The tradition of managing forest with a working plan or management plan dates back to about 150 years. The need for systematically prepared management plans that provided for management and development of protected areas in accordance with an appropriate range of conservation objectives, is a clause of the Bali Action Plan of the World Park Congress held in 1982. The development of guidelines and a manual for the preparation of wildlife management plan forms a major recommendation of the National Wildlife Action Plan 1983. A management plan institutionalises the management approach, thus ensuring realisation of national policies and objectives and obviating whims and fancies of individuals. Management plans ensure continuity of policy and objectives in the field of forest resource and wildlife management. At present, there are three kinds of management plans that exist in the forest department: (1) An exclusive Wildlife Management Plan for a National Park; (2) A Wildlife Management Plan concurrently with a forest-working plan, both relating to the same area; and (3) A Wildlife Management Plan for a wildlife sanctuary that incorporates with wildlife and forest management objectives.

Management, Game The art of producing sustained annual crops of wild game for recreational purposes.

Management, Method of The organized application of any particular silviculture procedure and regulation of fellings in order to attain the objects of management in a forest.

Management, Objects of The purposes for which it is proposed to manage a forest. *See* management plan, objectives of; objectives of management.

Management, Plantation Plantation management is about maximizing the benefits and minimizing the negative externalities. It encompasses planning, implementation and control of plantation. Plantations are normally assiduously planned and designed to complement the management of neighbouring natural forests. Besides, it is also ensured that such plantations are integrated with other land uses in order to conserve native flora and fauna, to maintain ecological sustainability and to maximize social benefits, while providing a productive resource base. Plantation management covers all aspects pertaining to plantation, its harvesting, and managing local biodiversity and use. Generally, it encompasses aspects such as: (a) Plantation planning, (b) Species selection, (c) Soil and site management, (d) Planting and maintenance, (e) Crop management, and (f) Pest and disease management.

Management, Range The scientific management of range land for the continuous production of forage and livestock, as consistent with use of land for other purposes.

Management, Sustained Yield Management of a forest to give equal annual or periodic returns in perpetuity.

Management, Watershed The administration and regulation of the watershed. *See* watershed.

Management, Wildlife The conservation and control of wildlife in accordance with scientific principles and national policy laid out.

Mango (plural **mangoes or mangos**) It is is a tropical fruit of the mango tree. Mangoes belong to the genus *Mangifera* which consists of about 30 species of tropical fruiting trees in the flowering plant family Anacardiaceae. The exact origins of the mango are unknown, but most believe that it is native to Southern and Southeast Asia owing to the wide range of genetic diversity in the region and fossil records dating back 25 to 30 million years. Mangoes retain a special significance in the culture of South Asia where they have been cultivated since time immemorial. Reference to mangoes as the "food of the gods" can be found in the Hindu Vedas and the leaves are ritually used for floral decorations at Hindu marriages and religious ceremonies. Mango trees (*Mangifera indica*) are large, reaching 35-40 m in height, with a crown radius of 10 m. The leaves are evergreen, alternate, simple, 15-35 cm long and 6-16 cm broad; when the leaves are young they are orange-pink, rapidly changing to a dark glossy red, then dark green as they mature. The flowers are produced in terminal panicles 10-40 cm long; each flower is small and white with five petals 5-10 mm long, with a mild sweet odour suggestive of lily of the valley. After the flowers finish, the fruit takes from three to six months to ripen. The mango fruit is a drupe; when mature, it hangs from the tree on long stems. They are variable in size, from 10-25 cm long and 7-12 cm diameter, and may weigh up to 2.5 kg. The ripe fruit is variably coloured yellow, orange and red, reddest on the side facing the sun and yellow where shaded; green usually indicates that the fruit is not yet ripe but this depends on the cultivar. When ripe, the unpeeled fruit gives off a distinctive resinous slightly sweet smell. In the centre of the fruit is a single flat, oblong seed (as big as a large stone) that can be fibrous or hairless on the surface, depending on cultivar. Inside the shell, which is 1-2 mm thick, is a paper-thin lining covering a single seed, 4-7 cm long, 3-4 cm wide, 1 cm thick.

Mangrove Conservation Programme Government of India has launched Mangrove Conservation Programme in 1987 and, has so far, identified 35 mangrove areas for intensive conservation and management in the country. These mangrove areas are identified on the recommendation of National Committee on Mangroves and Coral Reefs on the basis of their unique ecosystems, biodiversity etc. 100 per cent central assistance is given under Management Action Plans (MAPs) for undertaking activities like raising mangrove plantations, protection, catchment area treatment, siltation, control, pollution abatement, biodiversity conservation, sustainable resource utilization, survey and demarcation, education and awareness, etc. This is further supplemented by research and developmental activities which can give scientific inputs for smooth execution of Management Action Plans.

Mangrove Swamp A swampy or tidal area dominated by tropical trees or shrubs.

Mangroves Mangroves plants are that survive high salinity, tidal extremes, strong wind velocity, high temperature and muddy anaerobic soil — a combination of conditions hostile for other plants. Mangroves are successfully adapted in colonizing saline intertidal zone at the interface between the land and sea along the deltas, shallow lagoons, mud flats, bays and backwaters in tropical and subtropical sheltered coast lines. Mangroves not only protect the coastal communities from the fury of cyclones and coastal storms, but also promote sustainable fisheries and prevent sea erosion. In addition, they provide medicine and fuelwood. They also serve as the home of a wide range of flora and fauna including crocodiles and tigers. The Orissa Super-cyclone of 1999 and the life saving role of mangrove forests became very apparent because areas adjoining mangrove forests either withstood the fury of the cyclones or suffered far less damage than other areas. This generated awareness among local communities of the importance of mangrove forests, and encouraged them to raise mangrove nurseries and plant saplings in degraded areas. In spite of all such gifts they confer, many mangrove ecosystems have been cleared for aquaculture ponds and other alternative uses. Still others have been unsustainably exploited, leading to their degradation. Of late, the fragile mangrove ecosystems have been subjected to various anthropogenic and biotic pressures resulting in habitat destruction, loss of bio diversity, affecting avifauna and their migration paths. Unsustainable aquaculture, siltation, weed infestation, uncontrolled discharge of waste-water, industrial effluents, surface run-off, encroachment around these water bodies, etc. is resulting in shrinkage of their area. Obviously, effective measures are needed to save the mangrove ecosystems. However, a lot of good work has been done in this regard. Recognizing the importance of mangrove ecosystem, the number of mangrove areas in India has since grown from 15 to 35. The mangroves in India comprise 69 species under 42 genera and 28 families. India is home to some of the best mangroves in the world. The Government of India has established a National Mangrove Genetic Resources Centre in Orissa. Two mangrove species are endemic to India. One species is *Rhizophora annamalayana,* occurring in Pichavaram, Tamil Nadu. Another species is *Heritiera kanikensis* that exists only in Bhitarkanika of Orissa and Sunderbans of West Bengal. Both have been included in the World List of Biosphere Reserves by UNESCO. They represent the largest stretch of mangroves in the country.

Manhattan Distance The method used to calculate distance between cells in a raster data layer by counting the distance along the sides of the raster cells.

Mantle The unconsolidated organic and inorganic materials, together with more highly disintegrated bedrock, found on land surfaces as the result of geological weathering.

Manual Digitizing The process of digitizing maps and aerial photographs using a table digitizer.

Map 1. A reproduction of some portion of the earth's surface. 2. A representation of whole or part of earth's surface in miniature. 3. A conventional delineation of the earth's surface or a portion there of, on a flat sheet. 4. A reduced facsimile of the features on earth's surface. 5. A hand-drawn or printed document describing the spatial distribution of geographical features in terms of a recognizable and agreed symbolism. 6. Graphic representation of the physical features (natural, artificial, or both) of a part or the whole of the Earth's surface, by means of signs and symbols or photographic imagery, at an established scale, on a specified projection, and with the means of orientation indicated.

Map Algebra A method of combining raster data layers. Mathematical operations are performed on individual cell values from two or more input raster data layers to produce an output value.

Map Overlay The process of combining the data from two or more maps to generate a new data set or a new map. This is a fundamental capability of GIS.

Map Projection 1. The basic system of co-ordinates used to describe the spatial distribution of elements in a GIS. 2. A systematic drawing of lines on a plane surface to represent the parallels or latitude and the meridians or longitude of the Earth. 3. A mathematical and/or geometric method used to transfer the spherical surface of the earth onto a flat surface such as a map. Many different map projections exist, each with its own advantages and disadvantages.

Map, Base Map on which information may be placed for purposes of comparison or geographical correlation. The term "base map" was at one time applied to a class of maps now known as outline maps. It may be applied to topographic maps, also termed "mother maps" that are used in the construction of other types of maps by the addition of particular data.

Map, Cadastral Map showing the boundaries of subdivisions of land, often with the bearings and lengths thereof and the areas of individual tracts, for purposes of describing and recording ownership. It may also show culture, drainage, and other features relating to land use and value.

Map Characteristics A map should have the characteristics such as: (1) All objects on the map are in the same relative position as on the ground; (2) All angles between the lines drawn on the map are equal to the angles between corresponding lines drawn on the ground; and (3) The map covers much larger area and is drawn on a much smaller scale wherein detailed features cannot be represented.

Map, Choropleth Thematic map in which areas are coloured, shaded, dotted, or hatched to create darker or lighter areas in proportion to the density of distribution of the theme subject.

Map, Control 1. One of a set of maps, usually of 1: 15,000 scale (4 inch to one mile scale) maintained for illustrating the actual progress of forest operations under different heads for the purpose of comparison with corresponding prescriptions made in a working plan. 2. Sometimes used to refer to fire maps and similar maps illustrating the incidence of various forest offences, diseases and pests. It is a control record. The purpose of preparing such maps is to show progress of various forest operations/exercises. Various forestry operations are recorded by different colour wash and legends. Control maps are necessary for monitoring and evaluating forest works. When such maps are enclosed with control forms, they provide a full picture of past operations.

Map Digitization Conversion of map data from graphic to digital form.

Map, Isopleth Map consisting of lines connecting places of equal value of distribution for a given theme such as rainfall or temperature.

Map, Management A map prepared, normally as part of a working plan, to show the division of the forest area into management units, the layout of roads, annual treatment coupes, etc. These maps are generally in the scale of 1:50,000. Such maps are prepared by working plan officers in the last leg of their planning exercise. A good management map is always prepared on the basis of topographical maps produced by the Survey of India. This, in addition to topographical features, shows features like working circles, felling series and annual coup boundaries. Each working circle is given a distinct colour wash to make it conspicuous. However, other features like proposed plantation sites, nursery and other relevant activities can also be shown on the map.

Map, Planimetric Map that presents only the horizontal positions for features represented. It is distinguished from a topographic map by the omission of relief in measurable form. The features usually shown on a planimetric map include rivers, lakes, and seas; mountains, valleys, and plains; forests, and prairies; cities, farms transportation routes, and public utility facilities; and political and private boundary lines. A planimetric map intended for special use may present only those features essential to the purpose to be served.

Map, Projection Orderly system of lines on a plane representing a corresponding system of imaginary lines on an adopted terrestrial or celestial datum surface. Also, the mathematical concept for such a system. For maps of the Earth, a projection consists of a graticule of lines representing parallels of latitude and meridians of longitude or a grid.

Map, Regeneration A map in which the distribution, frequency and size of regeneration of the desired species is shown.

Map, Site A map showing the site where the forestry operation is being carried out. It is large scale map showing topographical, forest stock and management features.

Map, Slope or Clinometric Map Map showing the degree of steepness of the Earth's surface by the use of various colours or shading for critical ranges of slope.

Map, Soil Map that shows the constitution, structure, and texture of the soil and identifies ongoing erosion. Soil map shows different kinds of soils and their extent on the landscape. Each delineated units in the soil map provides information on physiographic, soil characteristics and classification reflecting their potentialities and problems. The National Bureau of Soil Survey and Land Use Planning (NBSS&LUP), Nagpur prepared soil resource map of different states on 1:2,50,000 scale, using a 3-tier approach, that is (1) image processing, (2) field surveys and laboratory analysis, and (3) cartography and printing. The soil map was printed on 1:5,00,000 scale, without generalizing. The basic mapped units are at the level of soil family associations with dominant phases. These maps can be used for broad forest planning.

Map, Topographical Topographical maps are those which show such features like river, roads, village, and contours of the terrain. Such topographic maps are produced by the Survey of India, the pioneer and apex surveying and mapping institute in India on a common scale. The country has been divided into 4* × 4* sheets on 1:10,00,000 scale (numbered 45, 46, 47, etc.). These one million scale sheets are further subdivided into 16 equal sheets (numbered from A to P) on a scale of 1:250,000. These degree sheets are further subdivided into 16 equal sheets (Numbered from 1 to 16) on a scale of 1:50,000 with a 15* extent. Again, for some areas, such 1:50,000-scale map is divided into four 1:25,000 sheets of 7.5*. They are numbered as NE, NW, SE and SW. Topographic maps are available at Survey of India office at Dehradun and at sales branches of the institute in various cities. Map constructions or preparation is a highly skilled work. The scale or "representative fraction" of a map compares the apparent distance between two selected points on the map and the true distance between those points on the ground. Here, both the distances are expressed in the same unit of measurement. Sometimes, confusion arises about the references to "small" or "large" scale maps. As we knew, scale is defined as the ratio of the distance on the map to the distance on the ground (earth). The distance on the map is generally taken as unity or one.

Suppose we have two sets of map. One is stock map which is in the scale of 1:15,000 and the second one is topographic map which is in the scale of 1:50,000; since 1/15000 is a larger fraction than 1/50,000, it follows that 1:15000 stock map is a larger scale map than the topographical sheet drawn at 1:50,000.

Map, Stock A map showing the distribution of the different forest or stand types which have a bearing on management, with information about type of forests, crop composition, density, age of crop, site quality, distribution of dominant species and regeneration status. These maps are generally prepared in the scale of 1:15,000. The working plan office prepares stock maps after having completed the stock mapping exercise. For preparing this map, the topographical maps of the Survey of India having scale of 1:50,000 are taken as base maps and these base maps are enlarged to 1:15,000 scale maps. On these enlarged maps, forest attributes are portrayed during the stock mapping. *See* management map, site map, and type map.

Map, Suitability A plantation map showing areas suitable for different species.

Map, Thematic 1. Map designed to provide information on a single topic, such as geology, forest, rainfall, population. 2. Thematic forest maps are generally on 1:50,000 scale, showing forest types, major species composition, crown density and other land uses prepared by interpretation of satellite imageries, aerial photographs duly verified by ground truthing.

Map, Topographic Map that present the horizontal and vertical positions of the features represented; distinguished from a planimetric map by the addition of relief in measurable form.

Map, Type A map showing the boundaries of various types, e.g., soil or vegetation.

Map, Volume Volume map is a map showing mean volume of growing stock spatially. This sort of map is used for timber planning and management. The scale used is 1:50,000.

Mapping, Participatory Participatory mapping is a tool of Participatory Rural Appraisal (PRA) technique. It comprises spatial drawing of any one area. This is drawn generally on a piece of paper to show and explain locality, physical attributes and events. The objective is to use the mapping for further in-depth probing of any issues. Maps prepared under this exercise generally shows households, farms, water bodies, forest, road and institutions. Sometimes events like literacy and epidemic incidences are shown on the map. Maps can also be prepared on the basis of separate themes like deforestation, environmental degradations, crop failure and epidemic incidences etc. Participatory maps are generally drawn by key informants in the presence of other participants who help and qualify the mapping exercise. An intensive discussion among the participants, in the course of mapping, helps in adding new information and eliminating errors and omissions.

Mapping Unit A set of areas drawn on a map to represent a well-defined feature or set of features. Mapping units are described by the map legend.

Maps, Indicative Indicative maps are those topographic maps, which shows the rough positions of different forest blocks and compartments on the map. The scale of the map is generally 1:2,50,000. The objective of the map is to show the location of different compartments, other features and working circle areas on a broader perspective.

Maps, Vegetative or Vegetation A kind of map showing the distribution of vegetation in the forest and non-forest area of a state or country. In other words, the map shows the tree and forest resources indicating their distribution in the landscape.The purpose is to draw attention to the extent of vegetation on a miniscule map. It is used to compare the land use pattern of any two regions. The map follows the standard rules of drawing it by the method of representation of physiognomy with the help of definite patterns and the climatic analogies by colours. Colours play an important role in the system of vegetation mapping. Generally, white indicates the practice of agriculture and green and yellow colour represents natural vegetation. Blue colour indicates water bodies.

Maquis Scrub vegetation, generally rather dense, composed of much branched, thorny and often aromatic shrubs, found in the Mediterranean region.

Marginal Land Land which lies on the margin of productivity, i.e. one which due to unfavourable topography, climate, etc. will yield a harvest of products, which, when marketed at existing price levels, will barely cover the cost of cultivation.

Mark, Property A specific mark indicating ownership impressed on timber by means of a marking hammer. The property mark is valid if it is registered under the provisions of the Indian Forest Act or any other Acts.

Mark, to (Timber) To impress a mark on timber or wood usually by means of a marking hammer. Timbers or logs are marked in the depot before sale. *See* mark, property. *See* also marking.

Market Failure Market failures result from the failure of market prices to reflect the full value to society of a commodity. For example, most of the economic values of ecological resources and services are not reflected by markets, therefore, their increasing relative scarcity is not readily captured by price signals. *See* government failure; institutional failure.

Market-Based Instruments (MBIs) An approach to environmental policy, which modifies the market signals received by producers and consumers in order to induce more environmentally friendly behaviour. Examples of MBIs are pollution charges, subsidy for pollution abatement, marketable permits, product charges and full-cost resource pricing.

Markhor (*Capra falconeri*) Also known as **Markhoor.** This is a species of wild goat found in the valleys of Kashmir up to the snow line. It is an inhabitant of dense pine and birch forests whose grassy blades form their grazing ground. It usually lives in herds and under varying conditions. It is also found in Afghanistan.

Marking Selection of trees to be cut or retained in a felling or thinning, the selected trees being indicated by a mark made with a scribe, or with a chisel or marking hammer on a blaze. Marking of selection trees is done mostly in one year advance.

Marking Hammer An implement employed for impressing on timber, standing or felled, a mark denoting number, treatment or ownership.

Marl A calcareous material composed principally of carbonate derived from photosynthetic activity of algae and mollusk shells. It is light grey in colour. Calcareous clay used as a dressing to improve soils, particularly through the addition of clay of light soils.

Marsh 1. A water-saturated, poorly drained wetland area, periodically or permanently inundated to a depth of up to 2 m (6.6 feet) that supports an extensive cover of emergent, non-woody vegetation, essentially without peat-like accumulations. 2. A tract characterized by a predominately inorganic soil, supporting low vegetation, characteristically monocotyledons, less acid and less continuously wet than a bog — often only intermittently inundated.

Mass Storage System Auxiliary, large-capacity memory for storing large amounts of data. Usually optical or magnetic disk or tape.

Mast The fruit of trees, such as oak, beech or other species of fagaceae, which is of value for feeding livestock. A 'mast year' is one in which the fruit of any such species is abundant.

Mast Tree Trees yielding nuts or acorns (such as oak, beech, chestnut, etc.) suitable for feeding animals. They provide abundant food supplies for wildlife. About 10 trees per hectare are desirable.

Master Plan 1. An official document adopted by any authority or local government or landowner setting forth its general policies regarding the long-term physical development of a city or other area. Such plans are broad enough to include all aspects of a development or redevelopment programme as distinguished from sporadic, isolated, or piecemeal planning. The process of designing futures not only of three dimensional accomplishments in space but also social mechanisms such as laws, regulations, policies, and forms of organization. 2. It is a comprehensive plan typically includes: (1) A land plan map showing the location of all owned land, the inter-relationship between all of the uses proposed on such land, the circulation system required to serve the uses existing or proposed and the relationship between ownership within a reasonable area of influence; (2) Land use policies related to the resources management, conservation and disposal of public lands; (3) Land use policies related to the activities and the regulations as they affect portions of the land; (4) Implementation schedules which establish priorities for programmes in management, mapping, engineering, and public works; and (5) A Programme for co-ordinating land use, intensity, and activity programmes with central/federal, state, regional, other local agencies as well as with private applicants. Increasing emphasis is being laid on social, economic, and esthetic topics, moving plans beyond physical and land use documents.

Mathematical Model A model that uses one or more of a range of techniques, including deterministic, stochastic and optimization methods.

Matric System Decimal system of weights and measures based on the metre as a unit length and the kilogram as a unit mass.

Maturity 1.The stage at which a tree is capable of reproducing itself by seed and has attained its full height. 2. The stage at which a tree of a crop has attained exploitable size or age. *See* maturity, economic or financial.

Maturity, Economic or Financial The age at which a tree or stand will no longer increase in value fast enough to earn a satisfactory rate of interest.

Maximum Likelihood A method embodying probability theory for fitting a mathematical model to a set of data. It is used in image interpretation.

Mean The average, or most likely value.

Mean, Arithmetic The result of adding together a set of values and dividing by the number of values, due regard being paid to sign this is sometimes distinguished as the algebraic mean, the arithmetic mean then taking all the signs as positive.

Mean, Geometric A central value of a series obtained by extracting the n root from the product of n values. Employed chiefly for averaging ratios. Always less than the mean, arithmetic.

Mean, Harmonic A central value obtained by taking the reciprocal of the mean, arithmetic of the reciprocals of two quantities. Employed chiefly for averaging rates, such as price or time rates. Always less than the geometric mean.

Mean, Population or True The mean arithmetic value of a variable for all members of a population.

Mean, Sample or True The mean arithmetic value of a variable in a sample or in the plots of a particular experiment.

Mean, Weighted A form of a mean intended to take account of the different precisions in the observations (or other values) to be averaged. Each value is included a number of times in proportion to its supposed precision weighted average.

Measure, True The cubic contents of round timber assessed by multiplying the length by sectional area commonly taken at mid-length, or as the mean of two ends. *See* solid volume; true volume; solid content; cubic content.

Mechanistic A system that can be characterized exactly by the laws of physics and chemistry. *See* stochastic deterministic.

Median It is value of variate which lies mid-way when the variates are arranged in order of magnitude.

Meiosis The two consecutive nuclear (reduction) divisions that halve the chromosome number, e.g., from diploid to haploid. *See* mitosis.

Melanin Black Dark-brown or yellowish pigment, colouring many animals.

Melanism Abnormal development of dark pigmentation in the skin, hair, feathers etc.

Menagerie A place where animals are kept and trained, especially for exhibitions. In particular, a collection of wild or foreign animals in cages or enclosures, as in a circus.

Mendelian Inheritance That controlled by pairs of gene whose members are, in sexually reproducing organisms, derived respectively from the two parents. These genes do not contaminate one another, and have a low mutation rate, and exhibit segregation according to the laws of Mendel.

Menu A list of available options displayed on the computer screen and from that list the user can choose by using the key board or a device such as mouse.

Merchantable 1.The portions of a tree or crop, which can be marketed under given economic conditions. 2. A commercial size or grade of logs, timber or other forest products. *See* bole, commercial.

Meridian Great circle on the surface of the Earth passing through the geographical poles and any given point on the Earth's surface. All points on a given meridian have the same longitude.

Mesic Site Environmental situations characterised by moderate to moderately high moist conditions due to the presence of springs or attributable to edaphic character. It excludes riparian systems (Thomas, 1979).

Mesic 1. Applied to a habitat that is neither dry nor wet. 2. Of sites or habitats characterized by intermediate moisture conditions, i.e. neither decidedly wet nor decidedly dry.

Mesophile Of organisms inhabiting sites which are decidedly neither wet nor dry.

Mesophyte A plant whose normal habitat is neither very wet nor very dry. A plant whose normal habitat is neither very wet nor very dry is called mesophytic.

Mesotrophic 1. Habitats of moderate nutrient capacity. 2. A water body or wetland with productivity intermediate between oligotrophic and eutrophic.

Metadata Information about the provenance, resolution, availability, age, ownership, price, copyright, and other matters concerning digital spatial data that is easily available to users.

Metalimnion The water layer of a stratified lake between the epilimnion and the hypolimnion characterized by a steep thermal gradient.

Metamorphic Rock Rocks derived from pre-existing rocks by mineralogical, chemical and structural alterations due to geologic processes originating within the earth. Igneous and sedimentary rocks may be changed to metamorphic rock or one metamorphic rock may be changed into another metamorphic rock.

Metapopulation A sub-population of a species linked to other sub-populations by more or less restricted migration.

Method Du Controle A method of forest management based on intensive inventories of growing stock and increment, applied mainly to irregular forest, with the object of maintaining or reaching maximum productive capacity.

MHz A million cycles per second.

Micro Planning Micro planning is a more detailed planning exercise. They are specific to particular villages. A micro plan is written in a plain, simple, straightforward style and readily understood by people who have no technical training. These are written in the local language, as far as possible. The descriptions are kept as brief as possible (to keep the document handy). With the adoption of sustainable development as the goal of present developmental planning, the relevance of micro planning has increased manifold. It is now an established fact that, before undertaking any planning for sustainable development of natural resources, the socio-economic and environmental systems have to be studied and assessed in the backdrop of local variations. Such a study can be conducted only with the participation of people. Based on such participatory method of study, a micro plan for development would be developed.

Micro Plans Micro plans are plans or a blueprint specific to a village or a group of villages. It is always a detailed plan. *See* micro planning.

Microbial Ecology The ecology of microorganisms, especially their roles in nutrient cycling, decomposition, and tree growth. *See* ecology.

Microclimate 1. The climate of small areas which for some reason differs significantly from the general climate of the area; more particularly the climate under a plant or other cover, differing in extremes of temperature, moisture, etc., from the climate outside that cover eco climate. 2. Generally, the climate of small areas, especially in so far as this differs significantly from the general climate of the region. 3. More particularly, the climate under a plant or other cover, differing in extremes of temperature and moisture from the climate outside that cover.

Microhabitat The specific combination of habitat elements in the locations selected by organisms for specific purposes and/or events. Expresses the more specific and functional aspects of habitat and cover. Separated from adjoining microhabitats by distinctive physical characteristics.

Microhabitat Element Small components of a habitat which by themselves seem insignificant but provide critical life history requirement of one or several species, and /or support ecological functions, e.g. snags, caves, etc. (Sawarkar, 1995). *See* special habitat and unique habitat.

Microrelief Small-scale differences in relief, including mounds, swales, or pits that are a few feet across and have differences in elevation up to about 6 feet.

Migration (Animal) The movement of animals, birds and fishes from one habitat or region to another, generally in large numbers, and especially done periodically. When applied to mammals, birds, fishes, etc. the term denotes migration or habitual or occasional movement from one region or climate to another. Migration is influenced by climate, food and such other factors. *See* Migratory.

Migration (Plant) Refers to the mass movements of plants from one place to another. It begins when the germule (spore, seed, fruit, offshoot or plant) leaves the parent area and ends when it reaches the final resting place.

Migration, Altitudinal Migration involving different elevations in a mountain country.

Migration, Anadromous Of fish, which ascend rivers from the sea at certain seasons for breeding. In salmon migration, the young go to saltwater for development and back to fresh-water for breeding.

Migration, Catadromous Of fish, living in fresh-water and going to the sea for breeding. Eels migrate to saltwater for breeding and back to fresh-water for maturing.

Migration, Diurnal Migration during the day. Most water fowls are diurnal migrants.

Migration, Nocturnal Migration during night. Small birds are mostly nocturnal migrants.

Milliacre An area of 1/1000th acre (usually 1/10th chain-6.6 feet or 2.01 metres, square) milliacre.

Mineral Soil A soil whose properties are dominated by the mineral matter, usually containing less than 20 per cent organic matter, or with only thin surface of organic layer.

Mineralization The conversion of an element that is immobilized in some organic combination or available form as a result of microbial decomposition.

Minerotrophic A wetland receiving water and minerals from surrounding physiographic regions, not just from precipitation.

Minicomputer A medium-sized, general-purpose single processor computer often used to control GIS (*see* workstation).

Minimal Area The smallest area that displays the characteristic features of a plant community. In European ecology, often the smallest area on which the species of a plant community are adequately represented, i.e., much smaller in extent than in the general definition above.

Ministry of Environment and Forests (MoEF) The Ministry of Environment and Forests working under Government of India is primarily concerned with the implementation of policies and programmes relating to conservation of the country's natural resources including lakes and rivers, its biodiversity, forests and wildlife, ensuring the welfare of animals and prevention and abatement of pollution. While implementing these policies and programmes, the Ministry is guided by the principle of sustainable development and enhancement of human well-being. The Ministry also serves as the nodal agency in the country for the United Nations Environment Programme (UNEP), South Asia Co-operative Environment Programme (SACEP), International Centre for Integrated Mountain Development (ICIMOD) and for the follow-up of the United Nations Conference on Environment and Development

(UNCED). The Ministry is also entrusted with the issues relating to multilateral bodies such as the Commission on Sustainable Development (CSD), Global Environment Facility (GEF) and of regional bodies like Economic and Social Council for Asia and Pacific (ESCAP) and South Asian Association for Regional Co-operation (SAARC) on matters pertaining to environment. The broad objectives of the Ministry are: (1) Conservation and survey of flora, fauna, forests and wildlife; (2) Prevention and control of pollution; (3) Afforestation and regeneration of degraded areas; (4) Protection of the environment, and (5) Ensuring the welfare of animals. These objectives are sought to be fulfilled by the Ministry primarily through: environmental impact assessment, eco-regeneration, assistance to organisations implementing environmental and forestry programmes, assistance to organisations including animal welfare programmes, promotion of environmental and forestry research, extension, education and training, dissemination of environmental information, international cooperation, and creation of environmental awareness among all sectors of the country's population.

Mire Slimy soil or deep mud. Also used for swampy ground, bogs or marshes.

Mitigation 1. Action taken to alleviate potential adverse effects on wetlands and fish habitat undergoing modification. 2. Also commonly used to mean compensation for damage done. In this usage, in-kind mitigation is replacement of a lost resource with one similar (stream for stream or species for species), while out-of-kind is replacement of one kind with another (lake for stream or one species for another).

Mitosis Vegetative nuclear division. The chromosome number of the daughter nuclei remaining the same as that of the parent meiosis.

MMU Minimum Mapping Unit. The smallest area (usually a polygon) mapped.

Mobility The tendency of the individual animal to change location during the day or so between seasons or years.

Mode That value of variable that occurs most frequently. *See* mean, arithmetic; median.

Model 1. A representation of attributes of features of the earth's surface in a digital database. 2. A set of algorithms written in computer code that describe a given physical process or natural phenomenon of the earth's surface. 3. A function fitted to an experimental variogram derived from sample data. 4. A statistical distribution or a con-capitalization of spatial variation.

Modem (Modulator-Demodulator) A device for the inter-conversion of digital and analogue signals to allow data transmission over telephone lines.

Modifiable Areal Unit Problem (MAUP) A problem arising from the imposition of artificial units of spatial reporting on continuous geographic phenomena resulting in the generation of artificial spatial patterns.

Module A separate and distinct piece of hardware or software that can be connected with other modules to form a system.

MOEF *See* Ministry of Environment and Forests.

Moisture Content The weight of water present in wood or other material, usually expressed as a percentage of the oven-dry weight.

Moisture Equivalent The weight of water, expressed as a percentage of the oven-dry weight that remains in a previously saturated soil after the moisture in it was reduced after centrifuging in a standard apparatus at a force 1000 times that of gravity.

Mongoose Archaic form Mungoose. This is an agile, keen-sighted, slender, ferret like, viverrine, flesh-eating mammal of India. It has a sharp stout and a long heavy tail. It captures and feeds on snakes, including the most venomous ones and on rodents. It can be domesticated. Species found in India are: COMMON MONGOOSE (*Herpestes edwardsi*): A tawny yellowish grey mongoose with a grizzled "pepper and salt" tinge. Three races are known: (i) Nyula of North and Central Indian; (ii) Ferrugineous, a desert form, and (iii) The typical edwardsi found in South India. CRAB-EATING MONGOOSE (*Herpestes urva*): Found in Assam, eastwards to Burma, South China and Malaya. It is an expert swimmer, and catches crabs, fishes, frogs, etc. in hill streams. SMALL INDIAN MONGOOSE (*Herpestes javanicus*): Found in North India from Kashmir eastwards to Assam and Orissa. It is only about 50 cm in length and lives in holes burrowed by itself. STRIPE-NECKED MONGOOSE (*Herpestes vitticollis*): The black neck stripe reaching backwards from the ear is distinctive. It is found in the Western Ghats from North Kanara southwards and in the adjoining South Indian hills.

Monitor Monitor is a display unit or an output unit of a computer system. The colour display capabilities of a monitor are measured by the number of bits used to represent each dot on the screen. To simplify things, this can be converted into the total number of colours that can be converted into the number of colours that can be reproduced: a 1-bit image is monochrome; 8-bit image supports 256 colours or grayscales; a 12-bit image supports 4096 colours; a 16-bit image has 65536 true colour (24- or 32-bit graphics).

Monitoring Monitoring is a continuous/periodic review undertaken by management, at every level of implementation, of an activity to ensure that input deliveries, work schedules, targeted outputs and other required actions are proceeding according to plan. Another way of defining monitoring is that it is a process of measuring, recording, collecting, processing and communicating information to assist project management decision making. However, precisely, it can be defined as an information system for decision making. A project's operation and performance are the aspects of concerns in monitoring with a view to keep track of the technical or economic "efficiency" of the project. In monitoring, the purpose is to ascertain whether project objectives are achieved or not. Therefore, the exercise of monitoring involves examination of the following points: (1) whether the various tasks are carried out according to schedule; (2) whether project impact is in according with project objectives; (3) whether project objectives/targets/ execution need adjustments; (4) thus monitoring is a management function. It begins with the initiation of the project and ends with the completion of the project.

Monitoring, Forest Monitoring is a part of forest management and is fundamental to the continual improvement aimed for. It is the process of collecting information about how effectively management prescriptions are being implemented, and what effects those prescriptions are having on forest management. It is an essential part of the management process. It helps the manager to ensure that action proposed is taken as per the plan. It also helps ensure that the avowed objectives are met. The results of monitoring provide a feedback into the planning process, which is further improved to provide better service to forest and the society. Therefore, monitoring should be a regular activity of any organization involved in sustainable forest management. The intensity of monitoring which should be carried out by an organization depends upon (1) objectives of management, (2) its size, (3) the criticality and complexity of operations, (4) performance standards, as well as (5) the resources available. Monitoring is carried out in a forest organization at two levels. One is at operational level and the other at strategic level. *Operational monitoring* helps forester or forest manager to identify whether practices are being properly implemented, or where the effects of certain operations are not as expected. It helps to identify successes and failures in forest management practices, to provide a basis for improvement in future management practices, and to identify areas where corrective steps are required. The activities which come under operational monitoring are marking, harvesting, forest road construction, silvicultural operations, plantation etc. Besides, post-harvest assessments also require close operational monitoring. It is because of the fact that harvesting and extraction operations have the greatest potential for environmental damage. Post-harvest assessment may cover the activities such as: (a) implementation of harvesting plan and guidelines, (b) assessing environmental effects of harvesting operations, (c) determination of status of regeneration of species harvested, and (d) assuring effect of harvest on the growth of forest stand. Post-harvest assessments are generally taken on a sampling basis. Different harvesting sites are selected randomly on the basis of a statistical model. This is usually done after one year of harvest operation. This provides to damaged saplings a time to die and upcoming seedling in coppice to come up vigorously. A clear picture of regeneration, therefore, emerges. But such exercise needs a clear method and procedure. The results of the assessment are analyzed and inferences are drawn. Based on such inferences, necessary steps are taken to improve upon the existing system in harvesting operation and silvicultural programmes. *Strategic monitoring* is a long-term process. It needs repeated and continuous observations/measurement of the environmental or social effects of forest management. It provides data about the long-term effects of the forestry operation, so that potential problem can be identified in proper time and resolved forthwith. Strategic monitoring of yields, growth rates and regeneration status is important to ensure sustainable harvest. Strategic monitoring aims at providing information about the results of management, which can be fed back into the management planning process. Before undertaking any such monitoring exercise, decision about parameter of monitoring is essential. Generally, certain key elements as the indicator are focused in monitoring exercise. The subjects that need strategic monitoring are site productivity, soil and water conservation, wildlife population, ecological restoration, and regeneration of forests, social development, impact of harvesting on regeneration. Key areas of strategic monitoring in forest practices include growth and yield monitoring, environmental monitoring, social monitoring and forest cover monitoring. Record prepared in the process of monitoring helps in improving the control system. Therefore, records produced and updated regularly facilitate monitoring and evaluation. Apart from this, monitoring procedures facilitate speedy working. As far as possible, a comprehensive monitoring programme should be drawn for the forest organization. The activities that can be taken for monitoring in a forest organisation are: (a) Timber and NTFPs yields, (b) Growth rates of forest stand, (c) Regeneration status of the forests, (d) Impact of forest management on flora and fauna in the forest, (e) Environmental, social and economic impacts of forest practices, (f) Cost, productivity and efficiency, (g) Effect of management practices on soil and water conservation, (h) Impact of protection measures on illegal activities in forests. *See* monitoring.

Monitoring of Social Impacts of Forest Practices The social impacts of forest management practices should be constantly monitored. This helps the management to assess the progress in the field of social issues. A systemic monitoring system also takes care of the changing social values in the society. Basic monitoring of social impacts by the forest organization itself enables it to know the real position of implementation of forest practices. This helps the forest organisation to identify problems and opportunities for development. Participatory approach to monitoring helps to obtain information about the perception of local community of its impacts. It helps the organisation to review and recast its policies and programmes. In other words, it provides the forest organization an opportunity to learn from its failings and shortcomings, so that necessary improvement can be made in the on-going management practices. Apart from this, monitoring of social issues provides a firm platform for regular face to face contact with different divergent stakeholders. This itself promotes understanding, mutual respect, trust, communication and consultation and collaboration.

Monocarpic Fruiting only once in its life, e.g. annuals.

Monoclimax Theory The hypothesis that in anyone environment there can be only one climax community, in contrast to the hypothesis that there can be several (polyclimax theory).

Monoecious Of flowering plants, having the male or female sexual elements borne separately on the same individual. *See* dioecious.

Montane 1. Relating to mountains. 2. Pertaining to climate, ecosystems, species particular to mountains.

Monte Carlo Simulation A statistical technique used to simulate the effects of random error in data analyses. Random 'noise' is added to the input data and analyses repeatedly to estimate the effects on the output data.

Moor An open, uncultivated tract with a more or less peaty soil supporting low vegetation, typically coarse grasses and sedges, and with sphagnum and cotton "grasses" at higher and wetter elevations; less dry than heath and at its wettest, a bog.

Moorhen A common term for the waterhen and related birds. Bird found in India are: INDIAN MOORHEN (*Gallinuala chloropus*): On land a typical waterhen; and in water like a small duck. Found throughout India up to 1800 metre elevation. PURPLE MOORHEN (*Porphyrio poliocephalus*): A handsome but clumsy purplish blue tail with long red legs. Found throughout the plains of India.

Mopping Up The act of making a fire safe after it has been controlled as by firing small unburned areas between the control line and the edge of a fire removing unburned inflammable materials in the area, extinguishing smoldering fires with earth or water etc. Rarely, if ever, completed until all of the fire has been put out.

Mor 1. A type of humus which is practically unmixed with the mineral soil and usually shows a well defined line of separation from it. Usually more or less matted and compacted, with very high acidity, poor nutrient supplies, very restricted fauna, and absence of earthworms. 2. 'A' horizon: the uppermost horizon of the mineral soil. Essentially a horizon of elevation (washing out.); 'B' horizon: essentially an alluvial horizon enriched with material washed down from a horizon and generally much amore compact; 'C' horizon: the uppermost layer of parent material which is in process of forming true soil under the influence of weathering; 'A/C' horizon: the mid-horizon of recently developed, generally calcareous soils, in which the quantity of unweathered rock increases with depth to merge into unweathered parent material; 'G' (or gley) horizon: this occurs between b and c horizons in soils with imperfect or impeded drainage.

Mortality Death or destruction of forest trees as a result of competition, disease, insect damage, drought, wind, fire and other factors.

Mosaic 1. A group of soils which always occur in association with one another in a manner not dependent on topographical features. 2. An arrangement of plant communities in a mosaic pattern, in contrast to zonation.

Moss To wrap up seedlings with a little earth round the roots, in moss and store them for planting out at later date.

Mould A fine fungal growth, or mildew, that forms on wood in damp stagnant atmosphere. Usually confined to the surface, and is the least harmful type of fungus.

Mould, Sooty A dull blackish coating on leaves or other plant parts, caused by saprophyte fungi that flourish on the excretions ("honey dew") of sucking insect.

Mouse A hand-steered device for entering data or commands to a computer.

MSS Multispectral scanner system that acquires images of four wavelength bands in the visible and reflected IR regions.

Mulch Plant residues and other materials used as a covering for the soil to conserve moisture, reduce run-off and erosion, check weed growth, protect from winter climate or improve the soil. Mulching materials are usually cut grass, foliage or straw, but may include compost, woodchips, saw-dust, paper, sand stones, etc. also to apply such covering to the soil.

Mull A type of humus layer having a loose crumb structure, mixed below with the mineral soil; associated with relatively low acidity, high nutrient supplies and rich soil fauna.

Multi-Criteria Evaluation (MCE) A method of combining several, possibly conflicting, criteria maps to derive suitability maps based on trade-off functions and user-specified criteria preference weights.

Multispectral Sensor (MSS) Device for sensing radian energy in several channels of the electromagnetic spectrum.

Multimedia Digital media presented in multiple forms including text, pictures, sound and video.

Multiple Forest Use A system of resource use where the forest resources in a given land unit serve more than one user.

Multiple Purpose Forest or other wooded land designated to any combination of production of goods, protection of soil and water, conservation of biodiversity and provision of socio-cultural services and where none of these alone can be considered as being significantly more important than the others (FRA, 2005).

Multiple Use The planned utilization of an area for a variety of purposes simultaneously. In forestry multiple use implies management designed to achieve maximum sustained yields of timber and, soil and water conservation, flood prevention, wildlife conservation, recreation and many other ecological services.

Multispectral Classification Process of sorting pixels into distinct classes based on their spectral characteristics in multiple band of electromagnetic wavelengths. Usually involves decision rules and cluster analysis.

Multispectral Refers to use of two or more bands in remote sensing.

Muntjac (Muntjak; Barking Deer) Any of various small-horned deer of South-Eastern Asia and Indonesia, constituting the genus Muntiacus. The animal found in India and Java. *Muntiacus muntjak* has well developed horns on bony pedicels. The male is distinguished by sharp exposed canine teeth and small upright antlers. Two forms are found in India: *Muntiacus muntjak viginalis* in North India, *Muntiacus muntjak aureus* in the south. *See* deer.

Mutation A change in the structure of a unit of heredity, i.e. the inception of a heritable variation.

Mutualism An interaction between the individuals of two or more species in which the growth, growth rate, and/or population size of both are increased in a reciprocally beneficial association.

Mycelium The vegetative portion of a fungus composed of hypha.

Mycorrhiza 1. The phenomenon of the association probably resembles symbiosis or at least virtually non-parasitic, between the root or rhizome of a green plant and a fungus. 2. The structure produced from the combination of the modified rootlet with fungal tissue.

Mynah (Myna or MINA) Any of a group of tropical birds of South Eastern Asia related to the starling and belonging to the genera Acridotheres, Gracula and Sturnus, Indian mynahs are: BANK MYNAH (*Acridotheres ginginianus*): This is found in the greater part of northern India, extending south up to about Bombay. It flocks in open country and human habitations. It is very similar to the common Mynah. It is a resident species, being a local migrant partially. BRAHMINY MYNAH (*Temenuchus pagodarum*): This is grey above and reddish fawn below, with glossy black crown and long recumbent crest and black wing quills. It is found almost throughout India, excepting the most arid and the humid evergreen regions. It is mainly resident but also a partial local migrant. It utters a pleasing little song in the breeding seasons. COMMON MYNAH (*Acridotheres tristis*): A dark brown single-crested bird with white tail tip and wing markings and bright yellow bill and feet. Often destructive to crops like grains, fruits, etc. It can live contentedly in a cage and can talk well. GREYHEADED MYNAH (*Sturnia malabarica*): This is a small trim bird, brownish silvery grey above and rusty brown below, with blackish wing quills. It is found almost throughout India. It is subject to considerable seasonal local migration. It inhabits open thinly-forested country and the neighbourhood of teak plantations and forest cultivation. JANGLE MYNAH (*Aethiopsar fuscus*). A local and patchily distributed species, similar in appearance to the common Mynah. HILL MYNAH (*Gracula religiosa*): It is remarkable for its capacity to mimic human speech. In India, it lives contentedly as a cage bird, being kept as a pet in homes. PIED MYNAH (*Sturnopaster capensis*; Syn. *S. contra*). It is common in North India and Assam.

Nn

Nadir Point on the ground directly in line with the remote sensing system and the centre of the earth.

NASA National Aeronautical and Space Administration. It is a space agency of USA.

National Biodiversity Strategy and Action Plan (NBSAP) The National Biodiversity Strategy and Action Plan (NBSAP), 2002 is an outcome of the widely felt need for a consolidated report on the direction that India should take for conservation, and sustainable and equitable use of biodiversity and biological resources, as also of the country's commitments under the UN Convention on Biological Diversity. It was a project initiative of Ministry of Environment and Forests (MOEF), Government of India funded by the Global Environment Facility through United Nations Development Programme (UNDP). India became a signatory to the Convention on Biological Diversity (CBD) in June 1992. The Convention came into force on December 29, 1993. Article 6 of the CBD requires parties to prepare NBSAP. The NBSAP is to serve as the main instrument for implementation of the CBD at a national level. Article 6b specifically mandates the integration of biodiversity conservation and sustainable use into various sectors. India's NBSAP had been prepared under this mandate.

National Natural Resources Management System (NNRMS) The main objective of National Natural Resource Management System (NNRMS) is utilization of remote sensing technology with conventional methods of monitoring of natural resources such as land, water, forests, minerals, oceans etc. for attaining sustainable development by addressing the following aspects: optimal utilization of the country's natural resources by a proper and systematic inventory of the resource availability, reducing regional imbalances by effective planning and in tune with the developmental efforts, maintain the ecological balance with a view to evolve and implement the environmental guidelines. The potential user agencies for utilizing the outcome/ information generated in the projects sanctioned by the Ministry of Environment and Forestry under NNRMS programme are the Central Government Departments/agencies, and the Ministry of Environment and Forests itself including the various organizations under its administrative control like FSI, ZSI, BSI etc.

National Park An area dedicated by State for all time, to conserve the scenery and natural and historical objects of national significance, to conserve wildlife therein, and to provide for the enjoyment of the same in such manner and by such means as will leave them unimpaired for the enjoyment of future generation, with such modifications as local conditions may demand (Indian Board for Wild Life, 1952). A national park is created under the Indian Wild Life Act, 1972. A "National Park" has come to have a special significance since the creation of the first national park in the world — Yellow Stone National Park in USA in 1872. In general National Park protects some of the outstanding forest and mountain sceneries and the abundance of wildlife of many species. These are administered by the Forest Departments of States. The Indian Board for Wild Life, founded in 1962, serves in a quasi-official advisory capacity. Four Wild Life Sanctuary established in India are of special importance in the survival of rare endangered species. The Gir Forest in Gujarat is the only remaining habitat of the Asiatic Lion (*Panthera leo persica*). The Kaziranga National Park in Assam is the principal remaining habitat of the Great Indian Rhinoceros (*Rhinoceros unicornis*). The Keibul Lamjao National Park is the only habitat of the browantlered deer (*Cervus eldi eldi*) feared to be near extinction. The Kashmir stag (*Cervus elaphus hanglu*) is protected in the Dachigam National Park in J&K. *See* Zoological Park; Park land.

Native Species 1. Indigenous species that is normally found as part of a particular ecosystem. 2. A native species is one which naturally exists at a given location or in particular ecosystem, i.e. it has not been moved there by humans. 3. A species that was present in a defined areas prior to European aggression. The term native species is synonymous with indigenous species.

Natural Analogue Model A model that uses actual events or real world objects as a basis for model construction.

Natural Capital Natural capital consists of a nation's environmental and natural resource reserves. It thus includes the stock of life-supporting systems, biodiversity, and renewable and non-renewable resources, but excludes both human capital and human-made capital. This concept is use full from two counts. Firstly, it highlights the extent to which environmental resources contribute to economic productivity and welfare. Secondly, it emphasises on the implications for the future of the depletion of environmental resources and damage to the environment's capacity to provide valuable services.

Natural Forest A forest composed of indigenous trees, and not classified as a plantation. In other words, natural forest excludes plantations. Natural forests are further classified using the following criteria: forest formation or type (closed or open), degree of human disturbance or modification and species composition (FAO, 2001).

Natural History Formerly the term used to include zoology, botany, geology, mineralogy and other subjects dealing with the animal, vegetation and mineral world. Now applied to a study of these subjects, especially animal and plant life, in a popular, non-technical manner.

Natural Pruning The natural death and shedding of branches on the stem of a tree from such causes as decay, or deficiency of light or water (self-pruning), or snow, ice and wind breakage.

Natural Range The geographical and altitudinal limits within which an organism occurs naturally.

Natural Regeneration *See* regeneration, natural.

Natural Resource 1. All things produced by nature as well as used to sustain or support life. Usually subdivided into two categories such as renewable and non-renewable resources. Renewable resources are resources such as sunlight, air, forest, vegetation cover, water and animals which either renew themselves by reproduction or are continued in supply by natural processes which can be aided or interfered with by man. Non-renewable resources are those resources which do not create or produce themselves. These include minerals, petroleum, gas, coal, etc.

2. Natural resource is a term generally used to indicate certain forms of land, water, and natural resources. It constitutes the physical bases for human life. Environmental resources are parts of nature that humankind considers to be useful or valuable. What is 'nature' can be debated endlessly, but for the sake of present discussion, it is simply the physical environment which includes, mainly air, sea, land, plants and animals. 'Useful' here relates to the production of material benefits, such as food, timber, while 'valuable means' able to produce valued experiences (Holmes Rolrton, 1988:272). He has listed about 14 different types of value associated with nature, ranging from economic and life-supporting value to religious and character-building value. Therefore, environmental resources can be defined as those parts of nature that can provide the goods and services sought by humans — including services such as opportunities for recreation, the appreciation of scenic beauty, or the disposals of wastes (Mather, A.S. *et. al.*, 1995). Natural resources can be grouped under three categories on the basis of their functions they form in the society. These three major groups of natural resources are: (a) The first group consists of raw materials and energy sources used by humans, usually as inputs into the economic system. These have been traditionally termed as natural resources. Use of such resources as raw material leads to production of goods and services. Examples of such resources are mineral ores, oil, coal, etc. (b) The second group comprises parts of the environment that can provide services rather than material goods. The examples of such resources are recreation and wildlife tourism. (c) The third group of natural resources provides the essential life support system for humans, including oxygen to breath and water to drink as well as material goods such as food and timber. It provides the sump or sink in which the wastes products generated from the human activities are assimilated. These three classes of natural resources may also be arranged vertically from higher to lower on the basis of their degree of expendability. The different classes of natural resources are: (a) Inexhaustible resources, e.g. solar energy; (b) Cyclic resources, e.g. water in the hydrological cycle; (c) Renewable resources, e.g. natural vegetation, and (d) Non-renewable resources, e.g. fossil fuels.

Natural Resources, Categories Natural resources can be grouped under three categories on the basis of their functions they form in the society. These three major categories of environmental resources are: (1) The first group consists of raw materials and energy sources used by humans, usually as inputs into the economic system. These have been traditionally termed as natural resources. Use of such resources as raw material leads to production of goods and services. Examples of such resources like mineral ores, oil, coal, etc. (2) The second group comprises parts of the environment that can provide services rather than material goods. The examples of such resources are recreation and wildlife tourism. (3) The third group of natural resources provides the essential life support system for humans, including oxygen to breath and water to drink as well as material goods such as food, timber. It provides the sump in which the wastes products generated from the human activities are assimilated.

Natural Science The systematic knowledge of nature and the physical world including zoology, botany, chemistry, physics, geology etc. distinguished from mental or moral science, abstract mathematics, etc.

Natural Selection In evolution the process by which the individuals (of a species) with characteristics that help them to become adapted to their specific environment tend to survive (Survival of the fittest) and transmit their characteristics while those less able to become adapted tend to die out, so that in the course of generations there is a progressive tendency in the species to a greater degree of adaptation.

Natural/Semi-Natural Areas Areas dominated by native or naturalized vegetation that has not been cultivated or treated with any annual management or manipulation regime. In cases where it cannot be assessed whether the vegetation was planted or cultivated by humans, the vegetation is considered "natural/ semi-natural."

Naturalized 1. Alien or exotic species that have become successfully established in an area. 2. A species is called naturalized when a species which is not native to a certain area, grows, reproduces and maintains itself.

Nature Reserves Particular tracks of land or pieces of landscape placed under strict protection from human interference. Such a protection preserves all plant species in the local community. *See* preserve.

Navigable 1. Generally, waters used by humans for transportation. 2. Legally, interstate waters; intrastate lakes, rivers and streams which are utilized by interstate travelers for recreational or other purposes. *See* navigation.

Navigation The science and technology of finding the position, course and distance travelled by a ship, plane or other craft. Traditional methods include the magnetic compass and sextants. Today the gyrocompass is usually used, together with highly sophisticated electronic methods. Satellite navigation uses satellites that broadcast time and position.

Navigation, Biological The ability of animals or insects to navigate. Although many animals can navigate by following established routes or known landmarks, many animals can navigate without such aids.

Nayan Great Tibetan Sheep (*Ovis Amon Hodgsoni*) This is the largest of all wild sheep, standing about 1.2 mt at the shoulder. It is horns are about 1 mt long. It is long in the leg, graceful and light, and suggests an antelope in build. It is found in North Ladakh and on the plateau of Tibet, but in quest of grazing it occasionally crosses into Spiti, Kumaon and North Sikkim.

Near Infrared (NIR) The shorter wavelength range of the infrared region of the Electro-Magnetic (EM) spectrum, from 0.7 to 2.5 μm. It is often divided into very-near infrared (VNIR) covering the range accessible to photographic emulsions (0.7 to 1.0 μm), and the Short-Wavelength Infra Red (SWIR) covering the remainder of the NIR atmospheric window from 1.0 to 2.5 μm.

Necrosis Death of plant cells, usually resulting in a darkening of the tissue.

Needle Cast Premature dropping of the needles in coniferous trees, frequently associated with attack by certain fungi, but also caused by physical agencies.

Neem (*Azadirachta indica, Syn. Melia azadirachta* L.) It is a tree under the family Meliaceae. It is one of two species in the genus ***Azadirachta*** and is native to Burma, India and Pakistan, growing in tropical and semi-tropical regions. Neem is a fast growing tree that can reach a height of 15-20 m, rarely to 35-40 m. It is evergreen but under severe drought it may shed most or nearly all of its leaves. The branches are wide spread. The fairly dense crown is roundish or oval and may reach the diameter of 15-20 m in old, free-standing specimens. The trunk is relatively short, straight and may reach a diameter of 1.2 m. The bark is hard, fissured or scaly, and whitish-grey to reddish-brown. The sapwood is greyish-white and the heartwood reddish when first exposed to the air becoming reddish-brown after exposure. The root system consists of a strong taproot and well developed lateral roots. The alternate, pinnate leaves are 20-40 cm long, with 20-31 medium to dark green leaflets about 3-8 cm long. The terminal leaflet is often missing. The petioles are short. Very young leaves are reddish to purplish in colour. The shape of mature leaflets is more or less asymmetric and their margins are dentate with the exception of the base of their basiscopal half, which is normally very strongly reduced and cuneate.The flowers (white and fragrant) are arranged axillary, normally more-or-less drooping panicles which are up to 25 cm long. The inflorescences, which branch up to the third degree, bear 150-250 flowers. An individual flower is 5-6 mm long and 8-11 mm wide. Protandrous, bisexual flowers and male flowers exist on the same individual (polygamous).The fruit is a glabrous olive-like drupe which varies in shape from elongate oval to nearly roundish, and when ripe are 1.4-2.8 × 1.0-1.5 cm. The fruit skin (exocarp) is thin and the bitter-sweet pulp (mesocarp) is yellowish-white and very fibrous. The mesocarp is 0.3-0.5 cm thick. The white, hard inner shell (endocarp) of the fruit encloses one, rarely two or three, elongated seeds (kernels) having a brown seed coat. The neem tree is noted for its drought resistance. Normally it thrives in areas with sub-arid to sub-humid conditions, with an annual rainfall between 400 and 1200 mm. It can grow in regions with an annual rainfall below 400 mm, but in such cases it depends largely on the ground water levels. Neem can grow in many different types of soil, but it thrives best on well drained deep and sandy soils (*p*H 6.2-7.0). It is a typical tropical/subtropical tree and exists at annual mean temperatures between 21-32°C. It can tolerate high to very high temperatures. It does not tolerate temperature below 4°C (leaf shedding and death may ensue).The active principles of the plant were provisionally named as nimbin, nimbinin, and nimbidin respectively. In India, the tree is variously known as "Divine Tree","Heal All","Nature's Drugstore", "Village Pharmacy" and "Panacea for all diseases". Products made from *neem* have proven medicinal properties as antihelmintic, antifungal, antidiabetic, antibacterial, antiviral and anti-infertility. Neem twigs are used for brushing teeth in India, Bangladesh and Pakistan. This practice is perhaps one of the earliest and most effective forms of dental care. All parts of the tree (seeds, leaves, flowers and bark) are used for preparing many different medical preparations. Neem oil is used for preparing cosmetics (soap, shampoo, balms and creams). Besides its use in traditional Indian medicine the neem tree is of great importance for its anti-desertification properties and possibly as a good carbon dioxide sink. Neem oil is useful for skin care such as acne, and keeping skin elasticity. Practitioners of traditional Indian medicine recommend that patients suffering from Chicken Pox sleep on neem leaves. Neem is a source of environment-friendly biopesticides. Among the isolated neem constituents, liminoids (such as Azadirachtin) are effective in insect growth-regulating activity. The unique feature of neem products is that they do not directly kill the pests, but alter the life-processing behaviour in such a manner that the insect can no longer feed, breed or undergo metamorphosis. Neem flowers are very popular for their use in Ugadi Pachadi (soup like pickle) which is made on Ugadi day in South India. Neem is also used in parts of mainland Southeast Asia, particularly in Cambodia, Laos and Vietnam.

Nested Sampling The measurements of data at a series of points whose locations are hierarchically structured.

Net Present Value (NPV) It is discounting of a stream of net benefits over time. It is an integral part of cost-benefit analysis.

Net Primary Production 1. Gross primary production minus biomass used in respiration by primary producers. 2. The amount of food in an ecosystem available for primary consumers.

Network 1. A special type of line entity used to represent interconnected lines that allow for the flow of objects (for example, traffic) or information (for example, telephone, calls). 2. Two or more interconnected computers used to facilitate the transfer of information. 3. Two or more interconnected computer systems for the implementation of specific functions. 4. Network database structure is a method of arranging data in a database so that links or pointers of a many-to-many type define explicit connections and relations. 5. A set of interconnected lines or arcs. 6. A network in computer system is the means by which computers share and exchange information and resources across either short distances (Local Area Network) or globally (Wide Area Network). Making the best use of network technology is about making better use of resources, enhancing productivity and efficiency, reducing costs and gaining competitive advantage. Network enables anyone in an organisation to communicate with and share resources with everyone else – giving them access to data held in individual PCs, by remote office sites and external suppliers and giving users the ability to share printers, fax and modern technology etc. *See* Network, Local Area and Network, Wide Area.

Network, Local Area (LAN) Local Area Network is a group of computers located relatively close to one another and connected through cabling system to enable them to share access to computing resources. LAN satisfies two fundamental requirements: sharing information and sharing computer resources. LAN consists of workstations, which are connected to a central computer called file server. Workstations are the nodal computers on which users do their work like executing their own application programme locally and sending request to the file servers for any of the network functions and receiving the response from the file server.

Network, Wide Area (WAN) When computers are spread over a larger geographical area, like inter-state, intercity, intracity, across building, etc. and still they are connected to one another in order to share information, the configuration is called Wide Area Network. WANs are extensions of LANs. Two LANs are connected by telephone lines and modems. A router and network operating system is required to establish the connections.

Neural Networks Classification system that looks forming a pattern and order in complex multivariate data sets. A key component of Artificial Intelligence (AI) techniques.

Neutralism The lack of interaction between two organisms (or species) and the phenomenon neither has any effect on the other.

Niche 1. A habitable position or the ultimate unit of the habitat, i.e., the specific place occupied by an individual organism. 2. By extension, the more or less specialized relationships existing between an organism, individual and its environment. 3. The specific set of environmental/habitat conditions that permit the full development and completion of the life cycle of an organism. 4. The place occupied by a species in relation to other species. The ecological niche of a species is the functional role of the species in a community; the fundamental niche is the totality of environmental variables and functional roles to which a species is adapted; the realized niche is the niche, which a species normally occupies.

Niche Environment The unique environment used to sustain the existence of an organism or species. *See* niche.

Nidifugous Of birds, which hatch in an advanced state of development and leave the nest almost immediately, e.g. fowl.

Nilgai Nilghai (*Boselaphus tragocamelus*). This is a large bluish-grey antelope of India. Both sexes have dark manes. The bulls have a distinctive tuft of stiff black hairs on the throat, and possess stout cone-like horns. The animal is found in India from the base of the Himalayas southwards to Mysore. It is absent in Bengal, Assam and the Malabar Coast. It avoids dense forests. The male is coloured bluish grey; the hornless female is tawny. The Nilgai is held sacred by the Hindus on account of its fancied kinship to the cow.

Nitrification The process by which nitrites and nitrates are formed in the soil by the action of certain aerobic bacteria from ammonium salts which are derived by the action of certain other aerobic and anaerobic microorganism on decaying vegetable residue. *See* denitrification.

Nitrogen Cycle The sequences of transformation undergone by nitrogen wherein it is used by one organism, later liberated upon the death and decomposition of the organism and is converted by biological means to its original state of oxidation to be re-used by another organism.

Nitrogen Fixation The conversion of elemental nitrogen to organic combinations, or to forms readily utilizable in biological processes, by nitrogen-fixing micro organism. When brought about by bacteria in the root nodules of leguminous plants it is spoken of as symbiotic; if by free-living micro-organisms acting independently, it is referred to as non-symbiotic-fixation.

Node 1. The point at which arcs (lines, chains, strings in a polygon network) are joined. Nodes carry information about the topology of the polygons. It is the point entity that represents the start or end point of a line or its intersection with another line. 2. Topological connection point between two or more arcs, within the GIS vector model.

Noise 1. Random or repetitive events that obscure or interfere with the desired information. 2. Irregular variations or error, usually short range that cannot be easily explained or associated with major mapped features or process in GIS and image interpretation.

Non-Marketed Goods Non-marketed goods are often environmental goods such as ecosystems and biodiversity. They are goods which do not have a market price, due to their position outside the market system. Ecosystem and biodiversity are two examples of resources which have no market price. The valuation of non-marketed goods is a major aspect of environmental economics. The main techniques of non-market valuation include the Contingent Valuation Method (CVM), the Travel-Cost Method (TCM) and hedonic pricing (Hanley *et al.*, 1997).

Non-Migratory That which does not migrate, or is resident.

Non-Native *See* exotic species.

Non-Porous Woods Those that do not contain vessels or pores. Applies to all conifers and a few broad leaved tree species.

Non-Removable Storage Computer data storage which cannot be moved easily and includes hard disks.

Non-Tariff Barrier An economic, political, administrative or legal impediment to trade other than a duty, tax or import quota.

Non-Use Values Values that individuals derive from natural resources without using them either directly or indirectly. This term is usually used synonymously with existence values. Sometimes a bequest value is also added to non-use values while computing.

Non-Vegetated A class with less than 1 per cent vegetation cover naturally or from which vegetation is removed and replaced by man-made surfaces or structures.

Non-Wood Forest Products (NWFPs) Non-wood forest products consist of goods of biological origin other than wood, derived from forests, other wooded land and trees outside forests. This working definition was adopted by FAO based on the recommendation of an interdepartmental meeting on definitions on NWFPs held in June 1999. According to the aforesaid definition, the three components of the term 'non-wood forest products' are interpreted as follows: (1) NON-WOOD. The term NWFP excludes all woody raw materials. Consequently, timber, chips, charcoal and fuelwood, as well as small woods such as tools, household equipment and carvings, are excluded. Non-Timber Forest Products (NTFPs), in contrast, generally include fuelwood and small woods; this is the main difference between NWFP and NTFPs. (2) FOREST: NWFPs should be derived from forests and similar land uses. FAO has elaborated definitions of 'forest' and 'other wooded land' in a working paper on terms and definitions for the Forest Resources Assessment 2000. Since plantations are included in the FAO definition of forest, NWFPs that are obtained from plantations, such as gum arabic (*Acacia Senegal*) or rubber (*Hevea brasiliensis*), are thus included in the definition of NWFPs. Many NWFPs are derived from both natural forests and plantations. The final definition of 'trees outside forests' is still in the process of elaboration. (3) PRODUCTS: In the proposed definition, the term 'product' corresponds to goods that are tangible and physical objects of biological origin such as plants, animals and their products. Forest services (e.g. ecotourism, grazing, bioprospecting) and forest benefits (e.g. soil conservation, soil fertility, watershed protection) are excluded. Services and benefits are even more difficult to assess and quantify than NWFPs and have therefore already been excluded from most publications dealing with NWFPs. A clear definition of forest service and benefits is still lacking (FAO, 2005).

Normal Forest A forest which for a given site or given objects of management, is constituted as regards growing stock, age-class distribution and increment and from which the annual or periodic removal or produce equal to the increment can be continued indefinitely without endangering future yields. It serves, as a standard with which to compare an actual forest so as to bring out latter's a deficiency for sustained yield management. It can be considered as one in which (a) trees of all sizes, classes or crops of all age-classes are present in correct proportion, to permit continued removal of an equal number of exploitable stems without affecting future yields, (b) each tree crop is putting on normal increment, and (c) no silviculture or other obstacles exist to the continuance of felling of exploitable stems.

Normal Growing Stock When age gradations or age classes are arranged normally and put on normal increment, then the forest is said to contain a normal growing stock. For the continued existence of forests, it is essential that in the annual or periodic felling, nothing but the annual or periodic increment of that forest is removed. If removal is in excess of increment, the forest will disappear sooner or later; if cut is less than the increment, the accumulation of timber will lead to congestion among the stems and rate of growth on the increment will fall. Therefore, if a forest is to be maintained at its maximum production, it must be in a state in which it can produce maximum increment. *See* normal forests.

Normal Kill The kill sustained by the most productive unit of the range of population.

Normal Population Age gradations should be in such proportion that as and when each age reaches maturity, the same quantity of produce should be available for felling. Occupation of equal area by each age is not essential. Rather, age gradations or age classes must occupy areas where yield will equal the same relative percentage of total yield of forest for the entire rotation. Thus theoretically, each of the age gradations must occupy in series of areas having equal productiveness. Such a proportion between various age gradations is known as normal proportion. *See* normal forest.

Normalcy Normalcy in a forest context, is an ideal state of perfection in all parts. In its simplest form, normalcy means an even distribution of stems of each age by area. In a natural forest, crop composition and its growth are the function of site quality and production is the function of site quality and age. The productivity of a given site is the element of management, which determines the species and their distribution in the crop. Thus for a given site, given distribution of age classes and given objects of management, there will be a normal forest which will be an ideal and ultimate forest with above reference. With the change of any of the above parameters the normal forest will change, and therefore, the concept of normalcy is not an absolute. It is more a dynamic concept. Thus, for a set of variables, as mentioned above, a normal forest is an ideal state of forest condition which serves as standard for comparison with an actual forest stand, so that the deficiency of the latter are brought out for the purpose of sustained yield management. From such a forest, annual and periodic yields equal to the increment, can be realized indefinitely, without endangering future yields and productivity of the site. There are four parameters of a given normal forest, which are: (1) Site quality, (2) Age classes, (3) Number of stems per hectare, and (4) Crop composition, i.e. number of species and their distribution. *See* normal growing stock.

Normalization Methods that are used to reduce redundancy and improve efficiency in a database.

Numerical Taxonomy Quantitative methods for classifying data using computed estimates of similarity.

Nursery An area where plants are raised for eventual planting out. Such nurseries have ordinarily both seedling and transplant beds. Nurseries are either permanent or temporary.

Nursery Stock Stock grown in a nursery for planting out; also plants supplied from a nursery.

Nursery, Bed A prepared area in a nursery where seed is sown, or into which transplant or cutting are put.

Nursery, Dry A nursery that is maintained without any irrigation or other artificial watering.

Nursery, Field A term sometimes used for a temporary nursery formed in or adjoining the planting areas. *See* nursery, temporary.

Nursery, Seedling A nursery in which seedlings only are raised, no transplanting being done.

Nursery, Temporary A term sometimes used for a temporary nursery formed in or adjoining the planting areas. Such type of nursery is generally established to reduce the cost of transportation on planting stock.

Nursery, Transplant A nursery into which seedlings are transplanted in preparation for planting stock. Transplanting technology provides rapid and robust growth to the planting stock.

Nursery, Wet A nursery that is maintained by irrigation or other artificial watering during the dry periods.

Nutrient Cycle The exchange of elements between the living and non-living components of an ecosystem.

Nutrient Cycling The transformation of chemical elements from inorganic form in the environment to organic form in living organisms, then back to inorganic form. This includes the exchange of elements between and among the biotic and abiotic components.

NWFP *See* Non-Wood Forest Products.

NWFPs Resource Management It is the management of NWFPs resources on the principles of sustainability. It basically includes: (1) Carrying out assessment studies and yield studies to specify sustainable harvest levels for important NWFP species, (2) Develop appropriate propagation, cultivation and harvesting techniques, particularly for aromatic and medicinal plants, and (3) Carrying out ecological and environmental studies to assess the impact of NWFP extraction on ecosystems.

Nymph A mobile immature stage of insects with incomplete metamorphosis.

Oo

Oak The term **oak** is used as part of the common name of any of several hundred species of trees and shrubs in the genus *Quercus* (from Latin "oak tree"). The genus is native to the northern hemisphere, and includes deciduous and evergreen species extending from cold latitudes to tropical Asia and the Americas. Oaks have spirally arranged leaves, with a lobed margin in many species; some have serrated leaves or entire leaves with a smooth margin. The flowers are catkins, produced in spring. The fruit is a nut called an acorn, borne in a cup-like structure known as a cupule; each acorn contains one seed (rarely two or three) and takes 6-18 months to mature, depending on species. Oaks are hardwood trees. Oak wood has a density of about 0.75 g/cm^3, great strength and hardness, and is very resistant to insect and fungal attack because of its high tannin content. Oak wood was used in Europe for the construction of ships until the 19th century, and was the principal timber used in the construction of European timber-framed buildings. Today oakwood is still commonly used in furniture making and flooring, and for veneer production. Barrels in which red wines, sherry and spirits such as Scotch whisky and Bourbon whiskey are aged and made from European and American oak. Japanese oak is used in the making of professional drums.

Objective of Silviculture. The objectives of silviculture are: (a) Enhancement of productivity of the forest ecosystem (b) Control of stand structure and process, (c) Control of composition, (d) Control of stand, (e) Increase of density, (f) Restocking of un-stocked or under-stocked or unproductive areas, (g) Protection of stand, (h) Control of rotational length,

(i) Facilitating of harvesting, and (j) Conservation of site quality and habitat.

Objectives of Management The principal objectives of Forest Management in India are guided by the National Forest Policy, 1988. These include the maintenance of environmental stability, conserving the nations' natural heritage by preserving remaining natural forests, preventing soil erosion and denudation of catchment areas, minimizing pressures on existing forests, and initiating participatory approach to forest management to achieve these aims. The policy stipulates that economic benefits of forestry are subordinate to environment and social objectives, although the provision of basic forest product needs for marginalised people is primary objective. A target has been set for one-third of the total land area of the country to be under forest, with a target of two-thirds in hilly and mountainous regions. Achieving this goal requires mobilisation of a major reforestation programme planned to establish around three million hectares of plantations annually, on scrub areas, available wastelands and marginal lands and on farm lands under social forestry pursuing suitable agroforestry systems. This target also includes planting to rehabilitate degraded natural forest areas. Forest management necessitates establishing corridors to link protected areas too.

Object-Oriented Approach Approach to organizing spatial data as discrete objects in a single map space.

Object-Oriented Database Structure The organization of data within a database defined by a series of predefined objects and their properties and behavioural characteristics.

Obligate Species Species-habitat relationship on account of which a species is almost completely dependent on a specific successional stage, community structure or composition for its existence (Thomas, 1979).

Obligate A species that is limited in its habitat to few environmental conditions. Usually this term is used in reference to a species occurrence in a wetland or upland habitat. If the species is very likely (> 99 per cent frequency) to be found in a wetland, it would be called an obligate wetland species. If the species is very likely (> 99 per cent frequency) to be found in an upland, it would be called an obligate upland species. This term can also be used for the frequency of an organism in a certain habitat or with other organisms.

Occlusion The healing over or closing of wounds in plants whether of natural or artificial origin.

Old Growth Forest 1. A forest relatively old and relatively undisturbed. 2. A forest dominated by mature or over-mature trees that has not been significantly influenced by human activity. The stand may contain trees of different ages and various species of vegetation.

Old Growth A stand that is past full maturity and showing decadence; the last stage in forest succession (Thomas, 1979).

Oleoresin A natural combination of resinous substances and essential oils occurring or exuding from certain plants.

Oligotrophic Habitats low in basic nutrients, usually characterized by a low accumulation of dissolved nutrient salts, supporting only a limited plant and animal life, and having a high oxygen content owing to the low organic content.

Ombrotrophic A wetland receiving hydrologic and mineral input only from precipitation.

Omnivore Animal that feeds on both plant and animal food. *See* carnivore and herbivore.

Omnivory 1. The process of animals eating both plants and other animals. 2. Feeding on prey from more than one trophic level.

Open Access A resource is said to be open access when it is not excludable, i.e. when access to the resource cannot be restricted to a limited group of people. The best-known example is forests. Because distinct property rights over forest are not in place. Unlimited access means that such resources may suffer from overexploitation and the so-called 'tragedy of the commons'.

Open Forest 1. Formations with discontinuous trees layer but with a coverage of at least 10 per cent and less than 40 per cent. Generally there is a continuous grass layer allowing grazing and spreading of fires (FAO-FRA- Terms & Definitions). 2. Open when the density of the forest is under 0.5. *See* crop density.

Open-Water Birds Fowls preferring the sea, wide estuaries etc. to more confined waters.

Operating System (OS) The control programme that co-ordinates or oversees all the operations of the computer such as Central Processing Unit (CPU), memory, keyboard, floppy drive, CD drive, Visual Display Unit (VDU), etc. In other words, operating system typically manages the following: multi-tasking, input and output, files, memory, networks, security, and system administration. The operating system is responsible primarily for managing the files in the disk and the communication between the computers and its peripherals. When the power is switched on to the computer, the operating system is first loaded, i.e., before user programme is entered and this process is called booting. All operating system have in-built commands and small programmes residing on the disk, which when run, behave like commands. The popular OS are Windows 95, 98, 2000, ME. XP and Linax.

Opportunity Cost The opportunity of an activity that uses scarce resources is the value of the next most economically productive use to which those resources could have been put. The concept of opportunity cost is widely used in economics in identifying the most efficient use of scare resources. If costs do not include opportunity costs of the resources used, and an activity's benefits outweighs the costs, then this indicates that an activity is financially viable. If the costs include opportunity costs and activity's benefits outweigh its costs, then this indicates that as well as being financially viable the activity is economically efficient. If an activity's benefits do not outweigh its costs, including the opportunity costs, this indicates that although the activity may be financially viable, an alternative use of the resources would be more economically efficient.

Optical Character Recognition (OCR) Software used to recognize the shape of alphanumeric characters in a scanned image and convert these to ASCII text files.

Orbit Path of a satellite around a body such as the earth, under the influence of gravity.

Ordinary Kriging A method for interpolating data values from sample data using regionalized variable theory in which the prediction weights are derived from a fitted variogram model.

Original Source The location of a native plant or plants from which seed or propagules were collected.

Orientation Establishing correct relationship in direction with reference to points of the compass; the state of being in correct relationship in direction with reference to the points of the compass.

Orophyte A plant inhabiting hills and mountains.

Orthophotograph A vertical aerial photograph from which the distortions due to varying elevation, tilt, and surface topography have been removed, so that it represents every object as if viewed directly from above.

Orthophotos A scale-correct photomap created by geometrically correcting aerial photographs or satellite images.

Other Wooded Land Land not classified as forest, spanning more than 0.5 hectares; with trees higher than 5 metres and a canopy cover of 5-10 per cent, or trees able to reach these thresholds *in situ;* or with a combined cover of shrubs, bushes and trees above 10 per cent. It does not include land that is predominantly under agricultural or urban land use (FRA, 2005 - Terms & Definitions).

Otter Any of a group of aquatic, fur-bearing, carnivorous, musteline mammals of the genus Lutra, and allied genera, related to the weasel and the munk, with webbed feet adapted for swimming, and a pointed long tail, somewhat flattened horizontally, acting as a rudder. The pelt is valued. In India, the common otter *Lutra lutra* or *L. perspicillata* is found only in Kashmir, the Himalayas and in Assam. The smooth Indian otter, *Lutrogale perspicillata* is found in the plains throughout India. The clawless otter *Amblyonyx cinerea* is the smallest of the otters, measuring only about 50 cm for the head and body with a tail of 30 cm. This is found in the Himalayan foothills from Kulu eastwards to Assam. In Great Britain, the otter *L. vulgaris* is much hunted with dogs.

Out Breeding Mating between individuals not closely related.

Output The results of processing data in a GIS; maps, tables, screen images, tape files.

Outturn 1. The quantity of produce obtained from any unit of a forest yield. 2. The quantity of sawn timber obtained from a given quantity of round logs.

Outturn Table A volume table giving the contents in terms of outturn.

Outwash Material, chiefly sand or gravel, which is washed from a glacier on account of melting.

Over Population An excess of population.

Overexploitation Felling of forests or exploiting forests at a rate too high to be sustained indefinitely. If the distribution of age classes in the forest is normal, the rate of fellings may correctly approximate the rate of net growth; but if younger age classes predominate, a rate of felling considerably lower than the net growth rate is justified. But overexploitation indicates felling at higher rate in both the cases. *See* under exploitation.

Overgrazing Grazing so heavily as to impair future forage production and cause range deterioration by damaging of the plants or soil or both grazing, conservative.

Overlap Extent to which adjacent images or photographs cover the same terrain, expressed as a percentage.

Overlay 1. The process of stacking digital representations of various spatial data on top of each other so that each position in the area covered can be analysed in terms of these data. 2. A data plane containing a related set of geographic data in digital form. 3. A combination of two or more map layers, within a GIS, to create one or more new map layers or new information. 4. A transparent sheet giving information to supplement what is shown on maps. 5. A tracing of selected details on a photograph.

Over-Mature The condition of a tree or crop which has passed (a) the exploitable age or size, or (b) the age after which it may be expected to become progressively unsound.

Overstocked A condition of overcrowding in tree crops. *See* crop density.

Overwood The upper most storey of a storeyed high forest or of any crop in which two or more distinct crown layers occur, either temporarily or permanently. For an example seed bearer over regeneration, standards over coppice or a crop of trees over bamboos underwood.

Ownership, Private Land owned by individuals, families, private co-operatives, corporations, industries, private religious and educational institutions, pension or investment funds, and other private institutions. Private owners may be engaged in agriculture or other occupations including forestry (FRA, 2005).

Ownership, Public Land owned by the state (national, state and regional Governments) or government owned institutions or corporations or other public bodies including cities, municipalities and villages (FRA, 2005).

Ozone Layer A form of oxygen (O_3) formed naturally in the upper atmosphere by a photochemical reaction with solar ultraviolet radiation and a major agent in the formation of smog. 2. Ozone, a tri-atomic molecule is formed naturally in the upper levels of the earth's atmosphere by high-energy ultraviolet radiation from the sun. The radiation breaks down oxygen molecules, releasing free atoms, some of which bond with other oxygen molecules to form ozone. About 90 per cent of all ozone formed in their way lies between 15 and 55 kilometres above the earth's surface, called the stratosphere. The stratospheric ozone layer absorbs all the harmful Ultra Violet (UV) radiation emanating from the sun. It protects plants and animals' life from UV radiation. UV radiation has the potential to cause skin cancer, eye damage, suppress body's immune system, decrease crop yield, cause damage to forests, etc. All these concerns in early seventies led to the adoption of the Vienna Convention in 1985 and the Montreal Protocol (1987). India produces CFC-11, CFC-12, CFC-113, halon-1211, HCFC-22, Halon-1301, Carbon-tetrachoride (CTC), Methyl Chloroform and Methyl Bromide. These Ozone Depleting Substances (ODS) are used in refrigeration and air conditioning, fire fighting, electronic, foams, aerosol fumigation applications.

Pp

Package A set of computer programmes that can be used for a particular generalized class of applications.

Paint To fill in an area with a given symbolism on a raster display device. It is a word used in cartography.

Paleoecology The study of the relationships of past organisms and the environment in which they lived. Also spelled palaeoecology.

Pan A compacted or cemented soil, horizons cementation may be affected by iron hydroxides, organic material SiO_2, $CaCO_3$ or other substances.

Panchromatic Imagery Single-band or monochrome imagery.

Panda, Lesser Red Panda (*Ailurus fulgens*) A carnivore of the Himalayas, somewhat larger beneath; the face is marked with white. It has a long bushy tail marked with pale rings. It is found in the Himalayas from Nepal and Sikkim eastwards to Upper Burma and Southern China, at medium elevations of 1800 to 3600 m. Also called Cat bear and Bear cat.

Pangolin (Scaly ant-eater) Any of several Asiatic and African mammals of genus manis and related genera of order Pholidota, that feed mainly on ants. The body is covered with large, flattened, reddish-brown imbricated, horny scales. It has a long sticky tongue and a long snout. It is able to roll itself into a ball when attacked. In India, the Indian Pangolin or Scaly Ant-eater, *Manis crassicaudata,* inhabits the plains and lower slopes of hill, south of the Himalayas. Another species, the Chinese Pangolin (*Manis aurita*) occurs in Assam.

Panorama A photograph of a wide expanse of terrain, taken from on or near the surface; a series of overlapping photographs.

Parakeet (*Parrakeet*) Any of numerous rather small, slender parrots with a long graduated tail. Birds found in India are: ALEXANDRINE or LARGE INDIAN PARAKEET (*Psittacula eupatria*): Found throughout India. A popular cage birds. ROSERINGED PARAKEET (*Psittacula krameri*). Found throughout the plains and locally up to 1500 metre. A popular cage bird. Learns to repeat a few words and to perform tricks. BLOSSOM-HEADED PARAKEET (*Psittacula cyanocephala*): Found throughout India and up to 1800 metre in the Himalayas.

Parallax Difference The difference in the distance on overlapping vertical photographs between two points, which represent two locations on the ground with different elevations.

Parallax Displacement of the position of a target in an image caused by a shift in the observation system.

Parallel of Latitude A circle, or approximation of a circle, on the surface of the Earth, parallel to the Equator, and connecting points of equal latitude; a circle of the celestial sphere parallel to the ecliptic, and connecting points of equal celestial latitude.

Parameter Any quantity in a problem or equation that is not an independent variable; can be assigned arbitrary values in solution of problem.

Parasite, Wound A parasite able to enter the host and establish itself only through wounds or injured tissue.

Parasite 1. An organism (plant or animal) that lives in or on another living organism of a different kind (host) and derives subsistence from it without returning any benefit. 2. An organism that draws a part or the whole of its nourishment from another living organism. Parasites are of two classes: (a) facultative, capable of existing independently of a living host; (b) obligate, incapable of existing independently of a living host. In the case of insects a parasite feeds on a single individual of its host. *See* predator.

Parasitism 1. The mode of life of a parasite, i.e. as between it and its host. 2. A close internal or external relation between two organisms, which is detrimental to one partner (the host) and beneficial to the other (the parasite). The latter derives nourishment and usually other benefits (as shelter and transportation) from the former, causing some damage, but not usually killing, directly and immediately. *See* parasite, symbiosis, and predatism.

Parasitization The act of infestation of an organism by a parasite.

Park 1. Usually a large enclosed piece of ground. 2. Enclosure in town or city ornamentally laid out for public recreation. 3. Large tract of land kept in natural state for public benefit. 4. A relatively small opening of grassland in a forest.

Park Land or **Parkland** Open grassland containing single trees or groups of trees. A grassland region with isolated or grouped trees, usually in temperate regions. The term can also be applied to a land with groups of cultivated trees or shrubs, suitable for use as a park. *See* savannah woodland.

Park, National An area owned by the state and dedicated to the cause of conservation of scenery and the natural and historic objects of national significance and conservation of wild animals and plants by such means as leave them unimpaired for the enjoyment of present and future generation. There is a provision for declaring a forest land as national park under the Indian Wildlife Act, 1972. *See* National Park.

Parrot Any of numerous tropical and sub-tropical birds of order Psittaciformes, with brilliant plumage, hooked bill and zygodactyl feet. They are excellent mimics and can simulate laughter and crying.

Parthenocarpy The development of a fruit without fertilization, as in the banana. Similar development of a (seedless) cone has been termed parthenocony.

Parthenogenesis Development of the egg without fertilization into a new individual.

Participatory Forestry Participatory forestry in India hovers around the concept of Joint Forest Management (JFM). In June 1990, Government of India issued notification and guidelines to all states and union territories to involve local communities in the rehabilitation and protection of degraded forests through Joint Forest Management. The concept formally recognises the importance of involving local people in protection, management and development of forests and envisages mobilizing communities through the formation of Village Forest Committees and empowering them to manage forests including degraded forest, on benefit sharing principle of care and share, although without the formal transfer of forest land ownership. JFM involves collaboration between forest departments and local community, with a local non-Governmental organisation, in many cases, serving as an interface between people and Government.

Community management is to be carried out according to well-developed micro-plan, which concentrates on technical and developmental aspects of forest management. Till 2005, most states have passed enabling resolutions and Joint Forest Management has been implemented on more than 17 million hectares of degraded forest through 63000 village forest committees. Joint Forest Management remains, however, an evolving concept. There are a number of issues, including devolution of authority and management functions, transfer of funding, training, information and technology dissemination, which need attention collectively, if JFM is to become a primary vehicle for development of forest resources and empowerment of people living in and around forest areas.

Participatory Micro-Planning This constitutes the village level planning stage. It commences after broad agreements between various participant agencies have been arrived at. This stage is the core of the entire planning exercise. Here the collection of information and data becomes more formal and structured and ideas start taking a concrete shape. It is now a common practice to adopt Participatory Rural Appraisal (PRA) techniques for undertaking ecodevelopment planning. PRA is a set of semi-structured methodology designed to facilitate a productive interaction with rural communities. Various exercises such as resource mapping, transact walk, Venn diagram, timeline, livelihood analysis etc. are aimed at eliciting people's perceptions about their lives, resources, development agencies, etc. The observations and perceptions emerged out of such PRA exercise can be used for any rural development planning work. The participatory planning process is a complex process involving PRA, collecting information of various Government plans, establishing contact and rapport with various agencies (both Government and non-Government), and setting up co-ordinating mechanisms at village, range and division/district levels. It also involves preparing comprehensive plans for various components of ecodevelopment such as joint forest management, watershed management, agricultural development, irrigation, cottage industries and handicrafts, apiculture, sericulture, fisheries, alternative energy and energy conservation programmes, etc. However, before taking up detailed PRA and planning work, the planning team has to strive to gain complete trust of the concerned people. Trust building involves such actions/gestures on the part of the planning team, which promotes mutual confidence between the PRA staff and the people. Trust building must start with the PRA staff as a clear understanding of the approach necessary for implementing it. *See* participatory rural appraisal.

Participatory Rural Appraisal (PRA) Participatory Rural Appraisal (PRA) is a methodology for interacting with villagers, understanding them and learning from them. It involves a set of principles, a process of communication and a menu of methods for seeking villager's participation in putting forward their points of view about any issue and enabling them to do their own analysis with a view to make use of such learning. It initiates a participatory process and sustains it. Its principles and the menu of methods help in organizing participation (Neela Mukherjee, 1993). It is a method of collecting variety of data, identifying and organizing intended groups and evoking their participation and initiating ways in which the said groups can interact and participate in different management processes like decision making, project design, implementation, monitoring and evaluation. Because of its participatory in nature, it is widely used to focus attention on people, their livelihoods and their interrelationships with socio-economic and environmental factors.

Partridge Any of a number of game birds resembling domestic fowls, as the grouse, pheasant, quails, etc. True partridges are similar to the quails. Partridges found in India are given below: BLACK (*Francolinus francolinus*). A typical partridge found in thick ground cover. It extends in various races throughout India. A resident species, ascending the western Himalayas up to 1500 m. It is an edible wild bird sold in Indian markets. It affords good sport. CHUKOR or CHIKAR (*Alectoris graeca*): It is distinguished by the black loop on the face and throat and by the beautiful bars on the flanks. Under the name of Greek Partridge, it has a wide distribution in Europe and Asia. In India the race *Alectoris graeca* is well known to sportsmen as Chukor. It is a resident bird found at elevations between 3000 and 4500 metre. It differs from the French partridge (*A. rufa*) in minor details. It is frequently found on barren hill-sides. GREY (*Francolinus pondicerianus*; Syn. *Ortygornis pondicerianus*):

A typical brown partridge. Two races are found in India. It is strictly a resident species. It is an edible wild bird sold in Indian markets. It is a popular cage bird, prized for its fighting qualities. It affords good sports. HILL PARTRIDGE (*Arborophila rufogularis* Syn. *A. torqueola*): This is found in the Punjab Hills, Himachal Pradesh, and eastwards up to Assam. PAINTED PARTRIDGE (*Francolinus pictus*). This is brownish black, profusely spotted and barred with white. It is found in Peninsular India south of a line running from Kutch to the Chilka Lake (Orissa), through Gwalior. It is an edible wild bird sold in the markets. It affords good sport.

Pascal A high-level computer programming language.

Pass In digital filters, it refers to the spatial frequency of data transmitted by the filter. High-pass filters transmit high-frequency data; low-pass filters transmit low-frequency data.

Passive Microwaves Radiation in the 1 mm to 1 m range emitted naturally by all materials above absolute zero.

Passive Remote Sensing Remote sensing of energy naturally reflected or radiated from the terrain.

Pastime Foods Food eaten principally for the purpose of spending time agreeably, i.e. for diversion or amusement, rather than for palpability or nutrition.

Path-and-Row Index It is a system for locating images before placing an order to remote sensing products for the purpose of image interpretation.

Pathogen An organism causing disease.

Pattern Regular repetition of tonal variations on an image or photograph.

Peacock (*Peafowl*) Any of a number of large related birds of genus Pavo. One species, common in India, is: COMMON PEAFOWL (*Pavo cristatus*): It is a native of India and Sri Lanka. The male has a crest and striking plumages and tails marked with iridescent ocelli ("eyes"); it is able to expand its tail erect, like a fan, to produce a gorgeous display. It is found almost throughout India, ascending the Himalayas up to 600 metre and locally up to 1500 metre. It is a purely resident bird. It has been declared as the national bird of India. It has deep ecological significance. It keeps down snakes and other poisonous reptiles in a habitat. When young they are good for eating.

Peat The residues of natural vegetation which have been affected by processes of anaerobic decomposition usually in water logging conditions.

Peck Order Pecking order. 1. The basic pattern of social organisation within a flock of poultry (extended to animals) in which each bird is permitted to peck another lower in the scale without fear of retaliation and is expected to submit to pecking by one of higher rank. 2. The status of each individual animal in the social hierarchy is equivalent to social rank. So called from the fact that birds enforce this social rank by pecking an inferior or being pecked by a superior. *See* hook order.

Pedology The scientific study of the soil.

Pelagic 1. Relating to the open ocean. 2. Open water areas away from the shore and the bottom. 3. Growing at or near the surface in water away from the shore.

Pelican Any of various large, gregarious, totipalmate, water birds of the genus Pelecanus, with a long neck, short legs, webbed toes. They have a large membranous distensible pouch which hangs from the lower bill and serves for storing fish. They live principally on fish but also on other aquatic animals. There is a fable that a pelican feeds or revives its young with its own blood. Pelicans found in India are: SPOTTED-BILLED PELICAN: GREY PELICAN (*Pelcecanus philippensis*): This is a huge squat pelican with an enormous beak, familiar to everyone through the zoo. It is found throughout the better watered tracts of India, wherever there are large expanses of water suitable for it to fish in. It is a resident bird, but capricious; also locally migratory. They fish by co-operative effort, swimming in a semi-circle and driving the fish before them into shallow waters, and scooping them upon their punch, which acts like a landing net. ROSY PELICAN (*Pelecanus onocrotalus*): Found near the Great Rann of Kutch.

Pen Plotter A device for drawing maps and figures using a computer steered pen.

Peneplain A land surface eroded to almost a plain.

Penning Site Sites inside forests set apart for use as cattle pens particularly during seasons of fodder and water scarcity in villages and outlying forests.

People and Forests Forests provide tangible and intangible benefits to millions of people all over the globe. Forests are home to 300 million people around the world. More than 1.6 billion people depend to varying degrees on forests for their livelihoods, e.g.

fuelwood, medicinal plants and forest foods. About 60 million indigenous people are almost wholly dependent on forests. Some 350 million people who live within or adjacent to dense forests depend on them to a high degree for subsistence and income. In developing countries, about 1.2 billion people rely on agro-forestry farming systems that help to sustain agricultural productivity and generate income. Mangrove forests, which cover only about 147,000 km^2 worldwide, are essential to the life cycles of the majority of the worlds commercial fish species (World Bank, 2004).

Perch A roost for a bird. Some birds need perches higher than the surface of the forest canopy. Removal of wolf-trees may evict them completely.

Perched Ground Water Ground water that is separated from the main body of ground water by unsaturated material. Also perched water table.

Percolation Generally used in the same sense as infiltration, but is better reserved for the movement of water below the surface soil. *See* infiltration.

Perennial A plant species that persists for several years. *See* annual.

Performance The degree to which a device or system fulfils its specifications.

Perigee The orbital point nearest the body about which a satellite is orbiting.

Period Age-class The number of years within the limits of a given age class.

Period Emergence The interval between the free appearance of the first and the last individuals of larvae or adults of a particular generation of an insect species.

Period, Conversion The period during which the change from one silvicultural system to another is effected.

Period, Preparatory 1. The period preceding a change of silvicultural system during which special operations are undertaken to prepare for conversion. 2. A period during which the conditions of canopy and soil are being modified with a view to rendering them suitable before regeneration fellings are begun. *See* felling, preparatory.

Period, Regeneration The period required to regenerate the whole of a periodic block. *See* regeneration interval.

Period, Working Plan The period for which detailed prescriptions are laid down in a working plan. It is the period for which the forest will be managed according to the prescriptions prescribed in the working plan. In the past the period used to be 15 to 20 years. But today as per the government guidelines it is 10 years.

Period A subdivision of rotation or conversion period.

Periodic Block 1. The part or parts of forest set aside to be regenerated or otherwise treated during a specified period. The regeneration block is called "floating" or "single" when it is the only periodic block allocated at each working plan revision. When all periodic blocks are allotted and thereby retain their territorial identity at working plan revision, they are termed "fixed" or "permanent". 2. In France, where uniform system was developed in the middle the 19th century, the procedure was to divide each forest into many self-contained periodic blocks. The number of these periodic blocks were equal to the period in the rotation. These periodic blocks were allotted once for all, each to its respective period of the rotation. This system is still followed in many countries of the world. The procedure of permanent allotment can be adopted where natural regeneration can be obtained within fixed time and risks of frost, storms, insects and fire damages are less. The method of self-contained periodic blocks facilitates tending and supervision. Logging and extraction are also comparatively cheaper. But the self-contained fixed periodic block presents many difficulties particularly in areas where serious damage occurs by winds, insects, fires, etc. The formation of large self-contained periodic blocks involves the artificial allotment of the crop to definite period, for which some part of the crop may be either too young or too old for the period for which they have been allotted. This problem is solved to a large extent by formation of the scattered periodic blocks. In this method each compartment or sub-compartment is considered separately and is allotted according to the age to appropriate period. The formation of fixed periodic blocks may be practicable in areas where there is no danger of wind, fire, insects damages and natural regeneration is easily and satisfactorily obtained. Such methods are not useful in cases of refractory species and an unfavourable site conditions where it is not possible to obtain complete regeneration within the prescribed time period. When regeneration is expected to witness problem, floating periodic blocks or Quartier Blue method is usually adopted. Under such method the area under regeneration is cartographically shown as blue in colour. When a working plan is revised, the area is allotted to periodic block according to the condition of the crop. The areas under regeneration are called Quartier Blue and area earmarked for augmenting regeneration in future is called Quartier Blanc. This system was first introduced in France and was followed in many countries later on.

Peripheral A hardware device that is not part of the central computer.

Perissodactyla Ungulate mammals which walk on hoofed toes, with weight-bearing axis along the third toe which is larger than the others in most cases, e.g. rhinoceros and horse.

Permafrost Areas of land which contain a layer that is always frozen and never completely melt, even at the height of summer. It is especially characteristics of the tundra and also of parts of the boreal forest biome.

Permeability The rate at which water moves through a soil under a standard pressure gradient. Usually defined as the amount of water traversing 1 square centimetre of soil surface under a pressure gradient of one dyne per centimetre.

Perspective Representation on a plane or curved surface of objects as they appear to the eye.

Pert (Programme Evaluation and Review Technique) A project management tool. This technique is used for evaluation of any ongoing or completed project.

Pf Value 1. The energy (force) with which water is held in a soil expressed as the logarithm of the height in centimetres of a column of water of equivalent weight; e.g., a pf value of 2 indicates that the force with which water is retained is equivalent to the weight of a water column 100 cm in height. The scale of values ranges from 0 which corresponds to a pressure of 1/1000th atmosphere, to 7 corresponding to 10,000 atmospheres. 2. The negative logarithm of the reciprocal of h ion concentration in a solution; *p*H value of 7 indicates neutrality, higher values indicate alkalinity and lower values acidity.

Phanerophyte 1. A land plant whose buds and shoot apices are destined to survive the unfavourable season and project into the air on stems that persist from year to year and often for many years.

Pheasant Any of various large, gallinaceous game birds, of the genus Phasianus and related genera of family Phasianidae, with a long, sweeping tail and brilliant feathers. They are most abundant in Asia and the adjacent Islands. Those found in India are: BLOOD PHEASANT (*Ithiginis cruentus*): Found in the mountains of India and China; remarkable for the bright red colour of the throat and breast. CHEER PHEASANT (*Catreus wallichii*): A buff or greyish pheasant found in the sub-Himalayan tracts. It shows a bare red eye patch and a long narrow tail. KALU PHEASANT (*Laphura lucomelana*): A crested Indian pheasant. Found at high elevations up to 3000m in the Himalayas (Kashmir, Himachal Pradesh, Arunachal Pradesh and other North-East States). MONAL PHEASANT: IMPEYAN PHEASANT (*Lophophorus impejanus*): A showy pheasant found at high altitudes in the Himalayas especially Kashmir, Bhutan, Sikkim, and the North-East States. PUKRAS: PUKRAS PHEASANT: KOKLAS PHEASANT (*Pucrasia macrolopha*): A pheasant found in North India and the Himalayas. The male is mostly crested with long black ear-tuffs. TRAGOPAN: HORNED PHEASANT (*Tragopan species*): A brilliantly coloured Asiatic pheasant, with the head of the male ornamented with a pair of fleshy erectile horns. Found in North-East States.

Phenology The science that deals with time of appearance of characteristic periodic events such as leaf shedding, etc., in the life cycle of organisms in nature especially as those events are influenced by environmental factors.

Phenotype An organism judged by its visible characters. *See* Genotype.

Pheromone A chemical substance released by animals, including insects, that influences the behaviour or development of other individuals of the same species, e.g., sexual attractants.

Phloem The tissues of the inner bark serving for the transport of elaborated foodstuffs and characterized by the presence of sieve tubes. *See* cambium.

Photogrammetry 1. Science or art of obtaining reliable measurements or information from photographs or other sensing systems. 2. A series of techniques for measuring position and altitude from aerial photographs or images using a stereoscope or stereoplotter.

Photographic UV Long-wavelength portion of the UV band (0.3 to

0.4 μm) that is transmitted through the atmosphere and is detectable by film.

Photometer An instrument for measuring the intensity of light.

Photomosaic A collection of aerial photographs which are joined to form a contiguous view of an area.

Photoperiodism Response in the ontogeny of an organism to the relative duration of day and night.

Photosynthesis Formation of carbohydrates in the chlorophyll containing tissues of plants exposed to light.

Phreatophyte A plant that derives its water supply from groundwater and is more.

Phyllosphere The micro-environment of leaves.

Phylogeny Evolutionary history of an organism or taxonomic group, e.g., species.

Phyrometer The living plant itself used as an instrument to measure the physical factors of the habitat in terms of physiological activities; for example, plants in sealed containers can be used to measure the rate of transpiration in different habitats.

Physical Weathering The breakdown of rock and mineral soil into smaller fragments by physical forces as by frost action. *See* weathering.

Physiognomic Class A level in the classification hierarchy defined by the relative per cent canopy cover of the tree, shrub, dwarf shrub, herb, and non-vascular life form (in the uppermost strata) during the peak of the growing season.

Physiognomic Group A level in the classification defined by a combination of climate, leaf morphology, and leaf phenology. Different variables are applied to this hierarchical level in the sparsely vegetated class.

Physiognomic Subclass A level in the classification determined by the predominant leaf phenology of classes defined by tree, shrub, or dwarf shrub stratum (evergreen, deciduous, mixed evergreen deciduous), and the average vegetation height for the herbaceous stratum (tall, medium, short). Different variables are applied to this hierarchical level in the sparsely vegetated class.

Physiognomy The structure and life form of a plant community.

Physiography A branch of geography dealing with the natural features of earth's surface; physical geography.

Phytogenic Soils Soils developed under the dominant influence of the natural vegetation, mainly in temperate regions.

Phytogeography The biogeography of plants. The scientific study of plant life with referent to the distribution of plants on earth and the mutual influence of environment and plants on each other.

Phytograph 1. A polygonal figure depicting the role of a species in a plant community, the polygon being formed by straight lines connecting points representing values on each of the chosen axes. The axes may represent such pertinent, quantitative data as basal area, frequency, and canopy density and for trees size class. 2. A polygonal figure depicting the role of species in a plant community. The polygon is formed by the straight lines connecting points on each of several axes. Such data as basal area, frequency and density, canopy may be represented on the axes.

Phytoplankton Microscopic plants, typically algae, suspended in the water column and subject to movement by waves and current. *See* plankton.

Picture Element In a digitized image, the area on the ground represented by each digital number. Commonly referred to pixel.

Pigeon Bird of the family Columbidae especially the rock-dove (*Columbia livia*) which haunts rocks and large buildings and is also domesticated. The carrier or homing pigeon is trained to fly home over long distances with message attached to its neck or leg. Birds found in India are: COMMON GREEN PIGEON (*Crocopus phoenicopterus*) found throughout India. BLUE ROCK PIGEON (*Columbia livia*). Found throughout India and locally up to 3900 m in the Himalayas.

Pilot Project An example of any micro level project or software application that shows the potential of a larger application. *See also* prototyping.

Pinch Period A season during which either food or water or both are minimal in their quantity, quality and distribution causing stress in animal populations. Generally the term addressees the need of welfare of herbivorous species.

Pintail Sometimes called sprigtail duck. A long-necked, slender and graceful duck (*Anas acuta*), with long neck and sharply pointed tail. It breeds in northern hemisphere. It is purely a winter visitor in India (October to March), being found throughout the country. It occurs in small flocks near the shore and feeds upon weeds, crustaceans and insects. It easily holds the first place among the ducks of India as a sporting bird, as a good bird for the table and for grace of shape and carriage.

Pioneer 1. A plant capable of invading bare sites (e.g. A newly exposed soil surface) and persisting there or "colonizing" them, until supplanted, by successional species. Pioneers often in large numbers invade over considerable areas. They are plant species that invade a bare area such as a newly exposed soil or rock surface. 2. Any new arrival in the early seral development of plant community, usually with particular reference to certain species whose presence appears to promote the establishment of more exacting (successor) species; often applied to a species planted to prepare a site for the latter. *See* succession.

Pit Method This is one of the most common methods for capturing elephants. A pit is dug in the usually path of wild elephants; it is partly filled with slash to execute the fall of the elephant, and is covered over with bamboos and earth so that there are no suspicious signs of the pit. When an elephant happens to walk along the path, it falls into the pit. It is then removed with the help of tame elephant.

Pit A depression on the surface of a digital elevation model that may represent a real feature or which may be an artefact of the gridding.

Pixel 1. A "picture element". 2. Contraction of picture element; the spatial variable defines the apparent size of the resolution cell and the spectral variable defines the intensity of the spectral response (at specified wavelength[s]) for that cell. 3. Contraction of picture element; smallest unit of information in a grid cell map or scanner image. 4. A single cell in a raster data model. It is a short form for picture element. *See* cell.

Plain Region of uniform general slope, comparatively level, of considerable extent, and not broken by marked elevations and depressions (it may be an extensive valley floor or a plateau summit); an extent of level or nearly level land; a flat, gently sloping, or nearly level region of the sea floor.

Plan A plan is a predetermined course of action to achieve a specified goal. In short, it is a blue print for action. *See* forest working plan, and management plan.

Planning Planning is deciding in advance what is to be done. It involves the selection of objectives, policies, procedures and programmes from among the available alternatives. A plan is a predetermined course of action to achieve a specified goal.

In short, it is a blue print for action. Different authors, however, have defined planning differently. Few of such definitions are: (1) David Cleland and William King: "Planning is the process of thinking through and making explicit the strategy, action and relationship necessary to accomplish an overall objective or purpose"; (2) George R. Terry: Planning is selecting and relating of facts and the making and using of assumptions regarding the future in the visualization and formation of proposed activities believed necessary to achieve desired results"; (3) Theo Haimann: "Planning is deciding in advance what is to be done. When a manager plans, he projects a course of action for the future, attempting to achieve a consistent, co-ordinated structure of operations aimed at the desired results"; (4) Koontz O'Donnell: "Planning is an intellectual process, the conscious determination of courses of action, the basing of decisions on purpose, acts and considered estimates"; (5) George B. Galloway: "Planning is the opposite of improvising. In simple words, it is an organized foresight plus corrective hindsight and conceived as a process. Planning embraces a series of steps: (i) the determination of objectives to be sought, (ii) reserch to understand the problem, (iii) the discovery of alternative solutions, (iv) policy making and chosing between alternatives, including the frequent choice of doing nothing, (v) the detailed execution of the chosen alternative known in physical planning as lay out or design"; (6) Alfrod and Beatty: "Planning is the thinking process, the organised foresight, the vision based on facts and experience that is required for intelligent action."

Plan, Benefits of 1. Planning has many benefits. They are: (1) It focuses management attention on objectives, that can generate results; (2) It helps management establish priorities; (3) It assists management to emphasize organizational strengths; (4) It helps management cope with ever-changing external environments; and (5) It facilitates control.

Plan, Features of a Good A good plan is that which (i) is based on a clearly defined objective, (ii) is simple, (iii) provides for a proper analysis and classification of action, i.e., which establishes standards, (iv) is flexible, (v) is balanced, and (vi) uses available resources to the utmost before creating new authorities and new resources. A good plan is always pragmatic and leads the organization forward on the path of progress and prosperity. A good plan opens up new avenues, and ways of doing things and reveals specific opportunities previously unknown to the planner.

Plan, Management Management plan is a document, which provides guidelines for working. It is available to everybody who is involved in decision making process. It is an indispensable tool for planning sustainable forest management operation. It states objectives clearly so that everyone involved in managing the forest shall work towards the same end. A management plan contains (1) The objectives of management, (2) A description of the resources available, and (3) The proposed methods of achieving the objectives.

Plan, Master An official document adopted by any authority or local government or landowner setting forth its general policies regarding the long-term physical development of a city or other area. Such plans are broad enough to include all aspects of a development or redevelopment programme as distinguished from sporadic, isolated, or piecemeal planning. The process of designing futures not only of three dimensional accomplishments in space but also social mechanisms such as laws, regulations, policies, and forms of organization. Comprehensive plans typically include: (1) A land plan map which shows the location of all owned land, the interrelationship between all of the uses proposed on such land, the circulation system required to serve the uses existing or proposed, and the relationship between ownership within a reasonable area of influence; (2) Land use policies related to the resources management, conservation and disposal of public lands; (3) Land use policies related to the activities and the regulations as they affect portions of the land; (4) Implementation schedules which establish priorities for programmes in management, mapping, engineering, and public works; (5) A programme for co-ordinating land use, intensity, and activity programmes with central/federal, state, regional, other local agencies as well as with private applicants. Increasing emphasis is being laid on social, economic, and esthetic topics, moving plans beyond physical and land use documents.

Plan of Operations A tabular statement showing the order and extent of all works to be carried out during one or more years.

Such a plan is based on the prescription of the working plan where one exists, otherwise on general silvicultural system as modified by financial provisions.

Plan, Felling-cum-Regeneration A detailed scheme for felling and regeneration where by arrangements are made to extract timber before regeneration begins. Such plan took its origin in Burma where there used to have long period (at least 5 yeas) which must elapse, after the teak is girdled, before extraction can be completed and regeneration started.

Planar Co-ordinates *See* 'cartesian co-ordinates'.

Planetable Instrument consisting essentially of a drawing board on a tripod and some type of sighting device (alidade) with attached straightedge, used for plotting the lines of survey directly from observation in the field.

Planimeter Planimeter is a mechanical integrator, which is used to find the area of any irregular figure. Now-a-days, instead of mechanical planimeter, digital planimeter are used to find the area of any irregular figure. The precision of such digital planimeter is very high.

Planimetry Plan details of a map – those having no indication of relief or contour.

Plankton Microorganisms suspended in the water having little or no power of locomotion, carried by waves, currents and other movements of water. Those are of two types: (1) Phytoplankton: microscopic floating aquatic plants; and (2) Zooplankton: microscopic floating aquatic animals; Based on the size, planktons are classified into: (i) Macroplankton: over 500 microns, (ii) Microplankton: 50-500 microns, (iii) Nanoplankton: 10-50 microns, (iv) Ultraplankton: 0.5 to 10 microns.

Planning, Forest Management Management planning is the foundation of a well-managed forest. It lays out the details of works, their rationale, and location. Management plan is the document, which provides guidelines for working. It is available to everybody who is involved in decision making process. It is an indispensable tool for planning sustainable forest management operation. It states objectives clearly so that everyone involved in managing the forest shall work towards the same end. A management plan contains (1) The objectives of management, (2) A description of the resources available, and (3) The proposed methods of achieving the objectives. Based on the size of forest operations, management plan can be categorized into three types. They are: (a) *Strategic plan*: It is the forest management plan prepared for an entire Forest Management Unit (FMU), over a long term, such as an entire rotation, or a period of twenty-five years, (b) *Tactical plan*: The forest management plan that sets out the activities planned, normally over a five-year period, in more detail. It may coincide with business plans, and (c) *Operation plan*: The forest operation plan or Annual Plan of Operation contains the details of the precise activities to be carried out over the next year. This will include month to month activities and should provide the direct control over operations. It is essential for carrying out operations in consonance with forest management plan. It is generally taken up along with annual budgeting. The tactical and operational plans are not only compatible with the strategic plan but also derived from it. They provide more detailed information and procedure. In many counties the strategic and tactical plans are amalgamated to form a 'management plan' or 'working plan' which covers a period of 10 to 20 years. A written management plan is revised periodically to ensure that it does not become static, irrelevant and unworkable. It also provides an opportunity to assess and revise objectives and methods of SFM. Revision of management plan should be a continuous process taking into account the changing situations within and outside the ambit of forestry. Induction of new technology and practices like information technology and biotechnology into the management process should be done periodically. Again with the increasing awareness of the public and need for community participation in management planning, the management plan should be made public. By making the management plan or a short summary of the management plan public, transparency and accountability of forest operations will be improved. This will go a long way not only in promoting better communication with myriad stakeholders but also in restoring confidence of local community in forest organization.

Plant Box or Tray A box or tray in which small plants are raised and transported to the forest for planting out. *See* transplant.

Plant Conservation This is concerned with the preservation of species of communities of plants that are of interest for their beauty, rarity or inherent scientific value. The meaning of forest conservation is different from that of plant conservation. Forest conservation is concerned with the proper methods for utilization of forest trees for timber and other useful products and services. This may also include preservation of individual tree species of special interest. *See* preserve; nature reserves.

Plant per cent Percentage of the number of the seeds in a sample (in nursery or plantation) that develops into seedlings at the end of the first growing season. Plant per cent is always lower than the germinative per cent. The number of plants that is likely to be obtained from a kilogram of seed depends upon the plant per cent. *See* germinative per cent.

Plantation Journal A register, in which all details of works carried out in a plantation, and other information pertaining to plantation are recorded from time to time.

Plantation, Productive Forest/other wooded land of introduced species and in some cases native species, established through planting or seeding mainly for production of wood or non-wood goods (FRA, 2005).

Plantation, Protective Forest/other wooded land of native or introduced species, established through planting or seeding mainly for provision of services. It includes all stands of introduced species established for provision of environmental services, such as soil and water protection, pest control and conservation of habitats to biological diversity. It also includes areas of native species characterised by few species, straight lines and even-aged stands (FRA, 2005).

Plantation 1. A forest crop raised artificially, either by sowing or planting. 2. Forest stands established by planting or/and seeding in the process of afforestation or reforestation. They are either: (a) Introduced species (all planted stands) or (b) Intensively managed stands or indigenous species, which meet all the following criteria; one or two species at plantation, even age class, regular spacing. (FAO-FRA — Terms & Definitions). 3. A plantation is an intentional planting of a crop, on a larger scale, usually for uses other than cereal production or pasture. The term is most often used for plantings of trees and shrubs. The term tends to be used for plantings maintained on economic basis other than that of subsistence farming. Crops may be called plantation crops because of their association with a specific type of farming economy.

Planting, *Dona* Planting out seedling or transplant from *donas* or cups made of big leaves in which they have been sown or transplanted earlier from the seed beds. It is a method of planting teak in Central India, now becoming rare. Instead polypots and root trainers are being used these days. *See* planting, basket.

Planting, Advance. Planting an area in advance of fellings.

Planting Out Transferring nursery stock of the planting site as contrasted with transplanting in the nursery.

Planting Plan A plan for an area to be planted. Showing the general layout of blocks, compartments, sub-compartments, firebreaks, and a road system and prescribing the areas and species to be planted in each year along with the method of planting.

Planting Series A series formed to control planting operations.

Planting, Ball Planting young trees with their roots undisturbed in a ball of earth.

Planting, Basket Planting young trees in the forest in loosely woven baskets in which they have been sown or transplanted.

Planting, Group Planting trees in groups. Often used for improving natural forest of scrub by planting groups of valuable species at wide intervals. *See* planting, line.

Planting, Improvement Planting of valuable tree species at relatively wide intervals in degraded or naturally poor forest or scrub, with a view to improve the value of the crop.

Planting, Line 1. Planting in line. 2. A method of improving natural forest or scrub by sowing or planting trees along widely spaced lines or on strips opened up through it.

Planting, Mound Planting in prepared mounds.

Planting, Notch Planting in notches, made with a mattock or spade, the notches being closed by pressure.

Planting, Patch Planting in small prepared patches.

Planting, Peg Planting in holes made with a stick, peg or a crowbar, the holes being closed by pressure. Teak stumps are planted in vertical holes made by crowbar.

Planting, Pit 1. A method of planting in pits from which the soil has been dug-out and replaced or exchanged. 2. Planting in prepared pits or natural depressions, with a view to collect and conserve moisture.

Planting, Pot Planting out young trees in pots of various materials in which they have been raised from seed or into which they heve been transferred from the seed bed.

Planting, Ridge Planting in prepared ridges.

Planting, Stump Planting of stump.

Planting, Trench Planting in a continuous trench.

Planting, Tube Planting out young trees in open tubes of various materials, e.g., bamboo, metal, paper, etc., in which they have been raised from seed, or into which they have been transferred from the seed bed.

Planting, Turf A method of planting on inverted turves, which are often cut from the drains.

Plot An area of ground or any other kind of experimental unit, such as a single tree or part of a tree, a sample of seeds used for a germination test, even an animal or a colony of insects. The essential feature is that the plots for an experiment are units selected to be as alike as possible, but thereafter to receive different treatments. *See* control plot.

Plot, Experimental 1. An area laid out to determine the effects of a certain method of treatment. 2. The major area unit of an established experimental study, requiring recurrent examination, often divided into sub-plots. *See also* design.

Plot, Linear Sample A plot laid out on a line usually of single sample trees or as the centre of a sample strip. If trees are measured periodically it is called a linear tree increment plot. *See* sample strip; transect plot.

Plot, Preservation A sample area of natural forest or plantation set apart for preservation in perpetuity mainly for purposes of ecological observations and growth studies covering the full life of the trees and crops.

Plot, Sample A plot chosen as representative of a larger area. In forestry, sample plots are used mainly in enumeration surveys and for studies of growth (e.g., preparing yield table or determining the effect of thinning treatments on the rate of growth). *See also* design.

Plotter A device used for drawing or producing maps and figures. Output device used to draw maps and other diagrams from digital data.

Plover (Family Charadridae) Any of a number of related gregarious, shore birds especially of genera Charadrius (e.g., ringed plover) and Squatarola (grey plover), with a short tails long pointed wings and usually brown or grey feathers, mixed white. The golden plover (*Pluvialis dominica*) is remarkable for its long migration between arctic breeding ground and its winter home in Patagonia. Plovers are highly esteemed for the table, and for this reason they are given little chance of increasing in numbers. The little Ringed Plover (*Charadrius dubius*) is found all over India and also in places having altitude up to 1200 mt in the Himalayas.

Pneumatophore A knee-shaped or spike-like projection of the roots of swamp trees enabling the sub-merged roots to obtain oxygen from air.

Poacher One who kills or takes game or fish illegally. One who shoots or otherwise destroys or captures wild life, violating the provisions of Wildlife Acts and Forest Acts and rules made under.

Pochard An Old World diving duck (*Aythya ferina* Syn. *Nyroca ferina*), with a chestnut red head. In India it is a winter visitor (November to March). It is found throughout northern India, scarcer towards the south upto Mysore. It gets its food consisting of roots and buds of aquatic plants by diving deep under water. It is mainly seen in the larger *jheels* and tanks.

Podzolization A soil forming process of cool, humid climates in which leaching by organic acids removes all alkaline earths in solution and translocates iron and aluminium sesquioxides from the a layer to the b, where they form the ortstein. A podzol possesses ao, a1, a and b and c horizons. The name refers to the ash like colour of the characteristic a2 zone. *See* soil horizons.

Point Dictionary Vector data structure in which all points are numbered sequentially and containing explicit reference which records which co-ordinates are associated with which polygon.

Point Mode Digitizing A method of manual digitizing whereby the operator decides where to record each co-ordinate.

Point of Resistance The minimum population or density necessary for recovery of productivity.

Point 1. A pair of co-ordinates representing a location with dimensions. 2. A single (x, y) co-ordinate or pixel used to describe the location of an object too small to be represented as a polygon or area feature within the working scale of the GIS.

Point-in-polygon Overlay (PIP) The process of laying a point map over a polygon map to determine which points falls within which polygon.

Polar 1. Geographically, regions that have all months below an average temperature of 50 degrees Fahrenheit or 10 degrees Celsius. 2. Areas within the polar circle.

Polar Orbit An orbit that passes close to the poles, thereby enabling a satellite to pass over most of the surface, except the immediate vicinity of the poles themselves.

Pole A young tree from the time when the lower branches begin to fall off to the time when the rate of height growth begins to slow down and crown expansion becomes marked. *See* sapling.

Policy 1. Course or principle of action adopted or proposed by a government. 2. A rule or norm usually prescribed by governments to help behaviour or decision-making. National policy makers have become more aware of the complex nature of policy reforms and the uncertainty of their effects. The interrelationship between forests and other sectors of the economy are also better understood. There are policies for all sectors of the economy including forestry.

Pollard A tree whose stem has been cut off in order to obtain a flush of shoots, usually above the height to which browsing animals can reach. *See* coppicing.

Polluter Pays Principle (PPP) Polluter Pays Principle is an important economic instrument, which is required to be applied for operationalization of the concept of sustainable development. It represents property rights on the environmental assets to convince producer of pollution to pay the difference between the social cost and private costs of provision goods and services. Polluter Pays Principle has its application in the field of natural resource management and this was institutionally advocated by the OECD (1975) for adoption in its member countries, which are typically industrial and industrial economies. The principle focuses on two things: (a) Allocating costs of pollution prevention and control measures to encourage rational use of scarce environmental resources and to avoid distortions in trade and investment; (b) Reflecting the costs of these measures in the costs of goods and services, whose extraction or production or consumption cause pollution. This is internalisation of environmental costs. When environmental costs are taken into account the market fails to reflect these costs in the price system.

Pollution The presence of matter or energy whose nature, location or quantity produces undesired environmental effects.

Polygamous Species Species in which the males mate with more than one of the opposite sex. Such species are pheasants and deer, can be replenished satisfactorily by restricting the killing of females only.

Polygon Overlay and Intersection The creation of new polygons (entities) by the process of overlaying and intersecting the boundaries from two or more vector representations of area entities.

Polygon 1. Dimensional vector object (i.e. area). Polygons are defined by a set of arcs with a common topology. 2. A multi-sided figure representing an area on a map. 3. A multifaceted vector graphic figure used to represent an area and formed from a closed chain of points.

Polygon-on-polygon Overlay Process of overlaying two polygon maps to determine how the two sets of polygons overlap. There are three main types of polygon overlay: union, intersect and identity.

Polynomial An expression having a finite number of terms of the form ax + bx5 +... Nx.

Polyploid Having more than two chromosome sets; the individual so constituted are called triploid or tetraploid or pentaploid or hexaploid, etc.

Pond Body of standing water smaller than a lake.

Population 1. A finite (or infinite) set of 'objects' whose properties are to be studied in a survey. 2. The aggregate of all units, however, sampled, forming the subject of study. The term is used in statistics.

Population and Global Environmental Problems Population growth remains central to many of the global environmental problems. Over the last two centuries, population of the world increased menacingly. In the year 1800 the world population was one billion. It reached two billion in the year 1930, i.e., after a span of 130 years. Then it reached three billion in the year 1960, i.e., after thirty years. Then it took about eleven to fourteen years to add one billion to the world population. Now, as the present trend continues, another billion of people will be added to the existing global population in every eleven years until 2021. In the year 2025, it is expected that the world population will be about 8.5

billion. What is disturbing is the fact that most of the population growth takes place in the third world countries where the resource management is very poor. Apart from this, about 60 per cent of the future increase in population will be in those tropical countries. Among all the continents, Africa has the highest projected growth rate, followed by Asia and Latin America. The linkage between population and environmental degradation is always visible. With the passage of time, industrial growth led to multiplication of per capita consumption of natural resources. Consequently, per capita level of pollution and environmental degradation increased manifold. As that growth continues, air, water, and pollution and depletion of natural resources become more widespread. This cumulatively led to increase in toxic industrial production on living resources. Now, the world population touched 6 billion and world economic activity has quadrupled in the last century. The pressure of agricultural and industrial development has strained the ecosystem of the planet, which consequently led to the beginning of the phase where carrying capacity of the planets resources like soil, forests, oceans, estuaries and atmosphere are transgressed at an alarmingly rate. Since, population and economic activity still continue their explosive growth, the resources of the planet are under tremendous pressure. The rapidity of changes under way is spelled out justifiably in the following passages from 'Our Common Future': "The planet is passing through a period of drastic growth and fundamental change. Our human world of 5 billion must make room in a finite environment for another human world. The population could stabilize at between 8 billion and 14 billion some time next century, according to UN Projection ... Economic activity has multiplied to create a $13 trillion world economy, and this could grow five or tenfold in the coming century."

Population Cycle Periodic rise and fall of population of a species.

Population Pressure The sum total of all factors, such as increase in population, decrease in available food supply, etc. which tend to reduce the capacity of the environment to support the population. If the pressure is not released, migration or expansion of range, or extinction or decline in population will result.

Porcupine Any of a groups of related gnawing rodents, of the genus

Hystrix, having coarse hair mixed with stout erectile spines or quills. Three species are known in India. They are: (i) *H. leucura*, found from the Himalayas to Kanya Kumari in rocky hill-sides; (ii) *H. hodgsoni* found only in central and eastern Himalayas, Assam and lower West Bengal; and (ii) *Atherurus macrurus* the brush-tailed porcupine, found in lower West Bengal and Assam.

Postal Code Non-geographic co-ordinate system consisting of alphanumeric codes used to increase the efficiency of mail sorting and delivery. If linked to geographic co-ordinates, these can be a useful form of spatial reference. This system of linking non-geographic entity is used in USA.

Post-climax A community more exacting than the climax, climatic of a given region, and found under exceptionally favourable site conditions within that region. Also see Pre-climax, sub-climax and climax.

Potable Suitable or safe for drinking.

Prairie An extensive tract of level or rolling land that was originally treeless and grass covered. Generally characterized by a deep fertile soil. Similar but generally infertile tracts in South America are termed llano. Such areas are found in north of the Amazon; and Pampa south of it; in Asia, steppe; in south Africa, high Veld.

Precautionary Principle (PP) The precautionary principle states that, while embarking on developmental process, we should avoid risks or reject policies and practices that could have unsustainable outcome or negative impacts on the ecosystem. In other words, it advises to take sufficient precaution in any initiatives in natural resource management. Putting it in another way, it offers a way of living with uncertainties about limits and impacts of economic activity or new technologies on ecosystem. It is important for environmental governance. Montreal Protocol (1996) is considered as historic because of adaptation of this principle. It suggested Governments to adopt significant measures for environmental protection well before full scientific knowledge about the threat has been ascertained. Sustainable development cannot afford to ignore developmental policies that are based on incomplete and uncertain information. In addition to these features, system uncertainties or socio-economic changes or stochastic features of bio-geographical phenomenon do warrant a cautious approach, largely expressed as "Precautionary Principle". The precautionary principle is based on the idea that any uncertainty should be interpreted towards a measure of safeguard. The PP principle is equivalent in a sense to a 'better safe than sorry' principle. Agenda 21, Principle 15 of the Rio Declaration of the Earth's Summit (1992) states: 'in order to protect the environment, the precautionary approach shall be widely applied by states according to their capabilities'. Some of the key elements of a legal definition are: (a) A threshold of perceived threat against which advance action would be deemed justifiable; (b) A burden of proof on the activity contributor or entrepreneur to show that a proposed action will not cause actual harm.

Precipitation Deposits of atmospheric moisture in liquid or solid forms, i.e., rain, snow, hail, dew and frost.

Precision 1. The degree of concentration of estimates about their mean value in repeated sampling; or the reliability of the determination of the true mean value derived from such estimates. The reciprocal of the variance is a measure of the precision. 2. Degree of accuracy of numerical representation, generally refers to the number of significant digits of information to the right of the decimal point. 3. Statistically it is the degree of variation about the mean. 4. A (statistical) measure of the dispersion of the values observed when measuring a characteristic of elements in a population; a clustering of values about their average.

Precision and Accuracy These terms are frequently used in the field of sampling. The reciprocal of the variance is a measure of the precision The term 'precision' is indicated by the size of the sampling error and excludes the effects of biases. Accuracy refers to the size of the total error including the effect of biases. In a forest inventory, much emphasis is laid on accuracy of an estimate. We always aim at designing an inventory for the maximum precision that is achieved by reducing bias to a minimum. A well-designed sample yields best results. *See* precision.

Precision Forestry Precision forestry uses high technology sensing and analytical tools to support site-specific, economic, environmental, and sustainable decision making for the forestry sector. Its real potential lies in its ability to improve the forestry process, not only helping to collect information but to use it for better and more transparent decision making (IUFRO, 2006).

Preclimax The plant community in seral development immediately preceding the climatic climax of the region, and found under site conditions drier than are usual in the climate of the region. *See* pro-climax, sub-climax.

Predation Pressure The effect of predation on a natural community especially with reference to survival of species preyed upon.

Predatism The practice of living as a predator. *See* predator and parasitism.

Predator 1. An animal which preys on other inferior or weaker animals. Predators have an important role in regulating balance of nature. Predator-prey relationship is intricate. Different forms of predation can be recognized. CHANCE PREDATION: When the prey species is temporarily at a disadvantage and is seized by a predator. HABIT PREDATION: When a species or individual habitually preys on another weaker species. SUCKEER-LIST PREDATION: When mentally and physically deformed individuals are eliminated by predators. 2. An animal that preys externally on others. A predator usually destroys several host; an animal parasite usually lives in or on a single host.

Predator mediated co-existence The co-existence of species in a community, one or more of which would have become competitively excluded, was not for the presence of a keystone predator. *See* Keystone predator.

Predominant Taller trees among dominants whose crowns reach above the general level of the upper canopy and determine the top level of the canopy.

Pregermination The procedure of germination of seed, usually until the radicle just emerges, before sowing in the forest or nursery.

Prescribed burning Skilful application of fire to natural fuels under conditions of weather, fuel moisture, soil moisture, etc. that allow confinement of fire to an predetermined area and produce the intensity of heat and rate of spread to accomplish planned benefits to one or more objectives of silviculture, wildlife management, grazing or hazard reduction (USDA Forest Service, 1956).

Preservation Saving from or maintaining against injury or destruction. Keeping safe and undisturbed for private or public use.

Preserve An area (as a tract of land with water) restricted for the protection or preservation of animals, trees or other natural resources, e.g., a wild life preserve. *See* sanctuary.

Pressure Applied to wildlife management, a factor that tends to reduce a wildlife population, especially one which arises from human activity. *See* population pressure.

Pre-suppression, Fire Those fire-protection activities concerned with the organization training, instruction and management of a fire control force and with the inspection and maintenance of fire control improvements, equipment and supplies to ensure effective fire suppression.

Pre-treatment Various treatments applied to seed prior to sowing in order to increase the rapidity or completeness of germination.

Prevention, Fire Those fire-protection activities concerned with the attempt to reduce the number of fires through education, hazard reduction, rewards and concessions for co-operation in fire-protection, and imposition of penalties according to law in cases of incendiarism.

Prey An inferior or weaker animal which is preyed upon by a predator. An animal that is or may be seized by another to be devoured.

Prickout, to To transplant small seedling individually into nursery bed. *See* line out, to.

Primary Colours A set of three colours that in various combinations will produce the full range of colours in the visible spectrum. There are two sets of primary colours, additive and subtractive.

Primary Data Data collected through first-hand observation. Field notes, survey recordings and GPS readings are examples of primary data.

Primary Forest Forest where there are no clearly visible indications of human activities and ecological processes are not significantly disturbed (FRA, 2005).

Primary Function A designated function is considered to be primary when it is significantly more important than other functions (FRA, 2005).

Prime Meridian Meridian of longitude 0 degrees, used as the origin for measurements of longitude. The meridian of Greenwich, England, is the internationally accepted prime meridian on most charts. However, local or national prime meridians are occasionally used.

Primeval Primeval relates to the earliest ages of the world or human history. It is always natural, essentially uninfluenced by human activity. The use of the term in connection with forest, vegetation cover, etc., is deprecated, as it does not allow for evolution and other factors.

Principal Component Analysis (PCA) 1. It is a method of analyzing multivariate data in order to express their variation in terms of a minimum number of principal components or linear combinations of the original, partially correlated variables. 2. It is an analysis of covariance in a multiple data set so that the data can be projected as additive combinations into a new axes, which express different kinds of correlation among the data.

Prism 1. A polygonal solid; a polyhedron having parallel, polygonal, and congruent bases and sides that are parallelograms. 2. Sometimes used in GIS to indicate a 3d solid body delineated by irregular polygonal faces.

Probability 1. The frequency expressed as a proportion or percentage of the total frequency, with which a long series of trials, strictly comparable circumstances will produce a specified value of a variable rather than any other conceivable value. 2. The chance of an event or occurrence.

Probability Distribution Function A real-valued function (in the range 0, 1) whose integral over a set gives the probability of a random variable having a value within the set.

Proclimax A term applied to all communities that suggest something of the permanence or extent of a climax, but are not typical of existing climate. It includes sub-climax, sere-climax, pre-climax, post-climax and dis-climax.

Production Forest Forests or other wooded land designated for production and extraction of forest goods, including both wood and non-wood forest products (FRA, 2005).

Production 1. The process of producing organic material. 2. The increase in bio-mass, by individuals, species or species groupings, over time. 3. The process of producing and extracting forest goods, including both wood and non-wood forest products.

Productivity 1. The rate at which bio-mass is produced per unit area by any class of organisms. 2. Rate of new tissue formation or energy utilization by one or more organisms. 3. Capacity or ability of an environmental unit to produce organic material.

4. The ability of a population to recruit new members by reproduction. In other words, the rate at which mature breeding stock produces other mature stock or mature removable crop.

Profundal The deep, bottom-water area beyond the depth of effective light penetration. All of the lake floor beneath the hypolimnion.

Programme A set of instructions directing the computer to perform a task.

Project Elephant Project Elephant was launched in February 1992 to assist states having free ranging population of wild elephants to ensure long term survival of identified viable population of elephants in their natural habitats. The project is being implemented in 12 states, viz. Andhra Pradesh, Arunachal Pradesh, Assam. Jharkhand, Karnataka, Kerala, Meghalaya, Nagaland, Orissa, Tamil Nadu, Uttarakhand and West Bengal. States are being given financial as well as technical assistance in achieving the objectives of the project. Help is also provided to other states with small population of elephants for the purpose of census, training of field staff and mitigation of human-elephant conflict. Main activities of project elephant are: strengthening of measure for protection of wild elephants from poachers, development of scientific and planned management for conservation of elephant habitats and viable population of wild Asiatic elephants in India, ecological restoration of existing natural habitats and migratory routes of elephants, promotion of measures for mitigation of man-elephant conflict in problem areas and moderating pressures of human and live stock on crucial elephant habitats, eco-development, veterinary care, research on elephant issues relating to elephant conservation, public education and awareness programme and capacity building of field staff, *mahouts* and veterinarians.

Project Tiger "Project Tiger" was launched in 1973 with an objective "to ensure maintenance of a viable population of tigers in India for scientific, economic, aesthetic, cultural and ecological values, and to preserve for all times, areas of biological importance as a national heritage for the benefit, education and enjoyment of the people." The Project has been successfully implemented, and at present there are 281 Tiger Reserves in 17 states, covering an area of 37761 sq. km. The selection of reserves was guided by the need to conserve unique ecosystem / habitat types across the geographic distribution of tigers in the country. The network of tiger reserves include high mountainous terrains of Arunachal Pradesh, the heavy rainfall areas of Assam and West Bengal, the estuarine mangroves of Sunderbans, the dry forests of Rajasthan, the foothills of the Himalayas in Uttarakhand, Uttar Pradesh and Bihar, the Central Indian Highlands of Madhya Pradesh, Chhattisgarh, and Maharashtra, and the plateau of Chotanagpur (Jharkhand), the hilly tropical and evergreen forests of Orissa, the evergreen forests of Western Ghats in Kerala and Karnataka, the dry deciduous forests of Andhra Pradesh and the Southern moist deciduous forests of Tamil Nadu. 'Project Tiger' is undisputedly the custodian of major gene pool of the country and a repository of some of the most valuable ecosystem and habitats for wildlife. For the purpose of management, the tiger reserves are constituted on a 'core'-'buffer' strategy. In the core area, forestry operations, collection of non-timber forest produce, grazing, human settlement and other biotic disturbances are not allowed, and are singularly oriented towards conservation. The buffer zone is managed as a 'multiple use area', with conservation oriented land use, having the twin objectives of ensuring habitat supplement to the spillover population of wild animals from the core, apart from providing site specific eco-developmental inputs to fringe dwelling, stakeholder communities. The main thrust of the project is protection and mitigation of deleterious human impacts with a view to comprehensively revive the natural ecosystem in the reserves. Project Tiger has been rated as a role model and has been noted as one of the 56 events that changed India since independence.

Projection A model of the Earths surface for mapping (usually in 2 dimensions). *See* map projection.

Propagule Any spore, seed, fruit or other part of a plant or microorganism capable of producing a new plant and used as a means of dispersal.

Proposed Reserve An area notified under a Forest Act as one which is proposed to be constituted into a reserved forest.

Protected Area 1. An area constituted by order of a State Government in India, to give protection to wildlife in places other than parks and sanctuaries. 2. An area protected by legislation, regulation, or land-use policy to control the level of human occupancy or activities. Categories of protected areas include protected landscapes, national parks, sanctuaries, conservation areas, multiple-use management areas, and nature (wildlife) reserves.

Protected Areas, Classification of The Commission of National Parks and Protected Areas of IUCN classified the protected areas into the following categories: Category I: Strict Nature Reserve/ Wilderness Areas: Protected areas managed mainly for science or wilderness protection. Category II: National Park: Protected areas managed mainly for ecosystem conservation and recreation. Category III: Natural Monument: Protected areas managed mainly for conservation of specific natural features. Category IV: Habitat/ Species Management Areas: Protected areas mainly for conservation through management intervention. Category V: Protected Landscape/Seascape: Protected areas managed mainly for conservation and recreation. Category VI: Managed Resource Protected Area: Protected areas managed mainly for the sustainable use of natural ecosystem.

Protection Guarding against danger or injury. Partial protection of certain species is achieved by enforcing close seasons and restrictions on human activity. Total protection is achieved by constituting sanctuaries or national park or conservation areas under Wild Life Act.

Protection Forests 1. Forest area declared as protected forests under Indian Forest Act, 1927. Proposed name for forests protected from harvesting by policy. These forests usually protect sensitive sites, such as watersheds and steep slopes. Generally protection forests are those forests which are designated for protection of soil and water (FRA, 2005).

Protection Forestry The practice of forestry with the primary objective of (1) protecting lands whether those upon which the forest is situated or those at a distance from it, against wind and water erosion; (2) conserving water supplies for human consumption, fish culture, etc.; (3) reducing hazards from flood damage to human life and property; and (4) ameliorating adverse climatic effects.

Protective Colouration (or Colouring) The natural colouration of any of certain organisms by means of which it blends with its normal environment and is thus protected from destruction by its enemies.

Prototyping It is a software development and project management methodology that uses 'prototype', i.e. software applications to test ideas with potential users. *See also* 'pilot project'.

Provenance The geographical source or place of origin from which a given lot of seed or plants was collected; the material from such a source or origin; often restricted to imply material from a specified race. In other words, the geographical origin of seed is its provenance.

Proximity. The closeness of one item to another.

Prune, to To remove live or dead branches or multiple leaders from standing trees for the improvement of the tree or its timber. Pruning of dead branches is called dry pruning. Pruning of living branches is called green pruning.

Pruning, Natural The natural death and fall of branches of standing trees from such causes as deficiency of light, decay, snow and ice. A very important effect of closing up of the crop is the hastening of the natural dying off of the lower branches, undoubtedly owing to the reduction of the light reaching them. The denser and more uniform the crop, the effective is the process of natural pruning.

Pruning, Root The pruning of roots, particularly for the purpose of encouraging the development of a compact, fibrous root system.

Psammophyte 1. A plant adapted to sandy tracts like seashore, dunes etc. 2. A plant growing in sands or sandy soils.

Psychrometer An instrument for determining the relative humidity of the atmosphere.

Puddle, to 1. To dip the roots of young plants in thin mud to conserve moisture. 2. To work clayey soil with water to pasty condition.

Pulp Wood chips that have been ground mechanically into fibres and are used for the production of inexpensive paper, such as newsprint, or that have been chemically treated to remove the lignin and are used to manufacture higher quality papers.

Pulpwood Wood cut or prepared primarily for manufacture into wood pulp.

Pure Line A line homozygous for all elomorphs; a family genetically homogenous for all its characters.

Purity (of Seed) The percentage of gross weight of sample of seed remaining after the removal of all matters other than the seed itself with such part of the fruits as is sown with it.

Pushbroom System An imaging device consisting of a fixed linear array of many sensors which is swept across an area by the motion of the platform, thereby building up an image. It relies on sensors whose response and reading is nearly instantaneous, so that the image swathe can be segmented into pixels representing small dimensions on the ground.

Pyrophyte A species that is adapted to survive severe fires. *See* fire climax.

Python Any of various large non-venomous old world tropical snakes of genus Python, which kills by constriction. Common in Indian forest.

Qq

Quadrant A quarter of a circle measured in units of 90 degrees.

Quadrat 1. A small field study unit or sample area, usually a square metre or a milliacre in size, established for the purpose of detailed observation. 2. A small, clearly demarcated, sample area of known size on which ecological observations are made. The term was originally applied to square areas, but now rectangles and even circles are frequently used. Generally it represents an area having a square decimetre, or square metre, or square mile, or a milliacre.

Quadtree A data structure for thematic information in a raster database that seeks to minimize data storage. 2. A compact raster data structure in which geographical space is subdivided into variably sized homogeneous quarters. This term is used in GIS.

Quail Any of various game birds, native of Asia, Europe, Africa and America, resembling domestic fowls. It is a migratory bird, some what like a diminutive partridge in shape and general colouration. It is much esteemed for the table. COMMON or GREY QUAIL (*Coturnix coturnix*): A miniature partridge with sandy colouration. It has a wide distribution in many parts of the Old World. It is highly migratory. It is mostly a winter visitor, though a large number are resident. JUNGLE BUSH QUAIL (*Perdicula asiatica*): Netted on a large scale and may be usually had in most bird markets. MOUNTAIN QUAIL (*Ophrysia superciliosa*). RAIN or BLACK-BREASTED QUAIL (*Coturnix coromandelicus*): Distinguished from the common quail by the black breast. It is found practically throughout the whole of India. Ascending the Himalayas up to 2,000 m. In many areas it appears with the rains and leaves after breeding; hence the name rain quail. In other areas it appears to be resident. Netted on a large scale for illegal sale in markets.

YELLOW-LEGGED BUTTON QUAIL: INDIAN QUAIL (*Turnix tanki*; Syn. *T. dussumieri*). Order Hemipodii. It is resident in the greater part of India; ascending the Himalayas up to 2400 mt. It avoids thick forests, preferring corn fields and grassy plains.

Quaking Bog Accumulation of organic matter and living organisms in the littoral.

Quality, Site A measure of the relative productive capacity of a site for a particular species. The top height as it varies with age is generally the basis for classification of site. *See* site quality, site class.

Quantization The process of converting from continuous values of information to a finite number of discrete values.

Quaternary Triangular Mesh (QTM) A referencing system that tries to deal with irregularities on the earth's surface using a regular mesh of triangles. An alternative to the geographic (latitude and longitude) referencing system.

Quincunx A group of five points, four of which form the corners of a square with the fifth as centre. In planting, an arrangement in which an extra plant is placed in the centre of each square of four plants.

Rr

Race Generally considered as an element of a linnean species separable as occurring naturally in a part only of the geographical or ecological range of the species, but not so well-defined as to constitute a taxonomic variety. *See* strain.

Radar Acronym for Radio Detection and Ranging. Radar is an active form of remote sensing that operates in the microwave and radio wavelength regions.

Radiometric Correction Correction of variation in data values that is caused by sensor malfunctions and atmospheric conditions.

Radiometric Enhancement Techniques that correct and improve radiometric values of individual pixels.

Rain Forest Rain forests or evergreen forest are associated with a climate characterized by continual high humidity and abundant rainfall and a short or no dry season. Rain forests are found on or near the equator where the climate is hot and wet. Heavy rainfall results as the most air brought by the converging trade-winds rises because of the heat. Over half of the tropical rainforests are in Central and South America, the rest in South East Asia and Africa. They provide the bulk of the oxygen needed for plant and animal respiration. Tropical rain forests covered 14 per cent of the earth's land surface, but are now destroyed at an increasing rate as their valuable timbers harvested and the land cleared for agriculture, causing problems of deforestation. Although by 1991 over 50 per cent of the world's rain forests have been removed, they still comprise about 50 per cent of all growing wood on the planet, and harbour at least 40 per cent of the earth's species (plants and animals). Tropical rain forests are characterised by a great diversity of species, usually of tall broad-leafed evergreen trees with many climbers, ferns, etc. They comprise some of the most complex and diverse ecosystems on the planet and help to regulate global weather pattern. Clearing of rain forests may lead to a global warming of the atmosphere and contribute to green house effect.

Rain Shadow An area to the leeward of a high land mass, particularly a mountain range, which receives less rain than would be expected had the high land mass not been upwind of it. Normally the rain shadow area receives the residue of orographic rain.

Raised Bog Accumulation of organic matter with excellent capillarity that raises water level in the mat which can result in the bog being raised above the original soil surface.

Ramsar Convention on Wetlands The Ramsar Convention on Wetlands, signed in Ramsar, Islamic Republic of Iran, in 1971, is an inter-governmental treaty that provides the framework for national action and international co-operation for the conservation and wise use of wetlands and their resources. Unlike most environmental treaties, it is not part of the UN system, although it collaborates extensively with other secretariats and partners. As of August 2004, 1374 sites totalling more than 121.4 million hectares were designated for inclusion in the List of Wetlands of International importance. Since mangrove forests are underrepresented on this lists, Conference of the Parties (CoP) to the Convention adopted three resolutions emphasizing their ecological and socio-economic importance. *See* wetland.

Random Quadrats Random placement of fixed sampling areas for vegetation research. *See* quadrats.

Randomized Arrangement One determined entirely by chance, as for example, when one out of all possible arrangements is selected by lot. This is in vogue in statistics. *See* design.

Range 1. The region throughout which a kind of organism or ecological community naturally lives or occurs. It refers to geographical and latitudinal limits within which the species is found. Owing to seasonal migration the terms 'winter range' and 'summer range' are frequently used and in the case of vanishing species, the terms 'former range' and 'present range' are used. 2. An open region, over which cattle sheep and other live-stock may roam and feed, especially when unenclosed. 3. Land, including forest land that primarily produces natural vegetation suitable for livestock grazing. 4. The area in which a plant naturally lives and reproduces. 5. The known geographical distribution of a plant or animal during a defined period of time. 6. The area in which an animal seeks food and water. 7. In arithmetic, the difference between the largest and smallest values in a set. 8. In geostatistics, the distance at which a transitive variogram ceases to increase monotonically. *See* forest range.

Range, Home The area occupied by a given individual (of wild life). It denotes the area needed for food, for raising a family, etc. It indicates the potential population density for any species.

Range, Natural The geographical and altitudinal limits within which an organism occurs naturally. *See* habitat.

Raster 1. Common GIS data model made up of a grid of cells or pixels. Each pixel contains a single value. 2. A regular grid of cells covering an area. 3. The scanned and illuminated area of a video display, produced by a modulated beam of electrons sweeping the phosphorescent screen line by line from top to bottom at a regular rate of repetition.

Raster Data Model System of tessellating rectangular cells in which individual cells are used as building blocks to create images of point, line, area, network and surface entities.

Raster Data Structure A database containing all mapped, spatial information in the form of regular grid cells.

Raster Display A device for displaying information in the form of pixels on a computer screen or VDU.

Raster Format A means of representing spatial data in the from of a grid of Digital Number (DN), each line of which can be used to modulate the lines of a video raster.

Rasterization 1.The process of converting an image of lines and polygons from vector representation to a gridded representation. 2. The process of converting data from vector to raster format.

Raster Map A map encoded in the form of a regular array of cells.

Raster-to-Vector Conversion *See* vectorization.

Raw Humus or Litter The portion of the forest floor which is not in an advanced state of decomposition.

Rayleigh Scattering Selective scattering of light in the atmosphere by particle that are small compared with the wavelength of light.

Real Time Refers to images or data made available for inspection simultaneously with their acquisition. Real time tasks or functions executed so rapidly that the user gets an impression of continuous visual feedback.

Realization An equi-probable result of stochastic simulation based on a known probability distribution function.

Recessive Character A character that dose not develop unless the gene responsible for it is present in both members of the chromosome pair, i.e., unless homozygous dominant character.

Reciprocal Cross A cross involving the same characters as another, but with the sexes of the parents interchanged.

Re-classification The process of re-classifying values in a map layer to produce a new map layer.

Re-connaissance of Forest A preliminary inspection of survey of a forest area, made in order to gain a general knowledge of all facts likely to be useful in determining future management approaches.

Re-connaissance Report (Forest) A report made to the forest owner (government or other), based on a re-connaissance and a review of past management to be adopted, with any possible alternatives, in order to manage the forest area sustainably. Better known in India as the preliminary working plan report which after sanction, forms the basis of instructions given to the working plan officer.

Record A set of attributes relating to a geographicai entity; a set of related, contiguous data in a computer file.

Recreation Refreshment of mind and body by means of some pastime, agreeable exercise or other resource affording relaxation and enjoyment.

Recruit One of the individuals forming the recruitment or young regeneration in a natural forest.

Recruitment 1. Those trees which have entered a particular category during a specified period. 2. Seedlings which have recently appeared in regeneration area, or stem which have grown into a particular diameter or girth class.

Rectangular Co-ordinates *See* 'Cartesian co-ordinates'.

Rectification Making an image that conforms to a map projection system. It is a process of projecting or transforming a tilted or oblique photograph onto a horizontal reference plane, the angular relation between the photograph and the plane being determined by ground re-connaissance.

Red Data Books and Red Lists It an unique global initiative which provide fundamental baseline information on the status of biodiversity as it changes over time. The IUCN Red Lists are widely recognized as the most comprehensive, a political global approach for evaluating the conservation status of plant and animal species. The IUCN Red List Programme and its companion information management system (the Species Information Service) are evolving into a broader biodiversity assessments initiative, which will provide fundamental baseline information on the status of biodiversity as it changes over time. The goals of the IUCN Red List Programme are to: (1) Identify and document those species most in need of conservation attention if global extinction rates are to be reduced; and (2) Provide a global index of the state of degeneration of biodiversity. Since their inception, the IUCN (International Union Conservation of Nature and Natural Resources) Red Data Books and Red Lists have enjoyed an increasingly prominent role in guiding conservation activities of Governments, NGOs and scientific institutions. *See* IUCN Red List.

Redundancy The inclusions of data in a database that contribute little to the information content.

Re-entrant An introversion of land levels, as exemplified by bays, inlets and valleys and delineated in map contours, in contrast to their extroversion, i.e. extension, as in capes, promontories and spurs.

Reflectance Ratio of the radiant energy reflected by a body to the energy incident on it. Spectral reflectance is the reflectance measured within a specific wavelength interval.

Reforest, to To restock felled or otherwise cleared forests or woodland.

Reforestation 1.The re-establishment of trees on denuded forest land by natural or artificial means, such as planting and seeding. 2. Establishment of forest plantations on temporarily unstocked lands that are considered as forest (FAO, 2001).

Refuge An area designated for the protection of game animals, birds and fish. *See* sanctuary.

Refuge Cover Vegetation from which game cannot be driven.

Regenerate, to To renew a forest crop by natural or artificial means. It is also known as restocking.

Regeneration 1. The act of replacing old crop with younger ones either naturally or artificially is called regeneration or reproduction. 2. A parent tree's establishment of progeny. 3. Re-growth of the forest following harvesting, either through natural process of seed dispersal and germination of artificially by planting. 4. The renewal of a forest crop by natural or artificial means; also the new crop so obtained. The regeneration of tree species has been classified into categories such as: (a) *Recruit*: Plant of one year old and contains two to four leaves.(b) *Unestablished*: Includes all whippy and sub-whippy plants having collar girth of thumb size and height up to 1.25 Mt. (c) *Established*: Plants having collar girth more than thumb size and height more than 1.25 Mt.

Regeneration Area The area laid down, normally in a working plan or scheme, to be regenerated in a specified time.

Regeneration Block The periodic block under regeneration.

Regeneration Interval The interval between the seeding felling and the final felling on a particular area.

Regeneration Survey A survey for the assessment of regeneration (established and unestablished) generally by sample enumeration. Natural regeneration commonly in the form of recruits, half-established and established or pole crop, appears on the forest floor in different varieties of species as well as sizes. By observing the forest floor, it becomes difficult to make an estimate of regeneration status correctly. Besides, ocular method is also susceptible to various errors. Hence, there is always a need to develop a scientific method to determine the regeneration status in the forests. Since hundred percent enumeration of regeneration found on the forest floor is not possible, the only option lies on sampling or sample enumerations. Therefore, regeneration survey, by definition, is a survey for the assessment of recruits, half-established and established regeneration generally by the method of sample enumeration.

Regeneration, Artificial The renewal of a forest crop by sowing, planting, or other artificial methods. Sometime the crop so obtained is also called as regeneration.

Regeneration, Gap A method of artificial regeneration in gaps, occurring or created in a forest floor, usually for supplementing regeneration.

Regeneration, Natural 1. The renewal of a forest crop by self-sown seed, or by coppice or root suckers. 2. Sometimes regeneration denotes the crop so obtained. Successful natural regeneration from seed depends upon the success of the following broad processes: seed production, seed dissemination, germination of seed and establishment of seedlings. For sustainable development of forest resources, it is necessary that crop continues with natural regeneration. For natural regeneration to take place successfully, the ground conditions required in Indian context are: (a) Adequate seed supply; (b) Adequate light condition, i.e. obtained *via* the regulation of the density and composition of various strata or canopies; (c) Soil composition and degree of development of undergrowth to protect the seedlings from desiccation and biotic influences with out undue competition for light, moisture and nutrients and also to improve the soil structure and nutrient status; (d) Efficient protection from damage from all kinds, (e) Adequate drainage, infiltration and aeration in the soil mass; (f) Effective soil and moisture conservation. In a situation where the forest ground conditions are compatible and congenial to natural regeneration, renewal of forest is a continuous process. But when such conditions are not fulfilled, then the regeneration process is affected. As a result, regeneration does not take place or inadequate regeneration occurs.

Registration Making two images conforms to one another. Process of superposing two or more images or photographs so that equivalent geographic points coincide.

Regression 1. Reversion to some earlier stage of succession consequent on the introduction of an adverse factor retrogression. 2. The relationship between specified values of one variable and the means of all corresponding values of another variable dependent on the first.

Regression Co-efficient In a linear regression equation, the increase in the dependent variable corresponding to unit increase in the independent.

Regulation, Forest 1. A branch of forestry concerned with the technical aspects of organising and maintaining a forest for sustained development including yield. 2. A legal framework regulating forest and its development.

Re-introduce A term used when a plant or animal once existed in an area, has become extinct and is being re-introduced from elsewhere. In such cases only the identical species and not a kindred species should be brought back into an area.

Relational Database A computer database employing an ordered set of attribute values or records known as tuples grouped into two-dimensional tables called relations.

Relational Database Structure A method of structuring data in the form of sets of records or tuples so that relations between different entities and attributes can be used for data access and transformation.

Relations Two-dimensional tables of data in a relational database.

Relative Geo-referencing The referencing in space of the location of a point to a local base station rather than to a global grid.

Release The freeing of trees and other vegetation from growth overtopping or immediately surrounding them.

Releve Method 1. A method of vegetation classification that groups classes by presence and abundance of characteristic species that are neither ubiquitous nor rare – typically a European methodology (Braun-Blanquette method). 2. A method of systematic and comprehensive searches through an area to collect complete information on species diversity.

Relict A community or species which, through the operation of a compensatory or protective feature, has survived some important change that has altered the general vegetation of the surrounding territory.

Relief Shadows Areas calculated to be in the shadow of hills using a Digital Terrain Model (DTM). The amount of shadow varies according to the relative position of the sun as determined by the time of day and date.

Relief Vertical irregularities of a surface; local difference in elevations.

Remote Sensing Remote sensing is the science of deriving information about the earth's land and water areas from images acquired at a distance. It is all about collection and interpretation of information about an object without being in physical contact with the object. In other words, it is a process of detecting and (or) monitoring chemical or physical properties of an area by measuring its reflected and emitted radiation. It usually relies upon measurement of electromagnetic energy reflected or emitted from the features of interest. Often used to refer to earth observation from satellite platforms using electromagnetic sensors. An explicitly spatial method of using satellite imagery to conduct ecological research and decision-making. Acquisition of information about objects using photographic or electromagnetic sensors on airplane or satellite platforms.

Removable Storage Computer data magnetic or optical storage media which are portable and include examples such as floppy disks, DAT tapes, and CD ROMs.

Renewability Ability of an organism or community to restore to the original status. This is a critical concept which characterise the nature of renewable resources. All renewable resources are renewable in nature but their ability to renew themselves is of course dependent on the systems that supply moisture and nutrients and maintain the media of air and soil in which medium they grow. Apart from this, they also depend upon ecological efficiency and resilience of the ecosystem in which other renewable resources play an a critical role.

Renewable Resources Renewable resources are those resources which have the capability for renewal. However, the distinction between non-renewable or exhaustible resources is not altogether watertight. Renewable resources can be exhausted, destroyed, or depleted like exhaustible resources. Tropical forests are a case in point. The distinction generally adopted between renewable and non-renewable resources is based on the rate of formation or replenishment. Fossil fuels are created by their organic and geological process and this process still continues today. But the rate of formation is so slow that it is negligible in comparison to the time span considered for our interpretation. In contrast to this, forests which regenerate or have the capacity to regenerate well within a finite period of time are aptly classified as the renewable resources. *See* natural resources.

Replication Repetition of a treatment or set of treatment in several plots undertaken in order to provide an assessment of the variability amongst plots treated alike and to increase the precision of comparisons.

Report, Basic Information (Working Plan) Before commencing the working plan revision, the Working Plan Officer (WPO) needs some very basic information. The divisional forest officer of the concerned territorial division prepares the Basic Information Report (BIR) and submits to the working plan officer for initiating the preliminary revision of the last working plan.

Report, First Preliminary (Working Plan) First Preliminary report is the first report submitted by the working plan officer to the review committee set up for revision of the working plan. This report is generally submitted before initiating fieldwork. Normally, a working plan officer takes two to three months to prepare and submit this report. This report is primarily based on the Basic Information Report (BIR) of the concerned forest division and observation of ground conditions and preliminary assessment of the forests with respect to effects of last plan and the existing and emergent problems of forest management in the said division.

Report, Second Preliminary (Working Plan) This is a report prepared by the working plan officer after analyzing and interpreting the data collected from primary and secondary sources. Generally, it takes twelve to fifteen months from the date of submission of first preliminary report. At this stage, the working plan officer is in a position to visualize the problems and constraints of management and based on his assessment and evaluation of last plan, he presents a strategy for managing forest resources of the forest division for the next 10 years. The second preliminary report, which contains analysis, evaluation and future strategy, is submitted and presented to a review committee. The review committee consists of senior officers of the state forest department as well as Ministry of Forest and Environment, Government of India. The committee discusses different aspects of proposed management strategy in the context of problems and constraints. The committee after due deliberation finalises the broad strategy necessary for the evolving management plan prescriptions.

Representational Fraction Scale of a map or chart expressed as a fraction or ratio that relates unit distance on the map to distance measured in the same unit on the ground.

Reproduction 1. A synonym for regeneration but more usually applied in forestry to a forest crop obtained by natural methods. 2. The process by which an organism reproduces, e.g., sexual or reproduction, asexual.

Reproduction Potential The maximum or unimpeded increase in the rate of a species in an ideal environment.

Reproduction, Asexual in biology reproduction that does not involve the production and fusion of sex cells, nor the necessity of two parents. Asexual reproduction can therefore lead to a rapid population build-up. It does not involve gamete, but excludes parthenogenesis.

Reproduction, Vegetative Reproduction, asexual in plants from some part of the plant body, e.g., of trees by coppice or root sucker or from root, stem or branch cutting.

Reptile A class of cold-blooded, lung-breathing vertebrates, belonging to the order Reptilia. This includes snakes, lizards, crocodiles, turtles, and tortoises. Indian reptiles include the cobra, *Naja naja* and *N. tripudians*; the Russell's viper, *Vipera russelli*; the Krait, *Bungarus coeruleus* and two crocodiles: *crocodilus porosus* and *C. palustris.*

Resampling 1. Technique for transforming a raster image from one particular scale and projection to another. 2. The calculation of new DN for pixels created during geometric correction of a digital scene, based on the values in the local area around the uncorrected pixels. 3. Extrapolating pixels values for a new grid from values in an old grid. It is applied after an image is rectified to a projection system or registered to another image.

Reserve A reserved forest or a reserved tree.

Resilience The ability of a community to return to its former state after disturbance. In other words, the capacity of the living community to recover from any kind of disturbance is known as resilience. In nature, the physical environment poses continuous challenges to the life forms with disturbance of various kinds. Apart from the natural disturbance, the human factor also inflicts perturbations and major disruptions in the communities. The recovery of the communities to its original structural and functional state after a span of time reflects the community's resilience, i.e. inherent tendency and capacity of the community to attain a dynamic equilibrium.

Resin Channel A longitudinal channel made on the stem of a resinous tree, e.g., chir pine, to induce flow of resin.

Resin Duct Intercellular tubular cavities containing resin and surrounded by excreting cells common to many softwoods such as pines, firs, etc. Also occurs in many hardwoods, especially of the dipterocarpacae family.

Resinosis An abnormal exudation of resin or pitch from conifers; also the abnormal impregnation of their tissues by resin gummosis.

Resistance The ability of a community to avoid alteration of its present state by a disturbance.

Resolution 1. Resolution is commonly expressed as the most closely spaced line-pairs per unit distance that can be distinguished. Also called spatial resolution. 2. The degree of discrimination between objects. It is also the ability to separate closely spaced objects on an image or photograph. It can be spatial resolution, i.e., that is what the smallest size and object needs to be to be observed. Spatial resolution indicates the size of the smallest recording unit to the smallest feature that can be mapped and measured. It can be spectral resolution, i.e., that is what number and size of area of the electromagnetic spectrum is required. It can be temporal resolution, i.e., that is how often does the subject need to be observed.

Resource Anything which has a utility or value. It is the most elusive term. There are many types of meaning. In one hand resources can be 'stock resources', like coal or iron or 'flow resources' like air, forests. Erich Zimmerman (1951) gave a different view about natural resources. He took the functional view of resources. He described that resource does not refer to a thing or a substance but to a function which a thing or a substance may perform. By this he meant that 'resources are not, they become.' In other words, he meant that any part of nature could become a resource when people perceive it as having utility or value. Changing perceptions, technology and economy create resources. Likewise, resources are destroyed or their value or utility reduced, in the same way it is created. A more common form of resource destruction involves degradation of resources. Degradation takes place when the use of the resource goes beyond its carrying capacity. But if resource is used within its threshold limit, then it does not degrade. Therefore, use of resource can be managed in such a way that productivity of the natural system does not reduce. Intensive agricultural practices can lead to soil erosion, which in turn leads to decline in land productivity and crop yield. Likewise, in case of a forest, when resources are removed at a faster rate than it is replenished by biological processes, then degradation sets in. The degradation process generally encompasses a series of stages. A change in technology or increased demand may lead to renewed pressure on the resources, and it initiates a cascade of negative changes leading to final exclusion of the resource from the earth.

Resource Economics A branch of economics related to the exploitation, extraction and regulation of the use of natural resources.

Resource Management The control of the use of natural resources in order to maximise the benefits that resource provides, while preventing overexploitation or degradation of the resource base. This may include the use of economic instruments such as marketable permits for the extraction of resources or other forms of regulation. Resource management can be used to ensure that renewable resource extraction is both efficient and sustainable (Markendya *et al.*, 2002).

Resources, Conservation of Natural The protection, improvement and use of natural resources according to principles, which will assure their highest environmental, economic and social service.

Resources, Natural All things produced by nature to sustain or support life. They include all potentially useful materials, forces, capacities and conditions provided by nature. *See* resources; natural resources.

Response Time The time that elapses between sending a command to the computer and the receipt of the results at the workstation.

Restocking To re-establish a forest crop at a site by natural or artificial means. *See* regeneration.

Restoration Ecology The restoration of derelict land to the exact state it was in previous to the disturbance.

Retention Harvesting A system of harvesting designed to retain individual trees or groups of trees to maintain structural diversity over the logged area of the forest.

Reversion The reappearance of an ancestral character which was not exhibited by the immediate parents and which has usually not appeared for several generations.

Rhinoceros Any of various, large, ungainly, heavy, plant eating perissodactyl mammals of tropical Africa and Asia, with one or two upright horns on the snout. They have very thick, frequently folded skin. Family Rhinocerotidae. Five species are still extinct. All species of rhinoceros are confined to the Old World and they differ remarkably from one another in structure. In India, the Great One-horned Rhinoceros (*Rhinoceros unicornis*) is found in Assam and West Bengal. Though it prefers swamp and grass, it is also found in wooded jungles in ravines and low hills. This is one of the rare animals threatened with extinction and so it is given special protection in Kaziranga Wild Life National Park in Assam. *R. sondaicus* is known as the Lesser (or *Javan*) one horned Rhinoceros; *Didermocerus sumatrensis* is known as the Sumatran (or Asiatic) tow-horned Rhinoceros.

Rhizobia The bacteria capable of living in symbiotic relationship with leguminous plants in nodules on the roots, the association usually being capable of fixing nitrogen (from the generic name rhizobium).

Rhizome A stem of root-like appearance, lying on or under the ground.

Rhizosphere The zone of soil immediately surrounding plant roots that is significantly influenced by the presence of the root due to enrichment with carbon from the root, and characterized by more intensive biological activity than non-rhizosphere soil.

Rhododendron (from the Greek: *rhodos*, "rose", and *dendron*, "tree") It represents a genus of flowering plants in the family Ericaceae. It is a large genus with over 1000 species and most have showy flower displays. The Rhododendron is an interesting genus characterized by shrubs and small to (rarely) large trees, the smallest species growing to 10-20 cm tall, and the largest, *R. arboreum*, reported to 50 m tall. The leaves are spirally arranged; leaf size can range from 1-2 cm to over 50 cm, exceptionally 100 cm in *R. sinogrande*. They may be either evergreen or deciduous. Some of the best known species are noted for their many clusters of large flowers. There are alpine species with small flowers and small leaves, and tropical species such as subgenus *Vireya* that often grow as epiphytes. Rhododendron is a very widely distributed genus, occurring throughout most of the Northern Hemisphere except for dry areas, and extending into the Southern Hemisphere in southeastern Asia and northern Australasia. The highest species diversity is found in the Sino-Himalayan mountains from central Nepal and Sikkim east to Yunnan and Sichuan, with other significant areas of diversity in the mountains of Indo-China, Korea, Japan and Taiwan. In addition, there are a significant number of tropical rhododendron species from southeast Asia to northern Australia. Relatively fewer species occur in North America and Europe.

Rich Picture A graphical method for expressing the scope of a problem. The term is used in GIS.

Richness The number of species occupying a particular area. *See* evenness.

Rift Valley A long, narrow valley resulting from subsidence of strata between more or less parallel faults, or from the elevation of strata outside the latter.

Right, Commutation of Forest The payment of compensation in cash or kind to extinguish a right in a forest.

Rill A small intermittent water course with steep sides and no obstacle to agriculture machinery; usually a few inches in depth.

Ring, Annual A layer of wood produced by the growth of one year annual layer.

Ring, False The layer of wood less than a full year's growth and seldom, extending completely round the stem; formed when diameter growth is interrupted and resumed during the same growing season.

Ring, Growth A layer of wood produced in one growing season. In climates with alternations of seasons favourable and unfavourable to growth, such layers are correctly referred to as annual rings, and provide a reliable index to the age of the trees.

Ring, to 1. To girdle. 2. To cut away a complete belt of bark all round a log for measurement. 3. To perform the same act on the living tree for certain purposes, e.g., to stimulate flowering or to make the tree dye slowly.

Ring-porous Woods Hardwoods in which the pores of the spring wood are distinctly larger than those of the summer wood and form a well-defined zone or ring diffuse-porous woods.

Riparian 1. Of pertaining to, or situated on the banks of a stream or body of water, or other perennial aquatic environments (Hoover and Wills, 1984). 2. The term is further extended to include seasonal or ephemeral streams having characteristics bank vegetation (Thomas, 1979). 3. The physical and biological environment adjacent to a river or stream that significantly influences, and/or is significantly influenced by, the stream or river. It is the zone, which contributes organic matter to the river or stream; the zone that is wetted by periodic surface or subsurface water from the river or stream (riparian area). Trees forming a strip along a watercourse may be termed gallery forest.

Riparian Forest At a large scale, it is the band of forest that has a significant influence on a stream ecosystem or is significantly affected by the stream. At a smaller scale, it is the forest at the immediate water's edge, where some specialized plants and animals form a distinct community. *See* riparian; riparian zone.

Riparian Zone 1.Terrestrial areas adjacent to perennial or intermittent water bodies that provide functional linkages between terrestrial and aquatic ecosystems through coarse and fine organic matter input, bank stability, water temperature regulation, sediment and nutrient flow regulation, and maintenance of unique wildlife habitat. It is also called riparian area or riparian habitat. 2. An area identified by the presence of vegetation that requires free or unbound water or conditions more moist than normally found in the area (Minor and Smith, 1971; Franklin and Dryness, 1973).

Risk, Fire It refers only to the agencies that cause fires.

Riverain 1. Relating to rivers and streams. Used commonly in classifying and delineating wetlands and deep water habitats. 2. Of vegetation growing in the close proximity of watercourses, or on small islands in river beds. *See* Riparian.

Rodent An animal belonging to the Rodentia, the order of gnawing or nibbling mammals, that includes the mice, squirrels, beavers, etc.

Rogue Any individual of a species which diverges in certain characters from those shown by the majority of the population. Abnormal characteristics may be inherited, induced by environmental factors or associated with disease, e.g. rogue elephant.

Root Definition A clear statement of purpose in GIS. This may be a statement of why the GIS is required and the purpose it is to serve.

Root Graft A graft between roots, generally natural.

Root Pressure A pressure exerted on the sap in the vascular bundles of stem or root, and originating in the root tissues.

Root Sucker A shoot rising from the root of a woody plant sucker.

Root Swelling The thickened basal part of a tree stem. *See* buttress; fluting.

Root, Stilt An adventitious root which emerges from the butt of a tree above ground level. So that the tree appears as if supported on flying buttresses, e.g., mangroves of the genus rhizome prop-root.

Rosewood It refers to a number of richly hued timbers, brownish with darker veining. All rosewoods are strong and heavy, taking an excellent polish, being suitable for flooring, furniture, turnery, musical instruments, and wooden chess sets (black pieces). Many Chinese and Indian dynasties in the the 16th century used the reosewood profusely. The pre-eminent rosewood appreciated in the western world is *Dalbergia nigra,* Brazilian Rosewood. Now it is a CITES-listed endangered species. It is also known as Rio rosewood or Bahia rosewood. This wood has a strong sweet smell, which persists over the years, explaining the name "rosewood". Another classic rosewood is *Dalbergia latifolia* known as (East) Indian rosewood or sonokeling. The population of Indian rosewood species is on decline. Other rosewoods can be found in tropical America, Southeast Asia, and Madagascar. About a dozen species of the genus *Dalbergia,* are recognized as rosewoods.

Rot A state of decay in wood. Rot and decay are more or less interchangeable terms, though rot generally implies a more advanced and obvious stage. *See* decay.

Rotation The planned number of years that elapses between the formation of the crop (regeneration of a crop) and its final felling. In the case of a selection forest, an exploitable size is fixed and only such trees are selected for felling which have reached the exploitable size. Therefore, in selection forests there is no final felling and rotation. Length of rotation depends upon various factors such as site qualities, rate of growth, some inherent characteristics of the species such as its natural span of life, age of viable seed production, age of maximum production, etc.

Rotation, Financial A rotation determined by financial considerations, e.g., that yielding the highest rate of interest. This rotation takes into account the compound interest on all the expenditures and incomes which accrue during this period. The rotation aims to provide the highest profits. There are several methods used for determining financial rotation. The method which is commonly used is based on soil expectation value.

Rotation, Physical The rotation that coincides with the natural life of a species on a given site. The natural life of the trees varies greatly with species and the site. Natural life of the most species on poorer sites is shorter. This rotation is generally used in the case of protection forests. Some of the trees with long life are: teak (450-680 years), deodar (704 years), chir (325 years) and sal (200 years).

Rotation, Silvicultural The rotation through which a species retains satisfactory vigour of growth and reproduction capacity on a given site. Silvicultural rotation can be neither lower than the age at which tree starts producing viable seeds in sufficient quantity nor beyond the age at which production of viable seeds has ceased. Normally this time range in trees is large.

Rotation, Technical The rotation under which a species yields most material of specified sizes and suitability for economic conversion or special use. This rotation may be adopted for the production of timber sizes required for railway sleepers, ship building, match splints, telegraph poles, pit props of mines, etc.

Rotation of the Highest Income (or Rental) The rotation that yields the highest average annual net income, irrespective of the capital value of the forest. Private owners of the forest generally aims at achieving the highest possible net revenue by keeping the rotation period as short as possible.

Rotation of the Maximum Volume Production The rotation that yields the greatest annual quantity of material. It coincides with the age at which the mean annual increment (MAI) and the current annual increment (CAI) cross each other when plotted on a graph. This rotation aims at the production of the maximum volume of wood material per unit area at a given site. This type of rotation is particularly important when the production of total woody material is important and not the size of the material.

Route Tracing Application of network analysis to trace the route of flows through a network from origin to destination. This is particularly useful where flows are unidirectional (as in hydrological networks).

Routed Line Cartograms Maps in which routes are plotted as generalized lines showing the sequence of stops and connections rather than the actual route taken. An example is the map of the Delhi metro rail system.

Royalty A prescribed fee for forest produce payable to the owner of the forest.

Rubber Sheeting The method used to adjust the location of features in a digital map layer in a non-uniform or non-linear manner.

Ruderal A plant that grows on wasteland, old fields, waysides, etc. *See* pioneer.

Ruminants Any animal of the artiodactyl suborder or division, Ruminantia, which comprises, the various "cloven-roofed" and "cud-chewing" quadrupeds. This group includes cattle, bison, buffalo, sheep, goats, chamois, deer, antelopes, giraffes, camels, chevrotains, etc.

Run-off 1. The total stream discharge, including both surface and sub-surface flow, usually expressed in cubic feet, or in inches per acre per unit time. 2. The rate of the total stream discharge, usually expressed in cubic feet per second per square mile of drainage area.

Run-off, Surface The actual amount of water running off the surface of an area, not including seepage.

Russell's Viper (*Vipera russelli*) A highly venomous snake with distinctive markings; found in south-eastern Asia, including India.

Rust 1. A fungus characterized by obligate parasitism and as many as five spore forms, frequently with alternate hosts. Spores of the more evident stages are usually orange to rusty brown in colour. 2. A disease caused by a rust fungus.

Ss

Sal ***(Shorea robusta)*** is a tree species native to southern Asia, ranging south of the Himalaya, from Myanmar in the east to India, Bangladesh, and Nepal. In India it extends from Assam, West Bengal, Jharkhand, Orissa and Chhattisgarh and east Madhya Pradeh, west to the Shivalik Hills in Haryana, east of the Yamuna. The range also extends through the Eastern Ghats and to the eastern Vindhya and Satpura ranges of Central India. It is often the dominant tree in the forests where it occurs. Sal is moderate to slow growing, and can attain heights of 30 to 35 m and a trunk diameter of up to 2-2.5 m. The leaves are 10-25 cm long and 5-15 cm broad. In wetter areas, it is evergreen; in drier areas, it is dry-season deciduous, shedding most of the leaves in between February to April, leafing out again in April and May. Sal is one of the most important sources of hardwood timber in India, with hard, coarse-grained wood that is light in colour when freshly cut, and becoming dark brown with exposure. The wood is resinous and durable, and is sought after for construction, although not well suited to planing and polishing. Sal resin is burned as incense in Hindu ceremonies, and sal seeds and fruits are a source of lamp oil and vegetable fat.

Salmon A marine and fresh-water fish food, *Salmo salar* (Family Salmonidae), with pink flesh common in the North Atlantic Ocean.

Salt Lick A place where salty or sulphurous earth, mud or water is found on the surface and wild animals habitually resort to eat, lick or drink the stuff.

Sample 1. A subset of the target population chosen so as to be representative of that population. 2. A part of a population consisting of one or more sampling unit selected and examined as representative of the whole. 3. A subset of a population selected to obtain information concerning the characteristics of the entire population. *See* census; sample survey.

Sample, Random A sample selected in such a manner that all possible samples of the same size have equal chances of being chosen.

Sample, Stratified Random A sample from a stratified population consisting of a random selection of sampling unit from each stratum; the sampling fraction need not be the same for all strata. *See* stratification.

Sample Survey Surveying or recording a sample of a population. There is no choice when the population is continuous (that is, effectively infinite), but one can define a sample from either a finite or an infinite population. Normally surveys are done for several reasons. A sample survey costs less than a census of the equivalent population, assuming that relatively little time is required to establish the sample size. Whatever the sample size, there are 'establishment costs' associated with any survey. Once the survey has begun, the marginal costs associated with gathering more information, from more people, are proportional to the size of the sample. But remember that surveys are carried out to answer specific questions, and sample surveys answer questions about the whole population. A sample survey will usually offer greater *scope* than a census. This may mean, for example, that it is possible to study the population of a larger (geographical) area, or to find out more about the same population by asking a greater variety of questions, or to study the same area in greater depth. *See* sample.

Sample, Systematic A sample consisting of sampling unit selected in conformity with some regular pattern (e.g., the sample formed from every twentieth two-chain strip of forest, or from every tenth tree in every fifth row). *See* sampling, systematic.

Sample, to To select and measure or record a sample of a population. *See* sample.

Sampling 1. Sampling is collection of qualitative or quantitative information of population from sampling units which possess the characteristics. Quantitative characteristics are the one which can be measured in terms of irregular units of measure such as metre, cms, kgs, inches or enumerated as to the number of occurrences. 2. Sampling is the technique of obtaining a series of measurements to obtain a satisfactory representation of the real world phenomenon being studied.

Sampling Aim To estimate some characteristics of a population without measuring all population units. Aim in planning a survey should be to take enough observation to obtain desired precision — no more no less.

Sampling Fraction The proportion of a population included in a sample.

Sampling, Intensity of Intensity of sampling refers to the percentage of the areas of the population or universe to be included in the sample. It depends on the factors such as: objective of inventory, type of forest, kind or method of sampling adopted using of advanced sampling technique, degree of accuracy and precision aimed at, availability of time and money and adequacy and technical competency of staff. It is generally an accepted principle that the smaller the area is, the higher is need for the sampling intensity. In other words, the larger the area is, the required sampling intensity is less.

Sampling, Probability The basis of probability sampling is the selection of sampling units to make up the sample based on defining the chance that each unit in the sample frame will be included. If we have 100 units in the frame, and we decide that we should have a sample size of 10, we can define the probability of each unit being selected as one in ten, or 0.1 (assuming each unit has the same chance). There are various sampling methods that one can use to select the units. It is an important feature of probability sampling that each time we apply the same method to the same sample frame we will generate a different sample. For a finite population we can use simple combinatorial arithmetic to calculate how many samples we can draw from a particular sample frame such that no two samples are identical. It turns out that from any population of N objects we can draw ${}_{N}C_{n}$ different samples, each of which contains n sampling units. In fact, in probability sampling we are concerned with the probability of each sample being chosen, rather than with the probability of choosing individual units. If each sample is as likely to be selected as every other sample (assuming equal probabilities), then each sampling unit automatically has the same chance of being included as every other sampling unit.

Sampling, Simple Random This is the simplest way of selecting sampling units using probability. This method leads us to select n units (from a population of size N) such that everyone of the ${}_{N}C_{n}$ possible samples has an equal chance of being chosen. To actually implement a random sample, however, we 'reverse' the process so that we generate a sample by selecting from the sample frame by any method that guarantees that each sampling unit has a specified (usually equal) probability of being included.

Sampling, Spatial This is one of the sampling methods now widely practiced. We can use this sampling technique when the phenomenon we are studying has a spatial distribution (that is, the objects in the sample frame have a location in that they exist at specific points in two or three dimensions). This would be required, for example, if we want to sample continuous phenomena such as forest vegetation, soil on a hillside, etc. Such phenomena are obviously most common in geographical, geological and biological research. This requires a sample that can be expressed as a set of points in two-dimensional space, displayed as a map.

Sampling, Stratified In circumstances where the target population actually consists of a series of separate 'sub-populations', each of which may have, on average, different values for the properties we are studying, this method is applied. Here the sampling method takes such sub-populations into account. The process of splitting the sample to take account of possible sub-populations is called *stratification*, and such techniques are called *stratified sampling* methods. In all stratified methods the total population (N) is first divided into a set of mutually exclusive sub-populations N_1, N_2 ... N_L, such that

$$N = \Sigma(N_1 + N_2 + \ldots + N_L)$$

Usually the strata are of equal sizes ($N_1 = N_2 = \ldots = N_L$) but we may also decide to use strata whose relative sizes reflect the estimated proportions of the sub-populations within the whole population. Within each stratum we select a sample (n_1, n_2, ... n_L), usually ensuring that the probability of selection is the same for each unit in each sub-population. This generates a stratified random sample. This method is applied in forest inventory.

Sampling, Systematic It is an sampling method. It is often simpler to design and administer. In a systematic sample (as in other probability methods) we decide the sample size n from a population of size N. In this case, however, the population has to be organised in some way, such as points along a river, or in simple numerical order (the order of sample units is irrelevant in simple random or stratified random samples). We choose a starting point along the sequence by selecting the rth unit from one 'end' of the sequence, where r is less than n, and is usually chosen randomly. We then take the rest of the samples by adding k to r, where k is an integer number equal to $^N/_n$, or to the next lowest integer below $^N/_n$ if this division produces a real number. We do this repeatedly until we reach the end of the sequence. *See* sample, systematic.

Sampling Unit The ultimate unit of assessment or measurement in a sample. It may be the individual, any given number of individuals, a given area of ground, etc. *See* plot.

Sanctuary A sacred and inviolable asylum, or a place of refuge and protection for wildlife. In India, a sanctuary is 'an area constituted by the competent authority in which killing, hunting, shooting or capturing of any species is prohibited except by the person (authorized under the law) responsible for the management of the sanctuary'. In India a sanctuary is usually created by a Gazette Notification of the State government under the Wild Life Act, 1972. Sanctuary provides the protection and space critically needed by the larger predators and grassland dwelling big game and the freedom from human interference needed by nesting birds during the breeding season. In India sanctuaries are owned by the State Forest Department concerned. This facilitates the management of wildlife, food and cover resources to an extent which is rarely possible in privately owned lands. The social uses of wildlife include nature study, photography and simple enjoyment of the out-doors and other ecotourism activities. *See*, National Park.

Sanctum Sanctorum Literally, the most holy place. In India the term is applied to an inner sanctuary, 'sanctuary within a sanctuary', or portion of a wildlife 'sanctuary' or park in which no forest operation or management is allowed, and in which sometimes no entry by visitors is allowed, in order to prevent any kind of disturbance to wildlife. *See* refuge.

Sandalwood It is the fragrant wood of trees from the genus *Santalum*. Species of this tree are found in Nepal, Southern India, Sri Lanka, Hawaii, South Pacific Islands and Australia. It is used as fragrance in perfume and incense, and for woodworking. Jewelry boxes, fans, and ornate carvings continue to be made in many parts of Asia, especially India, using sandalwood. *Santalum album* is currently endangered and consequently very expensive. Although all sandalwood trees in India and Nepal are Government-owned and their harvest is strictly controlled, many trees are illegally cut down and smuggled out of the country. The demand for sandalwood essential oil prices is increasing day by day. Sandalwood from Mysore region of Southern India is generally considered to be of the highest quality available. New plantations have been set up with international aid in Tamil Nadu, in order to facilitate the economic benefits of sandalwood. *Santalum ellipticum*, known as Hawaiian sandalwood is also used and deemed of high quality. *Santalum spicatum* (Australian sandalwood) is used by some aromatherapists and perfumers. The concentration of constituent chemicals in its essential oil — and hence, its aroma — differ considerably from those of other *Santalum* species. To produce commercially valuable sandalwood with high levels of fragrance oils, harvested *santalum* trees have to be at least 40 years of age, but 80 or above is preferred. However, inferior sandalwood produced from trees at 30 years old can still fetch a decent price due to the demand for real sandalwood. Unlike most trees, sandalwood is harvested by toppling the entire *santalum* tree instead of sawing them down at the trunk. This way, valuable wood from the stump and root can also be sold or processed for oil. Sandalwood essential oil provides perfumes with a striking wood base note. In Hinduism, sandalwood is often used for rituals or ceremonies. Its embalming paste is used in Lord Shiva temples on Shivlings. A vast majority of Hindus wear a small mark of this paste on their forehead right above the middle of the eyes. Sandalwood essential oil, which is very expensive in its pure form, is used primarily for Ayurvedic purposes, and treating anxiety. It is said to have been used for embalming the corpses of Princes in Ceylon since the 9th century. In Buddhism, sandalwood is considered to be of the *Padma* (lotus) group and attributed to the Bodhisattva Amitabha. Sandalwood scent is believed to transform one's desires and maintain a person's alertness while in meditation. Sandalwood is also one of the more popular scents used for offering incense to the Buddha. Sandalwood, along with agarwood, is the most popular and commonly used incense material by the Chinese and Japanese in worship and various ceremonies.

Sanitation, Forest The destruction, removal or treatment of infected or infested material for the purpose of reducing disease and insect incidence in the forest.

Sap 1. The fluid contents of the living cell. Also called as cell sap. 2. The fluid in plant tissue.

Sapling A young tree from the time when it reaches 1 metre in height till the lower branches begin to fall. A sapling is characterized by the absence of dead bark and its vigorous height growth. Outside India, the lower height limit is not so precise. *See* seedling.

Saprogen An organism capable of producing decay in non-living organic material, such as dead wood.

Saprophyte A plant which is incapable of getting all its nutrient requirements from purely inorganic substances, and which depends on dead organic food parasite.

Sapwood The outer woody layers of the stem or log which, in the growing tree, contain living cells. The sapwood is generally lighter in colour than the heartwood.

Sapwood Trees Trees without any apparent distinction between hardwoods and sapwood. Sometimes the term is applied to trees that will not die when girdled.

Satellite Image Geographical image (usually in digital form) taken of the earth's surface using electromagnetic sensors on board an orbiting satellite or spacecraft.

Saturation Deficit The difference between actual and maximum vapour pressure at the same temperature and relative humidity level.

Saturation Point The maximum number of a kind of organism that can be carried on a particular locality or area under optimum conditions. There is a limit to which animal population may increase, usually indicated by the carrying capacity, sometimes controlled by psychological factors inherent in the animals themselves. *See* carrying capacity.

Savanna 1. Essentially lowland, tropical and subtropical grassland, generally with a scattering of trees and/or shrubs. 2. A savanna or savannah is a grassland with widely spaced trees, and occurs in several types of biomes. In savannas, grasses and trees are co-dominant vegetation types, with trees and grasses often alternating in dominance over time. The herbaceous layer is usually a mixture of grasses and herbs with trees and shrubs scattered individually or in small clumps. Savannas are frequently seen as a transitional zone, occurring between forest or woodland regions and grassland or desert regions. Savannas are targets of regular fires. Most savannas experience fire at least twice a decade and annual fires are common in many savanna types. These fires are usually confined to the herbaceous layer and do little long term damage to mature trees. However, these fires do serve to either kill or suppress tree seedlings, thus preventing the establishment of a continuous tree canopy which would prevent further grass growth. Browsing animals such as elephants, antelope and deer also play an important role in suppressing tree growth in savannas. Savannas appear to be the result of human use of fire. Some believe that the term savanna has originally come from a word describing "land which is without trees but with much grass either tall or short". By the late 1800 it was used to mean "land with both grass and trees". Some believe that word "savanna" derived from the Spanish word "Zavana" meaning a "grass-covered treeless plain". It now refers clearly to land with grass and either scattered trees, or an open canopy of trees.

Savanna Woodland Open tropical or subtropical forest having an undergrowth mainly of grass. The trees have moderate height and usually deciduous habits or if evergreen then trees tend to have small leaves. *See* savanna; prairie.

Scale (Maps) 1. The relation between the size of an object on a map and its size in the real world. 2. Ratio of distance on an image to the equivalent distance on the ground. 3. A comparison of measurement on a map to measurement on the Earth, usually represented by a fraction or ratio. Also, a measure of detail in a map. Geographers categorise the map with greater detail over a smaller area as large scale map. Geographers call this application on large scale because the scale fraction (e.g., 1/24,000) is a larger number than broad area scales (i.e., 1:250,000 is a relatively small number compared to 1/24,000).

Scale Analogue Model A model that is a scaled down and generalized replica of reality, such as a topographic map or aerial photograph.

Scale-related Generalization Cartographic simplification of mapped features, the level of which is directly related to the scale of the map being drawn.

Scanner Raster input device similar to an office photocopier used to convert maps and other analogue data into digital data using the raster data model. A device for converting images from maps, photographs, or from part of the real world into digital form. The scanning head is made up of a light or other energy source and a sensing device which records digital values of light reflected back from the surface.

Scarify 1.To break up a forest floor and/or top-soil preparatory to natural regeneration or direct sowing. 2. To wear down by abrasion or by acid treatment an outer, more or less impervious seed coat, in order to assist or hasten germination.

Scattering Multiple reflections of electromagnetic waves by particles in the atmosphere or from surfaces.

Scenario A result of a numerical simulation model in which certain input data may be given values to represent conditions not yet observed. Scenarios are often used to compare forecasts of how landscape changes may turn out.

Scientific Forest Management Scientific forest management incorporates the various elements of the German management approach, which includes: (1) Establishing firm administrative control over the forests; (2) Clarifying and formalizing ownership and customary rights; (3) Defining the physical dimensions of forest estate; (4) Investigating the silvicultural characteristics and wood properties of the main species; (5) Estimating growth rates and patterns; and (6) Prescribing sustained yield management regimes, combining yield control and replacement of the forest as it is utilised. *See* scientific management.

Scientific Management Scientific management by definition is "that kind of management which conducts business or affairs by standards established by facts or truths gained through systematic observation, experiment, or reasoning" (Babcock,1927). Talor (1967) in his book 'The Principles of Scientific Management' proposed four principles of scientific management. They are: (1) Develop a science of every job with standardized work tools, and efficient methods for all to follow; (2) Scientifically select workers with skills and abilities that match each job and train them in the most efficient ways to accomplish tasks; (3) Ensure co-operation through incentives and provide the work environment that reinforces optimal work results in a scientific manner; (4) Divide responsibility for managing and for working, while supporting individuals in work groups for what they do best; some people are more capable of managing, whereas others are better at performing tasks laid out for them (Holt, David, 1990). *See* scientific forest management.

Scion Any unrooted portion of a plant used for grafting or budding onto a rootstock. Shoots of woody plants from which scions are cut are termed scion wood.

Sclerophyllous Forest Forest characterized by the prevalence of species having leathery, generally small, leaves, and developed in a climate with relatively hot and dry seasons.

Sclerophyte 1. A plant adapted to a climate with a wet winter and a hot dry-summer characterized by thick, hard, usually small evergreen leaves capable of functioning during winter and withstanding the dry summer. 2. A plant with thick, hard leaves—generally small, evergreen and xerophytic. *See* xeromorphic; sclerophyllous forest.

Scorch Injury to bark, flowers, foliage or fruit by excessive sun heat, freezing, salt-laden, fume-laden, unduly strong winds or unbalanced nutrition. On leaves the injury is chiefly at the margins during sunscald winter.

Scrambler A plant which owing to lack of rigidity in its stem and absence of special climbing organs, uses other vegetation as its support.

Scrub 1. Inferior growth consisting of small or stunted trees and/or shrubs, generally of unmerchantable species. Where the trees are sufficiently numerous, then it is termed as scrub forest. 2. Any woody growth of low economic potentiality.

Season, Close A period, established by statute or other regulations during which it is illegal to fish, thus giving the fish freedom from interference during spawning. A similar period when hunting of animals is prohibited.

Secondary Data Data collected by another individual or

organization for another primary purpose. Many data sources used in GIS, including maps, aerial photographs, census data and meteorological records, are secondary.

Secondary Forests Forest regenerated largely through natural processes after significant human or natural disturbance or the original forest vegetation. The disturbance may have occurred at a single point in time or over an extended period. The forest may display significant differences in structure and /or canopy species composition in relation to nearby forest on similar sites.

Secondary Sexual Character Any of the characters of animals, which differ between male and female, e.g. beard, antler, and some plumage. Distinct from primary sexual organs (testis and ovary) and from accessory sexual organs.

Seed Bearer A tree used for, or capable of, providing a supply of seed, especially one reserved for this purposes during regeneration felling. Trees retained for such purposes are called as the mother tree or seed tree.

Seed Drill A device for sowing seed in lines. Also the line as sown.

Seed Garden A plantation raised or treated expressly for the production of seed, usually of superior race. Also called as seed orchard. *See* seed orchard.

Seed Kiln A chamber in which seed is extracted from fruit (cones, pods, etc.) usually by means of hot air.

Seed Orchards 1. A plantation of trees (pre-selected on the basis of their superior genetic traits) that has been isolated from genetically inferior outside sources, and intensively managed to improve the genotype and produce abundant seed crops. 2. Seed orchard is restricted to stands planted for seed production and composed of trees known to be of desirable genotypes from tests of their progeny. They are usually established by vegetative propagation from the chosen genotypes and must be isolated from sources of contaminating pollen. To maintain a large and variable gene pool in the progeny, it is desirable to start with enough trees to have at least a dozen genotypes represented in each orchard unit that ultimately becomes a single seed source. Trees of the same genotype should be separated so as to enhance cross-pollination.

Seed Pellet One or more seeds compressed in a matrix of various materials, e.g., clay, fertilizer rodent and insect repellents, to form a coherent ball. Often used in aerial sowing.

Seed Production Area Area set aside in forests for gathering large quantities of seed. The procedure is to set aside or establish stands of good genotypes and manage them intensively and exclusively, for seed production (Faulkner, 1975). Seed production areas are good stands, chosen by phenotypic characteristics, that are thinned or otherwise treated to stimulate seed production.

Seed Year 1. A year in which a given species bears seed abundantly. 2. Also used to designate a year in terms of production of seed by a particular species as good, moderately good and poor or very poor seedling year.

Seedbed 1. The soil or forest floor on which the seed falls. 2. In nursery practice, a prepared area in which seed is sown.

Seeding 1. The act of producing seed on the part of a plant. 2. The regeneration of forest from seed, usually by natural means, as in seeding felling. 3. A plant grown from seed, before it reaches the sapling stage. 4. In nursery practice, one that has not been pricked out in the nursery.

Seeding Felling A method of regeneration involving the removal of trees in a mature stand (to open the canopy) with the exception of a small number of seed trees.

Seedling, Whippy A seedling, which has not yet developed into a rigid woody stem.

Seedling Year 1. One in which a given species produces abundant first-year seedlings. 2. Also used to designate a year, in terms of the amount of natural seedling regeneration produced by a particular species, as a good, fair poor or very poor. *See* seed year.

Seepage A general term for the flow of water below the surface of the soil in contradiction to surface run-off. It includes both infiltration and percolation.

Segregation Separation of parental characters in inheritance.

Selection 1. Choice of superior types for breeding purposes. 2. Non-random differential reproduction of different genotypes. Natural selection is the process by which the genetic make-up of a population changes allowing for a better adapted phenotype to be produced. 3. Plant(s) that display(s) one or more desirable characteristics and are selected for a specific use.

Selection Felling or Cutting. Annual or periodic felling or cutting of trees in a stand in which the trees vary markedly in age. The objective is to recover the yield and maintain an uneven-aged stand structure, while creating the conditions necessary for tree growth and seedling establishment. Differs from selective felling or cutting, in which the most valuable trees are harvested without any consideration for the condition of the residual stand.

Selection System This is a silvicultural system in which felling and regeneration are distributed over the whole of the area and the resultant crop is so uneven-aged that trees of all ages are found mixed together over every part of the area. Such a crop is referred to as 'selection forest' or 'all-aged forest'. These systems necessitates removing of mature and over-mature trees singularly over a large area of forests, on a periodic basis, without creating any lasting gap in the forest canopy. This is especially suitable for the temperate and tropical forests areas with hilly terrain. In this system, the removal consists of the category of trees, (a) Dead and dying trees, (b) Diseased, and defective trees, (c) Trees lacking in vigour and trees of undesirable species intervening with better stems and (d) Trees of prescribed exploitable girth. Removal of aforesaid trees is followed by tending and regeneration operations. This system works well when regeneration in the forests is assured. If the natural regeneration fails, and we keep on removing mature and bad trees, over time, then the forest area becomes open and barren. This is happening in most of our forests in India today. It is because of the fact that in one hand, majority of our forests lacks natural regeneration due to forest fires and excessive grazing and in the other hand, mature trees are removed. However, there are several advantages in this system. It maintains constant forest cover and so continued soil fertility is assured. There is also a possibility in the system to maintain the original composition of the crop and uneven character of the stand. The system also provides immunity against insect pests to the crop. It helps to restore a suitable balance between pests and predators. Apart from this, the system is most natural one. Operations under it follow the footsteps of nature closely. This system is ideally suited for maintaining the ecological balance of any forest ecosystem. Besides, there is an assured seed source from the older trees, so even if an accidental fire destroys the younger crop or the regeneration in one year, there is a possibility for further recruitment. This is the most flexible system where one can manipulate to obtain a complete and balanced composition of forest trees. The system can also be adapted to grow wood to cater to the local needs. However, marking of selected trees for felling under this selection system requires considerable professional skill and expertise.

Self, to Fertilization of the female gamete by the male gametes of the same individual, whether in nature or artificially. Also the individual so formed. *See* cross.

Self-mulching Soil 1. A soil that cracks deeply and becomes so granular at the surface when very dry that the granular mulch washes into the cracks when rains begin, and then the whole soil swells enough as it becomes moist to force material upward between the former cracks. 2. A soil in which the surface layer becomes so well aggregated that it does not crust and seal under the impact of rain.

Self-sown Seed A green plant having its own root system, but partly dependent for its nutrition on functional connection with the roots of other plants.

Semi-Parasite A green plant having its own root system, but partly dependent for its nutrition on functional connection with the roots of other plants.

Sensitive Site A site vulnerable to rapid change in its biological attributes or physical character in the face of management activity or resource uses either due to its small size or due to species/communities on that site which are intolerant to change or are exacting in their habitat requirements, or fragile rock/soil formation (Sawarkar, 1995).

Sensitive Species A species intolerant to any alteration in its habitat, a species, which is exacting in its habitat requirements and rapidly exhibits adverse impacts as a consequence to minor disturbance (Sawarkar, 1995).

Sensor 1. That receives electromagnetic radiation and converts it into a signal that can be recorded and displayed as either numerical data or an image. 2. Technical means, usually electronic, to extend man's natural senses by detecting emitted or reflected energy. The energy may be nuclear, electromagnetic (including the visible and invisible portions of the spectrum), chemical, biological, thermal, or mechanical.

Seral Successional as contrasted with climax. *See* succession.

Seral Stage A temporal and intermediate stage in the process of plant succession.

Seral Unit According to Clements these units in descending order of complexity are associes, consecies, facies, locies, socies, colony and family. Climax units.

Sere 1. Series of plant community resulting from processes of succession. 2. Any recognizable stage in plant succession.

Sere-climax A pro-climax in which the development of vegetation is arrested and held indefinitely at some stage earlier to that of the sub-climax owing to the action of factors, natural or artificial other than the climate (After Clements). *See* Sub-climax.

Series An area forming the whole or part of the working circle, containing or aiming at a normal series or age classes. *See* felling series; planting series.

Serow A goat antelope of genus Capriconis, of Eastern Asia, related to the goral. The Indian species, *C. sumatrensis* is found at high elevation (1800 to 3000 mt) in the Himalayas from Kashmir to Mishmi hills in Assam. It is usually seen in association with goral, shapu, nayan, ibex, markhor and the Himalayan Tahr.

Server Servers are the computers on a client /server network from which applications, data and resources are managed. Basically, servers provide services. Servers should always be high performance, fast and efficient computers. A server can be centralized (handles all the single server specific networking tasks) or dedicated (handles all the single/multiserver specific tasks on a multiserver network). Clients are computers on a network that lets users access the server's information and resources. Client computers can range from diskless workstations to multimedia—enhanced, complete desktop systems. The smallest server is not very different from a personal computer. The standard features of a server are: hot-swappable SCSI hard drives, RAID (Redundant array of inexpensive disks) controllers, redundant power supplies, remote management capabilities and a lot more. *See* client.

Sesquioxides Oxides of iron and aluminium present in the soil.

Shade Demander A species requiring at least in its early stages some degree of shade for its normal development. Shade demander refers to the ability of the tree species to achieve

maximum photosynthesis under low light intensities. *See* light demander; shade tolerant; shade bearer.

Shade Tolerant A plant that is a better competitor under shaded conditions. *See* shade bearer.

Shade-bearer A species capable of persisting and developing under shade. Species shows varying tolerance to different light intensities at different ages in their ability to survive or put on growth. Generally speaking, trees are classified into shade bearer and light demander. In tropical moist forest, good shade bearers are: *Xylia, Schleichera, Mallotus philippensis*, etc. *See* light-demander; shade demander.

Shadow Price A price that should be used in cost-benefit analysis (CBA) and other decision making frameworks when market failures leads to market prices which do not accurately reflect economic values, and thus do not reflect the full opportunity costs of an action. Adjustments to market prices to obtain shadow prices are required when there are distortionary taxes and subsidies, when there are monopolies or other market imperfections that lead to the market prices being higher or lower than the economic opportunity cost.

Shallow Rooted Applied to species whose root system does not extend far enough into the soil to save them from relatively easy wind-throw.

Shannon-Weaver Diversity Index A measure of the diversity of a community: $h = --\sum_{i=1}^{s}(p_i \ln p_i)$ where h is the Shannon diversity index, s is species richness (number of species), p_i is proportion abundance contributed by the *ith* species to the total. *See* Simpson's diversity index, diversity index.

Sheet Erosion Erosion of a fairly homogeneous layer of material. It may be imperceptible, particularly when caused by wind, or else evidenced by numerous fine rills.

Sheldrake Any of several large wild ducks, that feed on fish, shell-fish, etc. and nest in furrows. The plumage is variegated and often brightly coloured. *Genus Tardorna*: It is frequently found on sandy coasts in Europe, North America and Asia. RUDDY SHELDRAKE: BRAHMINY DUCK (*Tadorna ferruginea* Syn. *Casarca ferruginea*). It is a winter visitor in India (October to April) and is found throughout in suitable places. It is a wary bird.

Shelterbelt A belt of trees and/or shrubs maintained for the purpose

of shelter and acts as a protective-belt against wind, sun, snow-drift, etc. Shelterbelts are generally more extensive than windbreak covering areas larger than a single farm and sometimes whole regions on a planned pattern. *See* windbreak.

Shelterwood System or Uniform System This is a system that, aims at concentrated regeneration, in which the canopy is uniformly opened up over the whole area of a compartment to obtain uniform regeneration. Under this system, the mature trees are removed by successive felling. Therefore, Troupe, the famous forester has aptly termed it as a "system of successive regeneration felling." Depending upon the methods of carrying out the regeneration felling and distributing them in time and space, several sub-systems have also been developed. It was widely practiced in European forests. With the incoming of European foresters in India, it was applied to the forests of Utter Pradesh, Himachal Pradesh and Madhya Pradesh. The system has advantages as well as disadvantages. It has the advantages of a selection forests too. However, the system had many disadvantages: (a) Less concentrated working per unit area compared to clear felling, (b) Younger regeneration takes more time for establishment, (c) It requires tremendous skill in managing successive operations to manipulate overwood and to bring out the younger crop.

Shifting Cultivation 1. Farming system in which land is periodically cleared, burned, farmed and then returned to fallow. 2. Shifting cultivation is an agricultural system in which a person creates a piece of land with another piece of land and uses it and abandons it a short while later. This system often involves clearing of a piece of land followed by several years of wood harvesting or farming until the soil loses fertility. Once the land becomes inadequate for crop production, it is left to be reclaimed by natural vegetation, or sometimes converted to a different long-term cyclical farming practice. This system of agriculture is often practised at the level of an individual or family, but sometimes may involve an entire village. An estimated population exceeding 250 million people in the world derive subsistence from the practice of shifting cultivation, and ecological consequences are often deleterious. Of these cultivators, many use a practice of slash-and-burn as one element of their farming cycle. Others employ land clearing without

any burning, and some cultivators are purely migratory and do not use any cyclical method on a given plot. Sometimes no slashing at all is needed where regrowth is purely of grasses, an outcome not uncommon when soils are near exhaustion.

Shootable Of game that can be shot legitimately.

Shooting Block A block of forest where shooting was allowed in the past under a licence subject to specified rules and restrictions.

Shrub 1. A woody perennial plant differing from a perennial herb in its persistent and woody stem and less definitely from a tree in its low stature and its habit of branching from the base. Often restricted to plants up to 20 feet in height (BCFT). 2. It refers to vegetation types where the dominant woody elements are shrubs, i.e. woody perennial plants, generally more than 0.5 metres and less than 5 metres in height at maturity and without a definite crown. The height limits for trees and shrubs should be interpreted with flexibility, particularly the minimum tree and maximum shrub height, which may vary between 5 metres and 7 metres (FAO, 2001).

Side Lap Extent of lateral overlap between images acquired on adjacent flight lines.

Side-looking Airborne Radar (SLAR) An airborne side scanning system for acquiring radar images.

Sieve Mapping The consecutive overlay of various maps to find a set of feasible areas that satisfy a given set of criteria.

Signal Information recorded by a remote sensing system.

Signature 1. Any characteristic or series of characteristics by which a material or object may be recognized in an image, photo, or data set. 2. Set of statistics that describes and defines a training sample or cluster. It is used in multispectral classification. *See also* spectral response pattern and spectral signature.

Significance, Test A calculation of the probability that an ascertained quantitative difference between the results of certain experimental treatments is of a magnitude to justify attributing it to the difference in treatment rather than to chance or to experimental errors. If this probability is less than an agreed small value (termed the level of significance and often accepted as 1:20), the difference is said to be significant. Not-significant difference does not constitute a proof that no difference may exist.

Silt 1. Soil particles between 0.002 and 0.02 mm in diameter.

2. Also applied to a soil whose texture and properties are preponderantly those of silt. *See* soil texture.

Siver Fir *Abies pindrow* known as silver fir is very tall, evergreen, dense tree with crown conical when it is young and cylindrical afterwards. It is light shade bearer but shows poor growth in shade. Geographical distribution ranges from Afghanistan to Nepal. It has white smooth wood, mostly used for packing cases. It is a species associated with heavy snow fall. Silver fir forests were earlier managed under selection system, but later it was found to be unsuitable mostly because concentrated regeneration operations was found to be essential for regeneration. This is how Punjab shelterwood system was adopted later on.

Silviculture 1. It is the science and practice of cultivating forest crops. 2. It is the art and science of cultivating forest crops. 3. Silviculture is the art of producing of and tending a forest. 4. The application of knowledge of silvics in the treatment of forests. 5. The theory and practice of controlling forest establishment, composition, structure and growth (Spurr and Bornes, 1980). 6. The art and science of controlling the establishment, growth, composition, health and quality of forest and woodlands to meet the targeted diverse needs and values of landowners and society on a sustainable basis (FAO, 2005). 7. Silviculture treats forests trees as crops which are established, tended, and harvested and then replaced by others (Packham, J.R. *et al.*, 1992). 8. Silviculture practice consists of the various treatments that may be applied to forests stands to maintain and to enhance their utility for any purpose. 9. Silviculture is normally directed at the creation and maintenance of the kind of forests that will best fulfil the objectives of the organization. If the objective of management is different then the silviculture shall be different. When the objective of management is single, then the silviculture will be simple. But with the adoption of multiple objectives of management of forests, the silviculture will be a complex one and most intricate. 10. Silviculture is concerned with the social as well as the biological aspects of forestry. The implicit objective of forestry is to make useful to society. The job of the forester is to analyze the natural and social factors bearing on each stand and then devise and conduct the treatments most appropriate to the objective of the management.

Silvicultural Operations, Subsidiary A general term for all operations carried out immediately after the main felling. Besides proper cultural operations, this might include other specific operations.

Silvicultural System 1. A planned programme of treatments throughout the life of the stand to achieve stand structural objectives based on integrated resource management goals. A silvicultural system includes harvesting, regeneration and stand, group or tree tending methods or phases. It covers all activities of the entire length of a rotation or cutting cycle. (IUFRO World Series Vol. 9-en). 2. Silvicultural system is a method of procedure worked out in accordance with accepted sets of silvicultural principles, by which crops constituting forests are tended, harvested and replaced by new crops of distinctive forms. In other words, it is a package of inputs applied to the forest crop throughout its life with an objective of giving the forest a predefined character. 3. Forest, a dynamic entity, needs to be managed in such a way that the renewable natural resources would be available to humanity in perpetuity. Forests are, therefore, managed according to sound principle of silviculture. Silviculture is the art and science of cultivating forest crop. A forest crop requires careful tending, harvesting and replacing by new crops according to certain silvicultural procedures. When a set of silvicultural procedure is initiated along with a homogenous set of objectives of management, then it is called silvicultural system. The selection of silvicultural system for any type of forests necessitates consideration of an array of factors. 4. A method of silvicultural procedure worked out in accordance with accepted sets of silvicultural principles by which crops constituting forest are tended, harvested and replaced by new crops of distinctive forms.

Silvicultural Systems in Practice A wide variety of silvicultural systems are applied in Indian forests and the following discussion provides a broad generalization of their application. Selection systems and selection-*cum*-improvement felling are applied to evergreen and semi-evergreen, moist deciduous and dry deciduous forests. Regeneration is generally natural although supplementary planting often occurs. Treatment is largely limited to the establishment stage with intermediate silvicultural interventions often neglected. The uniform system is applied in moist deciduous forests where natural regeneration of valuable species is adequate. Irregular shelterwood systems are applied to evergreen and moist deciduous forests where regeneration can be established only with considerable effort. In this system, trees below exploitable girth are retained, as advance growth and intensive tending is the norm. Clear-felling with replanting is used in moist and dry deciduous forests where natural regeneration is unsatisfactory or where a change in crop composition is desired. Silvicultural interventions include intensive post-establishment treatment, as well as pruning and thinning at later stages. Coppicing systems which includes simple coppice system, coppice with standards, and coppice with reserves are generally applied to dry deciduous forests.

Silviculture, Scope of Silviculture has enormous scope for sustainable forestry. Forest is a renewable resource. If it is managed sustainably, benefits can be reaped on a sustainable basis. Silviculture helps in managing the forest resources within the framework of sustainability. For instance, application of silviculture with an objective of timber production aims at growing trees having timber value, developing method for non-destructive harvesting and maintaining the capacity of the site and vegetation to produce the same quantum of benefit for the future also. With the increasing emphasis on multiple use of forests, the application of silviculture for achieving the objective of management is becoming more complex. Silviculture holds key to sustainable forest management. Forest management aims at using forest resources for the benefit of the people, present or future, in a given social and economic environment; whereas silviculture is concerned with efficient application of ecological sciences. But, forest management sets objectives and limitations for different silvicultural options or alternatives. Economics has a strong bearing with silviculture. The economic time scale of forestry practice is so large and unique that it apparently defies all economic theory. In no country practice of forestry is undertaken purely on the basis of economic consideration. Rather the decision to practice forestry is a matter of ethics, politics, and social and economic concern for the present and future generation. Therefore, practicing forestry is never an exercise in conventional economics. However, once the decision to practice forestry is taken, it becomes logical to apply economic analysis to determine how best to execute the details of the forestry programmes. Funds are scarcely available for implementing the programme. The holding of land for future production of wood or non-wood forests products or other ecological services involves opportunity cost. Therefore, it is imperative to undertake such treatments that will yield the greatest increase in value of social, economic and environmental benefits. As a result, the sustainability of the programme will be ensured.

Silviculture, Objective of The objectives of silviculture are: (a) Enhancement of productivity of the forest ecosystem, (b) Control of stand structure and process, (c) Control of composition, (d) Control of stand, (e) Increase of density, (f) Restocking of un-stocked or under-stocked or unproductive areas, (g) Protection of stand, (h) Control of rotational length, (i) Facilitating of harvesting, and (j) Conservation of site quality and habitat.

Silviculture and SFM Silviculture is important for sustainable forest management. It is the art and science of growing trees. It involves manipulating natural biological processes of the forest in order to achieve specific end results. It includes all operations that are done between one harvest and the next, such as planting, thinning, pruning, weeding. Harvesting operations are themselves major silvicultural treatment. Therefore, silviculture is one of the important tools for executing sustainable forest management.

Silvics The study of the life history and general characteristics of forest trees and crops, with particular reference to environmental factors, as the basis for the practice of silviculture.

Simple Kriging An interpolation technique in which the prediction of values is based on a generalized linear regression under the assumption of second order stationarity and a known mean.

Simple Raster Simplest raster data structure in which the value of each pixel is stored as a separate value in a matrix.

Simpson's Diversity Index A measure of the diversity of a community: sd = 1 / pi 2i=1 where d is Simpson's diversity index, s is species richness (number of species).

Simulation Using the digital model of the landscape in a GIS for studying the possible outcome of various processes expressed in the form of mathematical models.

Single-grained Applied to a structure less condition of the soil, each grain being independent, as in dune sand.

Sink A depression or hole in a low lying, poorly drained area formed by the dissolution of underlying rock, where waters collect or disappear by sinking down into the ground or by evaporation.

Site Index An expression of forest site quality based on the height, at a specified age, of dominant and co-dominant trees in a stand. *See* site quality.

Site Quality It is a measure of the relative productive capacity of a site for a particular species. Site indicates complex assemblage of physical and biological factors of an area. It determines the forest growth. Every site responds differently to different species. Site quality is measured on the basis of top height of the crop on a particular age. According to All India Teak Yield Table there are four site quality classes for teak. They are: (1) Site Quality I— Top height: 36.6 to 30.5 mt.; (2) Site Quality II — Top height: 30.5 to 24.4 mt.; (3) Site Quality III— Top height: 24.4 to 18.3 mt. and (4) Site Quality IV — Top height: 18.3 to 12.2 mt. The top height is attained at the age of 50 years. In case, the crop is young, the corresponding top height for that age has to be determined. In case of sal, there are again four-site qualities prevalent in forestry practice. They are based on the top height of the crop at 80 years. These site qualities are: (1) Site Quality I—Top height 36.6 - 30.5mt.; (2) Site Quality II—Top height 30.5 - 24.4 mt.; (3) Site Quality III—Top height 24.4 - 18.3.mt. and (4) Site Quality IV—Top height 18.3 - 12.2 mt. The site quality has a sufficiently long range of top heights between each of its subdivision against a particular age. In other words, the range of variation of top height in a same site quality is so large that sometime it is difficult to measure the productive capacity of a site for a particular species for the purpose of comparison with other sites. In order to describe the quality more correctly and precisely, the method of fractional quality such as I/II, II/III, etc. has been evolved. Fractional quality is the site quality expressed as a decimal sub division of the height range of half a quality class, the figure running 0.0 to 2.0 within the whole. In Madhya Pradesh and Chhattisgarh there is a slightly different site quality classification in vogue. There are seven site qualities with respect to teak and miscellaneous trees. They are: (1) Site Quality I—Top height over 30 mt. (2) Site Quality II—Top height

25 to 30 mt. (3) Site Quality III—Top height 20 to 25 mt. (4) Site Quality IVa—Top height 15 to 20 mt. (5) Site Quality IVb—Top height 12 to 15 mt. (6) Site Quality Va—Top height 9 to 12 mt. (7) Site Quality Vb—Top height up to 9 mt.

Site Quality of Bamboo It is a measure of the relative productive capacity of a site for bamboo. There are three site qualities prevalent in Madhya Pradesh and Chhattisgarh for *Dendrocalamus strictus*. They are: (1) Site quality I — height of tallest culm over 9 mt; (2) Site quality II — height of tallest culm ranging from 6 to 9 mt; (3) Site quality III — height of tallest culm up to 6 mt. However, the classification for site quality for bamboo prevalent in other parts of the country is somewhat different. These classifications are: (1) Quality class I — average culm height 6 mt. or more for *Dendrocalamus strictus* and 14 metres or more for *Bambusa arundinancea*; (2) Quality class II — average culm height 4 mt or more but less than 6 metres for *Dendrocalamus strictus* and 10 mt or more but less than 14 metres for *Bambusa arundinancea*; (3) Quality class III — average culm height 2 mt or more but less than 4 metres for *Dendrocalamus strictus* and 2 metres and more but less than 10 metres for *Bambusa arundinancea*.

Site 1. An area considered in terms of its environment, particularly as this determines the type and quality of the vegetation the area can carry. 2. The complex of physical and biological factors of an area that determines what forest or other vegetation it may carry. Sites are classified either qualitatively on the basis of their climate, soil and vegetation, into site types, or quantitatively on the basis of by their potential wood production or mean stem volume into site classes. *See* environment, locality and factors of habitat.

Size Class One of the intervals into which the range of size of trees, logs, etc., is divided for classification and use; also the trees, logs, etc., falling into such an interval. Diameter or girth usually, height or length sometimes, and volume rarely, constitutes the basis of the division. *See* diameter class; girth class.

Size, Exploitable The diameter or girth decided upon as the normal size for felling in order to fulfil the objects of management. For an example a girth of 120 cm in case of teak crop may be decided as the exploitable size. *See* Girth, exploitable; Diameter, exploitable.

Skeletonization The removal of the softer tissues of leaves leaving the mid-rib, veins, etc., as a skeleton.

Slash The unusable residue after logging, i.e., branches, tops, bark, unutilizable logs, uprooted stumps and broken or uprooted trees left on the area. Also any large accumulation of debris after wind or fire.

Slash Disposal The treatment or handling of slash for reducing hazards from fire, insects or fungi for the purpose of making the falling seeds able to access soil. *See* slash.

Slip Erosion A sliding downhill of the mantle rock, as a whole. Slip erosions in large-scale are termed landslides.

Sliver A narrow gap between two lines created erroneously by digitizing or during the process of vectorization.

Sliver Polygons Small, often long and narrow, polygons resulting from the overlay of polygons with a common but separately digitized boundary. It indicates errors in the digitizing process.

Slope 1. Percentage or degree of change in elevation over a defined distance. 2. The gradient of the surface of the ground, given either as the angle the surface makes with the horizontal or as the ratio, expressed as a fraction or percentage, between the vertical rise or fall and the horizontal distance in which the rise or fall has occurred. For an example; when the angle of slope is 20 degree, then the slope percentage is 36 per cent; when the angle of slope is 45 degree, then the slope percentage is 100 per cent; when the angle of slope is 60 degree, then the slope percentage is 173 per cent. 3. The steepness or gradient of a unit of terrain, usually measured as an angle in degrees or as a percentage. *See* slope level.

Slope Level It generally means the ratio expressed as percentage between the vertical rise or fall and the horizontal distance in which the rise or fall has occurred. The terms used to qualify different categories of slope are: (1) Level — 0 to 5°; (2) Gentle — 5° to 10°; (3) Moderate — 10° to 15°; (4) Steep — 15° to 25°; (5) Very steep — 25° to 45°; (6) Precipitous — Over 45°. *See* slope; aspect.

Slough 1. Low, swampy ground or overflow channels where water flows sluggishly for considerable distances. 2. A sluggish channel of water, such as a side channel of a stream, in which water flows slowly through low, swampy ground, or a section of an abandoned stream channel containing water most of the time or round the year, but with flow only at high water, and occurring in a flood plain or delta. 3. A marshy tract lying in a shallow, undrained depression on a piece of dry ground. 4. A term used for a creek or sluggish body of water in a bottomland.

Small Game Game birds and mammals not classified as big game. *See* Game.

Smallwood Wood below a certain girth or diameter, but often with a lower limit. For statistical work, wood below 20 cm girth over bark in Europe and between 20 cm and 5 cm diameter over bark in India, is considered a smallwood. Smallwood volume is ordinarily inclusive of bark.

Smoke Damage Injury of plants by smoke or airborne chemicals. Also called fume damage.

Smoothing A set of procedures for removing short-range, erratic variation from lines, surfaces, or data series.

Snag 1. A standing dead tree, whole or broken, at least 1.5 mt in height where broken, with a minimum of 20 cm dbh, with or without limbs or bark (Sawarkar, 1995). 2. A standing dead tree from which the leaves and most of the branches have fallen, or a standing section of the stem of a tree broken off at a height of 10 feet or more. By definition, a snag is a dead or partly dead tree above 10 cm in diameter at breast height and above 1.8 mt tall. 3. A broken branch projecting from a tree bole. Snags provide an important part of the life support system for many species of plants, invertebrates, birds and mammals. Many animals depend on snags for nesting or shelter. A majority of insectivorous birds plays a pivotal role in control of forest insect pests. Birds along with insectivorous small mammals, microbes and predatory insects help control population at endemic level and exert significant control, during early stages of outbreak. Therefore, it is said that absence of suitable nest site leads to emergence of limiting factor for cavity nesting birds. When the tree dies, the snag undergoes a series of successional changes from death of the tree to final decomposition stage. Each stage in the decay process has particular value to certain group of wildlife species.

Snipe Any of several long-legged, wading birds of genus Gallinago, related to the woodcock, living chiefly in marsh place and characterized by a long, straight, flexible bill used in digging for worms. Its erratic flight makes it a severe test of marksmanship. FANTAIL or COMMON SNIPE (*Gallinago allinago*, Syn. *Cappella Gallinago*): A small long beaked bird with dark brown, streaked plumage. It is found throughout India but more specifically in north of the Godavari as a winter visitor; it is known to breed in Kashmir and Santal Parganas. JACK SNIPE (*Lymnocryptes minimus* Syn. *Gallinago minima*): Similar to common snipe and pintail snipe, but it has twelve pointed feathers. PAINTED SNIPE (*Rostratula benghalensis*): It has wonderfully painted plumage. It is a resident species throughout India, ascending the Himalayas up to 1500 mt wherever suitable swamps are found. PINTAIL SNIPE (*Gallinago stenura* Syn. *Capella stenura*): It is similar to the common snipe except that it has twenty-six tail feathers of which the outermost eight on either side are stiff narrow and wire-like. It is a winter, visitor to eastern and southern India. WOOD SNIPE (*Gallinago nemiricola*). It breeds in the Himalayas at elevation above 600 m. It spends winter in the lower Himalayas and in the hills of south India.

Snow-break 1. A shelter-belt or other obstacle maintained against snow. 2. Snow breakage, i.g., the breaking of trees or branches by snow. 3. A tree or portion of a tree broken by snow.

SNR Signal to noise ratio.

Sociability The tendency of organisms to grow together with others of the same kind. Expressed by Braun-Blanquet on an arbitrary numerical scale from 1 (growing singly) to 5 (growing in great crowds or pure populations).

Social Analysis Social analysis is the methodology, which provides guidelines for studying and identifying the social, economic and political factors that may affect or be affected by project activities as well as the people who are expected to benefit, particularly local population. On the basis of this information, there is need to identify potential problems that may emerge during implementation of the project or plan and suggest ways in which they can be addressed. The application of social analysis implies that development projects have social objectives. Underlying this is a belief that sustainable development means increasing the potential of rural people to influence and control their future on a long term basis, a goal that can be achieved by strengthening capacity, supporting equity and fostering empowerment (Gow, 1988). For social analysis to make a significant contribution to design and implementation at both programme and projects levels within this broader context of sustainable development, a framework that is simple to capture the complexities and constraints that characterize development interventions is called for. The emphasis should be on concerns involving the environment and natural resource base, the political dimension of forest protection and resource use, institutional implications, national, regional and local. Social analysis is generally grouped under three major components: (a) Social feasibility, (b) Institutions and organizations, and (c) Social and distributional impact. Social feasibility analysis focuses on the extent to which planned interventions can respond to local needs, conditions, potentials and capabilities. A project or plan is socially feasible if it is sufficiently adapted to local conditions in such a way that people can see the advantages of making changes and modifying their practices to attain new benefits.

Social Capital In the analysis of sustainability and Sustainable Development (SD), various different types of capital, including human-made capital, human capital and natural capital play an important role. Social capital is now included in this analysis, as being one of the factors that contribute to social well-being. There are many competing definitions of social capital but most of them incorporate the following features: relations and trust, reciprocity and exchanges between individuals which facilitate co-operation; and common rules, norms and sanctions mutually agreed or handed down within societies, network and social groups. Cultural resources such as traditions are another aspect of social capital (Markandya *et al.*, 2002).

Social Cost The social cost of an activity is to calculate as the sum of the private cost and the external cost resulting from the activity.

Social Rank The place occupied by an individual animal in the social hierarchy among the animals with which it lives. *See* peck order.

Society 1. A society is a local community within a consociation or faciation characterized by one or more sub-dominant. It may constitute a seasonal aspect or a layer of the larger community of which it is a part. 2. A localized climax community, occurring within an area controlled by a single or a few dominant species, which is characterized by a single sub-dominate species.

Soft Data Data obtained by inspection, intuition, or from other parties. Not measured directly and therefore, often judged to be less reliable than hard data.

Soft Hardwoods *See* hardwoods.

Software General name for computer programes and programing languages.

Softwoods A conventional term for the conifers and their timber, as distinguished from broad-leaved trees and their timber which are called hardwoods. In India, however, the use of the term is not thus restricted, but extends generally to all timber that has no definite heartwood and species of rapid growth and relatively poor durability.

Soil The uppermost weathered layer of the earth's crust. The subdivisions of soil recognized are: (1) *Surface soil* (often spoken of as the soil): The more or less completely weathered surface layer, rich in soluble material and containing a relatively higher proportion of organic matter and fine earth. It is also called top-soil. It is also called as the zone of aeration and intense root and microbiological activity. (2) *Sub-soil*: The layer immediately below the surface soil which is incompletely weathered and contains much less of soluble ingredients, organic matter and fine earth.

Soil-air The combination of gases occurring in the gaseous phase in soil.

Soil Auger A tool for taking a sample of soil down to some depth from the surface. *See* soil borer.

Soil Class A group of soils having the same range in particle size and physical properties based on texture. For practical purposes, soil class can be grouped as (a) Coarse textured soils, viz., sands and sandy loams; (b) Medium textured soils, viz., loams and silt loams; and (c) Fine textured soils, viz., clays and clay loams.

Soil Colour The colour of soil differs from soil to soil.

Soil Conservation The preservation of soil against deterioration and loss by using the land within its capabilities and applying those conservation practices that are necessary for its protection and improvement. More especially it consists of the use of land within the limits of economic practicability and in safeguarding it against impoverishment or depletion by erosion deposition, exhaustion of plant nutrients (through leaching, excessive cropping or overgrazing), accumulation of toxic salts, burning, water logging, improper cultivation or any type of improper use or failure to protect the land from soil loss or impairment of productiveness.

Soil Drainage The process, natural or artificial, by which excess water in the soil is removed.

Soil Ecology The study of soil organisms, their activities, and their interactions within the soil environment and with each other.

Soil Illuvial A soil or soil, horizons into which material have been washed and deposited by infiltrating water. *See* eluvial soil.

Soil Immature A soil which has not reached the stage of development that might be expected under existing weathering and biological processes.

Soil Mantle All the layers laying above the unweathered rock.

Soil Monolith A vertical section taken out of a soil profile and mounted for display or study.

Soil Morphology 1. The constitution out of the soil body as expressed in kinds, thickness and arrangement of the horizons in the profile, and in the texture, structure, consistency, porosity and colour of each horizon. 2. The properties, collectively of the soil body or any of its parts. It includes physical, chemical, mineralogical and biological properties.

Soil Organic Matter The organic fraction of the soil. It includes plant and animal residues at various stages of decomposition, cells and tissues of soil organisms, and substances shed by the soil population.

Soil Pit A pit dug with one or more vertical faces in order to examine the exposed soil profile.

Soil Population All of the organisms living in the soil, the combined soil fauna and flora.

Soil Pores Interstices between soil particles (voids).

Soil Porosity The extent to which the gross volume of the soil is unoccupied by solid particles. The air space in a soil at field moisture capacity is termed "non-capillary porosity". The portion in a soil that is not filled by water when the soil is wet, but well drained, is known as "capillary porosity".

Soil Profile The appearance of a soil in vertical section with particular reference to the sequence of layers that may be differentiated. *See* soil, horizons.

Soil Reaction The acid or alkaline reaction of a soil as measured by one of a number of methods and expressed in terms of *p*H units. *See p*H value.

Soil Rental The net annual income per acre or hectare derived from the soil.

Soil Resources, Decline of Productive The earth's soil resource is degraded, rendered sterile and contaminated with toxic chemicals at a rate that will spell disaster for the ecosystem. According to some estimate 10 per cent of the land surface of the planet has been transformed by human activities from forest and rangeland into desert (Paul R. Ehrlich *et al.*, 1977) and as much as 25 per cent more is at risk (World Resource, 1986). Crop land is already scarce in most of the developing countries. It is getting more scarcer because of expending urban areas and increasing population. Asia is beset with land scarcer problems. In Latin American countries 95 per cent of arable land lies with 10 per cent of the population and so the rest of the population owns 5 per cent of the arable land. Apart from this, most of these people have land on steep slopes which are highly susceptible to erosion. This has resulted into a situation of subsistence farming for most of the farmers in such countries. Likewise, large tracts in Africa are under the influence of draught. If the present rate of expansion of cropland in South America and Africa continues, then the days of unsustainable cropping systems are not far away.

Soil Salinity The amount of soluble salts in a soil, expressed in terms of percentage parts per million, or other convenient unit.

Soil Separate Mineral particles, less than 2 mm. In equivalent diameter ranging between specified size limits. *See* soil texture.

Soil Series A group of soils with similar profiles derived from similar materials under similar conditions of developments, but differing in other characteristics such texture and soil type.

Soil Structure The arrangement of the individual soil particles into aggregates of definite size and shape. These aggregates maintain their specific shapes on further fracture.

Soil Texture The relative proportion of the various size groups of individual soil particles. The individual size groups are referred to as soil separates. The size groups recognized are: (1) Clay, particles smaller than 0.002 mm; (2) Silt, particles between 0.002 mm and 0.02 mm; (3) Fine Sand, particles between 0.02 mm and 0.2 mm; (4) Course Sand, particles between 0.2 and 2.0 mm, and (5) Gravel, particles over 2.0 mm in size.

Soil Tilth It is the structure of the surface layer of the soil resulting from tilling operations.

Soil Type A subdivision of a soil series based mainly upon the soil texture of the upper layers.

Soil Working Loosening of the soil around plants by means of a pointed stick, hoe or similar implement to depths progressively increased with age, with a view to promoting soil aeration and infiltration capacity and conserving moisture.

Soil Wounding The superficial loosening of the soil with a rake, horrow or hoe, to prepare it for sowing or natural regeneration.

Soil, Acid For all practical purposes, a soil in which the *p*H value of the soil solution is less than 6.7. The degrees of soil acidity distinguished are: (1) Very acid (*p*H 5.0 to 5.8); (2) Moderately acid (*p*H 5.8 to 6.2); (3) Slightly acid (*p*H 6.2 to 6.7); (4) Neutral (*p*H 6.7 to 7.0).

Soil, Aeolian A soil formed from materials transported and deposited by wind, e.g., sand dunes and wind deposits of fine volcanic ash.

Soil, Aggregate A single mass or cluster of many soil particles held together, such as clod, prism, crumb or granule. *See* soil structure.

Soil, Alkali *See* soil, saline.

Soil, Alkaline A soil on which the *p*H value of the solution is more than 7. The degrees of soil alkalinity usually distinguished are: (1) Basic to Neutral (*p*H 7.0 to 7.5); (2) Basic (*p*H 7.5 to 8.5); (3) Very basic (*p*H above 8.5).

Soil, Alluvial A secondary soil derived essentially from flood plain material and generally without horizons, though strata may be present owing to the varying nature of the material deposited by the water at different times. *See* colluvial soil.

Soil, Black Cotton A tropical or sub-tropical black plastic clay soil, often developed from basic igneous rocks or in depressions, and sometimes found in alluvial sites unlike chernozem which it resembles superficially. It has low organic matter content and owes its low organic matter content and black colour to other constituents of the soil.

Soil, Brown Forest Immature but stable soil of cool, humid and temperate climatic regions. The nature of the parent rock continues to some extent to influence the properties of the soil profile. This profile normally contains a, b and c horizons with a silica-sesquioxide ratio uniform throughout brown earth. *See* soil, horizons.

Soil, Calcareous A soil containing sufficient calcium carbonate (often with magnesium carbonate) to effervesce visibly to the naked eye when treated with hydrochloric acid. It is alkaline in reaction.

Soil, Classification Study of soils and their inter-relationship, description of their properties, naming and grouping them systematically. The taxonomic units are frequently regrouped for various purposes such as drainage requirements, crop adaptations, highway construction or forestry purposes.

Soil, Colluvial A secondary immature soil derived from soil material of older origin, deposited by local erosion or solifluxion, e.g., down-washed or creek soils on the lower slopes of gentle hills colluvial soil.

Soil, Complex A mapping unit used in detailed soil surveys where two or more defined taxonomic unit are so intimately associated geographically that they cannot be separated by boundaries at the scale used.

Soil, Degraded A soil that has been subjected to stronger leaching than the type of prevalent soils in the area. Hence degraded soil is always lower in fertility.

Soil, Eluvial A soil or soil horizons from which materials, soluble or insoluble, have been leached or washed out by infiltrating water. *See* alluvial soil.

Soil, Heavy a soil which offers resistance or difficulty while tilling it. A fine-textured soil, viz., clay or clay loamy soil characterized by low infiltration capacity, poor drainage and inadequate aeration. It is not very much suitable to tree growth.

Soil, Horizons The layer into which a soil profile is divisible by simple ocular examination. Subdivisions of horizons are termed zones, and are indicated by the use of a numerical after the letter symbol for the horizon. The horizons recognized are: (1) A00 Horizon: Surface litter (generally found in a forest); (2) A0 Horizon: Humus layers consisting of mull and mor; (3) A Horizon: The upper most horizon of the mineral soil and essentially it represents a horizon of eluviation; (4) B Horizon: Essentially an alluvial horizon enriched with material washed down from A horizon and generally much more compact; (5) C Horizon: The uppermost of parent material which is in process of forming true soil under the influence of weathering; (6) A/C Horizon: The mid-horizon of recently developed, generally calcareous soils, in which the quantity of unweathered rock increases with depth to merge into unweathered parent material; (7) G Horizon: This horizon occurs between B and C horizons in soils with imperfect or impeded drainage.

Soil, Lateritic A soil characterized by the presence of laterite on the surface or the upper layers. Found in humid, tropical climates, as on the West Coast and Ghats of peninsular India.

Soil, Light A coarse-textured soil, for an example sandy loam characterized by high infiltration and low water-holding capacity. *See* heavy soil.

Soil, Mature A soil which has reached the full development that might be expected under existing weathering and biological processes and is always in equilibrium with its environment.

Soil, Peat *See* peat. Relatively uncommon in India.

Soil, Prairie A mature soil developed under grass in cool, semi-arid or moderately humid climates. Resembles chernozem but receives sufficient rainfall to prevent accumulation of $CaCO_3$ or $CaCO_4$.

Soil, Saline-alkali 1. A soil containing sufficient exchangeable sodium to interfere with growth of most crop plants and containing appreciable quantities of soluble salt. The exchangeable sodium percentage is greater than 15 and the conductivity of the saturation extract is greater than 4 milli mhos per centimetre (at 25°C). The *p*H of the saturated soil is usually less than 8.5. A saline-alkali soil has combination of harmful quantities of salts and either a high alkalinity or high exchangeable sodium, or both, so distributed in the profile that the growth of most crop plants is reduced.

Soil, Saline A group of soils occurring in arid climates where surface evaporation exceeds infiltration during the major part of the year. Characterized by layers of soluble salts deposited near the surface. Two types are distinguished: (1) Solonchak (white alkali): Characterized by surface deposits of $NaCl_2$ and Na_2SO_4 with $CaCl_2$ and $MgCl_2$, but the soil mass is structure less and dusty; (2) Solonetz (black alkali): Characterized by Na_2CO_3 and columnar structure. *See* alkali soil.

Soil, Secondary A soil derived from pre-existing soils by translocation and redeposition.

Soil, Skeletal A soil resulting from predominantly physical rather than chemical weathering. It is generally characterized by a high proportion of coarse material, and a low organic content.

Soil, Thermogenic Soils in which the dominant soil formation factor has been the high temperature. It is developed in sub-tropical and equatorial regions.

Somatic Pertaining to the body of an organism as distinct from its reproductive germ cells.

Source Code A computer programme that has been written in an English language like computer language. It must be compiled to yield the object code before it can be run on the computer.

Sowing, Broadcast The scattering of seed more or less evenly over a whole area, either that on which a crop is to be raised directly or a nursery bed, as opposed to other forms of sowing such as patch or strip sowing.

Sowing, Direct Sowing seeds directly on an area where a crop is to be raised, as opposed to sowing in a nursery. There are two distinct methods of direct sowing: 1st Category: Broadcast sowing, line sowing, patch sowing, strip sowing and dibbling; 2nd Category: Pit, mound, trench or furrow and ridge sowing.

Sowing, Line Sowing in drills or single lines as distinguished from sowing in strips.

Sowing, Patch Spot sowing a number of seeds in specially prepared patches.

Sowing, Strip Sowing thickly in narrow strips prepared for the purpose, usually at definite intervals from one another.

Spaceman Economy A term popularised by Boulding (1966) as metaphor representing the limits to the supplies of natural resources and to the capacity of the Earth's environment to assimilate wastes. It is also known as the 'economics of spaceship Earth'. This concept suggests that in the contexts of resource scarcity, priority should be given to maintenance of stocks of, for example, natural resources and human knowledge, and the minimization of the throughput of natural resources. *See* sustainable development; environmental sustainability.

Spacing The distance between the trees put out in a plantation or standing in a crop espacement.

Sparsely Vegetated A class of vegetation types that covers the land mass with 1-10 per cent of the area only.

Spatial Anything pertaining to the concepts of space, place and location.

Spatial Analysis *See* 'geographical analysis'.

Spatial Autocorrelation Tobler's Law of Geography (1976), which states that points closer together in space are more likely to have similar characteristics than those that are further apart.

Spatial Data Data that have some form of spatial or geographical reference that enables them to be located in two- or three—dimensional space.

Spatial Data Model A method by which geographical entities are represented in a computer. Two main methods exist and they are raster and vector data models. *See* geographical data model.

Spatial Data Retrieval The process of selectively retrieving items from a GIS data based on the basis of spatial location.

Spatial Data Structure Approach used to provide the information that the computer requires to reconstruct the spatial data model in digital form. There are many different data structures in use in GIS.

Spatial Decision Support System (SDSS). A decision support system (DSS) with a strong spatial component and incorporating spatial data models and spatial analysis to assist the user in arriving at a solution.

Spatial Enhancement 1.Enhancing values of pixels in an image relative to surrounding pixels. 2. Modifying pixel values in an image to enhance certain feature over others.

Spatial Entities Discrete geographical features (points, lines and areas) represented in a digital data structure.

Spatial Environmental Planning Spatial planning is primarily used for land use plans, city planning, and is recently extended to regional planning as well. In the conventional town and country planning, environmental issues were not addressed to the desired level, which has resulted in environmental degradation and deterioration of the urban areas. Monitoring has revealed that levels of air, water and noise pollution are higher in the metro and mega cities compared to other areas. It is, therefore, imperative that the policy planners and enforcement agencies initiate the remedial measures. Hence, spatial environmental planning has been introduced as a technique for conservation of the environmental resources and for achieving developmental targets in an environmentally sound manner. In this context, Zoning Atlas for situating industries was initiated at the district level which has covered more than 21 States and Union Territories so far. Thereafter, the programmes for Industrial Estate Planning and Development of Eco Industrial

Estates, Environmental Management Plans, Regional Planning Studies and Mapping of Environmentally Sensitive Zones have been taken up. Recently, Urban Environmental Information System has also been evolved for collection of information about the basic demographic profile of the urban area.

Spatial Interaction Models Models that are used to help understand and predict the location of activities and the movement of materials, people and information.

Spatial Interpolation The procedure of estimating the values of properties at unsampled sites within an area covered by existing observations (Waters, 1989).

Spatial Model A model of the real world, incorporating spatial data and relationships used to aid understanding of spatial form and process.

Spatial Process Models Models that simulate spatial component. These are used to help evaluate and understand complex spatial systems.

Spatial Query Action of questioning a GIS database on the basis of spatial location. Spatial queries include 'what is here?' and 'where is......?'

Spatial Referencing The method used to fix the location of geographical features or entities on the earth's surface.

Spawning Process of fertilizing and shedding eggs in fish.

Special Habitat A habitat which has a special function not provided by plant communities and successional stages. It includes riparian zones, snags, dead and down woody material and edges. It is biological in nature and can be created or altered by management (Thomas, 1979).

Special Richness A measure or expression of the number of species of plants or animals present in an area; the more species present, the higher the degree of species richness (Thomas, 1979).

Speciation The formation of a new species by evolution.

Species The main category of taxonomic classification into which genera are subdivided, comprising a group of similar interbreeding individuals having a number of correlated characters. It is a term used in classification to denote a subdivision of a genus. Forming a group of closely allied, mutually fertile individuals, showing constant differences from allied groups. In the binomial nomenclature of plants and animals, the second name (i.e., the name by which the species is distinguished from other species of the genus) is termed the specific name. Species of tree are usually distinguished by the characteristics of their fruits, flowers, leaves, bark, wood, etc.

Species-area Curve The graph of species *versus* area that describes the asymptotic growth in number of species encountered as the area sampled increases.

Species Invasion The immigration and establishment of a species in an area it did not previously occupy.

Species Richness The number of species present in a community, ecosystem, landscape, region, etc. *See* special richness.

Species, Accessory A useful species of less value than the principal species. It assists in the growth of the latter and influences to a smaller degree the method of treatment auxiliary species wants.

Species, Auxiliary A species of inferior quality or size, of relatively little silvicultural value or importance, associated with the principal or secondary or accessory species.

Species, Principal The species first in importance in a mixed stand, either by frequency, volume or silviculture value. 2. The species to which the silviculture of a mixed forest is primarily directed. For an example, in a teak forest the species 'teak' is the principal species towards which the silvicultuer is aimed at. *See* forest, mixed Species, accessory; species, auxiliary.

Species, Succession A species, which supplants the pioneer species at all later stages of ecological development. *See* succession.

Spectral Band An interval in the electromagnetic spectrum defined by two ends of wavelengths.

Spectral Distance A decision rule for image classification that assigns pixels to a cluster based on the minimum difference in spectral values to other pixels.

Spectral Reflectance Reflectance of electromagnetic energy at specified wavelength intervals.

Spectral Response Pattern Degree to which an object reflects incident electromagnetic energy in different regions of the electromagnetic spectrum.

Spectral Signature Quantitative measurement of the properties of an object or material over one to several wavelength intervals; the diagnostic spectral response for that entity. *See* spectral response pattern.

Spectral Vegetation Index An index of relative amount and vigour of vegetation. Such index is used for vegetation mapping by using satellite imageries.

Spectrometer Device for measuring intensity of radiation absorbed or reflected by a material as a function of wavelength.

Spectrum Continuous sequence of electromagnetic energy arranged according to wavelength or frequency.

Spheroid 1. A geometric representation of the shape of the earth. 2. Mathematical figure closely approaching the geoid in form and size and used as a surface of reference for geodetic surveys. A reference spheroid or ellipsoid is a spheroid determined by revolving an ellipse about its shorter (polar) axis and used as a base for geodetic surveys of a large section of the Earth (such as the Clarke spheroid of 1866 which is used for geodetic surveys in the United States).

Spike 1. An overshoot line created erroneously by a scanner and its raster-vector software. 2. An anomalous data point that protrudes above or below an interpolated surface representing the distribution of the value of an attribute over an area.

Spinning (Fishing) Form of fishing in which natural or artificial bait is cast, and then wound back, so that its appearance and behaviour suggest a swimming fish and thus induce attack by predatory fish.

Spline 1. A polynomial curve or surface used to represent spatial variation smoothly. 2. Mathematical method of smoothing linear features, often used to interpolate between points digitized along a curved feature.

Spoon Bill (*Platalea Leucorodia*) A tall white bird, related to the ibis, immediately identified by the black spoon-shaped bill. It has long beck and legs, the toes being bordered by a membrane and webbed at the base. It lives in water and feeds on small crustaceans, mollusks, frogs and fish. It is found throughout India, except the drier and the more hilly regions. It is a resident bird.

Sporadic Habitually living, occurring and/or reproducing here and there or individually. *See* gregarious.

Sporophore A fruit body of large fungi; a spore-bearing structure.

Spot Height A single height value on a topographic map, usually representing the location and height of a prominent feature between contour lines.

Spruce It refers to trees of the genus *Picea.* A genus of about 35 species of coniferous evergreen trees in the Family Pinaceae, found in the northern temperate and boreal (taiga) regions of the earth. Spruces are tall and large trees, from 20—60 (—95) m tall when mature, and can be distinguished by their whorled branches and conical form. The needles, or leaves, of spruce trees are attached singly to the branches in a spiral fashion, each needle on a small peg-like structure called a *pulvinus*. The needles are shed when 4—10 years old, leaving the branches rough with the retained pulvini. Spruces are used as food plants by the larvae of some Lepidoptera species. Spruce is one of the most important woods for paper manufacture, as it has long wood fibres which bind together to make strong paper. Spruces are cultivated over vast areas for this purpose. Spruces are also popular ornamental trees in horticulture, admired for their evergreen, symmetrical narrow-conic growth habit. For the same reason, some (particularly *Picea abies* and *P. omorika*) are also extensively used as Christmas trees. Spruce wood, often called *white wood,* is used for many purposes, ranging from general construction work and crates to highly specialised uses in wooden aircraft and stringed musical instruments including guitars, mandolins, cellos, and violins.

SPOT This is a French earth observation system. This satellite captures either 10 m panchromatic or 20 m 3 band multispectral imagery.

Spur A structure of piles, rocks, brushwood bundles or other material extending into a stream to induce deposition in order to protect the bank.

Square Planting Planting in a square pattern, i.e., with the plants occupying the four corners of each of the successive squares.

Squirrel Any of the arboreal, bushy-tailed rodents constituting the genus Sciurus and allied genera (Family Sciuridae) as the common Indian five-striped squirrel (*Funambulus palmarum*). The term is also applied to the various other members of the family Sciuridae as the chipmunks, flying squirrels, wood-chucks, etc. The Indian Giant Squirrel *Ratufa indica* is found in the mixed deciduous and moist evergreen forests of the Peninsula.

Stability The extent to which the variation in an individual characteristic of an ecological system is less than the variation in the environmental variables which influence that characteristic.

Stabilization The state of maximum adjustment between organisms and an environment that is characteristic of an ecological climax community. The term is applied when animal population or animal habitat is brought to a desired optimum state either by natural or artificial means.

Stage Structure The demographic distribution of a population based on developmental stages rather than absolute age.

Stagheaded The condition of a trees with dead upper branches projecting above the green portion of the crown.

Staking Marking with stakes the position of plants in a plantation.

Stakeholders 1. Stakeholders are defined as any people who are directly or indirectly affected by or interested in any initiatives or exercise or work. 2. Stakeholders in forest management are people or interest groups interested in, or affected by, forest management and operations; for example, government agencies, local communities, employees, investors, environmental interest groups, Non-Governmental Organizations (NGO) and general public.

Stand 1. Plant communities, particularly of trees, sufficiently uniform in composition, constitution, age, spatial arrangement or condition to be distinguishable from adjacent communities; also, may delineate a silvicultural management entity (Ford-Robertson, 1971). 2. Loosely used as a synonymous for main crop. More precisely, an aggregation of trees or other growth possessing sufficient uniformity in composition, constitution, age arrangement or condition to be distinguished from adjacent crops and forming a silvicultural unit (BCFT modif).

Stand Condition The descriptive measurement of a stand by the criteria of composition, health, age, size, volume or spatial arrangement (Thomas, 1979).

Stand Density *See* density, stand.

Stand Development The stages through which a stand passes during its lifetime, viz., the seedling or coppice shoot or sapling pole and sample tree.

Stand Structure The configuration of elements, parts, or constituencies of a stand (Thomas, 1979).

Stand Table A table showing the distribution of stems by diameter classes for each of the series of crop diameters. In India, it is usually appended at the end of yield table of the species and distribution is presented thereby. It is often auxiliary to a yield table. The average diameter of the main crop stems and the stems removed in successive thinning can be ascertained from the yield table but the range of diameters comprised in these averages cannot be known unless stand table is also prepared. In normally stocked forests, stand table gives a clear idea of the distribution of different diameter classes and can be put to several uses.

Stand, Elite 1. A tree selected for retention till maturity or till the last thinning. 2. A stand selected for seed collection on account of its specially good quality. *See* tree elite.

Stand, Fully-stocked A stand in which all growing space is deemed to be effectively occupied by the forest crop, but in which adequate room is left for the best development of the trees. *See* density, crop.

Standard A tree selected to remain standing over a younger or new crop, for some special purposes such as shelter, production of quality timber, seed, etc.

Standard, 1st Class and 2nd Class Standards retained for one or two coppice rotations respectively.

Standardization The process of transforming data into a common scale of measurement. This is used to ensure comparability between criteria measured in different units and different scales of measurement.

Station 1. The exact place of occurrence of a species or individual within a given habitat. 2. A circumscribed area representing a complete and definite ensemble of conditions of existence, as reflected in the uniformity of the vegetation.

Stationarity A statistical name for expressing degrees of invariance in the properties of random functions. It refers to the statistical model, and not to the data. Most commonly used to indicate invariance in the mean and variance, but also in the variance of first differences (see intrinsic hypothesis).

Status A term often used to denote the (present) position of a species with regard to population, degree of protection given, etc.

Stem The principal axis of a plant from which buds and shoots are developed. In trees, stem, bole and trunk are synonymous.

Stem Analysis The analysis of a compete stem by measuring annual rings on a number of cross-sections at different heights in order to determine its rate of past of growth. *See* stump analysis.

Stem Class A class into which trees of a stand or crop are placed on the basis of some quality of the stem.

Stenothermic Of organisms having or tolerating a small range of temperature.

Stenothermous Of organisms, which cannot tolerate a wide variation of temperature in environment. *See* eurythermous.

Steppe A wide treeless plain of grassland, characteristically xerophyte.

Stereo Plotter A device for extracting information about the elevation of landform from stereoscopic aerial photographs. The results are sets of x, y, and z coordinates.

Stereoscopic Aerial Photography The use of overlapping vertical aerial photographs to determine height based on the parallax effect gained from viewing the same object from slightly different angles.

Stewardship, Forest Environmentally and socially responsible use, management and development of forest resources to maintain and enhance the value of the forest for present and future generations.

Sticky Point The moisture content (per cent) at which soil begins to stick to objects such as knife or paper. The extent of sticking is measured by mixing successive quantities of water with a dry, finely powdered sample.

Stochastic Referring to patterns resulting from random effects.

Stochastic Model A model that recognizes that there could be a range of possible outcomes for a given set of inputs, and expresses the likelihood of each one happening as a probability.

Stochastic Simulation Simulation using a probabilistic model to generate a range of allowable data values.

Stock A rooted plant on which a scion is grafted. *See* growing stock, nursery stock and root graft.

Stockholm Conference (1972) The Stockholm Conference is the landmark in the field of global environmentalism. It marks the coming of age of the environmental movement. It assumed significance because of the legitimacy that afforded to environmental issues in international relations (Thomas, 1992). The Conference adopted the Stockholm Declaration with 29 Principles and provided a permanent basis for international environmental co-ordination and diplomacy. The importance of this conference is indicated from the fact that representatives of about 113 countries and 19 inter-Governmental agencies attended the conference. The scale of this international gathering itself symbolised the significance of environmental issues. The Conference ended with a decision to set up the United Nations Environmental Programme (UNEP). It also initiated the process of forming the Convention on International Trade in Endangered Species. The Conference also helped to strengthen environmental groups and to expand their roles. Meeting of Non-Governmental Organisations and the interaction with Governmental representatives provided a forum and a means of international networking for these groups. This resulted into broadening of their interests away from narrow concerns such as species protection and towards wider issues such as funding policies, relation of environment to development, etc. All this led to an emergence of the concept of sustainability. Apart from this, the Conference initiated changes in many fields. It promoted the development of national environmental policies; it helped the setting of separate environmental agencies and ministries; it promoted a formal dialogue between developed and developing countries over their environmental concerns; it initiated a process of thinking environmental problems and developmental problems interconnectedly; it led to a realisation among the nations that a synthesis between conservation and development is the answer to environmental as well as economic crisis.

Stolen A creeping stem or runner capable of rooting and forming a new plant.

Stool A living stump capable of producing coppice shoots. *See* stump.

Storage The parts of the computer system used for storing data and programmes (see archival storage, magnetic media).

Storey A horizontal stratum or layer of canopy in a plant community. Forests often have two or more canopy layers, each canopy layer constitutes a storey. *See* stratification.

Stork Any of various large, mostly Old World, long legged, wading birds of Cinconia and allied genera with a long neck and long stout, sharp straight bill, forming the family Cinconiidae. Storks are related to the herons and Ibises. Often they are as tall as 1.2 metre. ADJUTANT STORK: ADJUTANT BIRD (*Leptoptilos dubius*): Probably so-called from its fancied resemblance to a military figure in a parade ground. A large stork, standing 1.2 metre high, with an enormous, wedge-shaped, yellow bill and with the neck and head bare of feathers. It feeds on carrion and on small aquatic animals or snakes. It is found in northern India, extending eastwards to Assam. OPEN-BILLED STORK (*Anastomus oscitans*): A small stork, similar to the white stork, characterized by a grooved bill, with the upper and lower parts touching only at the base and at the tip. Found throughout India. PAINTED STORK (*Ibis leucocephalus*): A typical large stork with long, heavy, yellow bill, slightly decurved near the tip. Found through out India. WHITE STORK (*Cinconia cinconia*). An egret like bird, pure white except for black wings. Found practically through-out India, rather rare in south of the Deccan. WHITE-NECKED STORK (*Dissoura episcopus*): This large stork is easily distinguished by its white neck and distinctive plumage. It has a wide distribution in South and East Asia. It is a resident species throughout India. It is found singly, in pairs, or in small parties in open well-watered country such as flooded or irrigated land, rice field or small patches of marsh. It ascends the Himalayas up to 1200 metres.

Storm, Dry A lightning storm with less than 0.10 inch of precipitation.

Storm, Ice A storm that leaves a heavy deposit of ice formed of frozen rain or show causing much breakage in tops of trees and young stands.

Strain It is a loosely used term synonymous for race. It is a group within a variety that constantly differs in one or more genetic factors from a member of the variety.

Strangulation Constriction of the bole of the living trees by metal bands or other means, with the object of stimulating flowering and seed production. It is generally used to stimulate production in case of Jack fruit.

Stratification 1. Differentiation of tree, shrubs and herbs in a natural forests into several stories, layers or strata. Stratification is frequently observed in natural forests. In all the more luxuriant types, as well as in unevenaged forests approximating to them in form, there appear to be more or less well defined strata for the tallest trees, which tend to stand singly or in groups well above a more or less continuous main canopy; below this may be successively smaller trees, shrubs and ground layers. In a general way one can infer that the more favourable the site to tree growth, the more intensive the stratification is. 2. The operation of storing seeds in, and often in alternate layers with a moist medium such as sand or peat, in order to maintain viability or overcome dormancy of seed. 3. Subdivision of a population into strata or blocks or sampling unit as a preliminary to sampling. Each stratum should be more homogeneous in respect of the variable being measured than the population as a whole.

Stratified Kriging Interpolation by any kriging method within a set of strata or divisions of the land into different classes. Used in GIS analysis.

Stream Mode Digitizing The method of manually digitizing lines whereby the digitizer automatically records a co-ordinate at a set time or distance interval.

Stream Order A hierarchical ordering of streams based on the degree of branching. A first order stream is an unforked or unbranched stream. Two first orders flow together to make a second order; two second orders combine to make a third order stream, etc.

Stress This term covers a group of physiological changes induced by crowding. It is a common and subtle force which acts as a limiting factors in population dynamics.

Strike, to To take or cause to take root.

Strip Cropping Growing crops in a systematic arrangement of alternate strips or bands which serve as vegetative barriers to wind and water erosion. *See* contour cropping.

Stripling A sapling grown in a nursery stripped of its leaves and branches and sometimes root-pruned, before planting out.

Stripping Removing bark in strips as practiced, e.g. in wattle industry.

Strong Sustainability An economy is said to be strongly sustainable if the stocks of each of its capital assets, including its natural capital assets, are non-decreasing.This contrasts with weak sustainability, which allows decreases in the value of one type of capital, for example natural capital, to be compensated for by increasing stocks of another type of capital, for example human-made capital or human capital (Perman *et. al.*, 1999). *See* sustainable development.

Structured Query Language (SQL) 1. A standard language for interrogating and managing relational databases. 2. The computer language developed to facilitate the querying of relational database. Also known as standard query language.

Structured Systems Analysis and Design Methodology (SSADM) A method used for the design of GIS projects.

Stubble Mulch The lower short stiff parts of the stem of crops are called stubble. The stubble of crop or crop residues left essentially in place on the land as a surface cover before and during the preparation of the seed bed and at least partly during the growing of a succeeding crop.

Stump The base of tree and its roots left in the ground after felling. *See* cutting, root and shoot.

Stump Analysis The analysis of cross-section of a stump by measuring growth ring in order to estimate the age of the tree and its past rates of growth. *See* stem analysis.

Stump, to To cut back a seedling to make a cutting, root and shoot for planting.

Stumpage The value of timber as it stands uncut in a forest royalty.

Stumpage Value The economic rent embodied in a standing stock of trees. This is the difference between the sale value of the timber and the costs of harvesting it (Pearce, Markandya and Barbier, 1990).

Sub-alpine The highest elevation of a mountainous areas that can support forests.

Sub-climax 1. A pro-climax in which the development of vegetation is arrested and held at some stage short of the normal climax owing to the action of factors, natural or artificial, other than the climate (after Clements.). 2. The (seral) stage in plant succession immediately preceding the climax. *See* seral stage; climax.

Sub-compartment A subdivision of a compartment, generally of a temporary nature, differentiated for special description and treatment (preferably designated by small letters a, b, c, etc.).

Sub-dominant 1. A component of a community, typically a species, which, though locally (co-) dominant, exerts much less dominance than the widespread dominant does. 2. A constituent of a plant community with less influence on its character than a dominant.

Sub-littoral Zone The part of a shore from the lowest water level to the lower boundary of plant growth. It is a transition zone from the littoral to profundal.

Sub-plot A subdivision of an experimental plot or sample plot.

Sub-polar Geographically, regions that have only one (warmest) month at an average temperature of 50 degrees Fahrenheit or 10 degrees Celsius or above.

Sub-scene A portion of an image that is used for detailed analysis.

Sub-sere A sere in secondary succession. *See* secondary sere.

Subsidies and Forest Development Subsidies are powerful tools of social change in developing society. They can accelerate the adoption of aptitudes and practices compatible to sustainable development of natural resources. Subsidies can be particularly beneficial if they are limited in duration and sharply focused on specific economic, social or environmental goals which cannot be achieved by other means (Earth Council, 1996). Therefore, subsidies can, in effect, play a crucial role in helping development become more sustainable. However, many of the present subsidies in many countries encourage practices that are economically perverse, trade distorting, ecologically destructive and socially inequitable. It is so because the subsidies are decided without adequate forethought and planning with respect to their social, environmental, and economic consequence. Consequently, the system of subsidy reduces the potential revenues and, therefore, deprives the society of developmental opportunities, possible from sustainable use of a country's forests. Undercharging of the value of timber and other forest products is a manifestation of indirect subsidy. It also leads to wanton consumption and mindless wastage of the vital resources. In India, concessions and privileges for the local communities, without a proper mechanism of distributional justice at the village level, has led to an unsustainable use of forest resources. Apart from this, the revenue forgone because of such unregulated concessions and rights reduces opportunities and choices for development in the rural areas. World Watch Institute (1997) estimates that more than US$ 500 billion per year of consumer's and tax payer's money is spent by government to subsidize deforestation and other environmentally destructive activities.

Subsidy It is a type of economic instrument. Subsidies take a number of forms, and may consist of direct transfers or pricing and tax policies that are favourable to certain economic activities. The subsidies must be less than the value of the positive externality. Otherwise, subsidies distort prices and thereby lead to inefficient allocations of investment (OECD, 1989b).

Sub-soiling Tillage of the sub-soil or soil horizons below the normal plough-depth to break a hardpan or plough-pan which impedes internal soil drainage, or to shatter and treat a clay pan layer or other slowly permeable sub-soil that limits the roots-penetration of the plants.

Sub-species 1. A category intermediate in rank between species and variety, based on a smaller number of correlated characters that are used to differentiate species and generally conditioned by geographical and/or ecological occurrence. It generally has a larger number of correlated characters than are used to differentiate varieties and also a wider geographical occurrence. 2. Sub-division of species into two or more groups based on possession of slightly differing characters. Sub-species can usually interbreed and often grade into one another.

Subterranean A termite which is essentially soil-inhabiting, entering wood only from the ground, and requiring a constant supply of moisture for its existence. It readily invades wood in contact with damp soil and is also able to build covered runways over impenetrable obstructions and thus reach wood removed from ground contact.

Sub-tropical Climate A climate hot in summer with a cool winter determined in India more by altitude than by latitude.

Sub-tropical (Geographically) Regions that have an average temperature of 50 degrees Fahrenheit or 10 degree Celsius or above for 5 to 8 months of the year.

Succession 1. A series of plants or animals following each other in time or place in a regular order. 2. The gradual replacement of one community by another in the development of vegetation towards a climax; succession is "primary" on sites which have previously not borne any vegetation and "secondary" after destruction of whole or part of original vegetation. 3. The gradual supplanting of one community of plants by another, the sequence of communities being termed a sere and each seral stage. A sere whose first stage is open water is termed a hydrosere, one whose first stage is dry ground, a xerosere. Succession is primary (by pioneers) on sites that have not previously borne secondary vegetation, after the whole or part of the original vegetation has been supplanted; allogenic when the causes of succession are external to and independent of the community (e.g. Accretion of soil by wind or water, or a change of climate) and autogenic when the developing vegetation is itself the cause. Plant succession is important for wildlife management as various stages of succession will support different type of wildlife in different number. 4. Ecological succession was formerly seen as having a stable end-stage called the climax, sometimes referred to as the 'potential vegetation' of a site, shaped primarily by the local climate. This idea has been largely abandoned by modern ecologists in favour of non-equilibrium ideas of how ecosystems function. Most natural ecosystems experience disturbance at a rate that makes a "climax" community unattainable. Climate change often occurs at a rate and frequency sufficient to prevent arrival at a climax state. Additions to available species pools through range expansions and introductions can also continually reshape communities.The development of some ecosystem attributes, such as pedogenesis and nutrient cycles, are both influenced by community properties, and, in turn, influence further community development. This process may occur only over centuries or millennia. Coupled with the stochastic nature of disturbance events and other long-term (e.g., climatic) changes, such dynamics make it doubtful whether the 'climax' concept ever applies or is particularly useful in considering actual vegetation.

Succession Stage A stage or recognizable condition of a plant community which occurs during its development from bare ground to climax, e.g. grass-forb-shrub seedling-sapling/pole-young-mature-old growth (Thomas, 1979).

Succession, Allogenic Succession brought about by allogenic factors.

Succession, Ecological It is a fundamental concept in ecology. It refers to more-or-less predictable and orderly changes in the composition or structure of an ecological community. Succession may be initiated either by formation of new, unoccupied habitat (e.g., a lava flow or a severe landslide) or by some form of disturbance (e.g. fire, severe windthrow, logging) of an existing community. The former case is often referred to as primary succession, the latter as secondary succession. The trajectory of ecological change can be influenced by site conditions, by the interactions of the species present, and by more stochastic factors such as availability of colonists or seeds, or weather conditions at the time of disturbance. Some of these factors contribute to predictability of successional dynamics; others add more probabilistic elements. In general, communities in early succession will be dominated by fast-growing, well-dispersed species. As succession proceeds, these species will tend to be replaced by more competitive (k-selected) species.

Suitability Map Suitability means relevancy according to a set of predefined criteria. A suitability map displays locations that fulfil all criteria.

Sunscald Winter Injury to bark and cambium resulting in wounds or canker localized on the side of the tree exposed to the mid-day and afternoon sun. Injury occurs as a result of freezing following the unseasonable warming of the bark by the sun in winter.

Sun-synchronous Earth satellite orbit in which the orbit plane is nearly polar and the altitude is such that the satellite passes over all places on earth having the same latitude twice daily at the same local sun time.

Supervised Classification Information extraction technique in which the operator provides training-site information that the computer uses to assign pixels to categories. The term is used in digital classification and interpretation of imageries.

Supervised Training Image classification procedure in which the analyst selects groups of pixels, determines their spectral response pattern (signature), and trains a computer system to recognize pixels based on this.

Suppressed Applied to plants or trees only 1/2 to 5/8 of the height of the best trees, with their leading shoots definitely overtopped by their neighbours or at least shaded on all sides by them. *See* dominant; dominated.

Supra-littoral Zone The portion of the shore adjacent to the water's edge.

Surface The entity type used to describe the continuous variation in space of a third dimension, such as terrain. The term is used in GIS.

Surface Drape The draping of an image on top of a 3d view of a terrain model for the purpose of landscape rendering or visualization.

Surrogate Market Techniques These techniques involve studying consumer behaviour in markets for goods and services that are related to non-market, environmental goods, in order to infer the value that consumers place on the environmental goods.

Surround An area maintained round an experimental plot or sample plot to ensure that the latter is not being affected by the treatment applied to an area outside them.

Survey 1. Orderly process of determining data relating to any physical or chemical characteristics of the earth and the associated data obtained in a survey. 2. An organization engaged in making a survey.

Survey, Forest Soil It is survey of forest soil and provides an inventory of different kinds of soil and soil types occurring in different parts of the forests. The primary objective of the survey is to classify soils into well-defined types to map different kinds of soil. The data collected during soil survey are used to correlate soil conditions with the character and growth of the existing forest vegetation and in deciding the suitability of specific blocks or areas for specific association of trees. It also helps in evaluating the potentiality of an area for specific management practices and in determining the ecological status. A careful correlation of soil characteristics with vegetation enables the delineation of natural homogeneous area exhibiting homogeneous soil properties.

Survey, Wildlife A wildlife survey is a fact-finding exercise. Scientific investigation by qualified persons into the wildlife resources and the habitat. The survey includes subjects such as availability and type of cover, water, food supply, factors adversely affecting wildlife, and so on. The results of survey provides inputs for planning wildlife management of a given area.

Survey, Forest An inventory of forest land to determine such data as area and topography together with the condition, composition and constitution of the crop(s) on it, but not strictly crop enumeration (BCFT).

Survey Line Plot A partial enumeration employing lines of sample plots usually laid out at regular intervals along parallel survey lines.

Survey, Pilot It is a survey before conducting elaborate forest inventory. It generally aims at determining the number of sample plots required minimally for archiving the desired precision in the inventory. On the basis of available attributes, forest will be stratified for allocation of sampling unit. This survey is a prerequisite to decide the most efficient survey design within the ambit of available time, money and manpower.

Survey, Strip A partial enumeration employing regularly spaced survey lines (strictly a linear survey) or strip of specified width, along which recording of data is continuous. *See* linear strip survey, linear survey.

Sustainability A broad definition of sustainability is that the economic, social and environmental systems that generate human well-being are being maintained over time, on a sustainable basis. There are many different aspects to sustainability. A more precise definition of sustainability primarily depends on the context one considers. Sustainability can best be explained in terms of different types of capital stocks that contribute to human well-being. Some of these stocks are: human-made capital which are used along with natural resources and human capital to provide goods and services; social capital which are used to contribute directly to well-being; natural capital which are used not only to provide inputs to production of goods but also create life-support functions on which the earth including all human and other animals depends for their survival. The danger to sustainability lies in the fact that each of these capitals can be depleted in order to increase current well-being. Depletion of any of such capitals means decrease of future well-being.

Sustainable A term applied to economies and to development. It implies that the 'capital' of the system is maintained and that societies live off the 'income'. In ecological and forestry terms, it generally implies stability through time and an absence of environmental degradation, howsoever that may be measured. Over the years the concept evolved to acquire more critical meaning. *See* carrying capacity; sustainability; sustainable development.

Sustainable Development Sustainable development has been defined in Brundtland Report in 1987 (WCED, 1987), as 'Development that meets the needs of the present without compromising the ability of future generations to meet their own needs'. It implies integrating traditional economic concerns with social and environmental considerations. The concept of sustainability was first placed on the international agenda by the Brundtland Report in 1987 (WCED, 1987). The concept has received widespread acceptance as an ethically laudable goal with respect to the use of natural resources. Over the years, myriad of definitions have been added to explain the meaning and connotation of sustainable development. In the context of forestry, the concept of sustainability first received international attention in the statement of Forest Principles and Chapter 11 of Agenda 21, which were formulated at the 1992 UN Conference on Environment and Development (UNCED). The Forest Principles, a 'non-legally binding authoritative statement of principles', aimed to 'contribute to the management, conservation and sustainable development of forests' and noted the need for setting relevant standards for forest use. The importance of considering the needs of future generations while managing a forest resource has in fact been recognized in the ancient past. A definition of sustainability was provided by the German forester Hartig as early as 1804 (Schmutzenhofer, 1992): '...to utilize [forest stands] to the greatest possible extent, but still in a way that future generations will have at least as much benefit as the living generation'. These words are clearly echoed in more recent definitions, such as that given by Duerr and Duerr (1975): 'To fulfil our obligations to our descendants and to stabilize our communities, each generation should sustain its resources at a high level and hand them along undiminished'. This definition implies that there are social and economic aspects to an overall concept of sustainability within forestry. The concept of sustainability was for many years equated with the principle of sustained yield. But only in the last few decades the concept broadened to include environmental and socio-economic aspects. The basic elements of sustainability with relation to natural resources are based on principles such as: (a) The stock of the natural capital should not diminish and it should be conserved in sufficient abundance; (b) Rate of exploitation or use of natural resources should be linked with the rate of regeneration; (c) Demand should be linked with the rate of sustainable use; (d) The price of the product should reflect the economic price encompassing the environmental costs; (e) There is need to identify or develop substitutes for the natural resources; (f) The rate of discharge of wastes must not exceed the rate at which these flows can be assimilated without impacting ecosystem negatively.

Sustainable Forest Management (SFM) Sustainable forest management is a process of managing forest to achieve one or more clearly specified objectives of management with regard to the production of a continuous flows of desired forest products and services without undue reduction of its inherent values and future productivity and without undue undesirable effects on the physical and social environment. SFM is a process, rather than a fixed state. As such, universal prescriptions for SFM are over simplistic. Elements may include participatory and equitable approaches to decision-making geared towards maintaining ecosystem and landscape functions while also meeting broad economic, social and cultural needs. The management context is all-important.

Sustainable Forest Management, Components of Several recent international meetings have suggested that the following seven thematic elements are key components: (1) *Extent of forest resources*: The theme expresses an overall desire to have significant forest cover and stocking, including trees outside forests, to support the social, economic and environmental dimensions of forestry. For example, the existence and extent of specific forest types are important as a basis for conservation efforts. The theme encompasses ambitions to reduce deforestations and to restore and rehabilitate degraded forest landscapes. This theme also includes the important function of forests and trees outside forests to store carbon and thereby contribute to moderating the global climate; (2) *Biological diversity*: The theme concerns the conservation and management of biological diversity at the ecosystem (landscapes), species and genetic levels. Such conservation, including protected area with fragile ecosystems, ensures that diversity of life is maintained, and provides opportunities to develop new products, for example medicines, in the future. Genetic improvement is also a means to improve forest productivity, for example to ensure a high wood production in intensively managed forests; (3) *Forest health and vitality*: Forests need to be managed so that risks and impacts of unwanted disturbances are minimized, including wildfires, airborne pollution, storm felling, invasive species, diseases and insects. Such disturbances may impact social, economic as well as environmental dimensions of forestry; (4) *Productive functions of forest resources*: Forests and trees outside forests provide a wide range of wood and non-wood forest products. The theme expresses the ambition to maintain a high and valuable supply of primary forest products, while at the same time ensuring that productions and harvesting are sustainable and do not compromise management options of future generations; (5) *Protective functions of forest resources*: The theme addresses the role of forests and trees outside forests to help moderate soil, hydrological and aquatic systems. This includes to maintain clean water including, e.g. healthy fish population, as well as to reduce risks or impacts of floods, avalanches, erosion and droughts. Protective functions of forest resources also contribute to ecosystem conservation efforts. Protective functions of forest resources have strong cross-sectoral aspects, as the benefits to agriculture and rural livelihoods are high; (6) *Socio-economic functions*: The theme addresses the contributions of forest resources to the overall economy, for example through employment, values generated through processing and marketing of forest products and energy, trade and investments in the forest sector. The theme also addresses the important functions of forest to host and protect sites and landscapes that have high cultural, spiritual or recreational values, and thus include aspects of land tenure, indigenous and community management systems, and traditional knowledge: (7) *Legal, policy and institutional framework*: The theme includes the legal, policy and institutional arrangements necessary to support the above six themes, including participatory decision-making, governance and law enforcement, and monitoring and assessment of progress. The theme also addresses broader societal aspects, including fair and equitable use of forest resources, science research and education, infrastructure arrangements to support the forest sector, transfer of technology and capacity building, and public information and communication. These thematic elements are based on the criteria of the nine on-going regional/international processes on criteria and indicators for sustainable forest management, and were acknowledged by the International Conference on Criteria and Indicators in Guatemala in February 2003 and by the FAO Committee on Forestry in 2003. In February 2004, the FAO/ITTO Expert Consultation on Criteria and Indicators recognised that these elements are important for facilitating international communication on forest related issues (FAO, 2003).

Sustainable Livelihoods A livelihood comprises the capabilities, assets and activities required for a means of living. A livelihood is sustainable when it can cope with and recover from stresses and shocks and maintain or enhance its capabilities and assets both now and in future, while not undermining the natural resource base (Carney, 1998). The assets, which are the building blocks of livelihoods, are not only natural, physical and financial capital, but also social and human capital (kinship and network, nutrition and health). A range of assets is, therefore, needed to achieve sustainable livelihoods. The ability to move out of poverty or food insecurity is critically dependent on access to such an array of assets. Forests constitute a major source of sustainable livelihoods in the rural sector. They provide employment and income to rural people on a sustained basis. Forestry operations generate employment opportunities in small scale processing and trading activities, which require little financial capital or skill. They provide a wide range of wood and non-wood forest products, which are not reflected in the financial transaction. They, though necessary for living in rural areas, do not reflect in the income profile of economy. But, they play a very critical role in the life of poor people living in the villages.

Sustainable NTFP Yields Methods for calculating sustainable Non-Timber Forest Products (NTFP) yields are not yet fully developed in any part of the world. This poses a great deal of problem for operationalizing sustainable forest management. Sustainable management for non-wood products means balancing optimal productivity and controlling ecological change so that environmental equilibrium is maintained (Wickens, G.E., 1994). The range of management requirements for forest species providing non-wood products may complicate their management process, and their integration with timber production system may decrease the revenue outturn from timber sale, but could make the practice more environmentally efficient. But, sustainably managed forests for non-wood forest products provide a range of environmental services as well as goods. One of the best known of these services is soil and water conservation and other ecological life support services. Moreover, income generation, livelihood security, increased food security and enhanced well-being are some of the important social benefits that might nullify the increased cost of management of such forests.

Sustainable Tourism Tourism can, in any part of the world, involve environmental risks, since it involves relatively large number of people visiting what are often fragile ecosystems, such as coastal ecosystem, coral reef, rain forests. Sustainable tourism requires that the environment assets, which attract tourists, are not degraded by the activities of tourisms, and it also requires the participation and cooperation of the local community.

Sustainable Use Sustainable use is a commonly used phrase. According to The Biological Diversity Act, 2002 sustainable use means the use of components of biological diversity in such manner and at such rate that does not lead to the long term decline of the biological diversity, thereby maintaining its potential to meet the needs and aspirations of present and future generations. What is important is the fact that how to establish practices compatible to sustainable use of natural resources. The priority requirements under sustainable utilisation have been enumerated by World Conservation Strategy (IUCN, 1980). Few of the important requirements (as mentioned in different paragraphs of the IUCN document) are: (a) Determine the productive capacities of exploited species and ecosystems and ensure that utilization does not exceed those capacities (para 7.1); (b) Adopt conservation management objectives for the utilisation of species and ecosystems (para 7.2); (c) Ensure that access to a resource does not exceed the resource's capacity to sustain exploitation (para 7.3); (d) Reduce excessive yields to sustainable levels (para 7.4); (e) Reduce incidental take as much as possible (para 7.5); (f) Equip subsistence communities to utilise resource sustainably (para 7.6); (g) Maintain the habitats of resource species (para 7.7); (h) Regulate international trade in wild animals and plants (para 7.8); (i) Allocate timber concessions with care and manage them to high standards (para 7.9); (j) Limit firewood consumption to sustainable levels (para 7.10); (k) Regulate the stocking of grazing lands to maintain the long-term productivity of plants and animals (para 7.11); (l) Utilise indigenous wild herbivores, alone or with livestock, where domestic stock alone would degrade the environment (para 7.12).

Sustained Yield Production of forest products on a perpetual basis, ensuring that the rate of removal of forest products does not exceed the rate of replacement over the long term.

Sustained Yield Forestry The yield of defined forest products of specific quality and in projected quantity that a forest can provide continuously at a given intensity of management.

Sustenance Foods, Classes of During the critical winter season, game animals eat different types of food according to availability. These are: (1) *Preferred food*: They provide delicacies but are available only in the earlier part of winter; (2) *Staple food*: They form the foundation of winter sustenance; (3) *Emergency food*: They are capable of sustaining life but insufficient to maintain weight, vitality and resistance; (4) *Stuffing food*: They have no nutritive value but serve only to fill the digestive organs; (5) *Pastime food*: These foods are taken for enjoyment rather than for nutrition.

Swamp 1. Any area, such as a marsh or bog, where the ground saturated with water throughout much of the year, but during most of the year, the surface of the soil is not deeply submerged. 2. A tract generally characterized by a soil that is slightly acid, neutral, or slightly alkaline, and a water table at or above the soil surface (the water often moving perceptibly), supporting not only low vegetation, e.g. sedges, but also reeds and woody vegetation, including trees. In tidal areas, it is termed as a tidal swamp. 3. Tree or tall shrub dominated wetlands that are characterized by periodic flooding and nearly permanent subsurface water flow through mixtures of mineral sediments and organic materials, essentially without peat accumulation.

Swarm The simultaneous emergence or assembling in one place of large numbers of an insect species.

Swath Width The overall plane angle or linear ground distance covered by a scanner in the across-track dimension.

Symbiosis 1. A broad term covering a variety of close relationship between two or more kinds of organisms, particularly when the relationship appears to be mutually beneficial. 2. A relationship between two or more kinds of living organisms wherein all (the symbionts) benefit and which is sometimes obligatory for all. A non-obligatory relationship may be termed proto-cooperation. In the extreme condition of conjunctive symbiosis, the symbionts form a single body or organ, as in mycorrhizae and lichens.

Synchronous Satellite An equatorial west to east satellite orbiting the Earth at 34,900 km, at which altitude it makes one revolution in 24 hours synchronous with the Earth's rotation.

Synecology 1. Study of relationships of communities of organisms to their environment as opposed to those of individual species. 2. The study of biotic communities and the interaction of organisms that compose them. *See* ecology; autecology.

Syntax A set of rules governing the way statements can be used in a computer language.

Syntype A member of a taxonomic type series when no holotype is designated.

Synusia Any component of a community of one or more species, belonging to the same life-form, having similar environmental requirements and occurring in similar habitat, e.g. a layer of moss plants.

System, Conversion A method of silvicultural procedure designed to change forest crops from one system or one (set of) species to another, e.g., coppice to high forest, selection forest to uniform, or hardwood to conifer.

System, Improvement Felling A method of treatment involving essentially the removal of inferior growing stock and tending the better elements of the crop, usually in an irregular forest. It is not a silvicultural system as it does not aim at regeneration.

Systematic The study of biological diversity and evolutionary relationships among organisms. The term is sometimes used interchangeably with taxonomy.

Tt

Tablet A small digitizer used for interactive work on a graphics workstation.

Tahr This is a beardless, wild goat of genus Hemitragus, found in two different widely separated regions of India. The two species are: HIMALAYAN TAHR (*Hemitragus jemlahicus*): This is a wild goat with thick recurving horns, heavy body, robust limbs and with tangled masses of coarse and flowing hair on the body. The colour is deep reddish brown. It is found throughout the Himalayas, in precipitous terrain of towering cliffs, rocks and dense scrub or forest below the tree line, i.e. below 3000 to 3600 metre. NILGIRI TAHR (*Hemitragus hylocrius*): This is a close relative of the Himalayan species and is slightly larger. It is found in the Nilgiri hills, the Anamalai hills and southwards along the Western Ghats at elevations of 1200 to 1800 metre. Often called as the *Nilgiri ibex*.

Taiga Northern, sub-arctic, coniferous forests of Europe, Asia and North America, typically open or interspersed with bogs, which form a transition zone between the denser forests to the south and the tundra to the north.

Tally A system of recording trees counted during a timber cruise or inventory.

Talus 1. The accumulation of broken rocks that occurs at the base of cliffs or other steep slopes (Thomas, 1979). 2. Talus constitutes one of the unique habitats. It is formed when fragments of rocks and other soil materials are accumulated by force of gravity at the foot of cliffs or steep slopes. The microhabitat in the form of talus promotes vertebrate animals like frogs, lizards, snakes, birds and small mammals. The larger the talus is, the more stable and suitable it is for becoming wildlife habitat. Talus supports an edge of herbaceous vegetation that provides the food supply for species living within it.

Tangible Benefits Benefits to which a monetary value can be reasonably assigned. *See also* intangible benefits.

Tape Drive A device for reading and writing digital information from and to magnetic tapes.

Tape, Diameter A specially graduated tape by means of which the diameter may be read directly when the tape is placed round a tree or log.

Tape, Quarter-girth A specially graduated tape by means of which the quarter-girth may be read directly when the tape is placed round a tree or log.

Taper The decrease in diameter of the stem of a tree or of a log from the base to upwards. *See* form.

Taproot 1. The main root of a tree which strikes downward with or without heavy branching until it either reaches an impenetrable layer or one so lacking in oxygen or moisture that further downward growth is impossible. 2. The primary descending root formed in direct continuation of the radicle of the embryo; in trees, usually a stout root descending vertically from the centre of the tree (BCFT).

Target A clear and concise statement used to express planned results to be reached within a stated time period.

Taungya 1. Hill vegetation (Burmese: Taung – hill; ya – cultivation). 2. The method of raising forest plantations in combination with field crops, otherwise known as agri-silvi methods or agri-silviculture, and to the plantations themselves. *See* cultivation, shifting.

Taxonomy 1. The science of classifying organisms. 2. The arrangement of organisms into systematic groups such as species, genus, family, and order. It is the theoretical study of classification including its bases, principles, procedures and rules. 3. A classification of plants and animals according to their natural relationships. 4. Orderly classification of plants and animals according to their presumed natural relationships, forming a basic biological discipline, involving the firm establishment of binomial nomenclature and the static concept of fixity of species.

Teak (*Tectona*) It is a genus of tropical hardwood trees in the family Verbenaceae, native to the south and southeast of Asia, and is commonly found as a component of monsoon forest vegetation. They are large trees, growing to 30-40 m tall, deciduous in the dry season. The name teak comes from the Malayalam word *Thekku.* There are three species of Tectona: *Tectona grandis* (Common Teak) is by far the most important, with a wide distribution in India and Indo-China. *Tectona hamiltoniana* (Dahat Teak) is a local endemic species confined to Myanmar, where it is endangered. *Tectona philippinensis* (Philippine Teak) is endemic to the Philippines, and is also endangered. The timber is used in the manufacture of outdoor furniture, boat decks, and other articles where weather resistance is desired. It is also used for indoor flooring and as a veneer for indoor furnishings. Teak is easily worked and has natural oils that make it suitable for use in exposed locations, where it is durable even when not treated with oil or varnish. Teak cut from old trees grown slowly in natural forests is more durable and harder. Teak from young trees grown in plantations is more prone to splitting and water damage. Teak is used extensively in India to make doors and window frames, furniture and columns and beams in old type houses. It is very resistant to the attack of termites. The mature teak fetches a very good price. The age of the tree can be assessed from the annual rings formed every year inside the trunk. Teak is grown extensively by forest departments of different states in forest areas. Its popularity has led to growth in sustainable production throughout the seasonally dry tropics in forestry plantations. The Forestry Stewardship Council offers certification of sustainably grown and harvested teak products. Experiments are on to arrive at vegetative propagation from one year old stem cuttings. Teak is one of the most sought-after types of vintage furniture. Teak is used as a food plant by the larvae of moths of the genus *Endoclita* including *E. aroura, E. chalybeatus, E. damor, E. gmelina, E. malabaricus, E. sericeus* and *E. signifer* and other Lepidoptera including Turnip Moth. Much of the world's teak is exported by Indonesia and Myanmar.

Teal Any of a large group of small, short-necked, fresh-water ducks of Anas (*A. crecca*) and other allied genera widely distributed in Europe, Asia, America. The several species are beautifully marked. COMMON OR GREEN WINGED TEAL (*Anas crecca*): It is distinguished from other Indian species by the conspicuous emerald green and black speculum and the pale cinnamon bar on the coverts. It is well distributed in India during winter. Most commonly and abundantly netted for food. COTTON TEAL (*Nettapus coromandelianus*): It is the smallest of the Indian ducks. It is a resident species in the plains, being locally migratory. It spends all the time in water and dives well, seldom venturing into land. GARGANEY or BLUE WINGED TEAL (*Anas querquedula*): It is a winter visitor found throughout India. It is commonly and abundantly netted for food. WHISTLING TEAL (*Dendrocygna javanica*): This is a heavy dark-brown duck with round wings, found in over-grown swamps. Its whistling call is distinctive. It is a resident bird found all over India. It prefers tanks, backwaters and swamps with abundant growth of weed and vegetation.

Technocentric A world view common today that science and technology are the keys to material prosperity and that any problem thus created can be solved by the application of more science and technology.

Technological Change The increase in society's ability to solve problems or increase efficiency by technical means with time. Availability of alternative or completely new technical methods for solving problems associated with land uses and the inevitable evolution and development of new ideas.

Technological Solution The application of the devices or techniques developed by science for practical purposes. Often these are completely new technical methods for solving current or potential problems for which no "technological solutions" presently exist. The distinction between "technical solutions" and "engineering solutions" is that the first refers just to the development of new technical means while the last applies to the application of any technical means (new or old) to solving potential problems.

Telemetry Automatic transmission of data to a point remote from the sensing instrument. Use of small radios to monitor animal location, movement, behaviour, and physiology is an example of telemetry.

Telluric Moisture Water present in a site. Derived from sources other than direct precipitation on the site, e.g., from seepage or springs.

Temperate Climate A climate, which is warm in summer and has a definite winter season. Determined in India more by altitude than latitude. *See* sub-tropical climate.

Temperate Geographically, regions that have an average temperature of 50 degree Fahrenheit or 10 degree Celsius or above for only 2 to 4 months of the year.

Temperature A measure of the intensity of heat energy present.

Temporal Data Data that can be linked to a certain time or period between two moments in time.

Tending Generally an operation carried out for the benefit of a forest crop, at any stage of its life. It essentially covers operations on the crop itself and on competing vegetation. Examples of tending operations are weeding, cleaning, thinning, improvement felling, pruning, climber cutting and girdling of unwanted growth. Felling operations and ground operations like soil working, drainage, irrigation, controlled burning do not come under tending.

TENDU (*Diospyros melanoxylon*) It is also known as East Indian Ebony, or Tendu in Hindi. It is a member of the genus *Diospyros* and one of the plants commonly known as ebony. Its leaves are widely used in India for the manufacture of *bidis*, or hand-rolled tobacco cigarettes. Coromandel ebony wood is variegated brown and black. It is considered a highly valuable wood for turnery, fine cabinet work and joinery and is also excellent for best quality carving. The tree grows to some 20 metres under favourable circumstances. Since Coromandel ebony has been a favourite wood for woodworkers for centuries, most of it has been felled and used in high quality furniture. However, some trees can still be found and the wood is still being used on a small scale. The natural area of distribution is thought to be the island of Sri Lanka, the southern Indian coastal regions (Kerala, Tamil Nadu, Andhra Pradesh, Pondicherry) and Central and Eastern India.

Terminal A device, usually including a computer screen or VDU and a keyboard for communicating with the computer.

Terminalia Arjuna It is a medicinal plant of the genus *Terminalia*, widely used by Ayurvedic physicians for its curative properties in organic/functional heart problems like angina, hypertension, deposits in arteries, diabetes etc. According to Ayurvedic texts it is also very useful in the treatment of pain due a fall, ecchymosis of all types, spermatorrhoea and sexually transmitted diseases like gonorrhoea. Arjuna Bark (*Terminallia arjuna*) is thought to be beneficial for the heart.

Terminalia Chebula It is a plant species belonging to the genus Terminalia, family Combretaceae. It is a flowering evergreen tree called in English the Myrobalan or sometimes the Chebulic Myrobalan. In Urdu, Persian or Hindi it is also called Hardad, Haritaki or Harada respectively. It is native to the Indian subcontinent and the adjacent areas such as Pakistan, Nepal and the south-west of China stretching as far south as Kerala or even Sri Lanka where it is called *Aralu*. This tree yields small, ribbed and nut-like fruits which are picked up when still green and then pickled, boiled with a little added sugar in their own syrup or used in preserves or concoctions. The seed of the fruit, which has an eliptical shape, is an abrasive pit enveloped by a fleshy and firm pulp. *Terminalia chebula* can reach heights of 20 metres. The myrobalan is highly regarded as an universal panacea in the Ayurvedic medicine.

Termite A member of the order isopetra white ant. There are three ecological classes of termites.

Terrace, Bench A terrace approximately on the contour, having a steep or vertical drop to the slope below, and having a horizontal or gentle sloping part.

Terrace, Drainage A broad channel-type terrace used primarily to conduct water from an area at a low velocity. It is adapted to less absorptive soil and high rainfall.

Terrace A level plain bordering a stream, river, or lake.

Terracing Constructing a level or sloping platform of earth across a slope to detain or control surface run-off and check soil erosion. *See* bench terraces.

Terrain 1. A tract of country considered with regard to its natural features, configuration, etc. which especially affects its advantages, fitness for use. 2. Surface of the earth.

Terrain Analysis The process of interpreting a geographical area to determine the effect of the natural and human-made features on a particular activity, actual or proposed. This interpretation includes the influence of weather and climate on those features.

Terrain Factor Terrain factors are attributes of land forms, drainage features, ground features, vegetation, etc.

Terrain Model Surface model of terrain. *See* 'Digital Terrain Model (DTM)', 'Digital Elevation Model (DEM)' and 'Triangulated Irregular Network (TIN)'.

Territoriality The behaviour by which an organism claims an area and displays, threatens, and defends it against members of its own species.

Territory 1. The area, which an animal defends, usually during breeding season, against intruders of its own species. Territories are smaller and are normally located within an animal's home range. 2. The ground belonging to a single individual animal, or to a pair, or to a social unit (or group represented by the chief individual). Usually defended against intruders, and often made distinctive by various means. Widely observed in mammals, birds, fishes particularly during the breeding season. Several territories may be contained within a biotype.

Tessellation The process of dividing an area into smaller, contiguous tiles with no gaps in between them.

Tetraploid The individual so constituted that it has four chromosome sets.

Texture Frequency of change and arrangement of tones on an image.

Thematic Data 1. Data that relate to a specific theme or subject. 2. Qualitative and categorical raster data, usually map or land cover classes such as pasture, urban areas, standing water, etc.

Thematic Map 1. Map pertaining to one particular theme or subject. 2. A map displaying selected kinds of information relating to specific themes, such as soil, land use, population density, suitability for arable crops, and so on. Many thematic maps are also choropleth maps, but when the attribute is modelled by a continuous field, representation by isolines or colour scales is more appropriate. 3. A map designed to demonstrate particular features or concepts.

Theodolite A survey instrument for measuring horizontal and vertical angles using a rotating and tilting telescope. 2. Precision surveying instrument for measuring horizontal and vertical angles.

Thermal Band Generally, refers to thermal IR intervals associated with atmospheric windows at 3-5 and 8-14 micron wavelengths.

Thermal IR Generally, the IR region from 3 to 1000μm; specifically connotes the two intervals employed in remote sensing (3-5 and 8-14 micron). This spectral region spans the radiant power peak of the earth.

Thermocline The zone of water depth within which temperature rapidly changes between the upper warm water layer (epilimnion) and lower cold water layer (hypolimnion).

Thermograph A self-registering thermometer.

Therophyte 1. A class of Raunkiaer's form, life consisting of annuals or ephemerals passing unfavourable season as seeds and thus completing the life cycle from germination to ripe seeds within a single growth period. 2. A plant that completes its life cycle, from germination to ripe seed, within a single growth period, e.g. an annual. *See* life form.

Thicket 1. A crop composed of sapling or a sapling crop. 2. A dense growth of small trees, bushes, bamboos etc.

Thiessen Polygons 1. A tessellation of the plane such that any given location is assigned to a tile according to the minimum distance between it and a single, previously sampled point. Also known as dirichlet tessellation or voronoi polygons. 2. An exact method of interpolation that assumes the values of unsampled locations are equal to the value of the nearest sampled point to produce a mesh of irregular convex polygons.

Thinning 1. A felling (Cutting) made in an immature crop or stand in order to accelerate the diameter increment (annual growth) of the residual trees but also, by suitable selection, to improve the average form of the trees that remain, without permanently breaking the canopy. 2. A felling made in an immature stand for the purpose of improving the growth and form of the trees that remain, without permanently breaking the canopy. Thinning is a tending operation carried out in a crop beyond the sapling stage and up to the beginning of regeneration period. The thinning principles have been developed on the basis of natural development of the stand. A typical stand starts its life with large number of trees, usually many thousand per hectare at the beginning. The number of trees per hectare starts decreasing with the increase in their size and age. The decrease is much faster in the beginning but latter slows down when the crop grows larger. When the crop is mature only few hundred per hectare remains. Thus a continuous reduction in number of trees is primarily due to struggle for life and survival of the fittest, the most important law of nature (Dwivedi, 1980).

Thinning, Advance Thinning done in a regular crop in anticipation of suppression. It is a method developed by Craib and O' Connor for wattle and pine plantations in South Africa.

Thinning, Crown A method in which thinning is primarily directed to the dominant trees in a regular crop, the less promising ones being removed in the interest of the best available individuals. The dominated and suppressed stems are retained unless they are dead, dying or diseased.

Thinning Cycle The planned interval which elapses between successive thinning in the same area.

Thinning, Free A method devised by Heak, in which attention is concentrated on evenly spaced selected stems (called elites or alpha stems) which are retained until maturity or till the last thinning or two thinning being directed to the removal of other stems hindering their optimum development. Applied to regular crops. Also known as elite thinning.

Thinning Grade Thinning grade refers to the relative extent to which a crop is opened up in thinning. Standard thinning grades are: light thinning, moderate thinning, heavy thinning and very heavy thinning. These grades are in reference to the extent to which stem are removed. *See* thinning intensity.

Thinning Intensity A term generally used to indicate in numerical terms the extent to which a crop is thinned.

Thinning, Maximum A method, developed by Gehrhardt, which is a further development on Heak's free thinning and it aims at putting as high a proportion as possible of the total potential increment of the area on the retained stems; from an early stage the number of such stems is limited to the minimum that can fully utilize the growing space. It is applied to regular crops.

Thinning, Mechanical A thinning in which the trees to be cut are selected by some rule-of-thumb, e.g. trees in alternate rows or every second, third, fourth, etc. Line, or a minimum spacing gauged by a standard stick ("stick thinning"). Applied to regular crops.

Thinning, Ordinary The method in common use. It consists of removal of inferior individuals of a crop, starting from suppressed class, then taking the dominated class and lastly some of the dominant class. It is applied to regular crops.

Thinning, Selection 1. A method of thinning directed to obtain and/or maintain selection composition in a crop, with all diameter-classes adequately represented. 2. In American terminology, it refers to a thinning in which largest dominant trees and the poorest suppressed trees possessing a positive net conversion value are cut.

Threatened and Endangered Species A species or sub-species of animals or plants whose prospects of survival and reproduction are in immediate jeopardy (endangered), or likely to become so within the foreseeable future (threatened).

Threatened Species Any species that is likely to become an endangered species within the foreseeable future throughout all or a significant portion of its range, if certain pressures are not reversed.

Threshold Level The minimum concentration or amount of a given substance or condition necessary to produce a measurable physiological or psychological effect. Also, the point at which a major change occurs, e.g., the change of water to ice at zero degrees centigrade.

Tidal Flat Tide land that has little elevational variation, and is often muddy or marshy.

Tidal Marsh Low, flat marshland traversed by interlaced channels and tidal sloughs and subject to tidal inundations; normally, the only vegetation present is salt-tolerant bushes and grasses.

Tidal 1. A water body influenced by tides. 2. Of vegetation within reach of the influence of tides.

Tie-point A point on the ground which is common to two images. Several such points are used in the registration of images.

Tiger (*Panthera tigris* Syn. *Felis tigris*) A large, fierce, carnivorous mammal of the cat family, having a tawny yellow coat with black transverse stripes and white belly, and a long untufted tail that is ringed with black. It is typically larger than the lion with a total length usually of 2.7 to 3.0 metre, but sometimes of more than 3.6 metre. It lives usually on the ground, feeding chiefly on the larger mammals such as deer, antelope, etc., when these are not abundant, it will attack domestic cattle. Some become man-eaters. It has an extensive habitat ranging from Persia across Asia to Malaysia to Siberia and Manchuria. In its habitat, eight races are known. The Indian race, designated as the typical tiger, is found practically throughout India from the Himalayas to Kanya Kumari, except in the arid zone of the Punjab, Rajasthan and Kutch. *See* Project Tiger.

Tight Coupling A method of linking models to GIS in which the link between the GIS and the model is hidden from the user by an application interface and GIS and model share the same database.

Tile A part of the database in a GIS representing a contiguous part of the earth's surface. By splitting a study area into tiles, considerable savings in access times and improvements in system performance can be achieved.

Tiling The creation of a seamless spatial coverage by joining contiguous areas (tiles) together.

Tilt The angle between the optic axis of the camera or sensor and the plumb line to a given photo or image.

Tilth The physical condition of a soil in respect to its fitness for the growth of a specified plant.

Timber Inventory A collection of information about a timber stand made by measuring tree and stand characteristics such as tree volume, grade, site quality and stand density.

Timber, Saw Log suitable in size and quality for the manufacture of sawn timber. *See* timber sawn.

Timber, Sawn Timber sawn to size, with or without wane. *See* lumber.

Timber, Secondary Species of timber that are unacceptable as primary but are nevertheless actually or potentially marketable.

Timber, Standard Timber in round from the ground level down to 20.7 centimetres (8 inch) diameter over bark, volume being taken exclusive of bark.

Timber, Round Timber in the log, i.e., unconverted timber; also prepared timber in round, e.g. telegraph poles, pit-props, etc.

Timber 1. Categories of wood other than firewood. 2. For statistical record, wood down to a minimum diameter or girth; 21 cm girth over bark for small timber in Central India. Timber volume is ordinarily exclusive of bark in India and Malasiya. 3. Sometimes the term is used to denote standing trees, usually of commercial size. *See* timber, standard.

Timbers, Primary Species of timber that command a much higher price than others occurring with them and are, therefore, selectively exploited in preference to the latter. *See* timber, secondary.

Time Preference Time preference is related to the fact that, generally speaking, people prefer to enjoy a benefit in the present rather than to delay it into the future. The rate of time preference is the rate at which the present value of utility declines as the time at which it is enjoyed moves further into the future. This rationale is applied to make discounting the net benefits of projects in cost-benefit analysis.

Tolerance 1. The capacity of a tree to develop and grow in the shade of, and in competition with, other trees. 2. The capacity to withstand other factors as well as shade used in this sense, when some indication should always be given of the factor that is tolerated, e.g. shade tolerance, frost tolerance, etc. 3. The ability of an organism or biological process to subsist under a given set of environmental conditions. 4. Resistance of an organism to high levels or excesses of a substance or the deficiency of an element or a condition in its environment. 5. The capacity of a tree to develop and grow in the shade of and in competition with other trees. Trees able to grow in full or partial shade are considered "tolerant". Trees requiring full sunlight for survival are considered "intolerant". The range of these under which it can subsist, representing its limits of tolerance, is termed its ecological amplitude. For trees, the tolerance of most practical importance is their ability to grow satisfactorily in the shade of, and in competition with, other trees. If intolerant of shade, they are termed light demanders and if tolerant, they are termed as shade bearers. *See* shade tolerant. 6. For wildlife, it is its ability to adjust to different or disturbed habitats.

Tolerance, Ecological 1. The positive response of an organism to the excess or the deficiency of an element or a condition in its environment. 2. The capacity of an organism to endure or adapt to (usually temporary) unfavourable environmental factors. 3. An organism's capability to withstand a condition indefinitely and through all life stages. Short-term "tolerance" should be redefined in terms of stress.

Ton (cubic) In terms of timber volume, a unit of 40 cu. ft. Of timber on which shipping freight rates are usually based. In India, Myanmar and Malaysia the ton is treated as equal to 50 cubic foot. Of sawn timber or 50 hoppus feet of round timber that latter known as hoppus ton. In terms of weight, a metric ton is equal to 1000 kilogrammes.

Tone Each distinguishable shade of gray from white to black on an image.

Topocline A cline in respect of topographic factors.

Topographic Factors Those pertaining to the configuration of the land surface such as altitude, slope, aspect and exposure.

Topographic Inversion An optical illusion that may occur on images with extensive shades. Ridges appear to be valleys, and valleys appear to be ridges. The illusion is corrected by orienting the image so that the shadows trend from the top margin of the image to the bottom.

Topographic Maps 1. Maps whose primary purpose is to indicate the general feature of the land. These maps generally show terrain, basic land use, transport networks, administrative boundaries, settlements and other man-made features. 2. A map showing the surface features of the earth's surface (contours, roads, rivers, houses, etc.).

Topography The configuration and relations of a surface including its relief, elevation and the position of its natural and human-made features. The physical or natural features of an object or entity and their structural relationships.

Topology 1. The geometric relationship between objects located in space. A term used to refer to the continuity of space and spatial properties, such as connectivity, that are unaffected by continuous distortion. In the representation of vector entities, connectivity is defined explicitly by a directed pointer between records describing things that are somehow linked in space (for example a junction between two roads). In regular and irregular tessellations of continuous surfaces (e.g. grids) the topological property of connectivity between different locations may only be implicitly defined by the spatial rate of change of attribute values over the grid. The topology (connectivity) of gridded surfaces can be revealed by computing first, second, or higher order derivatives of the surface. 2. Method of determining spatial relationships in vector data models (tells computer what is inside or outside a polygon or which nodes are connected by arcs).

Total Station A theodolite or EDM combined with data logger and automated mapping software.

Toxic A substance or the excessive amount of a substance that may cause death, stress, or impairment. Characteristics of things called poisons or toxins.

Trace Elements Chemical elements appearing in minute quantities in natural systems or media. They may occasionally be concentrated by specific organisms. Nutrients such as P, though in minute quantities, are not usually called trace elements.

Trade-offs The combination of benefits and costs which are gained and lost in switching between alternative courses of action. "Trade-offs" include only those portions of benefits and costs that are *not* common to all alternative courses of action under consideration. The total estimated amount of resource programme outputs (market and non-market) foregone by (1) Modifying an existing programme or substituting one resource programme for another or (2) Due to switching among alternative courses of action. The economic value of this trade-off represents the opportunity cost.

Tragedy of the Commons This occurs where incomplete property rights lead to the overuse of renewable natural resources. Hardin (1992) suggests some possible policy measures to avoid such overexploitation and degradation of the resource, including privatization or allocation of permits for access to the resource.

Training Site Area of terrain with known properties or characteristics that is used in supervised classification.

Trampling Damage to plants or soil brought about by foot movements or congestion of livestock and/or people.

Transect 1. A set of sampling points arranged along a straight line. 2. A line, belt, strip or profile, as of vegetation chosen for study and charting vegetation profile. 3. A narrow sample strip or a measured line laid out through vegetation specifically chosen for study, i.e. for analysis, profiling and charting. *See* vegetation profile.

Transfer Function 1. A numerical method of transferring spatial data from one projection to another. 2. A numerical model for computing new attribute values from existing data using regression models or other algorithms.

Transform It is the process of changing the scale, projection, or orientation of a mapped image.

Transformation The process of converting data from one co-ordinate system to another.

Transgenic (Plant) Genetically engineered plant or offspring of genetically engineered plants.

Translocation 1. The movement of food and other materials within the tissues of a plant. 2. Move from one place to another. Generally used in wildlife management.

Transpiration 1. The loss of water in vapour form from a plant, mostly through the stomata and lenticels. 2. The process by which water vapour leaves the foliage or other parts of a living plant and is released to the atmosphere.

Transplant 1. A tree which has been removed from its original seedbed and replanted one or more times in a nursery. 2 A seedling after it has been moved one or more times in a nursery in contrast to a seedling planted out direct from the seedling.

Transportation Network All existing and planned roads, rails, bridges, airfields, and other transport facilities wholly or partly within or adjacent to and serving a planning area.

Travel Cost Method (TCM) This is a method to estimate the recreational demand for a site when market prices are not available. The methodology uses the cost of travel to a site as proxy for the entrance price to a site. Regression analysis is used to relate visitation rates to travel cost and socio-economic variables, such as income.

Travel Influence Zone Areas comprising existing or anticipated significant public outdoor recreational occupancy, use, and enjoyment along existing and planned overland routes of travel. These are areas in and around existing or planned developed recreation sites. In such areas beauty of the landscape and other aesthetic values are key management considerations and are an important part of the outdoor environment. These areas offer significant opportunities for existing, planned, or anticipated recreational use and enjoyment by people visiting or travelling through the zone.

Traverse Sequence of lengths and directions of lines connecting a series of stations, obtained from field measurements, and used in determining positions of the stations.

Tree Cavities Hollow cavities in trees that provide resting or nesting places for wildlife.

Tree Class or Tree Classification 1. Anyone of the classes into which the trees of a stand or crop may be divided for a variety of purposes. 2. Trees in an even-aged crop are classified into mainly three broad classes: (a) Dominant trees which form the uppermost canopy and include predominant, the tallest trees determining the general top level, and the rather shorter codominants; (b) Dominated trees, about three quarters the height of the predominants, filling up the minor holes in the dominant canopy; and (c) Suppressed trees which are little more than half of the height of the predominants and stand under the shade of the taller trees. *See* stem class; crown class.

Tree Compass An instrument of special design used for measurement of the diameter of tree or log.

Tree Line A loose term for the limit beyond which trees cannot or do not occur. The limiting factor is most commonly altitude or geographical latitude but may also be factors, such as aridity, flooding, etc. A distinction may be drawn between tree line and timber line, the latter being roughly the limit of timber rather than isolated trees.

Tree Trap A dead or girdled standing tree left to attract insects and facilitate their destruction.

Tree, Weed A tree of a species having little or no economic value on the site in question.

Tree, Wolf A vigorous tree, usually of bad form, occupying more space than its future value warrants and threatening potentially better neighbours, usually a broad-crowned dominant.

Tree, Elite 1. A tree selected for seed collection or for vegetative propagation on account of some especially good characteristics it may possess such as exceptional rate of growth, fine form, or timber quality and resistance to adverse climatic factors and to diseases and pests. 2. A tree selected for retention till maturity or till the last thinning. *See* stand, elite.

Tree, Nurse A tree grown or retained to protect or foster the growth of other trees during their youth.

Tree, Protected 1. As a good example, setting apart an important species for preservation as long as possible. 2. Protected trees are called as reserved trees. They are selected trees temporarily retained in a crop that are being regenerated for some specific purpose such as producing seeds, protecting regeneration or putting on increment. Reserved trees are trees or species in which the government has reserved special proprietary right under a forest act or other law and the felling of which is prohibited except under the rule. For an example royal tree or a certain kind of fruit bearing tree.

Tree, Reserved 1. A selected tree temporarily retained in a crop that is being re-generated for some specific purpose, e.g., to produce seeds, to protect re-generation or to put on increment. 2. A tree or species in which a Government has reserved special proprietary right under a forest act or other law and the felling of which is prohibited except under rule. *See* tree, protected.

Tree, Royal A kind of tree, reserved which is the property of Government wherever it may stand, e.g., teak in Burma and sandalwood in Mysore.

Tree, Sample A tree chosen as representative of a given population for detailed study of one or more of its characteristics. It is a tree whose diameter is equal or nearly equal to the mean diameter of the group it represents, and whose height, stem form and crown are also typical of the group.

Tree 1. A large woody perennial plant having a single well-defined crown. 2. As a legal term defined in forest law, it includes not only trees as defined above, but also plants as shrub, bamboos, canes and even stump and brushwood. 3. A woody perennial with a single main stem, or in the case of coppice with several stems, having amore or less definite crown. It includes bamboos, palms and other woody plants meeting the above criteria (FAO, 2001). 4. The stage of growth beyond the pole stages, when the rate of height growth begins to slow down and crown expansion becomes marked. 5. A woody plant having a well-defined stem, more or less definitely formed crown and usually attaining a height of at least 10 feet.

Trees Outside Forests (TOF) 1. Trees outside forests include all trees found outside forests and outside other wooded lands: stands smaller than 0.5 ha; tree cover in agriculture land, e.g. agroforestry systems, home gardens, orchards; trees in urban environments; along roads and scattered in the landscape (FAO, 2001). 2. Extensive tree wealth exists outside continuous forested areas in every country, termed as "Trees Outside Forests (TOF)", these are in the form of small woodlots and block plantations, trees along linear features, such as roads, canal bunds, etc. and scattered trees on farmlands, homesteads, community lands and urban areas. Inventory of trees outside forest areas is of great importance in planning as this, together with the forest inventory, provides a complete picture of wood/forest resources.

Trees Outside Forests (TOF), Assessment Forest Survey of India (FSI) has been carrying out TOF assessments since early 1990s. However, an accurate estimate at the national level at a specific time frame is still not available. FSI has divided the country into two types of area for survey. The first is rural area and the second is urban area. The methodology adopted by FSI is as follows: (1) *Trees Outside Forests (Rural):* The study area for this survey is considered as rural areas outside forest areas of the district. For any survey, an investigator requires a sampling frame. Sampling frame for rural areas has been prepared with the help of remote sensing technique and Digital Image

Processing (DIP), Protected Area Network (PAN), data for the respective districts and necessary data are procured from NRSA, Hyderabad. Toposheets for the same district are identified and geo-referenced. These toposheets are then used to rectify panchromatic data. After rectification, these PAN data are used to rectify the multi-spectral data (LISS). The panchromatic and multi-spectral data are then fused together and classified into various classes to obtain the three stratum of TOF, i.e. block, linear and scattered). (2) *Trees Outside Forests* (*Urban*): The study area for this survey is considered as urban centres as defined in district census book. Sampling frame for urban areas has been prepared by an agency called National Sample Survey Organisation (NSSO) under the Ministry of Statistics and Programme Implementation, Government of India. This organization conducts surveys by the name of Urban Frame Survey (UFS). They divide the whole urban centres of a district in blocks called UFS. These blocks are having clear-cut well defined natural boundaries. These blocks are formed on the basis of 600-800 population or 120-160 households and cover the whole area within the geographical boundary of town including vacant lands.

Trend Surface Analysis 1. A method for exploring the functional relationship between attributes and the geographical co-ordinates of the sample points. 2. A routine that interpolates a complex surface or series of data points to produce a much simplified surface showing the overall trend in the data.

Triangular Irregular Network (TIN) 1. A vector data structure for representing geographical information that is modelled as a continuous field (usually elevation) which uses tessellated triangles of irregular shape. 2. An irregular set of height observations in a vector data model. Lines connect these to produce an irregular mesh of triangles. The faces represent the terrain surface and the vertices represent the terrain features.

Triangular Planting Planting of plants in the pattern of an equilateral triangle, e.g., with the plants occupying the three corners of each of adjacent equilateral triangles.

Trim, to 1. To cut of branches from a felled or fallen tree. 2. To remove the buds and side shoots from young trees.

Triphala It is an Ayurvedic herbal *rasayana* formula consisting of equal parts of three myrobalans: Amalaki (*Emblica officinalis*), Bibhitaki

(*Terminalia bellirica*), and Haritaki (*Terminalia chebula*). Triphala is used to promote appetite and digestion, increase the number of red blood cells, and aid in removal of undesirable fat in the body. It is also used to clear congestion and headaches. Other claimed benefits include helping maintain normal blood sugar levels, as well as improvement in skin tone and colour. It is claimed that each of the three herbal fruits of Triphala takes care of the body by gently promoting internal cleansing of all conditions of stagnation and excess while at the same time it improves digestion and assimilation.

Triploid Having three chromosome sets.

Trophic Dynamics Energy flow through a community organized into several trophic levels.

Trophic Level Trophic level in ecology means the position occupied by a species (or group of species) in a food chain. The main levels are primary producers (photosynthetic plants), primary consumers (herbivores), secondary consumers (carnivores), and decomposers (fungi and bacteria). Green (photosynthetic) plants occupy the first trophic level, plant-eaters (i.e., herbivores) the second level, the carnivores (i.e., meat eaters) which eat the herbivores the third level, and secondary carnivores (i.e., carnivores which eat other carnivores) the fourth level.

Trophic Pertaining to food and nutrition.

Tropical 1. The region between the tropics of Cancer and Capricorn, i.e. 23½° north and south of the Equator. They are the limits of the area of Earth's surface in which the Sun can be directly overhead. The mean monthly temperature is over 20°C/68°F. 2. Geographically, regions characterized by a climate with high temperature, humidity and rainfall, and having very rare light frosts at night (an average temperature of 65 degree Fahrenheit or 18 degree Celsius for the coolest month).

Tropical Climate The prevailing weather condition in the tropical region. A climate which is hot with much rain and without a definite winter season.

Tropical Forests The forest assumes its character, composition and diversity on account of latitudinal gradient of the tropical region. Latitude plays a key determinant on which depends the rainfall of an area. With the increase or decrease in distance of a location from equator, rainfall tends to change. As the distance of a site from equator increases, rainfall decreases and the *vice versa*. On account of such factors, forests found in the tropical region have a distinct characteristics. Tropical forests are classed into two broad categories: (a) Tropical rain forests and (b) Tropical dry deciduous and moist deciduous forests. Tropical forests have an important role in the maintenance of microclimates, the protection of watersheds, the provision of unique habitats and supporting the economic livelihoods of indigenous people.

Tropism The response of an organism to an external stimulus by turning or bending.

Tropophyte 1. A plant that is adapted to a climate in which a very dry season is followed by a wet one, and is, therefore, alternately xerophilous and hygrophilous. 2. A plant that markedly changes its character, particularly its water requirements, with seasonal changes of climate, e.g. a deciduous tree.

Trout Any fish of genus Salmo, other than the Atlantic salmon (*Salmo salar*), including the trout of Europe (*S. trutta*). Also any of various fishes of the salmon family noted for their gameness and prized as food.

Truncated Soil Profile A soil profile that has lost its upper horizon(s) through erosion.

Tundra The zone of low vegetation in an arctic climate between the limit of the tree zone and perpetual ice or snow. Mountain or alpine tundra is the term sometimes used for the corresponding zone on high mountains. The zone of low, arctic vegetation between the tree line of the taiga to the south and the region of perpetual ice and snow. The corresponding zone on high mountains may be termed mountain tundra.

Tuple 1. A set of values of attributes pertaining to a given item in a database. Also known as a record. 2. Individual records (rows) in a relational database.

Turnkey System A GIS or CAD/CAM system of hardware and software that is designed, supplied, and supported by a single manufacturer ready for use for a given class of work.

Type Genus The genus which is formally taken and held to be most typical of the family or other higher group to which it belongs and gives it its name.

Type, Locality The locality in which a species is considered to be typically found (used when publishing a full description of a species). TYPE SPECIES is one designated as typical and definitive. TYPE SPECIMENS are known as HOLO-TYPE if the author designated a single specimen as the type of a species. If a new species is named from several specimens and the author does not distinguish between them, these specimens are known as SYN-TYPES, and it is open to another taxonomist to designate anyone of them as the type for the species whereupon it becomes the LECTO-TYPE. In certain cases when the holotype or the lactotype is believed to have been lost or destroyed, another specimen may be selected as the type specimen of the species concerned, and this is known as the NEO-TYPE.

Type, Species The species of a genus, which is regarded as the best example of the generic characters, i.e. the species from which a genus is named.

Type, Specimen 1.The original plant from which a description was drawn up. 2. That constituent part (i.e. an individual) of a taxon to which a botanical name is permanently attached. 3. One designated as the standard of a taxonomic group. An individual animal or plant, used as the basis for the scientific description of a species etc. *See* locality, type.

Uu

Ultisols Soils that are low in supply of bases and have subsurface horizons of alluvial clay accumulations. They are usually moist, but during the warm season of the year, some are dry. The particle-size class (texture) ranges mostly from sandy-loam to clayey.

Uncertainty Decision making in which there is no objective basis for assigning numerical probabilities to different possible outcomes or in which there is no way to describe the possible outcomes. A probability distribution is selected for analysis purposes based on experience, intuitive feelings, knowledge, and the lack of knowledge.

Under-planting 1. To plant young plants or seedlings or sow seed under an existing stand or standing crop. 2. Under-planting is a form of artificial regeneration applied in such forests in which the proportion of the more valuable species is too low, either naturally or through exploitation, and natural regeneration cannot be relied on. Here lines are cut through the undergrowth and lower canopy, and strong transplants putout along them, the lines being spaced. As the plants become established, the overhead cover is gradually removed by felling, girdling, or poisoning, until the crowns are fully free.

Undercut 1. In logging, the notch cut in a tree to govern the direction in which the tree is to fall and to prevent splitting. 2. In forest management practice, the harvesting of a quantity of timber less than the budgeted cut.

Under-exploitation Felling of forests or exploiting forests at a rate which can safely be increased. If the distribution of age classes in the forest is normal, the rate of fellings may correctly approximate the rate of net growth; but if younger age classes predominate, a rate of felling considerably lower than the net growth rate may be justified, but the rate of felling can safely be increased to a higher rate. *See* over-exploitation.

Undergrowth The lowest stratum of woody and other vegetation above the ground cover. *See* low cover, ground cover, and underwood.

Understocking 1. Placing a number of animals on a given area that will result in under-utilizing the available forage by the end of the planned grazing period. 2. A stand of trees so widely spaced that, even with full growth potential realized, crown closure will not occur. Understocking indicates a waste of resources, for certain purposes since the site is not fully occupied.

Understory 1. The lesser vegetation (shrubs, seedlings, saplings, small trees) within a forest stand which forms a layer between the overstory, the upper portions of adjacent trees and other woody growth, and the herbaceous plants of the forest floor. 2. The storey of a forest crop, e.g., a young crop under seed bearer, coppice under standards, or the lower storeys in a high storeyed forest.

Underwood Woody species growing under an overwood, i.e., the understorey. Also used for the coppice in coppice-with-standards. *See* understorey; undergrowth.

Undesirable Species Plant species that are not desirable because they are unpalatable or low in palatability, injurious to animals, poisonous, poor stabilizers of soil and water, etc.

Unevenaged Applied to crops in which individual stems vary widely in age, the range of difference being usually more than 20 years and, in the case of long rotation crops, more than 25 per cent of the rotation. The forest is called selection forest when trees of all or nearly all age gradations or age classes are present.

Unevenaged Management 1. Applying a combination of actions simultaneously to maintain continuous high-forest cover, recurring regeneration of desirable species, and the orderly growth and development of trees through a range of diameter or age classes to provide a sustained yield of forest products. Specifying the number or proportion of trees of particular sizes to retain within each area, thereby maintaining a planned distribution of size classes usually through felling regulations. Felling methods that develop and maintain uneven-aged stands are single-tree selection and group selection. 2. A combination of management practices for a stand, which maintains a range of age classes, by periodically selecting and harvesting individual trees or groups of trees (IUFRO World Series, Vol. 9).

Unevenaged Stand (All-aged Stand) A forest stand composed of trees that differ markedly in age and sizes growing together on a uniform site. By convention, a minimum range of 10 to 20 years is generally accepted, though with rotations of less than 100 years, 25 per cent of the rotation period may be the minimum.

Unexacting Tolerant of a wide range of soils or other environmental conditions. *See* tolerance.

Ungulate General term, now largely obsolete, for hoofed mammals, particularly Artiodactyla and Perissodactyla.

Union 1. The term in database connotes to the joining of two or more datasets together. 2. In case of Boolean logic, it connotes to the joining of two sets using the 'or' operator.

Unique Habitats Wildlife habitats of special function not included within plant communities and successional stages or special habitats; geomorphic in nature, e.g. cliff, caves, overhangs, shelves, or ledges, talus, crevices, etc.

United Nations Environment Programme (UNEP) The United Nations Environment Programme (UNEP) was established in 1972 with its headquarters at Nairobi, Kenya. India is a member of UNEP Governing Council. UNEP has a core mandate of playing a major role in development of scientific capacity and promoting scientific research related to environmental concerns in developing countries.

United Nations Framework Convention on Climate Change (UNFCCC) It is an International Treaty. It recognises the threats posed by Climate Change and attempts to find out solution to cope with the problem of global warming. India is a party to the United Nations Framework Convention on Climate Change (UNFCCC), which was adopted in May 1992 and came into effect on 21st March, 1994. The objective of the Convention is to achieve stabilization of greenhouse gas concentration in the atmosphere at a level that would prevent dangerous anthropogenic interference with the climate system. To give more concrete action plan to combat climate change, Parties to the Convention in 1997 adopted the Kyoto Protocol in recognition of the necessity for strengthening developed country's commitments under the convention in furtherance to the objective of the Convention. The Kyoto Protocol commits the developed countries, including economies in transition to reduce emissions of greenhouse gases by an average of 5.2 per cent below 1990 levels during 2008-2012. The Kyoto Protocol came into force on 16th February, 2005.

Universe A synonyms for population in statistics.

Unix A computer operating system.

Unpalatable Species Species that are not readily eaten by animals.

Unsupervised Training Image classification procedure in which the computer identifies inherent patterns in the spectral data and uses a clustering algorithm to order pixels into discrete classes.

Unsupervised Classification Digital information extraction technique in which the computer assigns pixels to categories with no instructions from the operator.

Upstream Element Map A map showing the cumulative catchment areas for each cell according to the topology of the local drain direction map.

Upwelling The rise of deeper, nutrient-rich water to the surface of the ocean along coasts.

Urban Forestry 1. The practice of forestry in an urbanized environment. 2. A specialized branch of forestry which deals with cultivating and managing trees in urban areas and evaluating their contribution to the physiological, sociological, psychological (and sometimes economic) well-being of urban society.

Urial or Shapu (*Ovis orientalis*) This is a wild sheep, living in steep grassy hill slopes above the forest line, i.e. above 3000 to 3600 metre in Ladakh, the Punjab and northwards in Tibet. The body colour is usually grey. It is distinguished from other sheep by its smaller size. It stands 0.9 metre at the shoulder, with horns of about 0.6 metre round the curves. In the Ladakh Urial the horns turn inwards at the tips, in the Punjab race the horns tend to form a circle. This is probably one of the ancestors of domesticated breeds of sheep.

Usar The local name for areas having saline alkali soil in the Indo-Gangetic plains.

Use (Utilization) Range management usage. The proportion of the current year's forage production that is consumed or destroyed by grazing animals. Forty or fifty percent of the annual forage growth (by weight) is often used as a rule-of-thumb on ranges in good or excellent condition that allows the amount of forage accelerated range rehabilitation.

Use Rights Rights for the use of forest resources that can be defined by local custom, mutual agreements, or prescribed by other entities holding access rights. These rights may restrict the use of particular resources to specific levels of consumption or particular harvesting technique.

Use Values The values derived from actual or potential future consumptions of a good or service.

User Charge A type of economic instrument. User charge are intended to recover the costs of public or community provision of a service, such as the treatment of effluent (including waste) and provision of water.

User Costs Values that users of a good or output pays to gain access or be able to use a good or service. Such costs include transportation costs, concession fees, and similar payments to other than the resource owner.

User Pays Principle (UPP) The UPP states that the beneficiaries should pay the full cost of using resources and their related services, together with the cost of losses for future generations following the intergenerational equity principle. Resource pricing often means increased resource prices for the users, forcing them to reduce their use of the services or of the natural resources (Markandya *et al.*, 2002).

USGS (United States Geological Survey) The USGS is an organization geared towards providing reliable scientific information to describe and understand the Earth; minimize loss of life and property from natural disasters; manage water, biological, energy, and mineral resources; and enhance and protect our quality of life. USGS is made up of 4 divisions: the National Mapping Division, the Biological Resource Division, the Water Resources Division, and the Geologic Division.

Usufruct Right This type of right conveys a right to use a natural resource, as opposed to an ownership right (Tietenberg, 1992 a).

Utilitarianism A political philosophy based on the principle of "the greatest good of the greatest number".

Utility 1. The usefulness or satisfaction-causing qualities of a good or service. 2. A term for system capabilities and features for processing data.

Utility Mapping A special class of GIS applications for managing information about public infrastructure such as water pipes, sewerage, telephone, electricity and gas networks.

Utilization per cent 1. The percentage ratio of normal yield to normal growing stock. 2. The percentage ratio between volumes as estimated from the standing tree or the log and the actual merchantable outturn in such categories as the estimate provides for.

Utilization Value The price of a standing crop would realize if offered for sale. *See also* exploitation value; devastation value.

UV *Ultra violet* region of the electromagnetic spectrum ranging in wavelengths from 0.01 to 0.4 m.

Vv

Validation The process of assessing by independent means the quality of the data products derived from the system outputs.

Valuation In environmental economic this refers to the estimation of the monetary value of an environmental asset, or to a change in the level of an environmental attribute. Two broad approaches are in vogue. First is direct valuation and second is indirect valuation method. Direct method includes technique such as the Contingent Valuation Method (CVM) and contingent ranking under which people are asked to state directly their strength of preference, or Willingness To Pay (WTP), for a proposed change. Indirect method attempts to get the preference from actual, observed, and market based information. They include hedonic price techniques, the Travel Cost Method (TCM), replacement cost techniques, etc.

Value Value is generally taken as the price, which is determined on the basis of relation between demand (based on diminishing marginal utility) and supply (based on cost of production).

Value-added Product / Value-added Production Adding value to a product by further processing it. Examples of value-added wood products include joinery stock, windows, doors, kitchen cabinets, flooring and mouldings. Value-added pulp and paper products include such items as packaging, diapers, coated papers, tissue, business papers and stationery, and other consumer paper products.

Value Added For a given enterprise, the market value of products or goods completed, less the cost of materials purchased from others.

Value, Capital The present worth of a forest capital. It may be expressed as a value, cost value, expectation value, market value, rental value or replacement value. The method of estimation will be conditioned by the circumstances of each case.

Value, Cost The capitalized present value of the total outlay on the acquisition and improvement of a property minus the capitalized present value of all incomes from the property, the capitalizing being done at the current rate of compound interest.

Value, Devastation The standing value of timber in a forest plus the value of the land.

Value, Expectation The discounted present value of all future returns from a property minus the discounted present value of all the future expenses necessary to earn those returns, the discounting being done at a given rate per cent.

Value, Exploitation The current value of the stands of a forest estimated on the assumption that all merchantable material is to be cut. *See* utilization value.

Value, Market The price that could be obtained by selling the forest as it stands. *See* sale value, exploitation value.

Value, Rental The value of a property expressed as the capital corresponding to the anticipated average rental and a given rate per cent of interest income value.

Value, Replacement The amount it would cost to build up the forest at present prices. Should be equal to cost value but for fluctuation in money values.

Value, Soil Cost Cost value of the forest soil.

Value, Soil Expectation Refers to the expected net productive value of the soil. *See* value, expectation.

Values (Value System) The particular (frequently subjective) positive point of view of an individual or the common point of view of a group on an issue, way of life, or concerning the worth of things or experiences. Values may range from those that are subjectively meaningful to a given individual to those that are shared cultural norms. They influence the selection of the means and ends of actions, and they serve as criteria by which objects or actions are evaluated.

Variable 1. A quantity which may take any one of a specified set of values. It is convenient to apply the same word to denote non-measurable characteristics, e.g. "sex" is a variable in this sense since any human individual may take one of two "values," male or female. It is useful, but far from being the general practice, to distinguish between a variable as so defined and a random variable or variate. 2. Any structural element in an ecosystem that varies over time, also "component". 3. A condition of a system in which elements or a performance measure take different values. 4. Any character which though common to the individuals of a population varies in extent or degree. The term is used in statistics. For an example, the height of tree, the volume of a crop produced on a hectare of land, the percentage of trees infected with disease or the colour of bark are all called as variable.

Variance 1. A measure of variability, being the square of the standard deviation or standard error. 2. A measure of the dispersion of the actual values of a variable about its mean. It is the mean of the squares of all the deviations from the mean value of a range of data. Used in statistics.

Variance, Analysis of A measure in statistics designed to differentiate and evaluate the total variation found experimentally, usually partitioned into the variation attributable separately to site treatment, and experimental error.

Variate In statistics, it is generally synonymous with variable, but sometimes limited to an individual observation or value of a variable.

Variation Variation in biology means a difference between individuals of the same species, found in any sexually reproducing population. Variation may be almost unnoticeable in some cases, obvious in others, and can concern many aspects of any organism. Typically, variation in size, behaviour, biochemistry, or colouring may be found. The cause of the variation is genetic, environmental, or more usually a combination of the two.

Variation, Co-efficient of The standard deviation expressed as a percentage of the mean of a population. It is a measure of dispersion.

Variety 1. Subdivision of species or sup-species from which it can be distinguished by one or more characters, but with which it can still interbreed. Many plants have varieties well known in horticulture. 2. A category intermediate in rank between species or subspecies. 3. Subdivision of a species having a distinct, uniform, though often inconspicuous difference, and typically breeding true to that difference. *See* ecotype.

Vector 1. Common GIS data model made up of points, lines, or polygons, with associated attributes. 2. The representation of spatial data by points, lines, and polygons in GIS. 2. In physics, it is a quantity having both magnitude and direction.

Vector Data Model A spatial data model using two-dimensional Cartesian (x,y) co-ordinates to store the shape of spatial entities.

Vector Data Structure A means of coding and storing point, line, and aerial information in the form of units of data expressing magnitude, direction, and connectivity in GIS.

Vector Format The expression of points, lines, and areas on a map by digitized cartesian co-ordinates, directions, and values.

Vectorization 1. The conversion of point, line, and area data from a grid to a vector representation. 2. The process of converting data from raster to vector format.

Vector-to-raster-conversion *See* rasterization.

Vegetation Management Management actions that change the composition or structure of plant communities.

Vegetation Profile 1. A diagram of the above-ground portions of plants along a line-transect presented in elevation, i.e. in their natural positions in contrast to a chart quadrat which shows in plan the location of and areas covered by each plant. A similar diagram showing the whole of the plants, i.e. roots and shoots, in one or more vertical profiles is termed a bisect. 2. A diagram of the vegetation in a forest along a line or narrow strip, presented in elevation profile diagram. *See* transect.

Vegetation Type A plant community, assemblage, or aggregation with distinguishable characteristics.

Vegetative Cover A broad term comprising the cover of all vegetation occupying an area.

Vegetative Manipulation Changing one vegetation type to another. It can be done by mechanical means, chemical, grazing, or fire. Usually, this is done to increase forage for wildlife.

Veneer Thin sheets of wood (usually less than 1/4" thick) produced by slicing or peeling a log.

Veneer log A log of high quality and desirable species suitable for conversion to veneer. Logs must be large, straight, of minimum taper, and free from defects.

Verification The process of proving that the system performance is within specification.

Vermin Noxious, mischievous or disgusting animals of small size and common occurrence, and difficult to control; these include various insects (e.g. flies, lice, bed-bugs), various mammals (e.g.

rats) and sometimes birds (e.g. hawks and owls). In wildlife management the term is restricted to mammals and birds which are injurious to crops, wildlife, etc. Generally applied to such mammals as rats, mice and such pests, but sometimes animals, which become too numerous and cause destruction are declared as 'vermin', such as wild dogs and crows.

Vernalization Treatment of seed by exposure to low temperature, short of freezing in order to accelerate germination, subsequent growth, and flowering.

Vernation After-ripening Biochemical or physical changes occurring in seeds, bulbs, tubers and fruits after harvesting when ripe in the ordinary way; often necessary for subsequent germination or growth.

Vernation The arrangement of leaves within a bud aestivation.

Vertebrate Any animal with a backbone.There are 41,000 species of vertebrate which includes mammals, birds, reptiles, amphibians, and fishes. They include most of the larger animals, but in terms of numbers of species they constitute only a tiny proportion of the world's animals.

Vertebrates Animals with backbones or spinal columns. Examples include mammals, fish, and amphibians.

Vertical Diversity 1. A term used to describe forest structure, proceeding vertically through a forest canopy. 2. The diversity in an area that results from the complexity of the above ground structure of the vegetation. The more tiers of vegetation or the more diverse the species make-up, or both, the higher the degree of vertical diversity.

Vertical Structure The structure formed by different layers of vegetation in a forest.

Vessels Cellular ducts containing and circulating sap in plants.

Veteran A standard in the coppice-with-standards system that has stood for four or more coppice rotations.

Viability 1. A population of sufficient numbers and reproductive potential to maintain its existence over time in spite of normal fluctuations in population levels. 2. The potential capacity of a seed to germinate. 3. In general term, it is that can be done or that will be successful.

Viable Populations A wildlife or fish population of sufficient size and reproductive potential to maintain its existence over time in spite of normal fluctuations in population levels.

Viewshed 1. Those parts of the landscape that can be seen from a particular point. 2 A polygon map resulting from a visibility analysis showing all the locations visible from a specified viewpoint.

Virgin Area Any area in which there has been virtually no human disturbances (such as burning, cutting, grazing) of the original vegetation. This may be defined as an area containing very little introduced species, with very little human disturbance.

Virgin Forest A natural, usually-mature forest never harvested and virtually uninfluenced by human activity. Also called "ancient" and "old-growth", these have the characteristic of little or no perceived human influence.

Virtual Reality (VR) The production of realistic looking computer-generated worlds using advanced computer graphics and simulation models.

Viruses A class of ultra microscopic, filterable, infectious agents, chiefly protein, which are typically inert except when in contact with certain living cells.

Visibility Analysis In GIS, it is an analysis of visible features on a terrain surface using a DTM.

Vista A point or area along a route of travel which affords a panoramic, unusual, or highly pleasant view.

Visual Character Type A large area of land that has common distinguishing visual characteristics of landform, rock formations, water bodies, and vegetation patterns. The "visual character type" concept and the types of land units it produces should be about the same as morphological region and physiographic regions. "Visual character type" units are used as a frame of reference for classifying the physical features of a given area as to their degree of scenic quality. It is a vocabulary generally used in United States.

Visual Display Unit (VDU). A computer screen used for graphical display.

Visual Landscape Character (Characteristic Landscape) The overall impression created by a landscape's unique combination of visual features (such as land, vegetation, water, structures) as seen in terms of form, line, colour and texture. The naturally established landscape being viewed as visually represented by the basic vegetative patterns, landforms, rock formations and water forms that are in view.

Volume The amount of wood in a tree or stand according to some unit of measurement, (cubic feet, cubic metre, etc.) or some standard of use.

Volume Table 1. A table of figures used to estimate the volume of wood contained in a standing tree, based on dbh and merchantable height. 2. A table showing for a given species the average contents of trees, logs or sawn timber for one or more given dimensions. The given dimensions may be (i) dbh alone (ii) dbh and height or (iii) dbh, height and some measure of taper. Volume table may be (i) general, (ii) regional or (iii) local, depending on the scope of their applicability. The main object of these tables is to estimate the volume of an average standing tree of known dimensions. The scope of applicability, therefore, depends on the sources of measurements on which the average given in the volume tables are based. Hence before using a table, it is necessary to see if the table is applicable to the locality where it is being used. In practice, volume table approach is correctly applied to group of trees only, not for a individual tree.

Volume Table, Commercial A volume table in which the contents are given as volume measured down to a thin end diameter down to which conversion is done, the stump volume being omitted. As the diameter level to which conversion is done may vary with time and place, the scope of applicability of these tables is limited to areas having the same closeness of conversion and to certain periods of time when standard of conversion is the same. *See* volume table; standard volume table; form quotient.

Volume Table, Form Quotient A volume table based on form quotient, normal as well as diameters and height.

Volume Table, General Volume table designed to cover the whole natural range and dimensions of a species. These volume tables are based on the average volume of trees growing over a large geographical area. These are, therefore, applicable to a wider range of distribution of the species. These tables are usually based on two variables, viz. diameter at breast height and total tree height. These tables show volume of trees by diameter class and in each diameter class by height classes. As these are based on measurement of trees growing in wider range of distribution of the species and as they require measurement of diameters and heights for their application, these tables have a limited direct field application. These tables are used for deriving local volume tables. Several kinds of general volume tables are met with depending on the kind of volume they show, e.g., standard volume table, commercial volume table, swan outturn table, assortment tables, etc.

Volume Table, Local These volume tables are compiled from the measurements of trees growing in restricted locality. These are generally based on one independent variable, viz. dbh (o.b.). These are, therefore, applicable to such restricted localities as coup or compartment because in such small areas, the assumption that the trees of the same diameter will have the same height, will hold good. The local volume tables are used for (1) estimating the volume of standing trees before felling with the object of regulating yield in accordance with working plan prescriptions or (2) for making confidential estimate of the volume of coupes. Usually derived from general or regional volume table. Generally prepared with dbh alone as the independent variable.

Volume Table, Regional Volume table designed to apply to a particular tract or region. This table is compiled from measurements of trees growing in region and therefore offers a limited applicability when compared to general volume table.

Volume Table, Standard A volume table in which the contents are given as volume measured down to the limits for standard timber and if necessary, small wood, with stump included. Mainly of use as a basis for reference and for deriving, by the application of suitable conversion, subordinate volume table in units and modes of measurement for specific local purposes.

Volume, Merchantable The amount of wood considered saleable in a tree or crop.

Volume, Stacked The space occupied by a stack as distinct from the cubic contents of the wood itself, i.e., the solid volume.

Volunteer A pioneer growth appearing in grassland or scrub.

Vulnerable Species A species that is considered at risk because it exists in low numbers or in restricted ranges, due to loss of habitat or other factors.

Vulture (Genus gyps; Family Vulturidae) Any of a number of large raptorial birds of prey, related to the falcons, eagles and hawks, with naked and usually, brightly coloured heads and dark plumage. They live on carrion, but are known to attack living animals; they are found in tropical and temperate regions. They have a hooked beak, with claws less strongly developed than those of the eagles or hawks. BLACK, PONDICHERY OR KING VULTURE (*Sarcogyps calvus*): A huge, black turkey-like vulture, found throughout India. GRIFFON VULTURE (*Gyps himalayensis*): A resident mountain species, found throughout the Himalayas. WHITE-BACKED OR BENGAL VULTURE (*Pseudogyps bengalensis*): A resident species, found throughout India and ascending up to 1500 metre in the Himalayas. This is the commonest vulture.

Ww

Wage The payment paid to labour for its assistance to any work or production.

Wage Rates These are the methods by which wages are calculated. There are a number of methods of calculating wages such as time-rates, piece-rates or task rates.

Waif Timber that is stranded along a floating stream or in the sea and bears no property mark, property. Often called 'waifwood' or 'driftwood'.

Walnut *Juglans regia* is known as walnut. In Hindi it is called as *Akkrat*. It is large deciduous tree having height more than 20 metres. It is distributed in Afghanistan, the Himalayas, Upper Burma hills, North China and Japan. In Himalayas it is indigenous usually at 1500 to 3500 metre height level. Wood is even grained, grayish brown with dark brown streaks, often beautifully mettled, used for furniture, cabinet making and are used for veneers. It is light demander, stands shade in youth. It has massive root system and is fairly wind-firm, but avoids generally exposed positions. It coppices well. Cultivated varieties are propagated by budding and grafting.

Warden An official, usually of the Forest Department, charged with supervisory duties relating to wildlife conservation and management. In India the designation "Wildlife Warden" refers to an officer of the rank of Deputy Conservator of Forests, and the designation "Chief Wildlife Warden" refers to an officer of the rank of a Chief Conservator of Forests or above.

Waste-land Land not capable of producing materials or services of value. A miscellaneous land type.

Water, Available The amount of water, plants can extract from unit volume of soil. It is mainly derived from capillary water and corresponds roughly to the water held by the soil between the limits of field moisture capacity and the wilting co-efficient.

Water Balance The ratio representing the difference between water assimilated into the body and that lost from that body (as urine, feces and sweat). Under average conditions, this is approximately equal to one.

Water Budget The balance of all water moving into and out of a specified area in a specified period of time.

Water Hole A natural hole or hollow containing water, as one in the dry bed of an intermittent river, or a spring in a desert, or a small pool or pond. Wild game comes to water holes during the dry weather.

Water Logging A condition in which the soil pores get filled with water to the exclusion of air. A rise in the water table due to excessive irrigation. Salinization of the land can also result, as rising water brings salts to the surface. A consequence of inadequate soil drainage.

Water Parting A summit of boundary line separating the drainage of two distinct streams or coasts. *See* watershed.

Water Pollution Any substance or energy form (heat, light, noise, etc.) which alters the state of a body of water from what would naturally occur. Especially associated with those altered states which prevailing laws have decreed as illegal.

Water Table That surface in a ground-water body at which the water pressure is atmospheric. The highest point in a soil profile where water saturates the soil on a seasonal or permanent basis. It is defined by the levels at which water stands in wells that penetrate the water body just far enough to hold standing water. In wells that penetrate to greater depths, the water level will stand above the confining upper bed of the aquifer.

Water, Capillary Water that is retained around the soil particles and in the capillary pores in the soil at forces approximately between values of pf value 2.7 and 4.5; capable of movement under the influence of surface tension, and the main source of supply to forest trees.

Water, Gravitational Water in the soil body in excess of the capillary capacity. Held by forces somewhat less than pf value 2.7 and incapable of being retained under conditions of free drainage.

Water, Ground The body of water in the ground, accumulated above impermeable layers that completely fills the pore space to a level whose depth below the surface varies from place to place and, generally from time to time. *See* water-table.

Water, Hygroscopic That portion of the soil water which is retained as a thin film by the soil particles at forces greater than pf value 4.5, i.e., after capillary water has been removed. It is incapable of movement by gravitational or surface tension forces, and is associated mostly with the colloidal part of the soil. Sometimes referred to as water of imbibitions.

Waterhole An impoundment constructed or maintained to provide a water source for wildlife and other uses.

Watershed (Drainage Basin, Catchment Basin, River Basin) 1. The word is loosely used as a synonym for catchment or drainage area. 2. The total region or area above a given point on a stream or lake that contributes water to the flow at that point. It is designated by the dividing line of area from which surface streams flow in two different directions. In other words, it is the line separating two contiguous drainage areas. 3. The area drained by a stream and its tributaries. 4. A region or area bounded peripherally by a water-parting and draining ultimately to a particular water course or body of water. 5. The region or area drained by a stream or river. It can also include regions and small watersheds in which rivers/streams lead into larger bodies of water. 6. Strictly a water parting, the dividing line between catchment areas. 7. The catchment area or drainage basin from which the waters of a stream or stream system are drawn. The country as a whole can be divided into three broad watersheds. They are: (1) Himalayan range with its Karakoram branch in the North, (2) Vindhyan and Satpura ranges in Central India, and (3) Sahyadri or Western Ghats on west coast. All the major rivers originate in one or the other of these watersheds. India is blessed with many rivers. As many as 12 of them are classified as major rivers whose total catchment area is 252.8 million hectares. Of the major rivers, the Ganga-Brahmaputra-Meghana system is the biggest with a catchment area of about 110 million hectares, which is more than 43 per cent of the catchment area of the all the major rivers in the country. The other major rivers with catchment area of more than 10 million hectares are the Indus (32.1 million hectares), the Godavari (31.3 million hectares), the Krishna (25.9 million hectares) and the

Mahanadi (14.2 million hectares). The catchment area of medium rivers is about 25 million hectare and the Subarnarekha with 1.9 million hectares catchment area is the largest among the medium rivers in the country.

Watershed Management 1. A combination of complementary practices of land treatment and structural works to maintain or improve total yield, quality, stability of flow of surface and subsurface water and prevention of damage and loss due to excessive and uncontrolled runoff, flooding, salination, and siltation. 2. Managing all the natural resources of a watershed to protect, maintain, or improve its desired water budget, both quantity and quality, over time.

Watershed Protection Managing all the natural resources of a watershed to protect, maintain, or improve its desired water budget, both quantity and quality, over time.

Water-table The upper surface of the zone of saturation of soil by ground water.

Water-table, Perched A water-table that is separated by unsaturated material from an underlying body of ground water in a different zone of saturation.

Wavelength Distance between successive wave crests or other equivalent points in a harmonic wave.

Weak Sustainability A type of rule for sustainability, which requires that the value of aggregate capital stocks including human-made capital, natural capital, human capital and social capital must not decline. Thus, reductions in the level of natural capital must under this rule be compensated for by investment in an alternative capital stock.

Weasel Any of a worldwide group of cunning, agile, carnivorous mammals of genus Mustela, related to the minks, stoats, martens, etc., with a long, slender body, short legs and a long bushy tail. They feed on rats, mice, birds, eggs, etc. The Himalayan weasel (*Mustela sibirica*) is distributed in the temperate and alpine regions of the Himalayas, in open grass and scrub, above the tree line at elevations ranging from 1500 to 5000 metre.

Weather (Meteorological Condition) The state of the atmosphere at a definite time and place with respect to air, temperature, humidity, wind, precipitation, cloudiness, etc. "Climate" is long-term and generalizes trends or types.

Weathering All physical and chemical changes produced in rocks, at near the earth's surface, by atmospheric agents, and which result in more or less complete disintegration and decomposition.

Weed 1. A valueless, troublesome, or noxious plant, often exotic, growing wild, especially one growing profusely. 2. A plant growing where it is not wanted. 3. A tree of a species having little or no economic value on the site in question. 4. Any unwanted plant that interferes or tends to interfere with the growth of individuals of favoured species.

Weeding A tending operation generally done in the seedling stage in a nursery or in a forest crop that involves the removal or cutting back of all weed.

Weighting Assigning numbers to express the relative importance of items (e.g., resource yields) in a group or series under consideration usually not be directly compared by existing techniques for quantification on some measurement scale. The assigned numerical values are usually referred to as "weights" or "multipliers". Weighting is usually done according to some objective sense of the relative importance of the different types of resource yields. While weightings are usually added (i.e., additive weighting) to obtain a measure of the total social value of resource uses or resource yield mixes for planning areas, they may also be multiplied or divided (or some combination of these processes) to facilitate decision making.

Weir 1. Notch or depression in a dam, embankment, or other barrier across or bordering a stream, through which the flow of water is measured or regulated. 2. A barrier constructed across a stream to divert fish into a trap. 3. A dam (usually small) in a stream to raise the water level or divert its flow, with water flowing over the top of the structure.

Well A hole dug or drilled into the earth, or a natural spring source of water.

Well-stocked The situation in which a forest stand contains trees spaced widely enough to prevent competition yet closely enough to utilize the entire site. Conventionally, forests having crown density above 0.4 or 0.5 are called well stocked forests.

Wetland 1. Land where saturation with water is the dominant factor determining the nature of soil development and the types of plant and animal communities living in the soil and on its surface. Soil or substrate that are at least periodically saturated with or covered by water, and differ from adjoining non-inundated areas. A general term for any poorly-drained, uncultivated tract, whatever its vegetation cover and soil. 2. Lands sometimes or always covered by shallow water or which have saturated soils where plants adapted for life in wet conditions usually grow. They represent areas that are permanently wet, or intermittently water covered, such as swamps, marshes, bogs, muskegs, potholes, swales, glades, and overflow land of river valleys. Salt marshes, and brackish marshes subject to saline and/or tidal influences are usually included. Large, open lakes are commonly excluded, but many kinds of ponds, pools, sloughs and holes may be included. These may also be any areas that are more or less regularly wet or flooded and where the water table stands at or above the land surface for at least part of the year. Shallow lakes and ponds, usually with emergent aquatic vegetation (such as reeds or cattails) as a conspicuous feature, are included in the definition, but the permanent waters of streams, reservoirs and deep lakes are not included. Neither are water areas that are so temporary as to have little or no effect on the development of moist-soil dependent vegetation. These are areas where the presence of water is a dominant factor and produces adverse effects on all vegetation except for aquatic plant communities. 3. Wetlands are lands transitional between terrestrial and aquatic system where the watertable is usually or near the water surface and land is covered by shallow water. They are life support systems for people living around and are effective in flood control, waste water treatment, reducing sediment, recharging of aquifers and also winter resort for variety of birds for shelter and breeding and provide a suitable habitat for fish and other flora and fauna. They also act as buffer against the devastating effect of hurricanes and cyclones, stabilize the shore-line and act as bulwark against the encroachment by the sea and check soil erosion. Apart from that, they are valuable for their educational and scientific interest and provide durable timber, fuelwood, protein rich fodder for cattle, edible fruits, vegetables and traditional medicines. Identification of wetlands can be attributed to the following three main factors: when an area is permanently or periodically inundated, when an area supports hydrophytic vegetation and when an area has hydric soils that are saturated or flooded for a sufficiently long period to become anaerobic in the upper layers. On these criteria, Ramsar Convention defines wetlands as areas of marsh or fen, peat-land or water, whether artificial or natural, permanent or temporary, with the water that is static or flowing, fresh, brackish or salt including areas of marine water, the depth of which at low tide does not exceed six metre. Mangroves, corals, estuaries, bays, creeks, flood plains, sea grasses, lakes etc. are covered under this definition. Nineteen sites have already been designated as Ramsar sites in India till date. *See* Ramsar Convention on Wetlands.

Whip A tall slender tree in the upper canopy, with very constricted crown and incapable of existence without the support of the neighbouring trees.

Wilderness 1. An area of undeveloped forest land retaining its primeval character and influence without permanent improvements of human habitation managed and protected so as to preserve its natural condition, and which (a) generally appears to have been affected primarily by the forces of nature with the imprints of man's work substantially unnoticeable; (b) has outstanding opportunities for solitude of a primitive and unconfined type of recreation. 2. In general, it is a term used to denote unspoiled area where wildness, vastness, remoteness and grandeur have a special appeal to naturalists and others wishing to escape the crowds and hurly burly of present-day life.

Wildfire (Forest Fire) 1. Any fire other than a controlled burn or a prescribed burn, occurring on wildland or forest. 2. A free-burning fire unaffected by fire suppression measures. They frequently need to be suppressed, but in some areas they are allowed to burn for ecological or economic reasons.

Wilding A natural seedling (in contrast to a nursery grown seedling) used in forest planting.

Wildlife (Protection) Act, the The Wildlife (Protection) Act, 1972 governs wildlife conservation and protection of endangered species. The Act prohibits trade in rare and endangered species. The Wildlife Act had been adopted by all states except Jammu & Kashmir, which has its own Act. The Centre provides financial assistance to stages for: (1) Strengthening management and protection of infrastructure of national parks and sanctuaries; (2) Protection of wildlife and control of poaching and illegal trade in wildlife products; (3) Captive breeding programmes for endangered species of wildlife; (4) Wildlife education and interpretation; and (5) Development of selected zoos.

Wildlife 1. Non-domesticated mammals, birds, reptiles, and amphibians living in a natural environment, including both game species and non-game species, whether considered beneficial or otherwise. 2. Living things that are neither human nor domesticated.

Wild-life Area Area devoted wholly or partly to wild-life purposes. It can be classified as: (1) SANCTUARY: Absolute protection of all animals is given; (2) REFUGE: Protection of certain species (or all species) during a part of the year; and (3) PRESERVE: Here wild-life is managed on a harvest basis.

Wildlife Conservation Conservation of wildlife, which includes an ever-widening group of animals, mammals, birds, fish, reptiles, amphibians, arthropods (e.g. lobster) and mollusks (e.g. oyster). Certain aesthetically and economically important animals tend to dominate the list. In India, the most serious threat to wildlife conservation is posed by habitat destruction. Expanding agriculture, industry, and urbanization, etc. are the causes of this destruction. Realizing the importance of wildlife resource and in order to prevent the gene erosion, India took the following measures: (1) enactment of Wildlife (Protection) Act (1972), (2) becoming a party to the Convention of International Trade in Endangered Species of Fauna and Flora (CITES,1976), (3) launching a national components of UNESCO's Man and Biosphere Programme (1972), and (4) starting conservation projects for individual endangered species like Hungal (1970), Lion (1972), Tiger (1973), Crocodiles (1974) and Brown-antlered Deer. There are 92 National Parks and 500 wildlife sanctuaries in the country covering an area of 15.67 million hectares. Twenty-eight Tiger Reserves have so far been set up in 17 States covering an area of about 37,761 sq.km. in the country. Project Tiger has been rated as a role model. Under the India Eco-development Project 572 eco-development committees have been formed in seven protected areas covering 75,600 families. For the first time information and communications technology is being used for linking important tiger reserves in the GIS domain for evolving a management support system including crime detection, dissemination of information through web and evolving a "National Tiger Monitoring and Habitat Evaluation System" with regional protocols. Total number of Elephant Reserves in the country stood at 23 as on 1st December, 2003. *See* wildlife management.

Wildlife Habitat All of the environmental conditions of a specific place occupied by a wildlife population. The native environment of an animal, ideally providing all elements required for life and growth, food, water, cover, and space.

Wildlife Institute of India The Wildlife Institute of India (WII) was established in 1982 under the Ministry of Agriculture and subsequently brought under the Ministry of Environment and Forests. The mandate of the Institute is to impart training, carry out research and advise on matter of conservation and management of wildlife. Wildlife Institute of India is an autonomous institute of the Ministry, with a 48-member WII Society headed by the Union Minister for Environment and Forests as the apex body.

Wildlife Management A branch of conservation which handles wildlife as a renewable natural resource. Concerned primarily with production, it also undertakes control measures that will preserve a species or hold its population in bounds. Wildlife forms an integral part of the land and hence wildlife management involves a type of land use.

Wildlife Trade International trade in live plants and animals, and in wildlife products such as skins, horns, shells, and feathers. The trade has made some species virtually extinct, and whole ecosystems threatened. Wildlife trade is prohibited or to some extent regulated by Wildlife Acts and CITES. Population of Rhino and Elephant (Asian as well as African) have declined drastically because of haunting for their horns and tusks, and poaching remains a problem where trade is prohibited.

Willingness to Accept (WTA) This refers to the amount of money an individual would be willing to accept as compensation for suffering a loss, such as environmental deterioration or for not receiving a benefit.

Willingness-to-Pay (WTP) An economic concept used either in non-market valuation of goods or when the prevailing price of a goods or service is thought to be different from its true value to an individual or society. It refers to the price an individual would be willing to pay rather than be deprived of the good or service (rather than to "go without it"). In other words, this indicates the maximum amount of money an individual is willing to pay to obtain a benefit or avoid a loss is usually assumed to reflect the values he or she attaches to the benefit or loss. Indications of willingness to pay may be obtained directly by questionnaires or indirectly by studies of payments for similar items in similar circumstances, or of related costs, such as transportation, paid to get to point of use. Validity and applicability of "willingness-to-pay" is dependent on who is assigned initial ownership rights to the good or service being evaluated. The concept has been used in the environmental valuation as a measure of the benefit to a consumer of a change in the price, quantity or quality of a good.

Wilt Disease 1. A plant diseases in which the drooping of foliage is the most conspicuous symptom. 2. A fatal virus disease of insect larvae which causes their bodies to become flaccid after death.

Wilting Coefficient The soil moisture content at which a specified standard plant permanently wilts.

Wind Blast Injury to leaves and/or twigs by strong wind.

Wind Fall A tree or trees thrown or uprooted by the wind.

Wind Firm A tree able to withstand strong winds without being thrown or broken.

Wind Throw A tree or trees uprooted by the force of wind.

Windbreak 1. A narrow shelterbelt of trees or other obstacle maintained against the wind. Also known as wind belt. 2. A wind barrier of living trees and shrubs maintained for the purpose of protecting the farm buildings, garden, orchard, etc. 3. Wind breakage, i.e. the breaking of trees or branches by wind.

Windfirm Trees able to withstand strong winds, i.e., able to withstand the force of wind without being uprooted (e.g., windthrown).

Window A band of EMR which offers maximum obtainable transmission and minimal attenuation through a particular medium with use of a specific sensor; wavelengths of optimum sensing.

Windows 95 It is an operating system used with personal computers and workstations.

Winter Drying The desiccation of foliage or twigs by dry winds at times when water conduction is restricted by freezing of the stem or of the ground. It may also occur on unfrozen but cold soil.

Windrow Slash, residue and debris raked together into piles or rows. Also the verb, to create the row.

Windthrow (Wind-fallen) 1. The tendency to be uprooted by the wind. Also, a tree or trees uprooted. Trees tend to develop root systems to support themselves against the forces they face. When either logging creates a new forest edge or selected trees from a group are removed, the remaining trees may face a significant increase in the force of the wind. The trees growing on the edge of a forest tend to shelter the interior trees, and trees in a group protect each other from the full force of the wind. If the remaining trees do not have root systems capable of absorbing this additional stress, they will be blown down. 2. A tree fallen because of high velocity of wind.

Witches Broom An abnormal bushy growth of parts of the branch system on trees or shrubs, markedly different from that of the normal plant and characterized by the shortening of the internodes and excessive proliferation, generally pathogenic origin.

Wolf Any of a large group of flesh-eating, dog like mammals of the genus Canis, widely distributed throughout the Northern Hemisphere with harsh gray or brownish-gray fur, erect pointed ears, and bushy tail, noted for fierceness, craftiness and rapacity. It is very destructive to game, sheep and cattle and will sometimes attack man, when several animals have gathered in a pack. The Indian wolf has a dingy reddish-white fur, some of the hairs being tipped with black. It is regarded as *Canis lupus pallipes*, or sometimes as a distinct species *Canis pallipes*.

Wolf Tree 1. A tree which occupies more space in the forest than its value justifies. Usually a tree which is older, larger, or more branchy than other trees in the stand. 2. A large, broad crowned, excessively branchy tree, which occupies more space than is justified by its timber value, although it may have high aesthetic and wildlife value. Wolf trees often provide abundant cover and heavy mast crops for animals.

Wood 1. Sometimes used to indicate firewood and small timber for domestic purposes as distinct from "timber". Sometime used to indicate timber as well as firewood. 2. Any area of land more or less covered with trees. *See* stand.

Wood Preservation Antiseptic treatment of wood to increase its durability.

Wood, Spring The less dense wood formed during the early period of growth of each false ring.

Wood, Summer The denser wood formed during the later period of growth of each false ring.

Woodland 1. Land bearing vegetation composed essentially of woody plants. There is a tendency to restrict the term to plant communities, in which trees, often small, are present, but form only an open canopy the intervening area being occupied by lower vegetation typically grass, in contrast to (close) high forest. 2. Land used primarily for the production of adapted timber crops and to provide tree cover for watershed protection, beautification, etc. It does not include farmstead and field windbreak plantings.

Woodland, Farm The wooded portion of a farm or the wooded land in connection with a farm.

Woody Plants Plants which live longer than two years and have a thick, tough stem or trunk covered with a layer of bark.

Word A set of bits (typically 16 or 32) that occupies a single storage location and is treated by the computer as a unit of information.

Working Circle A forest area (forming the whole or part of a working plan area) organized with a particular object, and under one silviculture system and one set of working plan prescriptions. For example, selection working circle, selection-*cum*-improvement working circle, coppice-with-reserve working circle. In certain circumstances working circles may overlap like the bamboo working circle, plantation management working circle.

Working Plan Management of any resource requires a plan. Forest, being an important resource since time immemorial necessitates a management plan. A management plan is largely about resolving conflicts, choosing goals, objectives and making decisions. If conflicts cannot be resolved, objectives are chosen wrongly or out of context and if decisions are wrongly taken, the plan will be a failure (Sawarkar, V.B., 1995). A management plan in forest parlance is called "Working Plan". Working plan had been defined variously by different authors in different context and at different point of time. This is the reason why there is wide variation in their content and tone. Few of such definitions are: 1. Working plan is a written scheme of management aiming at continuity of policy, controlling the treatment of a forest. 2. Working plan is the simplest possible statement of what is known about the working plan areas, its configuration, soil, climate, vegetation, its possibilities, what has been done in the past, what should be done in future, how it should be done and what records should be kept. 3. A working plan sets forth the purpose with which a forest should be managed so as to best meet the interests, and therefore, the wishes of the owner; and indicates the means by which this purpose may be accomplished. In other words, it is a forest regulation prescribing the application of certain cultural rules and the execution of certain works, in order to produce a given result (D'Arcy, W.E., 1910). 4. Working plan is the instrument of forest management practices in a unit area. The first working plan for India was prepared in 1837 by Mr. Munro for the forests of Travancore (Kerala). Instead of working plan, sometimes working scheme is also prepared. Working scheme is a plan of management not so detailed or so comprehensively developed as a working plan.

Working Plan Officer Forest management plan or forest working plan lasts for a definite period, say 10 to 15 years. Before the said plan expires, the working plan is revised. The job of revising working plan is assigned to a senior officer. The officer who undertakes the preparation or revision of working plan is called as working plan officer. The working plan officer has an array of complex tasks to accomplish. These tasks are: (1) Collection of basic information from the concerned territorial division, (2) Reconnaissance survey of the forest area for which the management plan is prepared,(3) Preparation of first preliminary (working plan) report, (4) Conducting fieldworks like stock mapping, inventory, socio-economic survey, stump and stem analysis, bio-diversity studies, evaluation of J.F.M. and plantation works, other studies and generation of data, (5) Analysis, processing and interpretation of data collected,

(6) Preparation of second preliminary (working plan) report along with preparation of maps, and (7) Preparation of final (working plan) report and maps.

Working Scheme A term used in some countries to denote a plan of management not so detailed or not so comprehensively developed as a working plan. It is a poor substitute of working plan. It is more of a contingency management plan.

Workstation A minicomputer or high-level personal computer used for local computations. It is often connected to other computers by a network. The operating system used for workstations is often Unix or Windows NT.

World Commission on Environment and Development The Commission was established by the United Nation's General Assembly in 1983. The said commission had the mandate (1) To examine critical environmental issues, (2) To formulate proposals for dealing with them, (3) To propose new forms of international co-operation, and (4) To raise levels of understanding and commitment to action on the part of individuals, corporations and Governments. Brundtland's Report coined the word 'sustainable development'. World Commission on Environment and Development launched the conservation strategy. The strategy focused on the theme of 'conservation' the intrinsic principle behind the concept of sustainability. But, the concept got a major boost with the publication of the report of the World Commission on Environment and Development (the Brundtland Report) in 1987 (WCED,1987). It focused on how development should be achieved. It also emphasised on the fact that environment degradation is inimical to development and economic growth. The report placed distinct emphasis on sustainable development. It provided an interpretational and functional framework to sustainable development. The Commission defined sustainable development as the development that meets the needs and aspiration of the present without compromising the ability to meet those of the future. It also advocated the continuation of economic growth as a means of solving the environmental problems. It accepted economic growth as key to solving poverty and underdevelopment. Sustainable development requires meeting the basic needs of all and extending to all the opportunity to fulfil their aspirations for a better life (WCED, 1987: 8). The report highlighted distributional issues like inter-generational, intra-generational and wide chasm between 'have-nots' and 'haves' in tackling environmental problems. It emphasised on the fact that economic growth should use the available stock of capital on sustainable basis and should not deplete the stock by using unsustainably. It sensitised the world community about the concept of sustainable development.

World Conservation Strategy (WCS), 1980 The World Conservation Strategy (WCS) was launched simultaneously in 40 countries in the year 1980. It reflected compromises, both among conservationists, and between conservationists and 'practitioners of development'. The strategy focused on three main groups of potential users—Governmental policy makers, conservationists and those directly concerned with living resources and developmental practitioners including aid agencies, industry and trade unions. Three main objectives were identified: (1) To maintain essential ecological processes and life supporting system, (2) To preserve genetic diversity, and (3) To ensure the sustainable utilisation of species and ecosystem. Therefore, conservation focused on 'preservation, maintenance, sustainable utilisation, restoration, and enhancement of the natural environment'. The strategy emphasised on practical benefits that would stem from the preservation of genetic diversity and sustainable utilisation of ecological resources. It also laid stress on the fact that human benefits would follow from appropriate forms of environmental management. Essentially, the strategy succeeded to a great extent to reconcile conservation and development goals by incorporating conservation principles into development rather than opposing development.

World Conservation Strategy, Second (1991) The concept of sustainability became popular with the publication of the Second Conservation Strategy (Caring for the Earth) in 1991. It was prepared by IUCN, UNEP and WWF. The strategy had two aims. One was to promote a new ethic for sustainable living, and to translate its general principles into practice. The other was to integrate conservation and development. It is said that the first strategy emphasised on the fact that conservation was not opposite to development and the second strategy sought to extend and embolden the concept. Therefore, the second strategy outlined few principles for building sustainable society. It provided a broader view of environment in its developmental context. It laid emphasis on developmental and distributional aspects. It also sought to promote ethics in economic development. Emergence of ethics led to the acceptance of a fact that purely technical solutions to environmental problems are not likely to succeed. The principles were: respect and care for community of life, improving the quality of human life, conserving the earth's vitality and diversity, keeping with the earth's carrying capacity, changing personal attitudes and practices, enabling communities to care for their own environments, providing a national framework for integrating development and conservation and creating a global alliance.

World Forestry Congress *See* Forestry Congress.

World Wide Web (WWW) Interconnected global network of computers and the software interface used to access and exchange digital information and multimedia.

Wrench To break the finer roots of nursery plants, without removing them from the soil by heaving the soil with a fork or similar implement, or by partly lifting the plant and refirming root pruning.

WTO and the Environment The WTO (World Trade Organisation) was created by International Treaty. It establishes the procedures that define 'fair trade practices'. A crucial principle of WTO is that import barriers cannot be established according to the techniques used in the production of goods.

Xx

Xerarch Succession Succession initiated in extremely dry situation, such as bare rock, wind blown sand, rocky slopes, etc. *See* hydrarch succession.

Xeric Applied to a habitat that is dry.

Xeromorphic (Scleromorphic) Having structural characteristics common among plants adapted to drought (i.e., small thick leaves with sunken stomata or revolute margins, surfaces that are heavily pubescent, waxy or highly reflective.

Xerophilous Inhabiting dry sites.

Xerophyte A plant that can subsist in dry situations.

Xerosere The different stages in a xerarch succession.

Xylem The tissues of the stem and root lying between the pith and cambium of a woody plant serving for water conduction, mechanical strength and food storage; characterized by the presence of wood vessels.

Xylometer An apparatus used for determining the volumes of irregular pieces of wood by measuring the amount of water they displace.

Yy

Yearling A one-year old seedling.

Yield 1. Yield is a measure of the output of forest products. 2. The quantity of products taken from the forest. 3. The volume or number of stems that can be removed annually or periodically, or the area over which fellings may pass annually or periodically, consistent with the attainment of the objects of management.

Yield Capacity The total quantity of material per annum, of given species, that an area is capable of producing under normal conditions, so long as the factors of the locality remain unchanged.

Yield, Determination of The calculation of the amount of material which may be removed from a forest annually or periodically over a stated period or of the annual or periodic area with the prescribed treatment and yield regulation. Requirements for determining sustained yield of forest products are: (1) Sustainable levels for timber and NTFP yield should be determined separately. (2) Authentic forest data including inventory should be collected in order to determine the level of sustainable harvest. Essential data required are: (a) Forest inventory data which provides information about the quantity of harvestable resources currently available; (b) Information about growth and yield pattern in order to determine how fast the resource will be renewed after harvesting; (c) Information about seed production and method of natural regeneration from studies and background knowledge and secondary sources; (d) Information about the status of natural regeneration in the forests; (e) Information about NTFPs and their pattern of exploitation and rate of replenishment; and (f) Growth and yield prediction requires analysis of results obtained from permanent sample and preservation plots. (3) Reliable method and sound rationale for the calculating the rate of harvest. Normally the 'Annual Allowable Cut' or 'Annual Cut' method is adopted to determine sustainable limit of timber yield. The annual cut is the volume of timber, which may be cut in one year in a given area. Calculation of annual cut is based on the volume of timber in the area, which can be harvested, while leaving enough stems in a selection forests to provide for the next crop. It depends on the currently exiting growing stock and the growth rate. (4) There should be acceptable and reliable method of control of such harvest operation. It is prudent to ensure that the production rate is kept slightly below the sustainable yield level. *See* yield regulation.

Yield Regulation 1. A term generally applied to the determination of the timber yield and the prescribed means of realizing it. 2. A technique for calculating and controlling the timber harvest level to ensure that sustained yield is implemented. *See* yield determination.

Yield Table, Money A table constructed from a volume yield in which the yields are expressed in terms of money instead of volume. Its main objective is to determine best financial rotation. As the selling rate of timber varies with size, the volume table cannot be directly converted into money yield table by simple multiplication.

Yield Table, Multiple A yield table in which data are given for different grades of thinning.

Yield Table A tabular statement which summarizes on an unit area (acre or hectare) basis all the essential data relating to the development of a fully-stocked and regularly thinned even-aged crop at periodic intervals covering the greater part of its useful life. Yield table gives different parameters of a crop such as number of trees, crop height, crop diameter, crop basal area, volume of standing crop, volume removed in thinning, MAI, CAI, etc. In short, it provides all the information regarding development of a crop. Yield table is not applicable to unevenaged forests because in its present form it has been compiled from even-aged pure crops and is therefore applicable to them alone. Yield tables for unevenaged crop have not been prepared so far because of the difficulties involved. The main difficulty is that there is no one representative average age in the unevenaged crop. Yield table differs from the volume table in many counts. Volume table gives the volume of an average tree by diameter and/or height classes, where as yield table gives different parameters of a crop as described above. *See* volume table.

Yield, Final 1. All the material that counts against the prescribed yield and which is derived from the main felling in a regular forest. 2. It is the sum of the main and subsidiary crop.

Yield, Financial The rate of compound interest realized during a rotation on all the money spent on a forest crop, taking into account all items of expenditure and income during that rotation.

Yield, Intermediate The material from thinning or operations preceding the main felling in a regular forest, or its cash equivalent. *See* subsidiary crop.

Yield, Intermittent The material of cash return obtained from time to time from a forest not organized for continuous production. see intermittent working.

Yield, Normal The yield from a normal forest.

Yield, Potential 1. The annual yield in material, of which a forest is capable, when maintained at its highest limit of productivity. 2. The estimated volume of products which might be obtained annually if the forest were managed in accordance with sustained yield principle.

Yield, Sustained 1. The material that a forest can yield annually (or periodically) in perpetuity. 2. Annual or periodic output of a constant volume of products in perpetuity. Sustained yield is only possible if sustained growth is maintained within the forest. 2. As applied to a policy, it indicates method or plan of management (sustained yield management). It implies continuous production with the aim of achieving, at the earliest practical time as well as at the highest practical level an approximate balance between net growth and harvest, either by annual or somewhat longer period.

Yield, Total 1. Total standing volume of a crop plus the total volume removed in thinning since its establishment in a more or less even-aged stand. 2. The sum of the final yield and intermediate yield.

Yak (*Bos grunniens* Syn. *Poephagus grunniens*). This is a large wild or domesticated ox of Tibet and adjacent elevated parts of Asia. It has short, smooth hair on the back and long wavy hair on the breast, sides, legs and tail. It is up to 1.8 metre high at the shoulder, and 550 kilogram in weight. It is smaller under domestication and lives as a beast of burden and source of flesh, milks, hide and hair. It is found in North Ladakh and sometimes it passes in east Kumaon.

Zz

Zero The origin of all co-ordinates defined in an absolute system. Where x, y, and z axes intersect.

Zero-based Budgeting A management process that provides for systematic consideration of all programmes and activities in conjunction with formulating Budget requests and programme planning.

Zonation An arrangement of different plant communities in more or less definite zone, following one another in a constant order due to a continuous change in the habitat factors.

Zone 1. One of the belts occupied by successive communities in a zonation. 2. Any of the five great latitudinal divisions of the earth's surface named according to the prevailing climate, specifically the torrid zone, bounded by the Tropic of Cancer and the Tropic of Capricorn, two temperate zones bounded by the Tropics and the polar circles and two frigid zones lying between the polar circles and the poles. *See also* Climatic Zones; Life Zones.

Zone of Influence The extent of area outside the legal PA boundaries over which wildlife damage problems of significance occur, excluding damage caused by itinerant elephant population not necessarily dependent on the PA and the extent of area settled by villages with people having a traditional PA based resource dependency, whichever is the greater area in extent. This is also considered as the buffer zone (Sawarkar, 1995).

Zone of Saturation The zone occupied by the ground water in the soil.

Zone, Roadside A strip of varying width along a highway of road on which the scenic values are safeguarded from impairment by excluding or restricting the utilization of natural resources, commercial development, and occupancy.

Zone, Waterfront A strip of varying width along a lake, pond, streams, ocean, or other water body, on which the scenic values are safeguarded from impairment by excluding or restricting the utilization of natural resources, commercial development and occupancy.

Zoning In general, separating a planning area into zones and establishing regulations to govern the use of the land (commercial, industrial, residential, type of residential, etc.) and the location, height, shape, use, and coverage of structures within each zone.

Zoning, Conservation Zoning which restrains development of unsuited areas such as steep slopes with fragile soils, areas of scenic beauty, and spaces with other natural values.

Zoning, Natural Resource A blanket term used to refer to all zoning which restricts the uses that are made of natural resource lands so as to maintain the benefits which flow from their natural capacities, productivity or material contents. For example, floodplain zoning, agricultural zoning and forest zoning are types of "natural resource zoning".

Zoo Abbreviation for zoological garden which is an area set aside for the exhibition of wild animals. Such wild animals are maintained in cages and artificial enclosures, in such a manner as to restrict their freedom almost completely. *See* Zoological Park; Central Zoo Authority.

Zoo Authority, Central Central Zoo Authority (CZA) was established in 1992 under the provisions of Wild Life (Protection) Act, 1972. The Authority consists of 10 members and one whole time member secretary and is chaired by the Minister, Environment and Forests, Government of India. Two committees, namely 'Administrative Committee' under the Chairmanship of Director General of Forests and Technical Committee under the Chairmanship of Additional Director General of Forests (Wildlife) have been constituted for carrying out the functions of the Central Zoo Authority. Main functions of the Central Zoo Authority are: specify minimum standards for housing, upkeep and veterinary care of the animals in the zoos, recognition of zoos on the basis of evaluation of their functioning, identify endangered species of wild animals for the purpose of captive breeding and assigning responsibility in this regard to zoos, coordinate the acquisition, exchange and loaning of animals for breeding, provide technical and other assistance to zoos for management and development on scientific lines. There are 165 recognized zoos in the country, and out of it 44 zoos are major and rest minor ones.

Zoo-geography A branch of biogeography concerned with the geographical distribution of animals and especially with the determination of land and marine area characterized by special groups of animals, and the study of the causes and significance of such groups.

Zoological Garden A place which aims at showing as large a number of mammals, birds, reptiles, fish etc., as possible, usually with a confined area in or near a city or town, for the recreation and education of the public, and to provide material for scientific study. The animals are usually kept in cages or restricted to small enclosures. *See* Zoological Park.

Zoological Park This is a zoo without bars. The animals are comparatively free and are exhibited in their natural surroundings as far as possible, with the barriers and restrictions hidden or camouflaged from view. Zoological parks can be constituted only where sufficient land is available and are generally situated on the outskirts of cities. *See* Zoological garden.

Zoological Survey of India The Zoological Survey of India (ZSI), a premier institute under the Ministry has been undertaking survey, exploration and research leading to the advancement of our knowledge on the exceptionally rich faunal diversity of the country since its inception in 1916. With its headquarters at Kolkata and sixteen regional stations located in different parts of the country, ZSI in recent years, has reoriented its plan of work by grouping the survey and studies under five major programmes, viz. (1) Fauna of states, (2) Fauna of conservation areas, (3) Fauna of important ecosystems, (4) Status survey of endangered species, and (5) Ecological studies.

Zoology 1. The study and classification of animals and animal life. 2. The science that deals with the classification of animals and the study of animal life. It is a division of biology distinguished from botany.

Zoom. A capability for proportionately enlarging or reducing the scale of a figure or maps displayed on a computer screen.

Zooplankton 1. Suspended or floating animal organisms usually drifting passively with water currents, e.g., protozoans, entomostracans, and various larvae. 2. The animal portion of the plankton.

Zooplankton Microscopic animals living within the water column. *See* plankton.

Zygote The cell formed by the sexual fusion of two gametes. Also the organism developing from such a cell fusion.

Bibliography

Anon (2002). *Biodiversity hotspots for conservation priorities Nature* 403: 853-858.

Bailey, R.G. (1988). *Ecogeographic Analysis*: A guide to the ecological division of land for resource management. Misc. Publ. No. 1465. USDA Forest Service, Washington, D.C. 16 pp. Begon.

Boyce, S.G. (1995). *Landscape Forestry*. John Wiley and Sons, New York, NY.

British Commonwealth Forest Terminology, Part I & II, Empire Forestry Association, London, (1957).

Brown, A.A. and Davis, K.P. (1973). *Forest Fire-control and Use*. New York, McGraw-hill. 686 pp.

Carpenter, R.A. (1995). A consensus among ecologists for Ecosystem Management. Bulletin of the Ecological Society of America 76(3): 161-162.

Champion, H.G. (1936). A preliminary survey of forest types of India and Burma. Ind. Gore. Rec(N.S) I.

Champion, H.G. and Seth, S.K (1968). A revised survey of the forest types of India. Government of India Publication 1968.

David, Reid (1996). Sustainable Development International Guide, DFID.

Dunstar, J. and K. Dunstar (1996). *Dictionary of Natural Resource Management*. UBC Press, BC.

Dwivedi, A.P. (1980). *Forestry in India*. Jugal Kishore and Company, Dehradun, India.

Emiliani, C. (1987). *Dictionary of the Physical Sciences*. Oxford University Press, New York, NY. p. 365.

Eyre, F.H. (1980). *Forest Cover Types*. Society of American Foresters, Washington, D.C. p. 148.

FAO. (2005). State of the World's Forests 2005. Rome.

FAO/ECE. (1986). Forest Fire Statistics. 3rd edition. New York, UN. p. 30.

Faulkner, R. (Ed.) (1975). *Seed orchards*. U.K. For. Comn. Bul. 54. p. 149.

Forest Research Institute (1936). Glossary of technical terms for use in Indian Forestry, Forest Bull. No New Series, 1911 and Indian Forest records (new Series) Vol II, No. 1.

Forest Terminology for Multiple-Use Management 1 Adobe Acrobat Portable Document Version William Hubbard, Christopher Latt, Alan Long 2.

Forman, R.T.T., and M. Godron. (1986). *Landscape Ecology*. Wiley and Sons, Inc. N.Y. p. 619.

Green, R.N., R.L. Trowbridge, and K. Klinka. (1993). *Towards a Taxonomic Classification of Humus Forms*. Forest Science Monograph 29. p. 49.

Hartl, D.L. (1981). A primer of population genetics. Sinauer Associates, Inc. p. 191.

Groombridge, B. and Jenkins, MD (2000). *Global Biodiversity*: Earth's living resources in the 21st century UK: World Conservation Monitoring Centre. p. 246.

Gulati, N.K. (1986). *A Glossary of Forestry Terms*. International Book Distributors, Deheradun.

Haskell, B.D., B.G. Norton, and R. Constanza Lawrence, E. (eds.). (1995).

Henderson's dictionary of biological terms. Eleventh Edition. Wiley and Sons, NY, NY. p. 693.

IUCN/UNEP/WWF (1991). *Caring for the Earth*. A strategy for Sustainable Living. Gland, Switzerland.

Jeff Hemphill, Remote Sensing Research Unit, UCSB, website for the class, Aerial Photogrammetry.

John A. Helms (editor) *The Dictionary of Forestry* (1998). 210 pages. The Society of American Foresters, 5400 Grosvenor Lane, Bethesda, MD 20814.

M.J. Harper, and C.R. Townsend (1990) (2nd edition). *Ecology*, individuals, populations and communities.. Blackwell Scientific Publications, London, p. 945.

Manual of Remote Sensing, Leonard Bowden, American Society Photogrammetry and Remote Sensing, Falls Church VA, (1975).

Markandya, A., P. Harou, L. Bellu and V. Cistulli (2002). *Environmental Economics for Sustainable Growth*: A handbook for Practitioners, Edward Elgar, Cheltenham

MoEF (1999). *National Policy and Macrolevel Action Strategy on Biodiversity*, New Delhi: Ministry of Environment and Forests, Government of India. p. 74.

MoEF (2000 Annual Report 2000-2001). New Delhi, Ministry of Environment and Forests, Government of India.

MoEF (2006 Annual Report 2005-2006). New Delhi, Ministry of Environment and Forests, Government of India.

Myers, N. (1988). *Threatened biotas*: 'Hotspots' in tropical forests. Environmentalist 8: 187-208.

Myers, N., R.A. Mittermeier, Mittermeier, C.G., da Fonseca, G A B, Kents, J. (2000).

National Wetlands Working Group (1988). Wetlands of Canada. Ecological Land Classification Series, No. 24. p. 452.

NOAA (USA) (1994). *Report to the Nation*: El Nino and climate prediction. Washington DC: University Corporation for Atmospheric Research p. 22.

Odum, E.P. (1971). *Fundamentals of Ecology*. W.B. Saunders Co., Philadelphia, p. 574.

Perman, R.Y. Ma, J. McGilvary (1996). *Natural Resource and Environmental Economics*, 2nd edition, Longman, Harlow

Pickett, S.T.A. and P.S. White (1985). *The Ecology of Natural Disturbance and Patch Dynamics*. Academic Press, New York. p. 472.

Puri, G.S. (1960). *Indian Forest Ecology*. Oxford Book and Stationery Co. New Delhi.

Putman, R.J. (1994). *Community Ecology*. Chapman and Hall, London, p. 178.

Ricklefs, R.E. (1990) (3rd edition). *Ecology*. W.H. Freeman and Company., New York, NY. p. 896.

Rodgers, W.A. and Panwar H.S. (1988). *Planning a Wildlife Protected Area Network in India*, (vol. 1) Dehra Dun: Wildlife Institute of India. p. 341.

Science Council of Canada (1974). A National Statement by the Schools of Forestry at Canadian Universities. Ottawa, Canada.

Spurr, S.H. and B.V. Barnes. (1980) (2nd edition). *Forest Ecology*. Ronald, New York. p. 571.

Stanners, D. and P. Bordeau (eds)(1995). *Europe's Environment*: The Dobris Assessment, Earthscan, London

The Dictionary of Forestry (1998). John A. Helms (editor). 210 pages. The Society of American Foresters, 5400 Grosvenor Lane, Bethesda, MD 20814.

The Society of American Foresters (SAF). 370 page book, *Terminology of Forest Science Technology*, Practice, and Products.

USDA Forest Service (1990). *Forest Service Manual-title 5100*, Fire Management, Washington, DC.

Waring, R.H. and W.H. Schlesinger (1985). *Forest Ecosystems, Concepts and Management*. Academic Press, Inc. p. 340.

Wetzel, R.G. (1983) (2nd edition). *Limnology*. Saunders College Publishing, Fort Worth, Texas. p. 858.

World Resource Institute (1994, tables 19.1, 23,2) and Sandler (1997).

World Resources Institute (1994, table 23.3). (Stephen H. Schneider, 1988). Source: Sandnes (1993, tables C6, C13).